POINTS *of* DEPARTURE

MULTICULTURAL VOICES

LITERATURE FROM THE UNITED STATES

FOREWORD BY
RITA DOVE

ScottForesman

A Division of HarperCollins*Publishers*

EDITORIAL OFFICES: Glenview, Illinois
REGIONAL OFFICES: Sunnyvale, California · Tucker, Georgia
· Glenview, Illinois · Oakland, New Jersey · Dallas, Texas

FOREWORD
Rita Dove

CONSULTANTS
James Masao Mitsui, *English teacher,* Hazen High School, Renton, Washington.
■ Anna J. Small Roseboro, *English teacher,* The Bishop's School, La Jolla, California.
■ Mary Sasse, *Writer-consultant,* formerly English teacher and department chair, Carbondale Community High School, Carbondale, Illinois. ■ Carmen Tafolla, *Educational consultant to school districts,* including Dallas I.S.D., San Antonio I.S.D., and Texas Association for Bilingual Education. ■ Barbara M. Winborn, *English teacher,* Armstrong High School, Richmond, Virginia.

PHOTOGRAPH CREDITS

Back cover: Fred Viebahn/Courtesy Vintage Books
1 Ulrike Welsch
2 Courtesy Arte Público Press
9 Courtesy John F. Kennedy Library
14 Courtesy Coffee House Press
15 The Bettmann Archive
21 Reprinted with the permission of Four Winds Press, an imprint of Macmillan Publishing Company from CALENDAR ART written and illustrated by Leonard Everett Fisher. ©1987 Leonard Everett Fisher.
30 Nat Fein/New York Herald Tribune
36 David Grier Photography/Courtesy New Directions Publishing Corporation; Michael Nye; Courtesy Fulcrum Publishing
42 Courtesy of the author
56–57 Ted Kawalerski/The Image Bank
58 Fred Viebahn/Courtesy Vintage Books
62 ©Tribune Media Services. All rights reserved.
67 Michael Dorris/HarperCollins; L. Tom
72 Courtesy of the author
96 Courtesy Gail Mathabane
100 Courtesy of the author
106 Courtesy University of California Davis News Service
110 Courtesy of the author
120–121 Joel Gordon Photography
122 Courtesy University of New Mexico
133 Courtesy National Council of Teachers of English
138 Ben Manlove/Courtesy of the author
152 Third World Press
156 Courtesy Francine Ann Yep
168–169 Michael Dwyer/Stock Boston
170 Robyn Stoutenberg

178 Jean Weisinger/Courtesy Harcourt Brace Jovanovich
190 Michael Nye/Courtesy University of Texas Press
206 Arte Público Press
214 Courtesy of the author
219 Courtesy Lewis & Clark College; Courtesy of the author
240 Giraudon/Art Resource
244 Mottke Weissman/The Dell Press
252 Courtesy University of Washington Press
268 Courtesy of the author
271 Courtesy Carmen Tafolla
292–293 Eugene Richards/Magnum Photos
294 Robert Foothernp/Courtesy Putman Publishing Group
309 Fred Viebahn/Vintage Books; Courtesy Lilly Mitsui
314 Jeff Stanton/Courtesy of the author
322 George Johnson
326 AP/Wide World Photos
328 Bob Adelman/Magnum Photos
336 The Silver Image/Morrow
346 Kate Kunz/Plume
358–359 Jean-Claude Lejeune/IBID.
360 The Estate of Carl Van Vechten, Joseph Solomon Executor
374 Rubén Guzmán
378 Courtesy Macmillan Publishing Company
388 Courtesy The Contemporary Forum
404 Courtesy HarperCollins; Courtesy Carolyn Soto
410–411 Bruce W. Talamon/Onyx
412 Courtesy Arte Público Press
418 AP/Wide World Photos
422 UPI/The Bettmann Archive; Pat Wolk/Courtesy of the author
426 Georgia McInnis

Acknowledgments for quoted matter are included in the acknowledgments section on pages 483–484. The acknowledgments section is an extension of the copyright page.

ISBN: 0–673–29427–7

1314-DQ-0403

Contents

Foreword

by Rita Dove

School supplies. My ten-year-old daughter makes a beeline to the rows of notebooks, pencil packs, and lunch boxes. Like me, she harbors a fondness for writing supplies, and these shopping sprees the week before school are intensely pleasurable for both of us.

She returns out of breath, with a small packet of crayons, the front of which portrays a group of smiling children from different ethnic backgrounds standing before a globe. *United Colors of Benetton,* I think, then notice the label: *Crayola Multicultural. Skin, Hair, and Eye Colors. 16 Crayons.*

I can't resist: I buy the packet. On the way home we wonder aloud what new names these special crayons might have: Cleopatra Bronze. Harriet Tubman Brown, Geronimo Sienna, Confucius Yellow. For my daughter's benefit (she is biracial) I tell the story of my first box of crayons, how I slipped up my grandmother's stairs and into the sacred guest bedroom so that I could crack open the carton (*64 colors!*) in private — and the shock of discovering the one sinister wax stick labeled "flesh." From then on, it seemed that I spotted this misnomer (or its sly accomplice, "nude") everywhere — its outrageous designation on items slated for every person's use, regardless of whether every complexion qualified as "flesh"-colored or not: Band-Aids, lingerie, Clearasil. To see this pale tint declared the representative of all flesh, when three-fourths of the world's population did not fit such description, was a slap in the face, a door slammed shut.

When my daughter and I get home, we sit down on the family room rug and spill out the crayons. What a disappointment! For many of the old names remain: burnt and raw sienna, goldenrod and apricot, cornflower blue and olive green, white and black and brown and tan. The statement on the back of the packet reads: *This Multicultural assortment contains 16 different skin, hair, and eye colors for coloring people around the world.*

My daughter doesn't notice my dejection and begins matching up crayons to our skin and hair. At least there's no "flesh"—I'm a sturdy "brown," and "apricot" is her complement. Then I understand what she had never known as otherwise: there should be no histories attached to colors. Just as that "flesh" crayon was wrong, wishing for politically correct labels was not right, either.

*　*　*

Imagine this: on a table lies a rectangular object whose dimensions are six by nine inches, or perhaps four by seven. It looks a little like a brick, but softer and flakier. Although it comes covered in navy-tinted linen or tooled burgundy leather or laminated patterned paper, the object can be lifted out of this exterior wrapping like a body from a coat.

No, it's more like a box than a brick. And like a box, you can lift the lid and look inside . . . then lift the next lid, and the next . . . until you have leafed through the entire package and in the process witnessed battles and train wrecks, cried over family tragedies and guffawed through social farces, learned about white whales and Arctic wolves, heard flies buzzing while hunchbacks muttered and bells tolled, sniffed jasmine tea over Dim Sum or nibbled a piece of wedding cake as the bride and groom embrace.

Welcome to the world of books!

But imagine if the hero were always the same person—5'10" tall, say, and wearing wing tip shoes, suspenders, and a bow tie. And imagine that everyone he meets either looks like him or wishes he or she did. And now, imagine that everyone in the book shares the same political convictions and religious beliefs, even the same tastes in movies and vacation spots and cars. If their opinions meshed so completely, what would they ever find to say to each other?

Gets old pretty quick, doesn't it?

As a child, I read book after book and became acquainted with many different characters, but I didn't find anyone resembling me in all those pages. So I grew to prefer foreign authors and historical novels. I could identify more readily with the characters in *War and Peace* than with Nancy Drew—as long as I journeyed to strange and wondrous worlds or landed on the faraway shores of the past, I could suspend my disbelief by becoming absorbed in an exotic social order.

When I became a teenager, however, I thirsted sometimes for a more immediate identification with the protagonist: what a bitter taste it left, this search for joy or solace, guidance or distraction in the literature of my country, a literature in which my white peers found themselves so readily reflected! In young adult novels, I tried to relate to the breathless excitement of the heroine—would he kiss her at the end of the date or not?—but there were never brown shoulders like mine emerging from the velvet caress of that strapless prom dress.

*　*　*

> *I do not like thee, Doctor Fell,*
> *The reason why I cannot tell;*
> *But this I know, and know full well:*
> *I do not like thee, Doctor Fell!*

Of course, there was a very good reason why this child behind the "I" in this rhyme does not like the doctor—he might give her nasty-tasting medicine, perhaps even a shot. And the reason she "cannot tell" might be because the adults declare her "silly" and override her objections. In contrast to such "childish" aversion, however, many people cannot tell the reason why they "do not like thee" because there really is none: they don't like the other person simply because that other person is DIFFERENT. And to overcome the anxiety of dealing with someone DIFFERENT, those who share some common ethnicity, tradition, and culture may convince themselves that they are intrinsically better human beings than the strangers.

Xenophobia is insidious, a close relative to racism: I remember being advised in ninth grade to choose German or French as my foreign language because, in the words of the school counselor, "Spanish is too easy: it won't impress the college admissions boards." That this judgment was the rule in those days (and I dare say still reigns tacitly as the "preferred" college prep course of action today) is all the more absurd when one considers that some of the greatest literature of the twentieth century has been written in Spanish. Such prejudiced counsel may well prove to be self-destructive advice: after all, the largest (and fastest-growing) "minority" in the United States is the diverse group of people who claim Spanish as the language of their heritage.

One scorching summer day when my daughter was three, we were on our way to the store to buy the odds and ends—socks, baby shampoo, Q-tips—toddlers seem to require in steady supply. Suddenly, out of the sheer blue, she piped up from the back seat: "Everybody was inside someone else once!" She pronounced this emphatically, then clapped in delight, applauding her discovery.

What a simple undeniable thought! That each of us, no matter which crayon tint matches our skin—black, brown, or peach, burnt or raw sienna, tan or apricot—each of us has spent the first months of life inside of another person. Each of us has been nested, nourished, carried, and labored over by someone else before ever seeing the light of this world. In the face of such a thrilling plain truth, how can we speak of insurmountable differences between people? The bottom line is that we are all human beings—*Homo sapiens*, two-legged mammals with an upright gait and opposable thumbs. Each of us knows what it's like to prick a finger or bump a funny bone, to cry and laugh and hope and remember.

The way we think about the world matters, and the words used to describe that way of thinking are powerful persuasions. For example, take the phrase *The American Dream.* Collectively, we hold that the dream includes a better life for ourselves and for future generations. But America's various constituent groups—ethnic, social, political, gender, and religious—may interpret the idea of "Life, Liberty, and the Pursuit of Happiness" in dramatically different ways. Liberty for one person or group could mean oppression or even enslavement of another; for one group, the pursuit of happiness may mean the right to live on the land of one's ancestors, a belief that could clash with another group's desire to build an eighteen-hole golf course at the foot of the mountains. The idea of a single dream is misleading, and yet we thoughtlessly utter this phrase as a symbol of unity. Can there be one American dream? Is that even desirable? (Would you want to dream someone else's dream?)

Another troublemaker is the concept of the Melting Pot. I remember relishing (excuse the pun!) this metaphor when I was young: at times I would envision a gigantic kettle aglow with molten alloys of gold, silver, and other precious metals;

each of us was a priceless ore, and the resulting amalgam would be the brightest, strongest metal imaginable. At other times I pictured a pot of soup in which each individual ingredient contributed to the mixed flavors of a thick, rich stew. When I was feeling pessimistic, the kettle became a cauldron bubbling with a sorcerer's concoction so ingeniously brewed, there was no way of telling what evil indelicacies — *eye of newt, and toe of frog* — one had to ingest in order to attain magical powers.

Regardless of which image prevails at any particular moment, there's one frightening thing wrong with the whole concept: in order to be in the melting pot, the individual has to disappear. All of the special talents and attitudes, all the idiosyncrasies and gestures that go into what we call "personality," must be melted down; to avoid being regarded as "un-American," one must "blend in." A more insidious term for this process is "assimilation," and it has been the instigator behind so much of the intolerance in the history of our world — witch burnings and anti-Semitic pogroms, Red-baiting and Ku Klux Klan murders, tribal wars and *ethnic cleansing.* "Why do they dress that way?" — "Their food smells funny." — "My God is the only god."

*　*　*

I prefer to think of our nation not as a melting pot, but as a mosaic. In a mosaic, hundreds and thousands of individual tiles are pieced together to assemble a scene, much like a jigsaw puzzle. Each piece has its unique colors and shape; each piece is essential to the whole which, when viewed from afar, forms one piece of art. Like a puzzle, if you take away one tile, the picture immediately develops a hole; it is incomplete. Like a quilt, each piece has a history, its own distinctive story, to contribute. Part of the delight of looking at a mosaic is precisely the paradox of seeing many tiny pieces within the whole. The individual tiles give the picture texture and contours. They make it interesting.

Consider each of the pieces in this textbook — essay or memoir, poem or short story — as a tile in the mosaic of the United States. Enjoy each piece as a window into the lives and feelings of those special human beings as they interact with a particular environment — and then step back to get the whole picture that *Multicultural Voices* provides: a comprehensive landscape of our abundant and many-faceted land.

$\mathscr{S}$idewalks $\mathscr{A}$ of merica

If you want a picture of real, everyday life in the United States, focus on its sidewalks and streets — the moods and foods, the people and places, the signs and the sights. Stop and look around. Take some snapshots. Listen to the voices. Immerse yourself in the smells, tastes, and texture of the communities. See if you agree that the Sidewalks of America are where the cultures of the world cross.

1

ABOUT **JUDITH ORTIZ COFER**

Judith Ortiz Cofer says that her memories of past events serve as a "jumping off" point for her writing. Her memories are indeed special because she enjoyed a bilingual, bicultural childhood. Born in Puerto Rico in 1952, she shuttled between her homeland and New Jersey while she was growing up. The stories she heard, the people she knew, and the places she lived are vividly translated into the art of her poems, nonfiction, and fiction. A writer who captures both the warmth of the tropics and the blustery noise of the north, Ortiz Cofer has published two poetry collections, *Terms of Survival* and *Reaching for the Mainland;* a collection of personal essays and poems, *Silent Dancing;* and a novel, *The Line of the Sun.*

American History

I ONCE READ in a "Ripley's Believe It or Not" column that Paterson, New Jersey, is the place where the Straight and Narrow (streets) intersect. The Puerto Rican tenement known as *El Building* was one block up from Straight. It was, in fact, the corner of Straight and Market; not "at" the corner, but *the* corner. At almost any hour of the day, El Building was like a monstrous jukebox, blasting out *salsas* from open windows as the residents, mostly new immigrants just up from the island, tried to drown out whatever they were currently enduring with loud music. But the day President Kennedy was shot there was profound silence in El Building; even the abusive tongues of viragoes, the cursing of the unemployed, and the screeching of small children had been somehow muted. President Kennedy was a saint to these people. In fact, soon his photograph would be hung alongside the Sacred Heart and over the spiritist altars that many women kept in their apartments. He would become part of the hierarchy of martyrs they prayed to for favors that only one who had died for a cause would understand.

On the day that President Kennedy was shot, my ninth grade class had been out in the fenced playground of Public School Number 13. We had been given "free" exercise time and had been ordered by our P.E. teacher, Mr. DePalma, to "keep moving." That meant that the girls should jump rope and the boys toss basketballs through a hoop at the far end of the yard. He in the meantime would "keep an eye" on us from just inside the building.

It was a cold gray day in Paterson. The kind that warns of early snow. I was miserable, since I had forgotten my gloves, and my knuckles were turning red and raw from the jump rope. I was also taking a lot of abuse from the black girls for not turning the rope hard and fast enough for them.

"Hey, Skinny Bones, pump it, girl. Ain't you got no energy today?" Gail, the biggest of the black girls had the other end of the rope, yelled, "Didn't you eat your rice and beans and pork chops for breakfast today?"

*T*HE OTHER GIRLS picked up the "pork chop" and made it into a refrain: "pork chop, pork chop, did you eat your pork chop?" They entered the double ropes in pairs and exited without tripping or missing a beat. I felt a burning on my cheeks and then my glasses fogged up so that I could not manage to coordinate the jump rope with Gail. The chill was doing to me what it always did; entering my bones, making me cry, humiliating me. I hated the city, especially in winter. I hated Public School Number 13. I hated my skinny flat-chested body, and I envied the black girls who could jump rope so fast that their legs became a blur. They always seemed to be warm while I froze.

There was only one source of beauty and light for me that school year. The only thing I had anticipated at the start of the semester. That was seeing Eugene. In August, Eugene and his family had moved into the only house on the block that had a yard and trees. I could see his place from my window in El Building. In fact, if I sat on the fire escape I was literally suspended above Eugene's backyard. It was my favorite spot to read my library books in the summer. Until that August the house had been occupied by an old Jewish couple. Over the years I had become part of their family, without their knowing it, of course. I had a view of their kitchen and their backyard, and though I could not hear what they said, I knew when they were arguing, when one of them was sick, and many other things. I knew all this by watching them at mealtimes. I could see their kitchen table, the sink, and the stove. During good times, he sat at the table and read his newspapers while she fixed the meals. If they argued, he would leave and the old woman would sit and stare at nothing for a long time. When one of them was sick, the other would come and get things from the kitchen and carry them out on a tray. The old man had died in June. The last week of school I had not seen him at the table at all. Then one day I saw that there was a crowd in the kitchen. The old woman had finally emerged from the house on the arm of a stocky, middle-aged woman, whom I had seen there a few times before, maybe her daughter. Then a man had carried out suitcases. The house had stood empty for weeks. I had had to resist the temptation to climb down into the yard and water the flowers the old lady had taken such good care of.

❋

Spanish Words

salsas Latin American dance music with Afro-Caribbean rhythms and elements of jazz and rock, p. 3

señorita young lady, p. 7

Dios mío exclamation meaning "My God," p. 9

Hija daughter, p. 10

Niña little girl, p. 10

luto mourning, p. 12

*B*Y THE TIME Eugene's family moved in, the yard was a tangled mass of weeds. The father had spent several days mowing, and when he finished, from where I sat, I didn't see the red, yellow, and purple clusters that meant flowers to me. I didn't see this family sit down at the kitchen table together. It was just the mother, a red-headed tall woman who wore a white uniform—a nurse's, I guessed it was; the father was gone before I got up in the morning and was never there at dinner time. I only saw him on weekends when they sometimes sat on lawn-chairs under the oak tree, each hidden behind a section of the newspaper; and there was Eugene. He was tall and blond, and he wore glasses. I liked him right away because he sat at the kitchen table and read books for hours. That summer, before we had even spoken one word to each other, I kept him company on my fire escape.

Once school started I looked for him in all my classes, but P.S. 13 was a huge, over-populated place and it took me days and many discreet questions to discover that Eugene was in honors classes for all his subjects; classes that were not open to me because English was not my first language, though I was a straight A student. After much maneuvering I managed "to run into him" in the hallway where his locker was—on the other side of the building from mine—and in study hall at the library where he first seemed to notice me, but did not speak; and finally, on the way home after school one day when I decided to approach him directly, though my stomach was doing somersaults.

I WAS READY for rejection, snobbery, the worst. But when I came up to him, practically panting in my nervousness, and blurted out: "You're Eugene. Right?" he smiled, pushed his glasses up on his nose, and nodded. I saw then that he was blushing deeply. Eugene liked me, but he was shy. I did most of the talking that day. He nodded and smiled a lot. In the weeks that followed, we walked home together. He would linger at the corner of El Building for a few minutes then walk down to his two-story house. It was not until Eugene moved into that house that I noticed that El Building blocked most of the sun, and that the only spot that got a little sunlight during the day was the tiny square of earth the old woman had planted with flowers.

I did not tell Eugene that I could see inside his kitchen from my bedroom. I felt dishonest, but I liked my secret sharing of his evenings, especially now that I knew what he was reading since we chose our books together at the school library.

One day my mother came into my room as I was sitting on the window sill staring out. In her abrupt way she said: "Elena, you are acting 'moony.' " *Enamorada* was what she really said, that is—like a girl stupidly infatuated. Since I had turned fourteen and started menstruating my mother had been more vigilant than ever. She acted as if I was going to go crazy or explode or something if she didn't watch me and nag me all the time about being a *señorita* now. She kept talking about virtue, morality, and other subjects that did not interest me in the least. My mother was unhappy in Paterson, but my father had a good job at the bluejeans factory in Passaic and soon, he kept assuring us, we would be moving to our own house there. Every Sunday we drove out to the suburbs of Paterson, Clifton, and Passaic, out to where people mowed grass on Sundays in the summer, and where children made snowmen in the winter from pure white snow, not like the gray slush of Paterson which seemed to fall from the sky in that hue. I had learned to listen to my parents' dreams, which were spoken in Spanish, as fairy tales, like the stories about life in the island paradise of Puerto Rico before I was born. I had been to the island once as a little girl, to grandmother's funeral, and all I remembered was wailing women in black, my mother becoming hysterical and being given a pill that made her sleep two days, and me feeling lost in a crowd of strangers all claiming to be my aunts, uncles, and cousins. I had actually been glad to return to the city. We had not been back there since then, though my parents talked constantly about buying a house on the beach someday, retiring on the island — that was a common topic among the residents of El Building. As for me, I was going to go to college and become a teacher.

*B*UT AFTER MEETING EUGENE I began to think of the present more than of the future. What I wanted now was to enter that house I had watched for so many years. I wanted to see the other rooms where the old people had lived, and where the boy spent his time. Most of all, I wanted to sit at the kitchen table with Eugene like two adults, like the old man and his wife had done, maybe drink some coffee and talk about books. I had started reading *Gone with the Wind*. I was enthralled by it, with the daring and the passion of the beautiful girl living in a mansion, and with her devoted parents and the slaves who did everything for them.

I didn't believe such a world had ever really existed, and I wanted to ask Eugene some questions since he and his parents, he had told me, had come up from Georgia, the same place where the novel was set. His father worked for a company that had transferred him to Paterson. His mother was very unhappy, Eugene said, in his beautiful voice that rose and fell over words in a strange, lilting way. The kids at school called him "the hick" and made fun of the way he talked. I knew I was his only friend so far, and I liked that, though I felt sad for him sometimes. "Skinny Bones" and the "Hick" was what they called us at school when we were seen together.

*T*HE DAY MR. DEPALMA came out into the cold and asked us to line up in front of him was the day that President Kennedy was shot. Mr. DePalma, a short, muscular man with slicked-down black hair, was the science teacher, P.E. coach, and disciplinarian at P.S. 13. He was the teacher to whose homeroom you got assigned if you were a troublemaker, and the man called out to break up playground fights, and to escort violently angry teenagers to the office. And Mr. DePalma was the man who called your parents in for "a conference."

That day, he stood in front of two rows of mostly black and Puerto Rican kids, brittle from their efforts to "keep moving" on a November day that was turning bitter cold. Mr. DePalma, to our complete shock, was crying. Not just silent adult tears, but really sobbing. There were a few titters from the back of the line where I stood shivering.

"Listen," Mr. DePalma raised his arms over his head as if he were about to conduct an orchestra. His voice broke, and he covered his face with his hands. His barrel chest was heaving. Someone giggled behind me.

"Listen," he repeated, "something awful has happened." A strange gurgling came from his throat, and he turned around and spat on the cement behind him.

"Gross," someone said, and there was a lot of laughter.

"The President is dead, you idiots. I should have known

that wouldn't mean anything to a bunch of losers like you kids. Go home." He was shrieking now. No one moved for a minute or two, but then a big girl let out a "Yeah!" and ran to get her books piled up with the others against the brick wall of the school building. The others followed in a mad scramble to get to their things before somebody caught on. It was still an hour to the dismissal bell.

A little scared, I headed for El Building. There was an eerie feeling on the streets. I looked into Mario's drugstore, a favorite hangout for the high school crowd, but there were only a couple of old Jewish men at the soda bar talking with the short order cook in tones that sounded almost angry, but they were keeping their voices low. Even the traffic on one of the busiest intersections in Paterson—Straight Street and Park Avenue—seemed to be moving slower. There were no horns blasting that day. At El Building, the usual little group of unemployed men were not hanging out on the front stoop making it difficult for women to enter the front door. No music spilled out from open doors in the hallway. When I walked into our apartment, I found my mother sitting in front of the grainy picture of the television set.

She looked up at me with a tear-streaked face and just said: "Dios mío," turning back to the set as if it were pulling at her eyes. I went into my room.

Though I wanted to feel the right thing about President Kennedy's death, I could not fight the feeling of elation that stirred in my chest. Today was the day I was to visit Eugene in his house. He had asked me to come over after school to study for an American History test with him. We had also planned to walk to the public library together. I looked down into his yard. The oak tree was bare of leaves and the ground looked gray with ice. The light through the large kitchen window of his house told me that El Building blocked the sun to such an extent that they had to turn lights on in the middle of the day. I felt ashamed about it. But the white kitchen table with the lamp hanging just above it looked cozy and inviting. I would soon sit there, across from Eugene, and I would tell him about my perch just above his house. Maybe I should.

In the next thirty minutes I changed clothes, put on a little pink lipstick, and got my books together. Then I went in to tell my mother that I was going to a friend's house to study. I did not expect her reaction.

"You are going out *today*?" The way she said "today" sounded as if a storm warning had been issued. It was said in utter disbelief. Before I could answer, she came toward me and held my elbows as I clutched my books.

"*Hija*, the President has been killed. We must show respect. He was a great man. Come to church with me tonight."

$\mathcal{S}$HE TRIED TO EMBRACE ME, but my books were in the way. My first impulse was to comfort her, she seemed so distraught, but I had to meet Eugene in fifteen minutes.

"I have a test to study for, Mama. I will be home by eight."

"You are forgetting who you are, *Niña*. I have seen you staring down at that boy's house. You are heading for humiliation and pain." My mother said this in Spanish and in a resigned tone that surprised me, as if she had no intention of stopping me from "heading for humiliation and pain." I started for the door. She sat in front of the TV holding a white handkerchief to her face.

I walked out to the street and around the chain-link fence that separated El Building from Eugene's house. The yard was neatly edged around the little walk that led to the door. It always amazed me how Paterson, the inner core of the city, had no apparent logic to its architecture. Small, neat, single residences like this one could be found right next to huge, dilapidated apartment buildings like El Building. My guess was that the little houses had been there first, then the immigrants had come in droves, and the monstrosities had been raised for them—the Italians, the Irish, the Jews, and now us, the Puerto Ricans and the blacks. The door was painted a deep green: *verde,* the color of hope, I had heard my mother say it: *Verde-Esperanza.*

I KNOCKED SOFTLY. A few suspenseful moments later the door opened just a crack. The red, swollen face of a woman appeared. She had a halo of red hair floating over a delicate ivory face—the face of a doll—with freckles on the nose. Her smudged eye make-up made her look unreal to me, like a mannequin seen through a warped store window.

"What do you want?" Her voice was tiny and sweet-sounding, like a little girl's, but her tone was not friendly.

"I'm Eugene's friend. He asked me over. To study." I thrust out my books, a silly gesture that embarrassed me almost immediately.

"You live there?" She pointed up to El Building, which looked particularly ugly, like a gray prison with its many dirty windows and rusty fire escapes. The woman had stepped halfway out and I could see that she wore a white nurse's uniform with St. Joseph's Hospital on the name tag.

"Yes. I do."

She looked intently at me for a couple of heartbeats, then said as if to herself, "I don't know how you people do it." Then directly to me: "Listen. Honey. Eugene doesn't want to study with you. He is a smart boy. Doesn't need help. You understand me. I am truly sorry if he told you you could come over. He cannot study with you. It's nothing personal. You understand? We won't be in this place much longer, no need for him to get close to people—it'll just make it harder for him later. Run back home now."

I couldn't move. I just stood there in shock at hearing these things said to me in such a honey-drenched voice. I had never heard an accent like hers, except for Eugene's softer version. It was as if she were singing me a little song.

"What's wrong? Didn't you hear what I said?" She seemed very angry, and I finally snapped out of my trance. I turned away from the green door, and heard her close it gently.

Our apartment was empty when I got home. My mother was in someone else's kitchen, seeking the solace she needed. Father would come in from his late shift at midnight. I would hear them talking softly in the kitchen for hours that night. They would not discuss their dreams for the future, or life in Puerto Rico, as they often did; that night they would talk sadly about the young widow and her two children, as if they were family. For the next few days, we would observe *luto* in our apartment; that is, we would practice restraint and silence—no loud music or laughter. Some of the women of El Building would wear black for weeks.

That night, I lay in my bed trying to feel the right thing for our dead President. But the tears that came up from a deep source inside me were strictly for me. When my mother came to the door, I pretended to be sleeping. Sometime during the night, I saw from my bed the street-light come on. It had a pink halo around it. I went to my window and pressed my face to the cool glass. Looking up at the light I could see the white snow falling like a lace veil over its face. I did not look down to see it turning gray as it touched the ground below.

RESPONDING

1. **Personal Response** Think of a national crisis or tragedy that you have lived through and describe your reaction to it. Compare your response to the narrator's reaction to Kennedy's death.

2. **Literary Analysis** Writers often reveal the personalities of *characters* indirectly through their thoughts and actions. How does the narrator reveal that family life, nature, and reading are important to her? Would you like to have this person for a friend? Explain.

3. **Multicultural Connection** How does the narrator indicate the importance of faith and religion to the Puerto Rican community?

LANGUAGE WORKSHOP

Fragments and Run-ons A *sentence fragment* is punctuated like a sentence but does not express a complete thought. You can correct fragments in two ways.

• Add or delete words to create a complete sentence.

• Attach the fragment to another related sentence.

A *run-on* is two or more sentences run together without proper punctuation between them. You can correct run-ons in several ways.

• Join them with a period, with a comma and a conjunction, or with a semicolon.

Correct these fragments and run-ons.

(1) El Building was a tenement in Paterson. At the corner of Straight and Market Streets. (2) Lots of noise came from El Building it blasted out *salsas* from windows. (3) The chain fence that separated El Building from the only house on the block.

WRITER'S PORTFOLIO

Interview someone who has vivid memories of November 22, 1963, the day President Kennedy was shot. Find out what she or he was doing, wearing, and feeling when the news arrived. How does this person feel about the event more than thirty years later? Record or take notes on the interview and write an essay.

ABOUT **FRANK CHIN**

Frank Chin — a Chinese American playwright, fiction writer, and critic born in Berkeley, California, in 1940 — detests stereotypical, Hollywood-derived images of Asian Americans. He prefers to call himself a "Chinatown Cowboy" (to associate himself with the men who built the railroads in the American West). Considered the father of Asian American writing for his pioneer efforts to publish works that express the genuine spirit of Asian American culture and history, Chin is the first Chinese American to have a play, *The Chickencoop Chinaman*, produced on the New York stage. Its focus, the search for identity in a racially divided society, is a theme Chin explores frequently. In his novel *Donald Duk* (1991), Chin presents a cartoon-like character, Donald,

who learns to see himself as a true individual.

From *Donald Duk*

WHO WOULD BELIEVE anyone named Donald Duk dances like Fred Astaire? Donald Duk does not like his name. Donald Duk never liked his name. He hates his name. He is not a duck. He is not a cartoon character. He does not go home to sleep in Disneyland every night. The kids that laugh at him are very smart. Everyone at his private school is smart. Donald Duk is smart. He is a gifted one, they say.

No one in school knows he takes tap dance lessons from a man who calls himself "The Chinese Fred Astaire." Mom talks Dad into paying for the lessons and tap shoes.

Fred Astaire. Everybody everywhere likes Fred Astaire in the old black-and-white movies. Late at night on TV, even Dad smiles when Fred Astaire dances. Mom hums along. Donald Duk wants to live the late night life in old black-and-white movies and talk with his feet like Fred Astaire, and smile Fred Astaire's sweet lemonade smile.

Fred Astaire a dancer and movie actor known for elegant attire including tails and top hat, p.15

The music teacher and English teacher in school go dreamy eyed when they talk about seeing Fred Astaire and Ginger Rogers on the late-night TV. "Remember when he danced with Barbara Stanwyck? What was the name of the movie…?"

"Barbara Stanwyck?"

"Did you see the one where he dances with Rita Hayworth?"

"Oooh, Rita Hayworth!"

Donald Duk enjoys the books he reads in schools. The math is a curious game. He is not the only Chinese in the private school. But he is the only Donald Duk. He avoids the other Chinese here. And the Chinese seem to avoid him. This school is a place where the Chinese are comfortable hating Chinese. "Only the Chinese are stupid enough to give a kid a stupid name like Donald Duk," Donald Duk says to himself. "And if the Chinese were that smart, why didn't they invent tap dancing?"

$\mathcal{D}$ONALD DUK'S father's name is King. King Duk. Donald hates his father's name. He hates being introduced with his father. "This is King Duk, and his son Donald Duk." Mom's name is Daisy. "That's Daisy Duk, and her son Donald." Venus Duk and Penny Duk are Donald's sisters. The girls are twins and a couple of years older than Donald.

His own name is driving him crazy! Looking Chinese is driving him crazy! All his teachers are making a big deal about Chinese stuff in their classes because of Chinese New Year coming on soon. The teacher of California History is so happy to be reading about the Chinese. "The man I studied history under at Berkeley authored this book. He was a spellbinding lecturer," the teacher throbs. Then he reads, "The Chinese in America were made passive and nonassertive by centuries of Confucian thought and Zen mysticism. They were totally unprepared for the violently individualistic and democratic Americans. From their first step on American soil to the middle of the twentieth century, the timid, introverted Chinese have been helpless against the relentless victimization by aggressive, highly competitive Americans.

"One of the Confucian concepts that lends the Chinese vulnerable to the assertive ways of the West is 'the mandate of heaven.' As the European kings of old ruled by divine right, so the emperors of China ruled by the mandate of heaven." The teacher takes a breath and looks over his spellbound class. Donald wants to barf pink and green stuff all over the teacher's book.

"What's he saying?" Donald Duk's pal Arnold Azalea asks in a whisper.

"Same thing as everybody — Chinese are artsy, cutesy and chickendick," Donald whispers back.

✳
Culture Notes

Chinese New Year Based on a lunar year of about 354 days, Chinese New Year falls somewhere between Jan. 10 and Feb. 19 on the Gregorian calendar (a solar year of about 365 days). p.17

Goong hay fot choy "Happy New Year" in Cantonese, p.17

Lawrence Ferlinghetti famous "Beatnik" poet during the 1950s and '60s, p.18

Oh, no! Here comes Chinese New Year again! It is Donald Duk's worst time of year. Here come the stupid questions about the funny things Chinese believe in. The funny things Chinese do. The funny things Chinese eat. And, "Where can I buy some Chinese firecrackers?"

And in Chinatown it's *Goong hay fot choy* everywhere. And some gang kids do sell firecrackers. And some gang kids rob other kids looking for firecrackers. He doesn't like the gang kids. He doesn't like speaking their Chinese. He doesn't have to — this is America. He doesn't like Chinatown. But he lives here.

*T*HE GANG KIDS KNOW HIM. They call him by name. One day the Frog Twins wobble onto the scene with their load of full shopping bags. There is Donald Duk. And there are five gang boys and two girlfriends chewing gum, swearing and smirking. The gang kids wear black tanker jackets, white tee shirts and baggy black denim jeans. It is the alley in front of the Chinese Historical Society Museum. There are fish markets on each side of the Chinatown end of the alley. Lawrence Ferlinghetti's famous City Lights Bookstore is at the end that opens on Columbus Street. Suddenly there are the Frog Twins in their heavy black overcoats. They seem to be wearing all the clothes they own under their coats. Their coats bulge. Under their skirts they wear several pairs of trousers and slacks. They wear one knit cap over the other. They wear scarves tied over their heads and shawls over their shoulders.

*T*HAT NIGHT, AFTER HE IS ASLEEP, Dad comes home from the restaurant and wakes him up. "You walk like a sad softie," Dad says. "You look like you want everyone to beat you up."

"I do not!" Donald Duk says.

"You look at yourself in the mirror," Dad says, and Donald Duk looks at himself in his full-length dressing mirror. "Look at those slouching shoulders, that pouty face. Look at those hands holding onto each other. You look scared!" Dad's voice booms and Donald hears everyone's feet hit the floor. Mom and the twins are out in the hall looking into his open door.

"I am scared!" Donald Duk says.

"I don't care if you are scared," Dad says. His eyes sizzle into Donald Duk's frightened pie-eyed stare. "Be as scared as you want to be, but don't look scared. Especially when you walk through Chinatown."

"How do I look like I'm not scared if I am scared?" Donald Duk asks.

"You walk with your back straight. You keep your hands out of your pockets. Don't hunch your shoulders. Think of them as being down. Keep your head up. Look like you know where you're going. Walk like you know where you're going. And you say, 'Don't mess with me, horsepuckie! Don't mess with me!' But you don't say it with your mouth. You say it with your eyes. You say it with your hands where everybody can see them. Anybody get two steps in front of you, you zap them with your eyes, and they had better nod at you or look away. When they nod, you nod. When you walk like nobody better mess with you, nobody will mess with you. When you walk around like you're walking now, all rolled up in a little ball and hiding out from everything, they'll get you for sure."

Donald does not like his dad waking him up like that and yelling at him. But what the old man says works. Outside among the cold San Francisco shadows and the early morning shoppers, Donald Duk hears his father's voice and straightens his back, takes his hands out of his pockets, says "Don't mess with me!" with his eyes and every move of his body. And, yes, he's talking with his body the way Fred Astaire talks, and shoots every gang kid who walks toward him in the eye with a look that says, "Don't mess with me." And no one messes with him. Dad never talks about it again.

Later, gang kids laugh at his name and try to pick fights with him during the afternoon rush hour, Dad's busy time in the kitchen. Donald is smarter than these lowbrow beady-eyed goons. He has to beat them without fighting them because he doesn't know how to fight. Donald Duk gets the twins to talk about it with Dad while they are all at the dining room table working on their model airplanes.

*D*AD LAUGHS. "So he has a choice. He does not like people laughing at his name. He does not want the gangsters laughing at his name to beat him up. He mostly does not want to look like a sissy in front of them, so what can he do?"

"He can pay them to leave him alone," Venus says.

"He can not! That is so chicken it's disgusting!" Penelope says.

"So, our little brother is doomed."

"He can agree with them and laugh at his name," Dad says. "He can tell them lots of Donald Duk jokes. Maybe he can learn to talk that quack-quack Donald Duck talk."

"Whaaat?" the twins ask in one voice.

"If he keeps them laughing," Dad says, "even if he can just keep them listening, they are not beating him up, right? And they are not calling him a sissy. He does not want to fight? He does not have to fight. He has to use his smarts, okay? If he's smart enough, he makes up some Donald Duck jokes to surprise them and make them laugh. They laugh three times, he can walk away. Leave them there laughing, thinking Donald Duk is one terrific fella."

"So says King Duk," Venus Duk flips. The twins often talk as if everything they hear everybody say and see everybody do is dialog in a memoir they're writing or action in a play they're directing. This makes Mom feel like she's on stage and drives Donald Duk crazy.

"Is that Chinese psychology, dear?" Daisy Duk asks.

"Daisy Duk inquires," says Penelope Duk.

"And little Donnie Duk says, *Oh Mom!* and sighs."

"I do not!" Donald Duk yelps at the twins.

"Well, then, say it," Penelope Duk says. "It's a good line. So *you* you, you know."

"Thank you," Venus says.

"Oh goshes, you all, your sympathy is so . . . so . . . so literary. So dramatic." Donald Duk says. "It is truly depressing."

"I thought it was narrative," Venus says.

"Listen up for some Chinese psychology, girls and boys," Daisy Duk says.

"No, that's not psychology, that's Bugs Bunny," Dad says.

"You don't mean, Bugs Bunny, dear. You always make that mistake."

"Br'er Rabbit!" Dad says.

"What does that mean?" Donald Duk asks the twins. They shrug their shoulders. Nobody knows what Br'er Rabbit has to do with Dad's way of avoiding a fight and not being a fool, but it works.

One bright and sunny afternoon, a gang boy stops Donald and talks to him in the quacking voice of Walt Disney's Donald Duck. The voice breaks Donald Duk's mind for a flash, and he is afraid to turn on his own Donald Duck voice. He tries telling a joke about Donald Duck not wearing trousers or shoes, when the gangster—in black jeans, black tee shirt, black jacket, black shades—says in a perfect Donald Duck voice, "Let's take the pants off Donald Duk!"

"Oh oh! I stepped in it now!" Donald Duk says in his Donald Duck voice and stuns the gangster and his two gangster friends and their three girlfriends. Everything is seen and understood very fast. Without missing a beat, his own perfect Donald Duck voice cries for help in perfect Cantonese *Gow meng ahhhh!* and they all laugh. Old women pulling little wire shopping carts full of fresh vegetables stop and stare at him. Passing children recognize the voice and say Donald Duk talks Chinese.

Culture Note

Asian lunar zodiac a belt of the heavens within which is the apparent annual path of the moon; divided in 12 divisions named after animals, p. 21

"Don't let these monsters take off my pants. I may be Donald Duk, but I am as human as you," he says in Chinese, in his Donald Duck voice, "I know how to use chopsticks. I use flush toilets. Why shouldn't I wear pants on Grant Street in Chinatown?" They all laugh more than three times. Their laughter roars three times on the corner of Grant and Jackson, and Donald Duk walks away, leaving them laughing, just the way Dad says he can. He feels great. Just great!

$\mathcal{D}$ONALD DUK DOES not want to laugh about his name forever. There has to be an end to this. There is an end to all kidstuff for a kid. An end to diapers. An end to nursery rhymes and fairy tales. There has to be an end to laughing about his name to get out of a fight. Chinese New Year. Everyone will be laughing. He is twelve years old. Twelve years old is special to the Chinese. There are twelve years in the Asian lunar zodiac. For each year there is an animal. This year Donald will complete his first twelve-year cycle of his life. To celebrate, Donald Duk's father's old opera mentor, Uncle Donald Duk, is coming to San Francisco to perform a Cantonese opera. Donald Duk does not want Chinese New Year. He does not want his uncle Donald Duk to tell him again how Daddy was a terrible man to name his little boy Donald Duk, because all the *bok gwai,* the white monsters, will think he is named after that barebutt cartoon duck in the top half of a sailor suit and no shoes.

RESPONDING

1. **Personal Response** Donald seems to idolize Fred Astaire, a famous dancer of the 1940s and '50s. Name a "star" you admire and tell why you do.

2. **Literary Analysis** What effect does the author's use of short, choppy sentences have on the story? Why do you think he uses this *style?*

3. **Multicultural Connection** Donald Duk says people ask stupid questions about the funny things Chinese believe in, do, and eat. Think about a misconception people have about customs, language, or holidays associated with your culture or someone else's. Then set them straight by giving them the facts.

LANGUAGE WORKSHOP

Stereotypes This loaded quote appears in "Donald Duk": "The Chinese in America were made passive and nonassertive ... totally unprepared for the violently individualistic and democratic Americans. From their first step on American soil to the middle of the twentieth century, the timid, introverted Chinese have been helpless against the relentless victimization by aggressive, highly competitive Americans."

Under two columns labeled *Chinese* and *American,* write at least five words used to describe each group. Then discuss the *stereotypes* implied in each label.

WRITER'S PORTFOLIO

Assess the signals Donald sends to others by his posture, eye contact, and other nonverbal cues. Add some tips of your own and prepare a brief list of instructions to appear in a survival manual for teens.

ABOUT **BRENT STAPLES**

The streets of small industrial towns and large metropolitan centers can be equally dangerous. Brent Staples, a journalist, literary and drama critic, and essayist, knows that only too well. While growing up in Chester, Pennsylvania, Staples avoided confrontations — and survived. Later, in Chicago and New York, he learned that plain avoidance was not enough. How Staples, who holds a Ph.D. in psychology from the University of Chicago, learned to cope with the reality of these mean streets is the subject of the following essay. Currently a member of the editorial board of the *New York Times,* Staples continues to probe the menace and meaning of America, most recently in *Parallel Time: Growing Up in Black and White* (1994).

Black Men and Public Space

*M*Y FIRST VICTIM WAS A WOMAN — white, well dressed, probably in her early twenties. I came upon her late one evening on a deserted street in Hyde Park, a relatively affluent neighborhood in an otherwise mean, impoverished section of Chicago. As I swung onto the avenue behind her, there seemed to be a discreet, uninflammatory distance between us. Not so. She cast back a worried glance. To her, the youngish black man — a broad six feet two inches with a beard and billowing hair, both hands shoved into the pockets of a bulky military jacket — seemed menacingly close. After a few more quick glimpses, she picked up her pace and was soon running in earnest. Within seconds she disappeared into a cross street.

That was more than a decade ago, I was twenty-two years old, a graduate student newly arrived at the University of Chicago. It was in the echo of that terrified woman's footfalls that I first began to know the unwieldy inheritance I'd come into — the ability to alter public space in ugly ways. It was clear that she thought herself the quarry of a mugger, a rapist, or worse. Suffering a bout of insomnia, however, I was stalking sleep, not defenseless wayfarers. As a softy who is scarcely able to take a knife to a raw chicken — let alone hold one to a person's throat — I was surprised, embarrassed, and dismayed all at once. Her flight made me feel like an accomplice in tyranny. It also made it clear that I was indistinguishable from the muggers who occasionally seeped into the area from the surrounding ghetto. That first encounter, and those that followed, signified that a vast, unnerving gulf lay between nighttime pedestrians—particularly women—and me. And I soon gathered that being perceived as dangerous is a hazard in itself. I only needed to turn a corner into a dicey situation, or crowd some frightened, armed person in a foyer somewhere, or make an errant move after being pulled over by a policeman. When fear and weapons meet—and they often do in urban America—there is always the possibility of death.

*I*N THAT FIRST YEAR, my first away from my hometown, I was to become thoroughly familiar with the language of fear. At dark, shadowy intersections, I could cross in front of a car stopped at a traffic light and elicit the *thunk, thunk, thunk, thunk* of the driver—black, white, male, or female—hammering down the door locks. On less traveled streets after dark, I grew accustomed to but never comfortable with people crossing to the other side of the street rather than pass me. Then there were the standard unpleasantries with policemen, doormen, bouncers, cabdrivers, and others whose business it is to screen out troublesome individuals *before* there is any nastiness.

I moved to New York nearly two years ago and I have remained an avid night walker. In central Manhattan, the near-constant crowd cover minimizes tense one-on-one street encounters. Elsewhere—in SoHo, for example, where sidewalks are narrow and tightly spaced buildings shut out the sky—things can get very taut indeed.

After dark, on the warrenlike streets of Brooklyn where I live, I often see women who fear the worst from me. They seem to have set their faces on neutral, and with their purse straps strung across their chests bandolier-style, they forge ahead as though bracing themselves against being tackled. I understand, of course, that the danger they perceive is not a hallucination. Women are particularly vulnerable to street violence, and young black males are drastically overrepresented among the perpetrators of that violence. Yet these truths are no solace against the kind of alienation that comes of being ever the suspect, a fearsome entity with whom pedestrians avoid making eye contact.

It is not altogether clear to me how I reached the ripe old age of twenty-two without being conscious of the lethality nighttime pedestrians attributed to me. Perhaps it was because in Chester, Pennsylvania, the small, angry industrial town where I came of age in the 1960s, I was scarcely noticeable against a backdrop of gang warfare, street knifings, and murders. I grew up one of the good boys, had perhaps a half-dozen fistfights. In retrospect, my shyness of combat has clear sources.

As a boy, I saw countless tough guys locked away; I have since buried several, too. They were babies, really — a teenage cousin, a brother of twenty-two, a childhood friend in his mid-twenties — all gone down in episodes of bravado played out in the streets. I came to doubt the virtues of intimidation early on. I chose, perhaps unconsciously, to remain a shadow — timid, but a survivor.

The fearsomeness mistakenly attributed to me in public places often has a perilous flavor. The most frightening of these confusions occurred in the late 1970s and early 1980s, when I worked as a journalist in Chicago. One day, rushing into the office of a magazine I was writing for with a deadline story in hand, I was mistaken for a burglar. The office manager called security and, with an ad hoc posse, pursued me through the labyrinthine halls, nearly to my editor's door. I had no way of proving who I was. I could only move briskly toward the company of someone who knew me.

Another time I was on assignment for a local paper and killing time before an interview. I entered a jewelry store on the city's affluent Near North Side. The proprietor excused herself and returned with an enormous red Doberman pinscher straining at the end of a leash. She stood, the dog extended toward me, silent to my questions, her eyes bulging nearly out of her head. I took a cursory look around, nodded, and bade her good night.

Relatively speaking, however, I never fared as badly as another black male journalist. He went to nearby Waukegan, Illinois, a couple of summers ago to work on a story about a murderer who was born there. Mistaking the reporter for the killer, police officers hauled him from his car at gunpoint and but for his press credentials would probably have tried to book him. Such episodes are not uncommon. Black men trade tales like this all the time.

Over the years, I learned to smother the rage I felt at so often being taken for a criminal. Not to do so would surely have led to madness. I now take precautions to make myself less threatening. I move about with care, particularly late in the evening. I give a wide berth to nervous people on subway platforms during the wee hours, particularly when I have exchanged business clothes for jeans. If I happen to be entering a building behind some people who appear skittish, I may walk by, letting them clear the lobby before I return, so as not to seem to be following them. I have been calm and extremely congenial on those rare occasions when I've been pulled over by the police.

And on late-evening constitutionals I employ what has proved to be an excellent tension-reducing measure: I whistle melodies from Beethoven and Vivaldi and the more popular classical composers. Even steely New Yorkers hunching toward nighttime destinations seem to relax, and occasionally they even join in the tune. Virtually everybody seems to sense that a mugger wouldn't be warbling bright, sunny selections from Vivaldi's *Four Seasons*. It is my equivalent of the cowbell that hikers wear when they know they are in bear country.

RESPONDING

1. **Personal Response** Like Staples, you have probably found yourself in a fear-provoking situation caused by stereotyping. Describe such an experience (for example, being stereotyped as a juvenile delinquent just because you are a teenager). Were any of your survival tactics similar to Staples's?

2. **Literary Analysis** Staples uses *humor* in his narrative to expose prejudice. Identify three humorous passages and discuss the message they contain.

3. Multicultural Connection The amount of public "space," the distance we prefer between ourselves and others, often varies depending on the situation and the culture. Describe Staples's experience with public space and his coping strategies. Compare or contrast them with your own strategies.

LANGUAGE WORKSHOP

Adjectives and Adverbs *Adjectives* modify nouns and pronouns. *Adverbs* modify verbs, adjectives, and adverbs. Modifiers that follow linking verbs such as *is, tastes, smells, looks, sounds,* and *feels* should be adjectives, not adverbs. (This pizza tastes *bad,* not *badly.*)
Identify the adjectives and adverbs in the following sentence from "Black Men and Public Space": "I came upon her late one evening on a deserted street in Hyde Park, a relatively affluent neighborhood. . . ."

Choose the correct word in each sentence below.
1. The woman was (*real, really*) afraid that she was being followed.
2. She walked (*nervous, nervously*) and quickly down the sidewalk.
3. The man felt (*bad, badly*) that he had frightened her.
4. The street sounded (*quiet, quietly*) except for soft footfalls.
5. (*Sudden, Suddenly*) a door slammed in the distance.

WRITER'S PORTFOLIO

As a self-styled "night walker," Staples sees people and places in unique ways. In your journal, contrast a walk you took or a sight you saw at night with one during daylight in the same environment. What effect does the dark have on quite ordinary people and things?

ABOUT **LORRAINE HANSBERRY**

Lorraine Hansberry's *A Raisin in the Sun* (1959) was the first play written by an African American woman to be produced on Broadway. *Raisin* won the New York Drama Critics Circle Award, making Hansberry the first African American and the youngest writer ever to receive the honor. Although several episodes in the play mirror Hansberry's own experiences, the theme is universal — the dreams and fears of ordinary people. In the following excerpt from *To Be Young, Gifted and Black*, an autobiographical collection developed into a two-act drama after her death in 1965, Hansberry sets down the "truth" of her "life and essences . . . which are to be found, first of all, on the Southside of Chicago," where she was born in 1930.

Chicago: Southside Summers

FOR SOME TIME NOW—I think since I was a child—I have been possessed of the desire to put down the stuff of my life. This is a commonplace impulse, apparently, among persons of massive self-interest; sooner or later we all do it. And, I am quite certain, there is only one internal quarrel: how much of the truth to tell? How much, how much, how much! It *is* brutal, in sober uncompromising moments, to reflect on the comedy of concern we all enact when it comes to our precious images!

Even so, when such vanity as propels the writing of such memoirs is examined, certainly one would wish at least to have some boast of social serviceability on one's side. I shall set down in these pages what shall seem to me to be the truth of my life and essences . . . which are to be found, first of all, on the Southside of Chicago, where I was born. . . .

ALL TRAVELERS TO MY CITY should ride the elevated trains that race along the back ways of Chicago. The lives you can look into!

I think you could find the tempo of my people on their back porches. The honesty of their living is there in the shabbiness. Scrubbed porches that sag and look their danger.

Dirty gray wood steps. And always a line of white and pink clothes scrubbed so well, waving in the dirty wind of the city.

My people are poor. And they are tired. And they are determined to live.

Our Southside is a place apart: each piece of our living is a protest.

I WAS BORN May 19, 1930, the last of four children.

Of love and my parents there is little to be written: their relationship to their children was utilitarian. We were fed and housed and dressed and outfitted with more cash than our associates and that was all. We were also vaguely taught certain vague absolutes: that we were better than no one but infinitely superior to everyone; that we were the products of the proudest and most mistreated of the races of man; that there was nothing enormously difficult about life; that one *succeeded* as a matter of course.

Life was not a struggle—it was something that one *did.* One won an argument because, if facts gave out, one invented them—with color! The only sinful people in the world were dull people. And, above all, there were two things which were never to be betrayed: the family and the race. But of love, there was nothing ever said.

If we were sick, we were sternly, impersonally and carefully nursed and doctored back to health. Fevers, toothaches were attended to with urgency and importance; one always felt *important* in my family. Mother came with a tray to your room with the soup and Vick's salve or gave the enemas in a steaming bathroom. But we were not fondled, any of us—head held to breast, fingers about that head—until we were grown, all of us, and my father died.

At his funeral I at last, in my memory, saw my mother hold her sons that way, and for the first time in her life my sister held me in her arms I think. We were not a loving people: we were passionate in our hostilities and affinities, but the caress embarrassed us.

We have changed little. . . .

Seven years separated the nearest of my brothers and sisters and myself; I wear, I am sure, the earmarks of that familial station to this day. Little has been written or thought to my knowledge about children who occupy that place: the last born separated by an uncommon length of time from the next youngest. I suspect we are probably a race apart.

The last born is an object toy which comes in years when brothers and sisters who are seven, ten, twelve years older are old enough to appreciate it rather than poke out its eyes. They do not mind diapering you the first two years, but by the time you are five you are a pest that has to be attended to in the washroom, taken to the movies and "sat with" at night. You are not a person—you are a nuisance who is not particular fun any more. Consequently, you swiftly learn to play alone. . . .

*M*Y CHILDHOOD SOUTHSIDE SUMmers were the ordinary city kind, full of the street games which other rememberers have turned into fine ballets these days, and rhymes that anticipated what some people insist on calling modern poetry:

Oh, Mary Mack, Mack, Mack
With the silver buttons, buttons, buttons
All down her back, back, back.
She asked her mother, mother, mother
For fifteen cents, cents, cents
To see the elephant, elephant, elephant
Jump the fence, fence, fence.
Well, he jumped so high, high, high
'Til he touched the sky, sky, sky
And he didn't come back, back, back
'Til the Fourth of Ju—ly, ly, ly!

I remember skinny little Southside bodies by the fives and tens of us panting the delicious hours away:

"May I?"

And the voice of authority: "Yes, you may — you may take one giant step."

One drew in all one's breath and tightened one's fist and pulled the small body against the heavens, stretching, straining all the muscles in the legs to make — one giant step.

It is a long time. One forgets the reason for the game. (For children's games are always explicit in their reasons for being. To play is to win something. Or not to be "it." Or to be high pointer, or outdoer or, sometimes — just *the winner.* But after a time one forgets.)

Why was it important to take a small step, a teeny step, or the most desired of all — one GIANT step?

A giant step to *where?*

*E*VENINGS WERE SPENT mainly on the back porches where screen doors slammed in the darkness with those really very special summertime sounds. And, sometimes, when Chicago nights got too steamy, the whole family got into the car and went to the park and slept out in the open on blankets. Those were, of course, the best times of all because the grownups were invariably reminded of having been children in the South and told the best stories then. And it was also cool and sweet to be on the grass and there was usually the scent of freshly cut lemons or melons in the air. Daddy would lie on his back, as fathers must, and explain about how men thought the stars above us came to be and how far away they were.

I never did learn to believe that anything could be as far away as *that.* Especially the stars. . . .

RESPONDING

1. **Personal Response** Hansberry says that writers quarrel about "how much of the truth to tell." In your experience, do you think that writers in general — or those you've met so far in this book — tell the truth? Do you think writers are entitled to alter the facts? Explain.

2. **Literary Analysis** Examine Hansberry's use of *setting*. Does Southside Chicago seem a pleasant or an unpleasant place to live? Why?

3. **Multicultural Connection** What picture of growing up in a big city during the 1930s and 1940s do you get from the details Hansberry provides? Explain how it compares or contrasts with growing up in the '90s in your community.

LANGUAGE WORKSHOP

Sentence Variety Try these tips to make your sentences more interesting.

- Begin with an introductory phrase, a question, or a quote.
- Sometimes put the object before the verb.
- Combine short, choppy sentences.
- Balance declarative sentences with other kinds.

Revise the paragraph below, using tips from this workshop.

Lorraine Hansberry was born in Chicago. She attended grammar and high school there. She attended the University of Wisconsin. Then she went to New York. She became involved in the theater. She wrote *A Raisin in the Sun.* She was the first African American to win the New York Drama Critics Circle Award.

WRITER'S PORTFOLIO

Write a letter to a person from another country explaining the rules of a game you played when you were young. Be sure to define terms or phrases carefully, since even the concept of "choosing sides," for example, may be unfamiliar to some.

NAOMI SHIHAB NYE Called a "quiet observer of the human condition," Naomi Shihab Nye published her first poems in *Wee Wisdom,* a children's magazine, when she was only seven years old. Born in St. Louis to a Palestinian father and an American mother, Nye lived in the Middle East and San Antonio, Texas, during her high school years. Since then she has been a writer in residence, a teacher, a songwriter, and a world-wide traveler who promotes international goodwill through the arts. Full-length collections of her poems include *Different Ways to Pray, Hugging the Jukebox,* and *Yellow Glove.*

MARILOU AWIAKTA Marilou Awiakta, a Cherokee/Appalachian writer whose last name means "eye of the deer," grew up on the high-tech, atomic frontier of Oak Ridge, Tennessee. A storyteller as well as a writer, Awiakta has been featured on PBS in the *Telling Tales* series, widely used in schools. Her works include *Abiding Appalachia: Where Mountain and Atom Meet,* which features poems about her Cherokee heritage; *Rising Fawn and the Fire Mystery,* a novella about the Choctaw Removal; and *Selu: Seeking the Corn-Mother's Wisdom,* a weaving of essays, poems, and stories.

DENISE LEVERTOV Born in England to a Welsh mother and an Anglican clergyman converted from Judaism, Denise Levertov received her schooling at home. She married an American, after serving as a nurse in World War II, and moved to the United States in 1948. At Black Mountain College, an experimental school in North Carolina, she found new rhythms that reflected her new surroundings and speech patterns. Today Levertov, the author of numerous volumes of poetry, is renowned for her precise images and direct statements.

West Side

NAOMI SHIHAB NYE

In certain neighborhoods
the air is paved with names.
Domingo, Monico, Francisco,
shining rivulets of sound.
Names opening wet circles
inside the mouth,
sprinkling bright vowels
across the deserts of
Bill, Bob, John.

The names are worn
on silver linked chains.
Maria lives in Pablo Alley,
Esperanza rides the Santiago bus!
They click together like charms.
O save us from the boarded-up windows,
the pistol crack in a dark backyard,
save us from the leaky roof,
the rattled textbook which never smiles.
Let the names be verses
in a city that sings!

The Real Thing

MARILOU AWIAKTA

for Berenice

"We're the most exclusive
Indian shop in New York City.
We only sell *the real thing*."
Coyote-smooth, the man
lured a covey of customers
to where he held up a weaving
three feet by two.
"This rug is genuine Navajo.
You know it by the tiny flaw
they always leave
to let the evil spirit out."
"Ah . . ." sighed the covey
and leaned closer.

Behind them a buckshot laugh
exploded
       scattered thoughts
    turned heads
toward a black-haired
four-square woman.
"I *am* Navajo," she said.

"My family makes rugs.
When I was a child
I herded our sheep,
helped Mother clean the wool.
Grandma spun and wove it.
We don't leave a flaw
'to let the evil spirit out.'
We leave it to show
what's made by humans
can't be perfect.
Only the Great Spirit
makes perfect things."

The covey stared
        blank
    silent
then closed back
to their smooth comfort—
"As I was saying . . .
This rug is genuine Navajo.
You know it by the tiny flaw
they always leave
to let the evil spirit out."

 Merritt Parkway

DENISE LEVERTOV

As if it were
forever that they move, that we
keep moving—

Under a wan sky where
as the lights went on a star
pierced the haze & now
follows steadily
a constant
above our six lanes
the dreamlike continuum . . .

And the people—ourselves!
the humans from inside the
cars, apparent
only at gasoline stops
unsure,
eyeing each other
drink coffee hastily at the
slot machines & hurry
back to the cars
vanish
into them forever, to
keep moving—

Houses now & then beyond the
sealed road, the trees / trees, bushes
passing by, passing
the cars that
keep moving ahead of
us, past us, pressing behind us
and
over left, those that come

> toward us shining too brightly
> moving relentlessly
>
> in six lanes, gliding
> north & south, speeding with
> a slurred sound—

RESPONDING

1. **Personal Response** Which of these poems do you relate to the most? Tell why.

2. **Literary Analysis** All three of these poets make exceptional use of *imagery,* or word pictures. In a poem of your own, create word pictures.

3. **Multicultural Connection** Describe how the *setting* of each poem provides a different picture of America.

LANGUAGE WORKSHOP

Figurative Language Poets use *figurative language*—language expanded beyond its ordinary literal meaning—to achieve new effects and provide fresh insights. For example, Naomi Shihab Nye might have merely observed that some names are more interesting, musical, or longer than others. Instead, she speaks of names such as Domingo "sprinkling bright vowels across the deserts of Bill, Bob, John." How might the first group of names "sprinkle bright vowels"? the second group seem like deserts? Work with classmates to provide a list of six "bright vowel" names and six "desert" names.

WRITER'S PORTFOLIO

Write a human-interest story on one of the following: (1) A survey of the people stopping at an interstate rest stop; (2) An interview with shoppers in an upscale shop in New York City; (3) A city council meeting about re-naming certain streets.

ABOUT **STEVE CHAN-NO YOON**

Steve Chan-no Yoon came to America from Korea in 1971 when he was one year old and has lived in southern California ever since. Currently he is working on a degree in psychology at the University of California at Santa Barbara, as well as writing his first book, which he says is "about a group of multicultural characters from the Wasted Generation." His hobbies include reading and writing, and sleeping and dreaming. His hopes and dreams include traveling around the world, meeting weird and interesting people,  writing a few good books, and never having to wear a suit. "Stoplight" was first written when Steve was sixteen.

$\mathcal{S}$toplight

$\mathcal{I}$T'S TIMES LIKE THESE that I wish I could be someone else. I mean, I love myself and all, and I wouldn't normally change a thing, but for right now, I just wish, I could be some other person in some other place. I mean I just can't imagine any kid my age feeling at ease with his parents, in an Italian restaurant, on a Saturday night.

"Are you ready to order?" says the waiter as he slithers over to our table. He is wearing black slacks and a white button-down shirt, and his head shines in the light from the pound of hair gel that he uses to slick back his hair.

I lean back in my chair, and I tap my fingers on the table, and I slowly look up at him. "No. We're still waiting for someone," I say, and with that the waiter walks away.

"When the Kims get here, I want you to be nice," my mom says as she looks at her deeply tanned face in the mirror of her compact. "They are coming all the way out here from South Pasadena, so be nice." She snaps her compact shut and levels a stare straight up at me.

Looking back at her cold dark eyes, and at that thin line of a mouth, I say with a sigh, "Fine."

The restaurant is as slick and glossy as the pages from a magazine. The walls are done up in a nice soft pastel color, and covering some of the larger spaces on those walls are paintings that depict wealth and sex in bright Day-Glo colors. There are spotlights brighter than daylight shining down on all the tabletops. The tables themselves are too high and the chairs are uncomfortable, but they look nice, and I guess that is all that matters in a place like this. The only thing that I like about the whole setup is a pair of red and green neon lights that circle the room. They blink on and off, and they hum softly to themselves when the restaurant lies silent.

*T*HE TABLES OF THE RESTAURANT are full of the rich white tan Americans who litter the streets of Los Angeles. Young white couples known as yuppies sit in their chairs sipping foreign light beers. One man sits at his table talking on a cellular phone while his wife flirts with the help. I can hear one couple, behind me, talking about how much money they have and about what they can do to make some more. Everybody in the restaurant has an almost dazed look about them, as if they had just finished selling off what little remained of their souls. They all look spent.

We are the only Asians in the whole restaurant, and this reminds me of a piano we once owned. All the keys were black or white except for one, and that key was stained a dull yellow. It looked more like plastic than ivory. I swear, it makes you feel kind of cheap and dirty in a weird sort of way.

"So, son, how is everything?" my father asks me, speaking in his native Korean language.

"Everything is fine," I answer, using my native English.

"Do you like your new school?" he asks me as he puts out his cigarette.

"Yeah, it's great. Why did we have to leave this time?"

His gaze drifts around the room, and with no emotion in his voice he says, "We left because of you."

"But I wanted to stay."

Ignoring what I just said, he looks down at his watch and lights another cigarette. You see, our family is one of those moving families. We move for whatever reason there is, and so far we've lived in almost every city in America. It's given me a good sense of what this country is all about, but what is that really worth?

It would be nice to call a place home for more than a few months. I sometimes wonder, when we are flying or driving to our newest home, what a normal life would be like. I wonder what it would be like to live in a three-bedroom house, with a two-car garage, and a dog barking in the backyard. I also wonder what it would be like to live with white skin, with white parents in this white world. It must be strange, that's for sure.

"Weren't they supposed to be here at nine?" my father asks my mom.

"There must be a lot of traffic. You know, they are coming all the way from South Pasadena. That's a long drive," my mom says as she twirls her diamond ring around her finger.

"Do you need anything?" my dad asks me.

"No. I'm fine," I answer. They do this to me every time we go out. They try and make up for a week's worth of neglect in one night by asking me if I need any money. I wish I could tell them that money isn't my problem, but I just can't.

"When are they getting here?" my father asks again.

But at that exact moment the Kims come into the restaurant. Mr. Kim is a short stout man of about fifty years. He looks like one of those average Asian men who work about twelve hours a day, seven days a week, for about thirty some odd years, until the stress gives them a heart attack. He's the type of guy who sacrifices his entire existence for the sake of his family, but what do you get off on, Mr. Kim? What is your drug?

*M*RS. KIM is a darkly tanned woman in her late forties. You can just tell that like my mom this woman loves the game of golf and a good session of gossip. Her specialties are a good back swing and an open flowing mouth.

The two men sit down at once, greeting each other with Buddha-like smiles. The women sit and smile affectionately at each other and start their usual talk. They talk about other people and other people's children, and about how so and so just got into Harvard, while so-and-so just got out of jail. In this community so long as you get good grades, you can murder someone and still be considered an angel. The stupid children are the bad ones, and the smart children are the saints. That's a fair way of doing things, isn't it?

When the waiter sees that our table is complete, he comes over. I look down at the menu, and I order for both my parents and myself. It's easier this way. I mean, my dad can order like no one else in any Oriental restaurant, but in a place like this it's almost embarrassing.

"How do you like Los Angeles, Austin?" Mrs. Kim asks me.

"It's different."

"You'll get used to it," she says with a big smile.

They leave me alone after that, which is fine with me. I just sit there eating, watching, and thinking, and before I know it, the dinner is over. My father and Mr. Kim argue over the bill for a few minutes, battling to see who will pay. To them it is an honor to pay and a disgrace not to. My father eventually grabs the check rudely out of the hands of Mr. Kim, and he pays the bill.

We walk out of the restaurant with mints rolling in our mouths. We stand there in the crisp night air waiting for our cars to be delivered. The sky above is clear, cleaned by the rains that fell earlier that day.

The streets are wet and the air still smells damp.

We get into our car and start on our way home. We are the only ones on the road, which is something that doesn't really happen that often in L.A. Usually these streets would be filled with mile upon mile of screaming cars, like a lava flow from some erupting auto plant. But tonight, the only actions in the intersection we are coming to is a lone newspaper drifting in the wind like a sagebrush in an old western ghost town. There is only one thing for me to look at, and this is the red stoplight.

I look up at the stoplight, and I try to figure out what it means. I know that the red light means stop and that the green light means go, but I cannot figure out what the blinking yellow light stands for. What does being yellow mean? The best answer that I can come up with is an in-between: go if you want to but stop if you don't. I hate being in between things, I really do, but it all doesn't matter because the light that is on is red, and all that it tells me is stop.

"Oh, look isn't that Mr. Lee at the side of the road?" my mom says as she looks through her side window.

I break the daze that I am in and look over to the side of the road. I have not noticed it before, but over to the side of the road sits a car with a flat, and around that car sits a family much like ours, but with a daughter and not a son. I look over closer at the girl sitting alone on the sidewalk staring down at the ground.

*S*HE HAS BLACK STRAIGHT HAIR flowing about her face in a way that only nature could have put it. Her face is oval shaped and covered in pearl-white skin. Her mouth is full and red, and her nose is pert, yet not conceited. Her eyes are large and brown, like those of a deer, and the only thought that is in my mind at that time is that she is a person I have to know.

"Hey, who's Mr. Lee?" I ask.

"It's one of your dad's employees," my mom says with a turn of her head.

"Why don't we help?" I say from the backseat.

"We should," my father says as he pulls over to the side of the street. He gets out of our car and goes over to his employee, and I go straight over to the girl sitting on the sidewalk.

"Hi. How's it going?" I say as I walk over toward her.

"Who are you?" she demands of me.

"My name's Austin. Our fathers know each other, and we pulled over to help," I say.

"Well, go ahead and help," she says, using her hand to point limply at the tire.

"You don't have to take that attitude about it," I say as I slowly walk away.

"Wait, I'm sorry. My name's Julie, and you just didn't pick the right time to try and talk to me. I'm a little annoyed right now," she says as she turns her head toward the tire.

"Well, do you think that maybe if I got your number and called you later, you would be in a better mood to talk?"

"Sure," she says with a smile, and she has a real nice smile. "That wouldn't be too bad."

Boldness with the females isn't usually my game, but sometimes it comes when the times call for it. All the way home I repeat her name and her number in my head as if it were a poem that will open up to some secret meanings. Julie, and Julie, I think in my mind.

*T*HE NEXT DAY I call her on the phone. We try and talk, but nothing comes out right. It's hard to have a conversation on the phone with someone you hardly know; so we decide to go out and talk in person. We both agree that a standard dinner-movie date won't do the job. Instead we plan a simple conversation over some coffee. We pick a nice little café on Pacific Coast Highway to be our meeting place. "We" is the new word for me, and I must admit that "we" sounds better than "I."

The air of the café is full of the smoke that billows from the few people who are smoking. The smell of freshly ground coffee beans penetrates the air like the smell of burning leaves on a windy October day. The smells, strangely enough, go well with the brown wooden furniture and the green plants that hang from the ceiling.

Mixed in with the constant whir of the coffee grinders and the espresso machines, the soft murmurs of people talking fill the sound waves of the room. The corner that I sit down in is right in front of a huge bay window that frames the beach scene outside. Sea gulls float in the sky like kites in a strong wind. The waves tumble under a bright-red sun that looks as if it is ready to crash down into the sea. I sit there in my seat waiting for Julie to come, and I am not even sure if she will show, but I don't worry about it too much. I just sit there, and I stare out the window.

I sit there for what seems like forever, until Julie finally walks in through the door. She is wearing a light sundress that clings to her body, leaving little room for the imagination but room enough. I can't help but think about how perfect she looks, and how much of a dream she is.

"Did you wait long?" she asks me.

"No, not that long."

"You know, I barely got out of the house today," Julie says as she sits down at the table. "My mom was making all these excuses for me not to go out. She finally told me that I shouldn't go out with a guy like you who has a bad reputation. Can you believe that?"

"I'm used to that. Trust me," I say as I take a sip of my coffee. "But that's just the thoughts of the older generation who overexaggerate things anyways. I mean, I don't think that just because I've made a few mistakes, I should be considered the devil reincarnated. Do you?"

*S*HE SHAKES HER HEAD, saying no. "Sometimes it's just so hard to understand our parents, isn't it?" she says as she plays with her coffee mug on the table. "We've got this huge generation gap to deal with, and on top of that we've got a cultural gap too. It really makes a conversation impossible sometimes."

"So it's just not me? Thank god — I thought I was going crazy there for a second." I say this and we both laugh for a second. "My mom tells me that you got into a pretty decent college."

"I just got accepted to Princeton."

"Really! Congratulations," I say.

"Thanks," she says with a soft humble smile.

"What are you going to study there?"

"I'm going to be a psychology major. I want to eventually study dreams."

"Wow, that's different. What do your parents think of this?"

She takes a sip of coffee and licks her liquid mustache with her tongue. "Well, of course they want me to become an accountant or something boring like that, but I've got to do what's going to make me happy, and not them. Right?" She says this in a way that makes me feel that she is in need of some reassurance.

"You know what I think?" I say while leaning forward as if to tell her a secret. "I think that they gave up their dreams and decided to live life in a stable way, and now they're miserable for it. So they feel jealous and resentful toward us for going for our dreams. That's why they discourage us."

"I guess that could be true. I honestly don't think that my parents have any dreams besides the ones that are connected to me," she says with a certain sadness in her eyes.

"God, for the longest time my parents wanted me to become an engineer, and take over the family business, but there's no way in hell I would ever do a thing like that," I say with determination in my voice.

"Then what do you want to do?" she asks as she puts her elbows on the table, and she rests her face in her hands.

"Me?" I say with a smile, and then whisper, "I was put on this earth to give my parents hell."

*J*ULIE LOOKS AT ME, and she tilts her head back as her mouth opens wide. She laughs—and not one of those geisha-girl giggles, either, but a real hearty laugh. "God, you are so weird," she says as she still laughs.

In an Asian society that is full of conforming mannequins who all dress the same, look the same, and act the same, it is always nice to be noticed. Most of the time being different or weird is the only way that some of us can have an identity that isn't generic.

"Thank you," I say smiling. "You're pretty weird yourself."

"A good weird, right?" she says with a smile.

"Right."

We continue our talk about all the things we hate, and

about all the things we love. We talk about all of the common things that we've shared, but basically we talk about how much we understand each other. To be understood, in this world that doesn't understand me, is one of the greatest things that I can ever feel. I mean, isn't that what we are all looking for, a little acceptance?

Sitting there in our own little world, I close my eyes and I wish to myself for this night to never end, but it does. The sun finally melts into the sea, and a blue darkness covers the sky. We both inhale the cool salty sea air as we walk outside toward the beach. There is a set of benches along the boardwalk that we sit down on.

"This is one thing that you don't get much of in New York," I say as I point out to the sea.

"Why did you move out here?"

"Do you want the truth or what my parents want me to tell you?"

She pauses for a second and then says, "The truth."

"Well, there was this Korean guy who owned a deli on our block. He was a J.O.J.—you know, just off the jet—and he spoke only a few words of English. He was from the old school, closed minded and a bit racist," I say, taking a breath to catch my thoughts. "One night a bunch of my friends and I went into the store and started messing with the deli man. I translated the things that he said, and the situation got out of hand. A fight broke out, but the deli man made it sound like we were robbing the store. He pressed charges on everyone but me."

"Why didn't he press charges on you?"

"Because my dad went in to talk to him. But after that there was a big demonstration because one of my friends was black. We moved because it got really uncomfortable for us to live there anymore."

"So you went in there to prove to your friends that you were on their side, but it all backfired," she says.

"All I wanted to do was to prove to everyone that just because we looked alike, it didn't mean that we thought alike," I say, looking down.

We sit there in silence for a few moments, and then we

walk over to the parking lot where both our cars sit. There is a fluorescent street lamp that flickers a yellow light across our faces. She walks up to her car and turns to me.

"I had a good time," she says. "Call me tomorrow."

"Sure," I say, walking closer. I look at her and move my head forward to kiss her.

Kisses can be childish or even meaningless at times. There is, however, a feeling one gets when two pairs of lips press up against each other that is neither childish or meaningless. It is as if this moment were meant to be.

*A*CTUALLY WE NEVER KISSED. Hell, I don't even know if Julie is her name. I don't even know if a girl like Julie does exist. I once read a book, though, that said that the subconscious does not distinguish between reality and fantasy. So in that sense she is real to me, and maybe someday I will meet a girl like Julie. Then maybe I won't have to feel like an alien, alone on a strange planet. The stoplight turns green. Our car moves forward, and this jars me out of my thoughts. We drive on home and the stoplight keeps changing.

RESPONDING

1. **Personal Response** Steve Chan-no Yoon wrote this story when he was sixteen. Do you think his feelings about parents, love, and pressure are typical of teenagers? Explain.

2. **Literary Analysis** In this selection, the author uses colors *symbolically.* Point out passages that employ colors. What is the significance of red, green, and especially yellow?

3. **Multicultural Connection** The narrator reveals a great deal about people and lifestyles in southern California. He also mentions some attributes ascribed to Asians.

Make two lists — *Southern California* and *Asian* and list appropriate details from the story under each head. Then discuss which of these details you consider stereotypical.

LANGUAGE WORKSHOP

Classifying Sometimes it is difficult to figure out what is real and what is not in a story with a dream sequence such as "Stoplight." *Classify* the following events into those that actually happened in the story and those that are imagined.

1. The Kims arrive at the restaurant.

2. Austin's father pays the check.

3. Austin's family stops to help a driver with a flat.

4. Austin and Julie make a date.

5. Austin's family drives on home and the stoplight keeps changing.

WRITER'S PORTFOLIO

Since this story is told from the first-person point of view, you do not hear Austin's parents' side of the story. With two partners, write a short dramatic scene in which Austin and his parents come together and talk out Austin's problems. Try to remain faithful to Austin's point of view but invent what Austin's parents say.

SIDEWALKS OF AMERICA

Projects

VISUAL DISPLAY

With a partner, make a collage, a mural, a slide-sound presentation, or a video that focuses on the multicultural nature of the United States. To accompany your visual presentation, write a script using quotes from some of the selections in this unit. Present your display to the class.

CULTURE TOUR

The writers in this unit represent different backgrounds: African American, Chinese American, British American, Native American, Korean American, Puerto Rican, and Palestinian American. Choose one group and research some highlights—its history, its famous people, its literature and art, and/or other contributions. If you wish to work in groups, be sure to cover several aspects. Present your findings to the class by taking them on a culture tour, complete with "props" such as artifacts, music, pictures, or photographs.

COMPOSITION ON BEING ALIKE

Writer Maya Angelou has said that "human beings are more alike than unalike and what is true anywhere is true everywhere . . . if we try to understand each other, we may even become friends." Using three of the selections from this unit, write an essay that establishes whether or not humans are indeed more alike than unalike.

Further Reading

The following books highlight cultural diversity in the United States.

Chin, Frank. *Donald Duk.* Coffee House Press, 1991. In this novel, Donald Duk, annoyed by his name and all things Chinese, gains a new racial pride through his dreams of Chinese workers on the Central Pacific Railroad and his own increasing self-assurance.

Ellison, Ralph. *Invisible Man.* Random House, 1952. This is the story of a young African American man from the South, who confronts a hostile society in New York City's Harlem.

Hansberry, Lorraine. *To Be Young, Gifted and Black.* The New American Library, Inc., 1970. In this special auto-biography — a representative sampling of Hansberry's works that serves as a self-portrait — readers get a vivid picture of the African American experience in mid twentieth-century America.

Nye, Naomi Shihab. *Different Ways to Pray.* Breitenbush Books, 1980. Lively poems with memorable images appear in this collection. Nye fans will also enjoy reading *Hugging the Jukebox* (an American Library Association Notable Book, 1982) and *Yellow Glove* (1986).

Poey, Delia and Suarez, Virgil, eds. *Iguana Dreams: New Latino Fiction.* HarperCollins, 1992. This is a showcase of writers from diverse Latino cultures in America — Mexican, Puerto Rican, Cuban, Chilean, and Dominican — who treat universal themes.

Yep, Laurence, ed. *American Dragons: Twenty-Five Asian American Voices.* HarperCollins, 1993. This collection of Asian American writing of various genres presents appealing vignettes of Americana.

Image Makers

How do people form their self-images? All too often the way we view ourselves is conditioned by image makers who distort and manipulate reality, telling us how we *might* be, *could* be, *should* be. Can you distinguish between the real you and the persona that movies, TV, and magazines have created? What's there beneath the clothes, the pose, and the labels? Who is that special person with a distinct character, particular background, and unique dreams?

ABOUT **RITA DOVE**

"To Be Young, Gifted and Black," the title of a drama based on Lorraine Hansberry's journals, are terms that characterize Rita Dove. A poet noted for her ability to pull readers into other lives, Dove published her first collection, *The Yellow House on the Corner* (1980), when she was twenty-eight. A later collection titled *Thomas and Beulah,* loosely based on the lives of her grandparents, won the Pulitzer Prize for poetry in 1987. In 1993, Dove was named Poet Laureate of the United States, the first African American to hold the position and the youngest person ever chosen. In addition to her poetry, Dove has published a collection of short stories and a novel, *Through the Ivory Gate* (1992), from which the following prelude is taken.

Prelude

From *THROUGH THE IVORY GATE*

"You don't want that one."

"Yes I do, please . . ."

"Look at it, Virginia!"

"Why can't I —"

"Just look. What color is it?"

"Black."

"And the mouth?"

"Red."

"And?"

"Big."

"What else?"

"He's smiling —"

"Grinning. What else?"

"Pretty eyes . . ."

"Pop eyes, chile, those are pop eyes. Don't you know who that is?"

"Just a doll a funny doll, Grandma, can't I have it?"

"Girl, don't you recognize an insult when you see one? That's supposed to be you! Shame on you," Grandma Evans said, handing Virginia over to her mother. "Belle, ain't this chile got no sense at all?"

On the bus Virginia eased the new purse out of its wrappings and studied it carefully. It was black and shiny; she could almost see herself in its flat surface. She unsnapped the clasp and peeked inside. A little mirror came with the purse; it dangled from a golden chain.

Culture Note

Tiger . . . night the opening lines of "The Tiger" by William Blake (1757–1827), an English poet who included the poem in *The Songs of Experience*, p. 60

Skin brown. Hair black. Eyes small and far apart. Un-smiling. *I don't look like that—why she say it's supposed to be me?* Her grandmother didn't say any of those other dolls looked like anybody.

> *There was a pickaninny cryin'*
> *Down in Tennessee one night,*
> *His little heart was nearly breakin'*
> *Just because he wasn't white!*

Her mother sang that song as a joke. Her mother had told her a story about another song; the white insurance man had come to the door and Aunt Carrie was changing the beds upstairs hollering in a loud voice:

> *Someone's gotta pick the cotton,*
> *Someone's gotta pick the corn,*
> *Someone's gotta keep on singin' a song—*

And Mom let the white insurance man in and ran up to the bedroom but not in time to catch Carrie at the top of the stairs:

> *That's why darkies were born!*

Virginia liked that story. She would have liked to be Aunt Carrie folding a fresh sheet bigger than herself, hollering at the top of her lungs:

> *That's why darkies were born!*

If you meet a paper tiger, he won't steal your clothes. A tiger in the forest might. That was another song:

> *Tiger, tiger burning bright*
> *In the forests of the night.*

A tiger is also part of a baseball team. A boy cousin from Detroit talked about going to "see the Tigers" and she wanted to go, too, but she was in the wrong state. Her father took her and her brother to see the Indians. It wasn't the same, going to see the Indians. A man stood up in the stands and poured all his whisky away. He must have been sad, because he hid the bottle under his coat and watched the stream of yellow until it gave out. Ernie Jr. snickered, and she pointed the man out to their father, who took them away for some popcorn.

T HE PUPPET'S NAME IS SAMBO. He is wearing red jacket blue trousers purple shoes with crimson soles and linings and a green umbrella. Oh what a friendly boy he looks to be! Too bad he is so silly! The Negro children laughed.

"Yes, Akron was young and struttin' those days. STANDING ROOM ONLY! the headlines said. Men with their families came up from Georgia to work in the rubber and oatmeal factories. And in the summer when that oats smell got headstrong and those rubber factories loudmouthed the heat, no one was nowhere but in the street. All day, all night the street was the respectable place to be.

"It was 1919, chile. I had on a striped sundress. In those days summers were hot like they supposed to be—that was before them astronauts got to fooling around with God's atmosphere. It was so hot that summer the men got to fainting at the machines. There were traveling minstrel shows, come down from Cleveland with vaudeville for the grown-ups and puppet shows for the children. We stood

Culture Notes

Sambo Little Black Sambo, a character in a children's story popular in the first half of the 20th century; a demeaning stereotype. In this story, tigers take Sambo's fancy clothes, but while they argue about which one is the finest tiger in the jungle, he recovers them. p. 61

Akron a booming industrial site in Ohio during the first half of the 20th century. Job opportunities created by World War I drew many African Americans there. p. 61

bareheaded in the sun to see them shows. My dress was red an' white, made out of an old coat lining. It had a yellow sash. When the show started up, Little Black Sambo strutted out in his bright clothes and green parasol. 'Look,' the minstrel said, 'look at little Sambo in his brand-new clothes! How he loves bright colors, little monkey that he is!' "

"I'll never wear bright colors again; I promise, Grandma."

"Hush, chile, don't be silly. But I'll tell you one thing: I don't care how many dolls they make in this world and how bad you might want them—I ain't going to buy you one till they can do them right."

THEN THERE WAS PENELOPE, Penelope with the long red hair and plump good looks of Brenda Starr, Penelope of the creamy skin and dimpling cheeks. Aunt Carrie had bought her, Aunt Carrie said she was cute as a penny, she thought up the name. There were also small pink curlers and a comb. Wash and set and place her in the sun to dry. As many as five hair styles a day—Penelope the Model, Penelope the God-Fearing Nurse, Penelope the Prize-Winning Journalist, Penelope the Girl Next Door, Penelope Had a Man and He Loved Her So. Never a hair out of place unless she shook it loose to let it stream in the wind. Virginia gave her a ride on her bicycle to make sure it streamed.

That summer was Virginia's ninth birthday. Birthdays had their ritual: she was allowed to drink coffee for breakfast, and she chose the dinner menu—chicken and applesauce and pork 'n' beans. She bicycled to Morry's Grocery for a dime's worth

Culture Note

Brenda Starr a comic strip character portrayed as a sophisticated female journalist; a forerunner of the Barbie Doll image, p. 62

of candy buttons and ate them all. Then she took Penelope to the park. When she got back, it was nearly dinnertime; the kitchen clanged and hissed. She had gone upstairs and just laid Penelope on the bed when her mother appeared in the doorway, holding a shiny yellow package.

"Something you've always wanted," she said. "From Grandma."

Virginia ripped the waxy gift paper away. In a blue display box lay a doll in a seersucker playsuit. It had brown skin. It looked like an overturned crab. And the eyes didn't close and—she felt tears coming—it had no hair. Those blistered, painted curlicues on that bulbous scalp could not be called hair.

"Just think, honey—now you finally have a doll who looks like you!"

"I don't want it." Backing away as the doll was thrust into her arms.

"What do you mean, you don't want it? Honey, where are you going? What are you doing—don't you dare—!"

Virginia threw the doll down the stairs.

Her father came running, newspaper fluttering at his ankles. "What's all the commotion about?" he demanded.

"Oh, nothing," her mother said, "nothing at all. Except that your daughter is ashamed of being a Negro. Look what she did to my mother's birthday present. She obviously prefers that fat redhead to her own color." She shook Penelope in Virginia's face.

"Do you know what you're telling us?" Belle spoke under her breath, but her voice was hard and shiny as scales. "You're saying you don't appreciate this doll. Your grandmother goes half across town to buy you the first Negro baby doll and you throw a fit, you throw her down the stairs like dirty laundry. You don't want it? You don't like it? You don't like being a Negro? For years we've fought so there would be Negro dolls for our children, and you'd rather play with—"

"Stop it, Belle."

Her father knelt down, took her gently by the shoulders. "Why did you throw Grandma's doll down the stairs?" he asked sadly. His hair smelled like ginger ale and fresh-cut grass; she knew it was just his hair pomade, but she couldn't help thinking it came directly from him like a magician's smoke, a halo of scent.

"Tell me," he said, "what it is you don't like about the doll."

He took the doll away from her mother and held it out quietly. Virginia stared at it—the bulging eyes, the painted head. She didn't look like that. And if she did, how could her own parents stand there and tell her so? How could they love her and show her at the same time that she was ugly?

"All right"—he sighed—"maybe you need a little time to think it over. I have a suggestion: Keep this doll for a day. Play with it for one day and then, if you still don't like it, we'll take it back. No questions asked. Okay? You tell us you don't like it, we'll take it back."

He put the doll on the bed.

"Come on, Belle."

Virginia was alone. They thought they could leave her up here and she would be too scared to say anything. They thought by tomorrow she'd calm down and say, "Yes, I'll keep it; I'll even give it a name"—and then they would take Penelope away and Virginia wouldn't even notice she was gone.

The new doll lay on the bed in its flimsy, striped sunsuit. She picked it up. It felt cheap—so lightweight, and the hard skin could be dented with the merest pressure from her thumb. She walked over to the window, unlatched the screen, and threw the pickaninny out, hard.

Oh, how smoothly it fell, a mindless spot in the air, toppling lazily, smiling its nonsense smile. A shallow *thwap* when it landed, skipping across the brick street like a ball and coming to rest against the far curb, its body a startled, upreaching claw.

"You crazy or what?" Ernie Jr. shrieked, making a sharp turn on his roller skates at the end of the drive. The front door slammed, Virginia's mother ran out and across the street; she scooped up the doll and stood there a moment looking up at the window in disbelief. Virginia did not step away.

SOMETIME AFTER the family had moved to Arizona, Penelope's left arm was punctured by something, a hairpin or a needle, and she soaked up water whenever she got a shampoo; every morning Virginia's pillow was wet. The white girls at the junior high began to iron their hair as if this were a new invention, some kind of revelation. Virginia straightened her hair as always; she cut bangs, used larger rollers, rinsed it sable brown.

She had a recurrent dream: in it she was wearing white shorts and a yellow T-shirt, and she was running through all the streets in the old neighborhood. Though the sun bore down fiercely and the cobbled bricks were precarious, she ran without the least effort. Her hair streamed behind her, long and shining, red as the tulip shedding and the cardinal flashing. *Isn't she lovely,* they whispered as she ran past, *a wild deer, an antelope.* And in the dream her skin was still dark.

YEARS LATER when Afros came into style, Virginia breathed a sigh of relief and got rid of the curlers. It was time to go to college: rummaging through the cartons in the storeroom, she came upon a shoebox. Penelope's hair lay matted and dusty around her rose-pink face; the arm with the puncture had turned dark green, as if rotten with gangrene. She was spongy; even the desert heat hadn't been able to suck all the water out. Virginia took her to show her younger sister.

"What did you ever see in such a fat thing, anyway?" Claudia mumbled, turning back to "Mister Rogers' Neighborhood."

That's when Virginia noticed the stuffing had mildewed. Penelope stank. She took the doll to the bathroom and laid her on the scale: She came to four pounds. There was nothing to do but throw her away.

RESPONDING

1. **Personal Response** Virginia's doll means a great deal to her. Tell about a favorite childhood toy or object you treasured and explain what became of it.

2. **Literary Analysis** References to hair provide an *image* pattern that helps tie the selection together. Discuss how different kinds of hair reflect Virginia's changing self-image.

3. **Multicultural Connection** Young Virginia has a confused image of herself. How do Penelope, Sambo, and the "first Negro baby doll" influence that image?

LANGUAGE WORKSHOP

Words from Greek Virginia's grandmother recalls events in 1919, before astronauts started "fooling around with God's atmosphere." *Astronaut* comes from the Greek *astron* or *astēr* meaning "star" and *nautēs* meaning "sailor." *Atmosphere* comes from the Greek *atmos* meaning "vapor" and *sphaira* meaning "sphere." Now explain the meanings of the following italicized words.
1. The *astronomer* answered our questions about Venus.
2. We refused to sail until we had *nautical* training.
3. In *astronomy* class we are studying the planets.
4. The basketball was *spherical*.
5. Indicate the Greek words with an *asterisk.*

WRITER'S PORTFOLIO

Imagine this scenario: You have created a line of toys that you will market under the brand name Image Makers. Write a brief ad promoting one of these toys. Direct your ad to nine-year-olds, "selling" the toy to them by emphasizing a desirable quality projected by it such as strength, beauty, popularity, excitement, or adventure. Feel free to use propaganda techniques. You might want to illustrate your ad.

LOUISE ERDRICH Louise Erdrich worked on highway construction crews and poured coffee in diners before breaking into the literary scene with *Love Medicine,* the highly acclaimed novel that won the National Book Critics Circle Award in 1984. Within a decade, she had written The *Beet Queen, Tracks,* and *The Bingo Palace* to complete the series. She has also written short stories; essays; and two collections of poetry, *Jacklight* and *Baptism of Desire.* Of mixed German American and Turtle Mountain Chippewa descent, Erdrich brings an uncommon perspective to multiethnic themes. She strives, she says, "to present Indian people as sympathetic characters, non-stereotypes, characters that any non-Indian would identify with."

CATHY SONG Cathy Song's very first collection of poems, *Picture Bride,* won the prestigious Yale Series of Younger Poets Award in 1983. Most of these poems, told from a first-person point of view, deal with family rela-tionships — both constructive and destructive. "Picture Bride," the title poem, sets up the major motifs of the volume: the Hawaiian set-ting, the family, and the pull of home. After earning degrees from Wellesley College and Boston University, Song returned to her native Hawaii. She has published another poetry col-

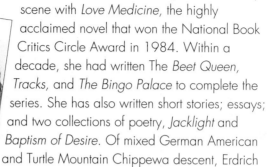

lection, *Frameless Windows, Squares of Light,* which displays again her special ability to fuse form and content in an easy, natural manner.

Dear John Wayne

LOUISE ERDRICH

August and the drive-in picture is packed.
We lounge on the hood of the Pontiac
surrounded by the slow-burning spirals they sell
at the window, to vanquish the hordes of mosquitoes.
Nothing works. They break through the smoke-screen
    for blood.

Always the lookout spots the Indians first,
spread north to south, barring progress.
The Sioux or some other Plains bunch
in spectacular columns, ICBM missiles,
their feathers bristling in the meaningful sunset.

The drum breaks. There will be no parlance.
Only the arrows whining, a death-cloud of nerves
swarming down on the settlers
who die beautifully, tumbling like dust weeds
into the history that brought us all here
together: this wide screen beneath the sign of the bear.

The sky fills, acres of blue squint and eye
that the crowd cheers. His face moves over us,
a thick cloud of vengeance, pitted
like the land that was once flesh. Each rut,
each scar makes a promise: *It is*
not over, this fight, not as long as you resist.

Everything we see belongs to us.

A few laughing Indians fall over the hood
slipping in the hot spilled butter.
The eye sees a lot, John, but the heart is so blind.
Death makes us owners of nothing.
He smiles, a horizon of teeth
the credits reel over, and then the white fields
again blowing in the true-to-life dark.
The dark films over everything.
We get into the car
scratching our mosquito bites, speechless and small
as people are when the movie is done.
We are back in our skins.

How can we help but keep hearing his voice,
the flip side of the sound track, still playing:
Come on, boys, we've got them
where we want them, drunk, running.
They will give us what we want, what we need.
Even his disease was the idea of taking everything.
Those cells, burning, doubling, splitting out of their skins.

Culture Notes

ICBM intercontinental ballistic missile, p. 68

sign of the bear Ursa Major (Latin for "great bear"),
the seven most conspicuous stars in the Big Dipper,
p. 68

Picture Bride

CATHY SONG

She was a year younger
than I,
twenty-three when she left Korea.
Did she simply close
the door of her father's house
and walk away? And
was it a long way
through the tailor shops of Pusan
to the wharf where the boat
waited to take her to an island
whose name she had
only recently learned,
on whose shore
a man waited,
turning her photograph
to the light when the lanterns
in the camp outside
Waialua Sugar Mill were lit
and the inside of his room
grew luminous
from the wings of moths
migrating out of the cane stalks?
What things did my grandmother
take with her? And when
she arrived to look
into the face of the stranger
who was her husband,
thirteen years older than she,

did she politely untie
the silk bow of her jacket,
her tent-shaped dress
filling with the dry wind
that blew from the surrounding fields
where the men were burning the cane?

RESPONDING

1. **Personal Response** Do you see any advantages to arranged marriages? How might your answer be different if you were a picture bride of generations ago rather than a teenager in the United States today?

2. **Literary Analysis** Find examples of *alliteration*—the repetition of similar sounds to create melody, mood, or dramatic effect—in both Erdrich's and Song's poems. Explain what effects are achieved.

3. **Multicultural Connection** The subjects of these poems—a picture bride and a group of Native Americans—seem at first to have little in common. In what respects do both appear to be victims of image makers? Do you think Native Americans are portrayed in movies today more or less accurately than they were in the past? Explain.

LANGUAGE WORKSHOP

Symbol A *symbol* is something concrete, such as an object, person, place, or happening, that represents something abstract, such as an idea or quality. Louise Erdrich ascribes symbolic characteristics to John Wayne, the legendary cinematic cowboy. What does John Wayne represent to the Native Americans at an outdoor movie? What, if anything, does John Wayne represent to you?

WRITER'S PORTFOLIO

Erdrich provides a memorable cinematic description of "arrows whining, a death-cloud of nerves/swarming down on the settlers/who die beautifully, tumbling like dust weeds." Recall a vivid scene from a movie or TV—or look for one in the next day or so—and describe it using figurative language. If you find you have the beginning of a poem, you might want to complete it.

ABOUT **NASH CANDELARIA**

A descendent of one of the pioneer
families that founded Albuquerque in 1706,
Nash Candelaria grew up in English-speaking
Catholic Anglo neighborhoods in Los Angeles.
Beginning his career as a scientist, he later
became a science writer and a fiction writer.
Candelaria has published three highly
regarded novels set within the framework of
New Mexican history that deal with the lives of
a fictional family. One of these novels, *Not by
the Sword*, won the American Book Award
in 1983. In both his
novels and short stories,
Candelaria aims "to give
Hispanics their proper
place in U.S. history,"
adding that "many of us
have been here a long
time, longer than most
Anglos."

The Day the
Cisco Kid Shot
John Wayne

Just before I started the first grade we moved from Los Rafas into town. It created a family uproar that left hard feelings for a long time.

"You think you're too good for us," Uncle Luis shouted at Papa in Spanish, "just because you finished high school and have a job in town! My God! We grew up in the country. Our parents and grandparents grew up in the country. If New Mexico country was good enough for them—"

Papa stood with his cup and saucer held tightly in his hands, his knuckles bleached by the vicious grip as if all the blood had been squeezed up to his bright red face. But even when angry, he was polite to his older brother.

"I'll be much closer to work, and Josie can have the car to shop once in a while. We'll still come out on weekends. It's only five miles."

Uncle Luis looked around in disbelief. My aunt tried not to look at either him or Papa, while Grandma sat on her rocking chair smoking a hand-rolled cigarette. She was blind and couldn't see the anger on the men's faces, but she wasn't deaf. Her chair started to rock faster, and I knew that in a moment she was going to scream at them both.

"It's much closer to work," Papa repeated.

Before Uncle Luis could shout again, Grandma blew out a puff of cigarette smoke in exasperation. "He's a grown man, Luis. With a wife and children. He can live anywhere he wants."

"But what about the — "

He was going to say orchard next to Grandma's house. It belonged to Papa and everyone expected him to build a house there someday. Grandma cut Uncle short: "Enough!"

As we bumped along the dirt of Rafas Road toward home in the slightly used Ford we were all so proud of, Papa and Mama talked some more. It wasn't just being nearer to work, Papa said, but he couldn't tell the family because they wouldn't understand. It was time for Junior — that was me — to use English as his main language. He would get much better schooling in town than in the little country school where all the grades were in just two rooms.

"Times have changed," Papa said. "He'll have to live in the English-speaking world."

It surprised me. I was, it turned out, the real reason we were moving into town, and I felt a little unworthy. I also felt apprehensive about a new house, a new neighborhood, and my first year in school. Nevertheless, the third week in August we moved into the small house on Fruit Avenue, not far from Immaculate Heart Parochial School.

I barely had time to acquaint myself with the neighborhood before school began. It was just as well. It was not like the country. Sidewalks were new to me, and I vowed to ask Santa Claus for roller skates at Christmas like those that city kids had. All of the streets were paved, not just the main highway like in the country. At night streetlights blazed into life so you could see what was happening outside. It wasn't much. And the lights bothered me. I missed the secret warm darkness with its silence punctuated only by the night sounds of owls and crickets and frogs and distant dogs barking. Somehow the country dark had always been a friend, like a warm bed and being tucked in and being hugged and kissed good night.

There were no neighbors my age. The most interesting parts of the neighborhood were the vacant house next door and the vacant lot across the street. But then the rush to school left me no time to think or worry about neighbors.

I suppose I was a little smug, a little superior, marching off that first day. My little sister and brother stood beside

Aunt Tillie and watched anxiously through the front window, blocking their wide-eyed views with their steaming hot breaths. I shook off Mama's hand and shifted my new metal lunchbox to that side so she wouldn't try again.

Mama wanted to walk me into the classroom, but I wouldn't let her, even though I was frightened. On the steps in front of the old brick school building a melee of high voices said goodbye to mothers, interrupted by the occasional tearful face or clinging hand that refused to let go. At the corner of the entrance, leaning jauntily against the bricks, leered a brown-faced tough whose half-closed eyes singled me out. Even his wet, combed hair, scrubbed face, and neatly patched clothes did not disguise his true nature.

He STUCK OUT A FOOT to trip me as I walked past. Like with my boy cousins in the country, I stepped on it good and hard without giving him even so much as a glance.

Sister Mary Margaret welcomed us to class. "You are here," she said, "as good Catholic children to learn your lessons well so you can better worship and glorify God." Ominous words in Anglo that I understood too well. I knew that cleanliness was next to godliness, but I never knew that learning your school lessons was — until then.

The students stirred restlessly, and during the turmoil I took a quick look around. It reminded me of a chocolate sundae. All the pale-faced Anglos were the vanilla ice cream, while we brown Hispanos were the sauce. The nun, with her starched white headdress under her cowl, could have been the whipped cream except that I figured she was too sour for that.

I had never been among so many Anglo children before; they outnumbered us two to one. In the country church on Sundays it was rare to see an Anglo. The only time I saw many of these foreigners — except for a few friends of my father's — was when my parents took me into town shopping.

"One thing more," Sister Mary Margaret said. She stiffened, and her face turned to granite. It was the look that I later learned meant the ruler for some sinner's outstretched hands. Her hard eyes focused directly on me. "The language of this classroom is English. This is America. We will only speak English in class and on the school grounds." The warning hung ominously in the silent, crackling air. She didn't need to say what we brownfaces knew: If I hear Spanish, you're in trouble.

As WE BURST from the confines of the room for our first recess, I searched for that tough whose foot I had stomped on the way in. But surprise! He was not in our class. This puzzled me, because I had thought there was only one first grade.

I found him out on the school grounds, though. Or rather, he found me. When he saw me, he swaggered across the playground tailed by a ragtag bunch of boys like odds and ends of torn cloth tied to a kite. One of the boys from my class whispered to me in English with an accent that sounded normal—only Anglos really had accents. "Oh, oh! Chango, the third grader. Don't let his size fool you. He can beat up guys twice as big." With which my classmate suddenly remembered something he had to do across the way by the water fountain.

"¡Ojos largos!" Chango shouted at me. I looked up in surprise. Not so much for the meaning of the words, which was "big eyes," but for his audacity in not only speaking Spanish against the nun's orders, but shouting it in complete disregard of our jailers in black robes.

"Yes?" I said in English like an obedient student. I was afraid he would see my pounding heart bumping the cloth of my shirt.

Chango and his friends formed a semicircle in front of me. He placed his hands on his hips and thrust his challenging face at me, his words in the forbidden language. "Let's see you do that again."

"What?" I said in English, even though I knew what.

"And talk in Spanish," he hissed at me. "None of your highfalutin Anglo."

Warily I looked around to see if any of the nuns were nearby. "¿Qué?" I repeated when I saw that the coast was clear.

"You stepped on my foot, big eyes. And your big eyes are going to get it for that."

I shook my head urgently. "Not me," I said in all innocence. "It must have been somebody else."

But he knew better. In answer, he thrust a foot out and flicked his head at it in invitation. I stood my ground as if I didn't understand, and one of his orderlies laughed and hissed, "¡Gallina!"

The accusation angered me. I didn't like being called chicken, but a glance at the five of them waiting for me to do something did wonders for my self-restraint.

Then Chango swaggered forward, his arms out low like a wrestler's. He figured I was going to be easy, but I hadn't grown up with older cousins for nothing. When he feinted an arm at me, I stood my ground. At the next feint, I grabbed him with both hands, one on his wrist, the other at his elbow, and tripped him over my leg that snapped out like a jackknife. He landed flat on his behind, his face changing from surprise to anger and then caution, all in an instant.

HIS CRONIES LOOKED DOWN at him for the order to jump me, but he ignored them. He bounced up immediately to show that it hadn't hurt or perhaps had been an accident and snarled, "Do that again."

I did. This time his look of surprise shaded into one of respect. His subordinates looked at each other in wonder and bewilderment. "He's only a first grader," one of them said. "Just think how tough he's going to be when he's older."

Meanwhile I was praying that Chango wouldn't ask me to do it a third time. I had a premonition that I had used up all of my luck. Somebody heard my prayer, because

Chango looked up from the dirt and extended a hand. Was it an offer of friendship, or did he just want me to pull him to his feet?

To show that I was a good sport, I reached down. Instead of a shake or a tug up, he pulled me down so I sprawled alongside him. Everybody laughed.

"That's showing him, Chango," somebody said.

Then Chango grinned, and I could see why the nickname. With his brown face, small size, and simian smile there could be no other. "You wanna join our gang?" he asked. "I think you'll do." What if I say no? I thought. But the bell saved me, because they started to amble back to class. "Meet us on the steps after school," Chango shouted. I nodded, brushing the dust from my cords as I hurried off.

That was how I became one of Los Indios, which was what we called ourselves. It was all pretty innocent, not at all what people think of when they see brown faces, hear Spanish words, and are told about gangs. It was a club really, like any kid club. It made us more than nonentities. It was a recognition, like the medal for bravery given to the cowardly lion in *The Wizard of Oz*.

❋

Spanish Words

Vaqueros y paisanos
Mexican cowboys and countrymen, p. 78

WHAT WE MOSTLY DID was walk home together through enemy territory. Since we were Los Indios, it was the cowboys and the settlers we had to watch out for. The Anglo ones. *Vaqueros y paisanos* were okay. Also, it was a relief to slip into Spanish again after guarding my tongue all day so it wouldn't incite Sister Mary Margaret. It got so I even began to dream in English, and that made me feel very uncomfortable, as if I were betraying something very deep and ancient and basic.

Some of the times, too, there were fights. As I said before, we were outnumbered two to one, and the sound of words in another language sometimes outraged other students, although they didn't seem to think about that when we all prayed in Latin. In parish it was a twist on the old cliché: the students that pray together fight together—against each other.

But there was more to Los Indios than that. Most important were the movies. I forgot the name of the theater. I think it was the Rio. But no matter. We called it the Rat House. When it was very quiet during the scary part of the movie, just before the villain was going to pounce on the heroine, you could hear the scamper of little feet across the floor. We sat with our smelly tennis shoes up on the torn seats—we couldn't have done any more harm to those uncomfortable lumps. And one day someone swore he saw a large, gray furry something slither through the cold, stale popcorn in the machine in the lobby. None of us would ever have bought popcorn after that, even if we'd had the money.

For a dime, though, you still couldn't beat the Rat House. Saturday matinees were their specialty, although at night during the week they showed Spanish-language movies that parents and aunts and uncles went to see. Saturdays, though, were for American westerns, monster movies, and serials.

Since I was one of the few who ever had money, I was initiated into a special assignment that first Saturday. I was the front man, paying hard cash for a ticket that allowed me to hurry past the candy counter—no point in being tempted by what you couldn't get. I slipped down the left aisle near the screen, where behind a half-drawn curtain was a door on which was painted "Exit." No one could see the sign because the light bulb was burned out, and they never replaced it in all the years we went there. I guess they figured if the lights were too strong, the patrons would see what a terrible wreck the theater was and not come back.

The owner was a short, round, excitable man with the wrinkles and quavering voice of a person in his seventies but with black, black hair. We kept trying to figure out whether it was a toupee or not, and if it was, how we could snatch it off.

For all his wrinkles, though, he could rush up and down the aisles and grab an unruly kid by the collar and march him out like nothing you ever saw. So fast that we nicknamed him Flash Gordo. We would explode into fits of laughter when one of us saw him zoom down the aisle and whispered "Flash Gordo" to the rest of us. He gave us almost as many laughs as Chris-Pin Martin of the movies.

I counted out my money that first Saturday. I was nervous, knowing what I had to do, and the pennies kept sticking to my sweaty fingers. Finally, in exasperation, Flash Gordo's long-nosed wife counted them herself, watching me like a hawk so I wouldn't try to sneak in until she got to ten, and then she growled, "All right!"

Zoom! Past the candy counter and down the aisle like I said, looking for Flash. I didn't see him until I got right up front, my heart pounding, and started to move toward the door. That's when this circular shadow loomed in the semi-dark, and I looked up in fright to see him standing at the edge of the stage looking at the screen. Then he turned abruptly and scowled at me as if he could read my mind. I slipped into an aisle seat and pretended I was testing it by bouncing up and down a couple of times and then sliding over to try the next one.

I thought Flash was going to say something as he walked in my direction. But he suddenly bobbed down and picked something off the floor — a dead rat? — when a yell came from the back of the theater. "Lupe and Carlos are doing it again! Back in the last row!"

Flash bolted upright so quickly my mouth fell open. Before I could close it, he rushed up the aisle out of sight, toward those sex maniacs in the last row. Of all the things Flash Gordo could not tolerate, this was the worst. And every Saturday some clown would tattle on Lupe and Carlos, and Flash would rush across the theater. Only later

Words to Know

Flash Gordo a Spanish twist to the name Flash Gordon, a character in a comic strip set in the future, p. 80

Gringos a sometimes derogatory name for white, English-speaking Americans, p. 81

¿Dónde están los mejicanos? Where are the Mexicans? p. 81

inglés English, p. 81

did I learn that there never was any Lupe or Carlos. If there had been, I'm sure Los Indios would have kept very quiet and watched whatever it was they were doing back there.

"Oh, Carlos!" someone yelled in a falsetto. "Stop that this minute!"

I jumped out of my seat and rushed to the door to let Los Indios in. By the time Flash Gordo had shined his flashlight over and under the seats in the back, we were all across the theater at the edge of the crowd where we wouldn't be conspicuous. Later we moved to our favorite spot in the front row, where we craned our necks to look up at the giant figures acting out their adventures.

While the movies were fantastic — the highlight of our week — sometimes I think we had almost as much fun talking about them afterwards and acting them out. It was like much later when I went to high school; rehashing the Saturday night dance or party was sometimes better than the actual event.

We ALL HAD OUR FAVORITES and our definite point of view about Hollywood movies. We barely tolerated those cowboy movies with actors like Johnny Mack Brown and Wild Bill Elliot and Gene Autry and even Hopalong Cassidy. Gringos! we'd sniff with disdain. But we'd watch them in preference to roaming the streets, and we'd cheer for the Indians and sometimes for the bad guys if they were swarthy and Mexican.

They showed the Zorro movies several times each, including the serials, with one chapter each Saturday. Zorro drew mixed reviews and was the subject of endless argument. "Spanish dandy!" one would scoff. "¿Dónde están los mejicanos?" Over in the background hanging on to their straw sombreros and smiling fearfully as they bowed to the tax collector, I remember.

"But at least Zorro speaks the right language."

Then somebody would hoot, "Yeah. Hollywood inglés. Look at the actors who play Zorro. Gringos every one. John Carroll. Reed Handley. Tyrone Power. ¡Mierda!"

That was what Zorro did to us. Better than Gene Autry but still a phony Spaniard, while all the *indios y mestizos* were bit players.

That was no doubt the reason why our favorite was the Cisco Kid. Even the one gringo who played the role, Warner Baxter, could have passed for a Mexican. More than one kid said he looked like my old man, so I was one of those who accepted Warner Baxter. Somebody even thought that he was Mexican but had changed his name so he could get parts in Hollywood — you know how Hollywood is. But we conveniently leaped from that to cheering for the "real" Cisco Kids without wondering how they ever got parts in that Hollywood: Gilbert Roland, César Romero, Duncan Renaldo. With the arch-sidekick of all time, Chris-Pin Martin, who was better any day than Fuzzy Knight, Smiley Burnette, or Gabby Hayes.

Spanish Words

indios y mestizos Indians and people of mixed Spanish and Indian ancestry, p. 82

Hasta la vista See you soon. p. 82

La huera (also la güera) the blonde, p. 83

"Sí, Ceesco," we'd lisp to each other and laugh, trying to sound like Chris-Pin.

We'd leave the theater laughing and chattering, bumping and elbowing each other past the lobby. There Flash Gordo would stare at us as if trying to remember whether or not we had bought tickets, thoughtfully clicking his false teeth like castanets. We'd quiet down as we filed past, looking at that toupee of his that was, on closer inspection, old hair blackened with shoe polish that looked like dyed rat fur. *Hasta la vista*, Flash, I'd think. See you again next week.

O NE SATURDAY AFTERNOON when I returned home there was a beat-up old truck parked in front of the empty house next door and a slow parade in and out. In the distance I saw a curious stare of a towhead about my age.

When I rushed into the house, my three-year-old brother ran up to me and excitedly told me in baby talk, *"La huera. La huera, huera."*

"Hush," Mama said.

Uncle Tito, who was Mama's unmarried younger brother, winked at me. "Blondie's wearing a halter top and shorts," he said. "In the backyard next door."

"Hush," Mama said to him, scowling, and he winked at me again.

That night when I was supposed to be sleeping, I heard Mama and Papa arguing. "Well," Mama said, "what do you think about that? They swept up the gutters of Oklahoma City. What was too lightweight to settle got blown across the panhandle to New Mexico. Right next door."

"Now, Josefa," Papa said, "you have to give people a chance."

"Halter top and shorts," Mama snipped. "What will the children think?"

"The only child who's going to notice is Tito, and he's old enough, although sometimes he doesn't act it."

But then my eyelids started to get heavy, and the words turned into a fuzzy murmur.

One day after school that next week, Chango decided that we needed some new adventures. We took the long way home all the way past Fourth Street Elementary School, where all the pagan Protestants went. "Only Catholics go to heaven," Sister Mary Margaret warned us. "Good Catholics." While her cold eye sought out a few of us and chilled our hearts with her stare.

But after school the thaw set in. We wanted to see what those candidates for hell looked like — those condemned souls who attended public school. And I wondered: if God had only one spot left in heaven, and He had to choose between a bad Catholic who spoke Spanish and a good Protestant who spoke English, which one He would let in. A fearful possibility crossed my mind, but I quickly dismissed it.

We rambled along, picking up rocks and throwing them at tree trunks, looking for lizards or maybe even a lost coin dulled by weather and dirt but still very spendable. What we found was nothing. The schoolyard was empty, so we turned back toward home. It was then, in the large empty field across from the Rio Valley Creamery, that we saw this laggard, my new neighbor, the undesirable Okie.

Chango gave a shout of joy. There he was. The enemy. Let's go get him! We saddled our imaginary horses and galloped into the sunset. Meanwhile, John Wayne, which was the name I called him then, turned his flour-white face and blinked his watery pale eyes at us in fear. Then he took off across the field in a dead run, which only increased our excitement, as if it were an admission that he truly was the enemy and deserved thrashing.

He escaped that day, but not before he got a good look at us. I forgot what we called him besides Okie *gabacho gringo cabrón*. In my memory he was John Wayne to our Cisco Kid, maybe because of the movie about the Alamo.

That then became our favorite after-school pastime. We'd make our way toward the Fourth Street Elementary School looking for our enemy, John Wayne. As cunning as enemies usually are, we figured that he'd be on the lookout, so we stalked him Indian-style. We missed him the next day, but the day after that when we were still a long block away, he suddenly stopped and lifted his head like a wild deer and seemed to feel or scent alien vibrations in the air, because he set off at a dogtrot toward home.

"Head him off at the pass!" Chango Cisco shouted, and we headed across toward Fifth Street. But John Wayne ran too fast, so we finally stopped and cut across to Lomas Park to work out a better plan.

We ambushed him the next day. Four of us came around the way he'd

Culture Notes

Okie a derogatory name for poor Oklahomans displaced during the 1930s partly as a result of severe drought, p. 84

gabacho gringo cabrón a string of derogatory terms: a person born of Spanish parents — consequently, more European than Mexican; a white American; a husband of an unfaithful wife. In this context, the terms combine to form an epithet such as "you white, redneck, son-of-a-gun," p. 84

¿Que hablas español? Do you speak Spanish? p. 85

expect us to, while the other two of us sneaked the back way to intercept him between home and the elementary school. At the first sight of the stalkers he ran through the open field that was too big to be called a city lot. Chango and I waited for him behind the tamaracks. When he came near, breathing so heavily we could hear his wheeze, and casting quick glances over his shoulder, we stepped out from behind the trees.

HE STOPPED DEAD. I couldn't believe anyone could stop that fast. No slow down, no gradual transition. One instant he was running full speed; the next instant he was absolutely immobile, staring at us with fright.

"You!" he said breathlessly, staring straight into my eyes.

"You!" I answered.

"¿Que hablas español?" Chango asked.

His look of fear deepened, swept now with perplexity like a ripple across the surface of water. When he didn't answer, Chango whooped out a laugh of joy and charged with clenched fists. It wasn't much of a fight. A couple of punches and a bloody nose and John Wayne was down. When we heard the shouts from the others, Chango turned and yelled to them. That was when John Wayne made his escape. We didn't follow this time. It wasn't worth it. There was no fight in him, and we didn't beat up on sissies or girls.

On the way home it suddenly struck me that since he lived next door, he would tell his mother, who might tell my mother, who would unquestionably tell my father. I entered the house with apprehension. Whether it was fear or conscience didn't matter.

But luck was with me. That night, although I watched my father's piercing looks across the dinner table with foreboding (or was it my conscience that saw his looks as piercing?), nothing came of it. Not a word. Only questions about school. What were they teaching us to read and write in English? Were we already preparing for our First Communion? Wouldn't Grandma be proud when we went to the country next Sunday. I could read for her from my schoolbook, *Bible Stories for Children*. Only my overambitious father forgot that *Bible Stories for Children* was a third-grade book that he had bought for me at a church rummage sale. I was barely at the reading level of "Run, Spot, Run." Hardly exciting fare even for my blind grandmother, who spoke no English and read nothing at all.

Before Sunday, though, there was Saturday. In order to do my share of the family chores and "earn" movie money instead of accepting charity, my father had me pick up in the backyard. I gathered toys that belonged to my little sister and brother, carried a bag of garbage to the heavy galvanized can out back by the shed, even helped pull a few weeds in the vegetable garden. This last was the "country" that my father carried with him to every house we lived in until I grew up and left home. You can take the boy out of the country, as the old saying goes. And in his case it was true.

I dragged my feet reluctantly out to the tiny patch of yard behind the doll's house in which we lived, ignoring my mother's scolding about not wearing out the toes of my shoes.

I must have been staring at the rubber tips of my tennis shoes to watch them wear down, so I didn't see my arch-enemy across the low fence. I heard him first. A kind of cowardly snivel that jolted me like an electric shock. Without looking I knew who it was.

"You!" he said as I looked across the fence.

"You!" I answered back with hostility.

Then his eyes watered up and his lips twitched in readiness for the blubbering that, in disgust, I anticipated.

"You hate me," he accused. I squatted down to pick up a rock, not taking my eyes off him. "Because I don't speak Spanish and I have yellow hair."

No, I thought, I don't like you because you're a sniveler. I wanted to leap the fence and punch him on those twitching lips, but I sensed my father behind me watching. Or was it my conscience again? I didn't dare turn and look.

"I hate Okies," I said. To my delight it was as if my itching fist had connected. He all but yelped in pain, though what I heard was a sharp expulsion of air.

"Denver?" the soft, feminine voice startled me, and I looked toward the back stoop of their house. I didn't see what Tito had made such a fuss about. She was blond and pale as her son and kind of lumpy, I thought, even in the everyday housedress she wore. She tried to smile — a weak, sniveling motion of her mouth that told me how Denver had come by that same expression. Then she stepped into the yard where we boys stared at each other like tomcats at bay.

"Howdy," she said in a soft funny accent that I figured must be Oklahoma. "I was telling your mother that you boys ought to get together, being neighbors and all. Denver's in the second grade at the public school."

DENVER BACKED AWAY from the fence and nestled against his mother's side. Before I could answer that Immaculate Heart boys didn't play with sniveling heathens, I heard our back door squeak open, then slam shut.

"I understand there's a nice movie in town where the boys go Saturday afternoons," she went on. But she was looking over my head toward whoever had come out of the house.

I looked back and saw Mama. Through the window over the kitchen sink I saw Papa. He's making sure she and I behave, I thought.

"It would be nice for the boys to go together," Mama said. She came down the steps and across the yard.

You didn't ask me! my silent angry self screamed. It's not fair! You didn't ask me! But Mama didn't even look at me; she addressed herself to Mrs. Oklahoma as if Snivel Nose and I weren't even there.

Then an unbelievable thought occurred to me. For some reason Denver had not told his mama about being chased home from school. Or if he did, he hadn't mentioned me.

He was too afraid, I decided. He knew what would happen if he squealed. But even that left me with an uneasy feeling. I looked at him to see if the answer was on his face. All I got was a weak twitch of a smile and a blink of his pleading eyes.

I was struck dumb by the entire negotiation. It was settled without my comment or consent, like watching someone bargain away my life. When I went back into the house, all of my pent-up anger exploded. I screamed and kicked my heels and even cried—but to no avail.

"You have two choices, young man," my father warned. "Go to the matinee with Denver or stay in your room." But his ominous tone of voice told me that there was another choice: a good belting on the rear end.

O F COURSE, this Saturday the Rat House was showing a movie about one of our favorite subjects where the mejicanos whipped the gringos: the Alamo.

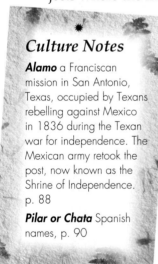

❋

Culture Notes

Alamo a Franciscan mission in San Antonio, Texas, occupied by Texans rebelling against Mexico in 1836 during the Texan war for independence. The Mexican army retook the post, now known as the Shrine of Independence. p. 88

Pilar or Chata Spanish names, p. 90

I had to go. Los Indios were counting on me to let them in.

I walked the few blocks to town, a boy torn apart. One of me hurried eagerly toward the Saturday afternoon adventure. The other dragged his feet, scuffing the toes of his shoes to spite his parents, all the while conscious of this hated stranger walking silently beside him.

When we came within sight of the theater, I felt Denver tense and slow his pace even more than mine. "Your gang is waiting," he said, and I swear he started to tremble.

What a chicken, I thought. "You're with me," I said. But then he had reminded me. What would I tell Chango and the rest of Los Indios?

They came at us with the rush. "What's he doing here?" Chango snarled.

I tried to explain. They deflected my words and listened instead to the silent fear they heard as they scrutinized Denver. My explanation did not wash, so I tried something in desperation.

"He's not what you think," I said. Skepticism and disbelief. "Just because he doesn't understand Spanish doesn't mean he can't be one of us." Show me! Chango's expression said. "He's — he's — " My voice was so loud that a passer-by turned and stared. "He's an Indian from Oklahoma," I lied.

"A blond Indian?" They all laughed.

My capacity for lying ballooned in proportion to their disbelief. I grew indignant, angry, self-righteous. "Yes!" I shouted. "An albino Indian!"

The laughs froze in their throats, and they looked at each other, seeing their own doubts mirrored in their friends' eyes. "Honest to God?" Chango asked.

"Honest to God!"

"Does he have money?"

Denver UNFOLDED a sweaty fist to show the dime in his palm. Chango took it quickly, like a rooster pecking a kernel of corn. "Run to the dime store," he commanded the fastest of his lackeys. "Get that hard candy that lasts a long time. And hurry. We'll meet you in the back."

Denver's mouth fell open but not a sound emerged. "When we see him running back," Chango said to me, "you buy the ticket and let us in." Then he riveted his suspicious eyes on Denver and said, "Talk Indian."

I don't remember what kind of gibberish Denver faked. It didn't have to be much, because our runner had dashed across the street and down the block and was already sprinting back.

Our seven-for-the-price-of-one worked as always. When the theater was dark, we moved to our favorite seats. In the meantime, I had drawn Denver aside and maliciously told him he had better learn some Spanish. When we came to the crucial part of the movie, he had to shout what I told him.

It was a memorable Saturday. The hard sugar candy lasted through two cartoons and half of the first feature. We relived the story of the Alamo again — we had seen this movie at least twice before, and we had seen other versions more times than I can remember. When the crucial, climatic attack began, we started our chant. I elbowed Denver to shout what I had taught him.

"Maten los gringos!" Kill the gringos! Then others in the audience took up the chant, while Flash Gordo ran around in circles trying to shush us up.

I sat in secret pleasure, a conqueror of two worlds. To my left was this blond Indian shouting heresies he little dreamed of, while I was already at least as proficient in English as he. On my right were my fellow tribesmen, who had accepted my audacious lie and welcomed this albino redskin into our group.

But memory plays its little tricks. Years later, when I couldn't think of Denver's name, I would always remember the Alamo — and John Wayne. There were probably three or four movies about that infamous mission, but John Wayne's was the one that stuck in my mind. Imagine my shock when I learned that his movie had not been made until 1960, by which time I was already through high school, had two years of college, and had gone to work. There was no way we could have seen the John Wayne version when I was in the first grade.

Looking back, I realized that Wayne, as America's gringo hero, was forever to me the bigoted Indian hater of *The Searchers* fused with the deserving victim of the attacking Mexican forces at the Alamo — the natural enemy of the Cisco Kid.

Another of my illusions shattered hard when I later learned that in real life Wayne had married a woman named Pilar or Chata or maybe both. That separated the man, the actor, from the characters he portrayed and left me in total confusion.

But then life was never guaranteed to be simple. For I saw the beak of the chick I was at six years old pecking through the hard shell of my own preconceptions. Moving into an alien land. First hating, then becoming friends with aliens like my blond Indian Okie friend, Denver, and finally becoming almost an alien myself.

RESPONDING

1. **Personal Response** The narrator's childhood fantasies and idols were significantly shaped by the movies. Who are movie heroes of the '90s? Can you identify with these heroes, or do you, like the narrator, have to redefine them?

2. **Literary Analysis** The narrator compares the Anglo and Hispanic students and the nun who teaches them to different ingredients in a chocolate sundae. Think of a *metaphor* that reflects your class, team, or group of friends. Illustrate your work if you wish. Post your comparisons on a class bulletin board or collect them in a booklet.

3. **Multicultural Connection** The narrator's family moves so that he will use English as his main language, a practice enforced by Sister Mary Margaret. Today several states have enacted "English Only" laws. Do you agree or disagree with such laws? Why or why not?

LANGUAGE WORKSHOP

Compare/Contrast Beginning with the title, Candelaria emphasizes cultural clashes by contrasting people, places, and languages as well as ethnic and religious groups. See how many contrasting pairs from the story you can list.

WRITER'S PORTFOLIO

The narrator says that his "gang" was really a kids' club and "all pretty innocent." In a short paper, compare or contrast the purpose and activities of Los Indios with the groups or clubs you have joined or have observed.

ABOUT **MAYA ANGELOU**

Born in St. Louis in 1928, Maya Angelou (ä′jə lü) was raised by her grandmother in Arkansas until she graduated from eighth grade. Then she joined her mother in San Francisco. After completing high school, she studied and taught dance. By the late 1950s, however, she had become committed to writing and to working in the civil rights movement. For her outstanding contributions to American literature, she has received many honorary degrees and the applause of the whole nation on January 20, 1993, when she

delivered her poem, "On the Pulse of Morning," at President Clinton's inauguration. Angelou is currently Reynolds Professor at Wake Forest University in Winston-Salem, North Carolina.

Getups

Because I was very keen that my son not feel that he was neglected or different, I went frequently to his school. Sometimes between my jobs I would just go and stand outside the fenced play area. And he would, I am happy to say, always come and acknowledge me in the colorful regalia. I always wore beads. Lots of beads. The cheaper they were, the more I got, and sometimes I wore head wraps.

When my son was six and I twenty-two, he told me quite solemnly that he had to talk to me. We both sat down at the kitchen table, and he asked with an old man's eyes and a young boy's voice, "Mother, do you have any sweaters that match?" I was puzzled at first. I said, "No," and then I understood he was talking about the pullover and cardigan sets which were popular with white women. And I said, "No, I don't," maybe a little huffily. And he said, "Oh, I wish you did. So that you could wear them to school when you come to see me."

I was tickled, but I am glad I didn't laugh because he continued, "Mother, could you please only come to school when they call you?" Then I realized that my attire, which delighted my heart and certainly activated my creativity, was an embarrassment to him.

When people are young, they desperately need to conform, and no one can embarrass a young person in public so much as an adult to whom he or she is related. Any outré action or wearing of "getups" can make a young person burn with self-consciousness.

I learned to be a little more discreet to avoid causing him displeasure. As he grew older and more confident, I gradually returned to what friends thought of as my eccentric way of dressing. I was happier when I chose and created my own fashion.

I have lived in this body all my life and know it much better than any fashion designer. I think I know what looks good on me, and I certainly know what feels good on me.

I appreciate the creativity which is employed in the design of fabric and the design of clothes, and when something does fit my body and personality, I rush to it, buy it quickly, and wear it frequently. But I must not lie to myself for fashion's sake. I am only willing to purchase the item which becomes me and to wear that which enhances my image of myself to myself.

If I am comfortable inside my skin, I have the ability to make other people comfortable inside their skins although their feelings are not my primary reason for making my fashion choice. If I feel good inside my skin and clothes, I am thus free to allow my body its sway, its natural grace, its natural gesture. Then I am so comfortable that whatever I wear looks good on me even to the external fashion arbiters.

Dress is important to mention because many people are imprisoned by powerful dictates on what is right and proper to wear. Those decisions made by others and sometimes at their convenience are not truly meant to make life better or finer or more graceful or more gracious. Many times they stem from greed, insensitivity, and the need for control.

I have been in company, not long to be sure, but in company where a purveyor of taste will look at a woman or man who enters a room and will say with a sneer, "That was last year's jacket." As hastily as possible, I leave that company, but not before I record the snide attitude which has nothing to do with the beauty or effectiveness of the garment, but rather gives the speaker a moment's sense of superiority at, of course, someone else's expense.

Seek the fashion which truly fits and befits you. You will always be in fashion if you are true to yourself, and only if you are true to yourself. You might, of course, rightly wear that style which is emblazoned on the pages of the fashion magazines of the day, or you might not.

The statement "Clothes make the man" should be looked at, reexamined, and in fact reevaluated. Clothes can make the man or woman look silly and foppish and foolish. Try rather to be so much yourself that the clothes you choose increase your naturalness and grace.

RESPONDING

1. **Personal Response** Imagine that Maya Angelou accompanies you the next time you buy clothes. Do you think she will agree that the clothes you choose enhance your self-image? If not, explain to her why you buy the clothes you do.

2. **Literary Analysis** How does Angelou's *tone* affect her message in this essay? For example, do you think she is informal? preachy? or something else?

3. **Multicultural Connection** Angelou explains that cardigan sets were once popular with white women. What groups today try to distinguish themselves by the clothes they wear? Do *you* have a "getup"? Explain.

LANGUAGE WORKSHOP

Proverbs Maya Angelou disagrees with the *proverb*, "Clothes make the man." Why? What does the following Ashanti proverb mean? "When a man is wealthy, he may wear an old cloth." What might be Angelou's reaction to this proverb?

WRITER'S PORTFOLIO

If money were no object, what would you choose to wear? Plan a complete wardrobe, including accessories, for at least one season. Describe your wardrobe in an ad with prices and pictures.

ABOUT **MARK MATHABANE**

Mark Mathabane (**ma′thä bān′**) was born in 1960 in Alexandra, South Africa. Poor and illiterate, his parents lived in fear of being deported to tribal reserves or "home-lands." Despite tremendous obstacles, he attended school and at thirteen took up tennis. In 1978, inspired by U.S. tennis star Arthur Ashe and aided by another U.S. tennis player, Stan Smith, Mathabane entered a U.S. college on a tennis scholarship. He graduated in 1983. In 1986, he published *Kaffir Boy*, an autobiography. Currently he makes a living as a writer and lecturer. In 1989, he published *Kaffir Boy in America: An Encounter with Apartheid*, and in 1992 he and his

wife, Gail, published a book called *Love in Black and White: The Triumph of Love over Prejudice and Taboo.*

Appearances Are Destructive

$\mathbb{A}$s public schools reopen for the new year, strategies to curb school violence will once again be hotly debated. Installing metal detectors and hiring security guards will help, but the experience of my two sisters makes a compelling case for greater use of dress codes as a way to protect students and promote learning.

Shortly after my sisters arrived here from South Africa I enrolled them at the local public school. I had great expectations for their educational experience. Compared with black schools under apartheid, American schools are Shangri-Las, with modern textbooks, school buses, computers, libraries, lunch programs and dedicated teachers.

But despite these benefits, which students in many parts of the world only dream about, my sisters' efforts at learning were almost derailed. They were constantly taunted for their homely outfits. A couple of times they came home in tears. In South Africa students were required to wear uniforms, so my sisters had never been preoccupied with clothes and jewelry.

They became so distraught that they insisted on transferring to different schools, despite my reassurances that there was nothing wrong with them because of what they wore.

I have visited enough public schools around the country to know that my sisters' experiences are not unique. In schools in many areas, Nike, Calvin Klein, Adidas, Reebok and Gucci are more familiar names to students than Zora Neale Hurston, Shakespeare and Faulkner. Many students seem to pay more attention to what's on their bodies than in their minds.

Teachers have shared their frustrations with me at being unable to teach those students willing to learn because classes are frequently disrupted by other students ogling themselves in mirrors, painting their fingernails, combing their hair, shining their gigantic shoes or comparing designer labels on jackets, caps and jewelry.

The fiercest competition among students is often not over academic achievements, but over who dresses most expensively. And many students now measure parental love by how willing their mothers and fathers are to pamper them with money for the latest fads in clothes, sneakers and jewelry.

Those parents without the money to waste on such meretricious extravagances are considered uncaring and cruel. They often watch in dismay and helplessness as their children become involved with gangs and peddle drugs to raise the money.

When students are asked why they attach so much importance to clothing, they frequently reply that it's the cool thing to do, that it gives them status and earns them respect. And clothes are also used to send sexual messages, with girls thinking that the only things that make them attractive to boys are skimpy dresses and gaudy looks, rather than intelligence and academic excellence.

The argument by civil libertarians that dress codes infringe on freedom of expression is misleading. We observe dress codes in nearly every aspect of our lives without any diminution of our freedoms—as demonstrated by flight attendants, bus drivers, postal employees, high school bands, military personnel, sports teams, Girl and Boy Scouts, employees of fast-food chains, restaurants and hotels.

In many countries where students outperform their American counterparts academically, school dress codes are observed as part of creating the proper learning environment. Their students tend to be neater, less disruptive in class and more disciplined, mainly because their minds are focused more on learning and less on materialism.

It's time Americans realized that the benefits of safe and effective schools far outweigh any perceived curtailment of freedom of expression brought on by dress codes.

RESPONDING

1. **Personal Response** How would you go about helping Mark Mathabane's sisters make a comfortable transition from their South African school to your own?

2. **Literary Analysis** Restate the main point of Mathabane's *essay* in a sentence.

3. **Multicultural Connection** Do you agree or disagree with Mathabane that many American "students seem to pay more attention to what's on their bodies than in their minds"? Explain. Are his criticisms of American schools justified? Why or why not?

LANGUAGE WORKSHOP

Word Origins Mathabane compares American schools to black schools in Africa under *apartheid* (ə pärt′hāt or ə pärt′hīt). This word, from Afrikaans, meaning "separate," refers to South Africa's system of legalized racism. Under this system, he was known as a *Kaffir*. This word, of Arabic origin, is a derogatory term used by whites to refer to blacks. Use a dictionary to find out the meaning and origins of these words used by Mathabane: *unique, ogling, pamper, extravagance, meretricious.*

WRITER'S PORTFOLIO

Write a letter to your school board for or against the adoption of a dress code as a way to protect students and promote learning.

ABOUT LONGHANG NGUYEN

Longhang Nguyen (**long häng we′ən**) is a Vietnamese American student who emigrated to the United States with her brother and father in 1979. Her mother rejoined them after two years of separation. During those two years, her father took care of her and her younger brother, in addition to attending school to reobtain his veterinary license. She is currently studying medicine in San Francisco. To Nguyen, "love is a complex of emotions. There aren't straightforward or universal answers to its questions. Perhaps the most fruit- ful approach to the fol- lowing story lies not in judging Linh's decision but in understanding the individual tiles, color by color, of the mosaic of her heart."

Rain Music

L INH AND I GREW UP penned in the same yard, so our sibling rivalry did not last very long. By third grade we had stopped physically assaulting one another and reached a permanent truce. At that time her hair was long and flowing, brushed daily by my mother as Linh closed her eyes and counted each stroke. It always felt like cool satin when I yanked it, her head jerking backward, mimicking the motion of my arm. In actuality, she was very kind and I was not too violent, so we became intimate friends. I have not had any trouble from her since.

She is the red rose of the family and I am the green thorn. We have both decided that we are beautiful, so she tells me, but I believe she is also very beautiful outside in face and gesture. I always pout when I accuse her of being a selfish firstborn, picking, stealing the best of our parents' genes and leaving me the rejected remainder. She has wide, almond-shaped eyes like black, pearl-black reflecting pools with brown-colored flecks swirling beneath the surface, light honey-color skin and even, velvet-smooth cheeks. Her nose is just slightly upturned, her lips rosebud shaped, her chin small and delicate. Her hair still looks and feels the same now as in third grade. The vision, taken together as a whole, is breathtaking. There is something about it, a wistful, dandelion, orchidlike kind of beauty that feels like notes in a chord being played separately, finger by finger, harmonizing back and forth. I marvel even now.

My mother and father have polished her until she shines. She graduated summa cum laude from the College

of Chemistry at Cal and double majored in Ethnic Studies. However, my parents don't count the latter. She is now a fourth-year student at UCSF preparing to enter the surgical residency program next fall. My parents are bursting at the seams, gorged with devouring so much blessedness and good fortune.

"Will your daughter become a surgeon?" our relatives ask.

"It's possible," my father says, beaming.

"She is friends with this young man in her class. He's tall, distinguished-looking, loyal and respectful to his parents, hard-working but generous. He was even born in Vietnam! But he came over here with his family in 1975. He went to Harvard"—my mother pauses to let the relatives gasp in unison—"on a full scholarship!" she smiles modestly, then lowers her eyes.

"A possible son-in-law?" they ask.

She shrugs and sighs. "That is up to God."

Linh hasn't told my parents about David. She met him five years ago during her final year at Cal. That semester they were in three classes together: a choral class, an Afro-American literature class, and a creative writing class. They became good friends.

David is a writer. His subjects are ordinary preoccupations of other writers: his mother, the father he has never seen or known, the friends of his childhood. Some of them are dead now. The others are spread out across the country. One is a construction worker in St. Louis. Another is a teacher in Baton Rouge. The third is a journalist in Washington, D.C. They write to him once in a while or call him. Linh hasn't met any of them, but she knows them all.

After David feverishly completes a story, Linh cooks him dinner. Afterward, she tucks him into bed and sits nearby in the wicker chair, legs drawn up and hugged tightly to her chest, to watch him while he sleeps. His soft, black curls rest against the white of the pillow, his closed eyelids and long lashes flutter minutely while he dreams, his breath whistles through the evenness of his teeth as the cover grazes the dark honey of his skin.

They always have a good time together, and he makes her laugh in many different ways, wherever they happen to be. He always gets close to finishing her off during a tennis set, but then she cries out that he has cheated and treated her unfairly and he has to start over again. He never wins. Sometimes they sing together, his clear resonant tenor melding with her flutelike, crystalline soprano. Then they have tea.

I know all about David. She won't stop talking about him, but I know less about Thanh, the Vietnamese friend at UCSF. I know he's nice but that's all. She woke me up this morning at ten thirty and said, "It's a bright, beautiful, Saturday morning. Let's go and have a picnic."

"No, no," I mumbled hazily in my sleep. "Take David. Leave me alone."

"I don't want to take David. I want to spend quality time with you, my darling sister. Get up, you piece of mutton. Toast on the table in five minutes and we're leaving in half an hour."

"Oh, lord," I groaned, "I'm being punished for sins from past lives."

We arrived at the park at twelve, lugged our ample picnic hamper heavily laden with cheese, fruits, sandwiches, ice, and bottles of juice from the car, and trudged into the heart of the lightly shaded, green forest. When I opened the basket and took out the butter, she started to talk.

"David kissed me last night . . ."

"He what?"

". . . or I kissed him. It just happened, I guess. He invited me to dinner, promised to cook a sumptuous Cajun feast with Vietnamese desserts. *Bánh flanc*, you know. My favorite." She plucked a blade of grass from its roots and twisted it back and forth, watching a streak of feeble, yellow sun play on its linear edges. "I expected it to be a celebration. He'd just finished his first novel, not quite a love story, he says, and he wanted me to read it." She spoke more softly. "When I arrived, he had set tiny blossoms in water dishes throughout the apartment. It smelled wonderful. The food was delicious, everything so lovely, so tranquil I didn't know where to begin. After dinner he led me into the living room.

" 'Rain music,' he said. 'It's for you.' After the last note on the piano had stopped to echo, he turned toward me and kissed me for a long, long time. I didn't know what I was doing. I just couldn't stop. I didn't breathe. When he let me go, I kept thinking of his hands and fingers, seeing them fly over the ivory keys like little Russian men dancing in their black fur hats and noticing how his brown was different from mine. I was raging inside, screaming in my head, 'Why can't his fingers be brown like mine, be my brown? Why is his hair curly, not straight like mine?' I saw brown pigments run across my eyes, all different colored browns. Those pigments keep us apart. How do I stand there and tell this man who writes me music and whose hands burn my cheeks that I can't be who he wants me to be?"

"But he doesn't want to change you."

"No, I can't be who he thinks I am. He's a damned starving writer. He can't give me anything, just himself. And he doesn't even know that I'm using him. Damn it! He doesn't even know." She choked on her tears, swallowed, and cried quietly, hugging her knees, until exhausted. The leaves rustled softly while I waited.

After a while she grew calm, her eyes gazing steadily at the flashing water of the stream below. "I love Thanh. I would never hurt him for anything. Throughout the four years at UCSF, he has been so patient, so kind, so dedicated to medicine for its own good, not for just its technology, even though he's brilliant and understands these details completely. He's so perfect for me, just perfect. It's like he stepped out of my story and came to life. We speak the same language and share the same past. Everything. And Mom and Dad, they've done so much for us. Now they think they've won the lottery from God for being good all their life."

"But how do you feel about Thanh? How does he make you feel?"

"He will be my lifelong friend. He'll make a wonderful father. That's what a husband should be. Our children will know the culture and customs of our homeland. They'll speak Vietnamese and English, just like us."

"And how does David make you feel?" I tugged at her gently.

She bowed her head for a long while reflecting. Then she softly murmured, "It's just not possible."

"But why? I don't understand."

The picnic basket remained quite full. Neither of us was hungry. It threatened to rain as we packed up to go home. On the drive back, we were silent. I watched the windshield wipers swing back and forth, clearing rain cascading down the front window.

RESPONDING

1. **Personal Response** If you had a friend in Linh's predicament, what would you say to her?

2. **Literary Analysis** What is the significance of rain in the *title* and at the end of the story?

3. **Multicultural Connection** Although Linh says that "pigments" keep David and her apart, what other reasons are revealed in the story?

LANGUAGE WORKSHOP

Punctuating Dialogue In *direct quotations,* quotation marks are placed before and after the speaker's exact words. If the direct quotation is interrupted, both parts are enclosed in quotation marks. Periods, commas, and usually question and exclamation marks are placed inside quotation marks. A comma sets off the speaker from the words spoken.

Punctuate the following: No, no I mumbled hazily in my sleep. Take David. Leave me alone.

WRITER'S PORTFOLIO

Write a letter from Linh to columnist Ann Landers seeking advice, along with Ann Landers's reply.

ABOUT **JACK FORBES**

Jack Forbes, whose Delaware and Powhatan ancestors lived on the Atlantic coast, was born in Southern California and spent his childhood in rural El Monte del Sur and urban Los Angeles. In 1959, after graduating from college, he began teaching and working with ethnic minority students. A tireless organizer on behalf of Native peoples, Forbes helped develop Native American Studies programs and Native institutions, including D.Q. (Digahawida Quetzalcoatl) University and Tecumseh Center at the University of California, Davis. His most recently published works are *Columbus and Other Cannibals* and *Black Africans and Native Americans*. An anthology of Forbes's fiction is scheduled for publication in 1995 by The University of Oklahoma Press.

Only Approved Indians Can Play: Made in USA

The ALL-INDIAN BASKETBALL Tournament was in its second day. Excitement was pretty high, because a lot of the teams were very good or at least eager and hungry to win. Quite a few people had come to watch, mostly Indians. Many were relatives or friends of the players. A lot of people were betting money and tension was pretty great.

A team from the Tucson Inter-Tribal House was set to play against a group from the Great Lakes region. The Tucson players were mostly very dark young men with long black hair. A few had little goatee beards or mustaches though, and one of the Great Lakes fans had started a rumor that they were really Chicanos. This was a big issue since the Indian Sports League had a rule that all players had to be of one-quarter or more Indian blood and that they had to have their BIA roll numbers available if challenged.

And so a big argument started. One of the biggest, darkest Indians on the Tucson team had been singled out as a Chicano, and the crowd wanted him thrown out. The Great Lakes players, most of whom were pretty light, refused to start. They all had their BIA identification cards, encased in plastic. This proved that they were all real Indians, even a blonde-haired guy. He was really only about one-sixteenth but the BIA rolls had been changed for his tribe so legally he was one-fourth. There was no question about the Great

Lakes team. They were all land-based, federally-recognized Indians, although living in a big midwestern city, and they had their cards to prove it.

Anyway, the big, dark Tucson Indian turned out to be a Papago. He didn't have a BIA card but he could talk Papago so they let him alone for the time being. Then they turned towards a lean, very Indian-looking guy who had a pretty big goatee. He seemed to have a Spanish accent, so they demanded to see his card.

Well, he didn't have one either. He said he was a full-blood Tarahumara Indian and he could also speak his language. None of the Great Lakes Indians could talk their languages so they said that was no proof of anything, that you had to have a BIA roll number.

The Tarahumara man was getting pretty angry by then. He said his father and uncle had been killed by the whites in Mexico and that he did not expect to be treated with prejudice by other Indians.

But all that did no good. Someone demanded to know if he had a reservation and if his tribe was recognized. He replied that his people lived high up in the mountains and that they were still resisting the Mexicanos, that the government was trying to steal their land.

"What state do your people live in?" they wanted to know. When he said that his people lived free, outside of the control of any state, they only shook their fists at him. "You're not an official Indian. All official Indians are under the whiteman's rule now. We all have a number given to us, to show that we are recognized."

Well, it all came to an end when someone shouted that "Tarahumaras don't exist. They're not listed in the BIA dictionary." Another fan yelled, "He's a Mexican. He can't play. This tournament is only for Indians."

The officials of the tournament had been huddling together. One blew his whistle and an announcement was made. "The Tucson team is disqualified. One of its members is a Yaqui. One is a Tarahumara. The rest are Papagos. None of them have BIA enrollment cards. They are not Indians within the meaning of the laws of the government of the United States. The Great Lakes team is declared the winner by default."

A tremendous roar of applause swept through the stands. A white BIA official wiped the tears from his eyes and said to a companion, "God Bless America. I think we've won."

RESPONDING

1. **Personal Response** If you were an official in the All-Indian Basketball Tournament, what would be your requirements for allowing players to participate?

2. **Literary Analysis** What is *ironic* about the term "official Indian"? about the BIA official who says, "God bless America. I think we've won"?

3. **Multicultural Connection** For years Native Americans were encouraged to give up Native ways and assimilate into the "mainstream." As this story reveals, what has been the result?

LANGUAGE WORKSHOP

Satire A technique that uses humor and/or wit to make fun of a subject, usually to inspire reform, is called *satire*. What is Jack Forbes satirizing? Find at least three words or phrases that help achieve satire.

WRITER'S PORTFOLIO

To be treated with prejudice by members of one's own group (whether based on religion, place of national origin, culture, or even social or professional activities) is not unusual. Draft a proposal aimed at reducing prejudice and/or conflict within a group with which you identify or belong.

ABOUT **WILMA ELIZABETH MCDANIEL**

Wilma Elizabeth McDaniel was born to a family of Oklahoma sharecroppers, part Cherokee, in 1918 and traveled to California in 1936 as part of the dust bowl migration. She began writing at age eight and crammed her poems on brown paper bags and the backs of envelopes when she could not afford writing supplies. Always a storyteller, McDaniel has written twelve books of poetry, four books of stories, one novella, and a play, all of which have been published in magazines and journals. Currently a resident of Hanford, California, in the San Joaquin Valley, she brings a special understanding to the dilemmas faced by displaced people coping with the demands of a new environment.

Who Said
We All Have to
Talk Alike

WHO KNOWS HOW NEFFIE Pike's speech pattern was formed? Her Ozark family had talked the same way for generations. They added an "r" to many words that did not contain that letter. In spite of this, or because of it, their speech was clear and colorful and to the point. Most people understood what they were talking about, exactly.

Neffie was her parent's daughter. She called a toilet, "torelet," and a woman, "worman," very comfortably. The teacher at the country school never attempted to change Neffie's manner of speaking. She said that Neffie had a fine imagination and should never allow anyone to squelch it. In fact, Neffie never really knew that she talked different from most other people.

People in the tiny community of Snowball really loved Neffie. She was a good neighbor, unfailingly cheerful and helpful. The appearance of her tall and bony figure at the door of a sickroom or a bereaved family meant comfort and succor. A great woman, everyone in Snowball agreed.

She would have probably lived her life out in the same lumber house if her husband had not died. In the months that followed his death she developed a restless feeling. Home chores, church and charity work did not seem to be enough to occupy her mind. She started to read big town newspapers at the library in nearby Marshall, something new for her. She became especially interested in the out of state employment want ads. She mentioned to neighbors, "They are a lot of good jobs out there in the world."

One day she came home from Marshall and stopped at old Grandma Meade's house. She sat down in a canebottom chair and announced, "I have got me a job in California. I am selling my house and lot to a couple of retired people from Little Rock. They will be moving in the first of June."

Grandma Meade sat in shocked silence for several seconds, then said, "Honey, I do not believe it. I mean that I never in the world imagined that you would consider leaving Snowball. You and Lollis was so happy together here." Her voice trailed off, "Of course nobody could foretell the Lord would call him so young."

Neffie looked stonily at her and said with her usual clarity, "A widder worman is a free worman, especially if she don't have no children. She ought to be free to come and go like she pleases. After all, I am only fifty-one years old. I can do as much work as I ever did. This job is taking care of two little girls while their mother works at some high paying job. She has already sent me a bus ticket. I would be a fool not to go. Everyone has been to California except me. I always hankered to see the state for myself. Now is my chance to see some of the rest of the world. It may sound foolish, but it will sort of be like having a dorter of my own and grandchildren. I aim to write you a long letter when I get settled down out there."

Neffie left for California on schedule. After two weeks Grandma Meade began to worry a bit. She said, "I thought that Neffie surely would have dropped us a line by now. The last thing she told me was that she would write me a long letter. Well, maybe she hasn't got settled down yet."

A month passed without any word from Neffie.

Bug Harrison was at Grandma Meade's house when Neffie returned the day after Snowball's big Fourth of July celebration.

Neffie put her suitcases down and began at the beginning. "Grandma, you was so right about so many things. I knowed I was in trouble hock-deep, only one minute after I stepped off that bus in California. A purty young worman come forward to meet me and said she was Beryl. I busted out and told her, 'My, you are a purty worman, even purtier than your pitcher.' She kinda shrunk back and looked at me like I had used a cussword. She stood there holding her little girls' hands and asked me, where on earth did you hear a word like worman, was it a female worm of some kind? She said, 'Worman is woe-man,' like you say woh to a horse.

"Her remark nearly knocked me off my feet. I felt like a fool, and I didn't even know why. My stomach started churning. I durst not say anything to defend myself, because I hadn't done anything wrong.

"We started walking to Beryl's station wagon in the parking lot. I told her that I never was blessed with a dorter or son, either. That set her off again. She said that her children were at a very impressionable age, that I would have to watch my speech and learn the correct pronunciation of words. She did not want them picking up incorrect speech patterns and something she called coll-oke-ism, something I had, and didn't even realize. I decided to shut up and get in the car. The worman had already paid for my fare. I felt that I had to at least give her a few months' service, if I could stand the punishment at all.

"On our way to Beryl's house, she stopped at a drive-in restaurant and ordered cheeseburgers and milkshakes for all of us. I decided to just eat and listen.

"It was sure a pleasurable drive on to Beryl's home. We followed the same county highway for the entire seven miles. The road was lined on both sides with pams, tall with them fronds waving in the breeze. It reminded me of pitchers I have seen of The Holy Land, really touched my heart. I forgot myself again and said that I never had seen pams before except in pitchers. Quick as a flash Beryl told me, 'They are pall-ms, not pams. There is an l in the word.' After that, I sure buttoned up my mouth. I just said yes or no to anything she asked me.

"Her house turned out to be a real nice place, bright and modern with every type of electrical gadget you could think of. There were four bedrooms, each with a bath. I was so tired and upset over Beryl's attitude that I begged off sitting up to visit with her and the little girls. I ran me a full tub of warm water and took me a long soaking bath. I fell into bed and went sound asleep. Worman, I plumb died away, slept all night without waking up. To show you how hard I slept, there was a fairly severe earthquake in the central part of California where Beryl lived. It even shook a few things off a living room shelf. I tell you, I wouldn't have heard Gabriel blow his horn that night.

"I woke up feeling relieved that it was Monday. Beryl left for work promptly at seven-thirty. That meant the girls and I had the house to ourselves. Worman, I am a telling you, they was two living dolls, Pat and Penny. I made them bran muffins for breakfast and scrambled some eggs. They ate until they nearly foundered. It seemed like they had never seen a bran muffin before, asked me if I would cook them the same thing each day.

"I told them I knew how to cook other good old homely dishes, too. Every day, I tried something new on them, biscuits and sausage and milk gravy, buttermilk pancakes, waffles, popovers, french toast, corn dodgers, fried mush. You name it, worman, I cooked it for those dolls. It wouldn't be no big deal for the kids here in Snowball, they was raised to eat like that, but it was hog heaven to Pat and Penny."

Grandma Meade had been listening intently, her eyes pinned on Neffie's face. Now she asked, "How did Beryl like your cooking?"

Neffie laughed heartily. She said, "To put it plain, she LOVED it. I can say that she never found any flaw in my cooking, only made one complaint connected with it. I boirled her a fine big cabbage and hamhock dinner and made cornbread for our supper one evening. When we started to sit down at the table, I said that is was a nice change to have a boirled dinner now and then. That set her off like a firecracker. She said, 'That is boil–ed, not boirled.' I decided to let that snide remark pass. I saw she started dishing up the food — she lit in on it like a starving hound-dog. That showed what she thought of my cooking, didn't it? My cooking sure helped me get through them weeks as good as I did."

Bug Harrison broke in, "What were your duties during the day?"

Neffie said, "I was hired to take care of the two little girls. That is what I done. I cooked because people have to eat. I always have, always will. That didn't put no extra strain on me. The girls and I played the most of the day. They would sit on each arm of my chair and listen to me tell them about my life back in Arkansas. I didn't hold back nothing. I told them about haunted houses, ghosts, robbers, bank holdups, tornadoes, snakes, tarantulas, times when the river flooded and we had to float on a rooftop to save our lives. Lordy, worman, they just ate it up. They would listen to me with their eyes as big as saucers. I don't quite know why I done it, but I asked the girls not to tell their mother about my stories. They were as secretive as little private detectives until a week ago. They got so excited over one of my stories that they forgot theirselves. I was busy in the kitchen putting some homemade noodles into a pot of chicken broth. I heard Pat tell her mother, 'Mom, back in Arkansas where Neffie used to live, they are wormans that can tell fortunes for people. They can look right through your face and tell if you are telling the truth or a lie. They can rub your warts with skunk oirl and say some words and all the warts will fall off, never ever come back.' I figured I was in bad trouble, but I kept on dropping the noodles into the broth. I was a hundred percent right about the trouble.

"Beryl blowed her stack. She marched right back to the kitchen with the girls at her heels. She stood in the door and said, 'I have been afraid of this very thing. Neffie, I just can't keep you on any longer.'

"At that point Pat and Penny throwed themselves down on the floor and started bawling like two young calves. Pat sobbed out real angry-like, 'Yes, you CAN keep Neffie! She is the best storyteller in the whole world and the best cooker. If she goes home to Arkansas, we won't never have no more biscuits and sausage and gravy.' The tears began to run down her little face.

"Beryl stood there with her face like a flintrock. It looked like she wanted to be nice to me, but that her duty come first with her. She drawed in her breath and said, 'Neffie, you are as good and kind and honest as you can be, exceptional, but your speech is totally unacceptable. My children are at a very impressionable age. I have tried to overlook it, but they are definitely being influenced in the wrong direction. They say dorter and orter with regularity. The pattern must be eradicated immediately. I shall be happy to pay your traveling expenses home. You can look on this trip out West as my vacation gift to you.' I could see that her mind was made up and she wasn't going to change it.

"I did think to ask her if she had some other baby-sitter in mind. I didn't want to run out and leave her in a bind without one. She said there was a young girl from the college who wanted day work, so she could attend night classes. She thought that would work out great. I got her point. The college girl would be different from me, more to suit Beryl.

"Well, to shorten my story, she bought me a big box of real expensive chocolates and put me on the bus with my paid ticket, just like she had promised. She and the girls stood there beside the bus waiting for it to pull out. Penny looked up at me and blew me a kiss. I heard her say as plain as plain could be, 'Neffie, you are a sweet worman.' Then I saw Beryl put her hand over Penny's mouth. Right then, the bus pulled out of the depot and I lost sight of them.

"Worman, I done a lot of thinking as that bus rolled along the highway. I would eat a chocolate and think over my experience with Beryl. Things kind of cleared up in my mind, like having blinders taken off of my eyes. I saw I had really been ignorant of some things that other folks knowed. I didn't talk right to suit some of them, but that wasn't my fault. *I didn't know we was all supposed to talk the same way.* I thought people hadn't all talked the same since before God tore down their tower at Babel and confused all their tongues. Folks all over the world have talked different ever since then. I guess some of them like Beryl want to go back to pre-Babel days. Anyway, it was sure an eye-opener to me, hurt me, too. Beryl just plain separated herself from me. It was like she took a sharp knife and cut a melon in half, and throwed away the half that was me. You know what you do with a piece of melon you don't want. You throw it with the rinds into the garbage can. Worman, who said that we all have to talk alike? Can anyone tell me that?"

RESPONDING

1. **Personal Response** Do you think that Neffie would be a good baby-sitter? Why or why not?

2. **Literary Analysis** McDaniel uses *eye-dialect,* a respelling of words to indicate pronunciation common to certain parts of the country and/or socioeconomic levels. How do such words help characterize Neffie?

3. **Multicultural Connection** Speech patterns, such as Neffie's, are clues to one's level of education, age, sex, occupation, and origins. What is acceptable to one group may not be acceptable to others. What speech patterns do you or your friends use that others may find unacceptable?

LANGUAGE WORKSHOP

Regionalisms Whether you call it *pop, soda,* or *sodee* depends on where you're from. What you call a *frying pan,* others might call *skillet* or *spider.* What are the meanings of the following *regionalisms,* used by Neffie?
1. "I always *hankered* to see the state for myself."
2. "I knowed I was in trouble *hock-deep.*"
3. "I *durst* not say anything myself."

WRITER'S PORTFOLIO

Write a brief dialogue between two people having different dialects or speech patterns reflecting different ages, education, geographical areas, interests, or occupations. For example, consider a Midwestern rapper, a Southern chef, or a person who is just learning English.

IMAGE MAKERS

Projects

MEDIA ALERT

Using a team approach, investigate the way Native Americans, Asian Americans, Hispanic Americans, and African Americans are depicted in the media today. Check out the movies, newspapers (including advertisements and comic strips), magazines, and television shows available during one full week for your information. Present your team's findings to the class and come to some conclusion about the validity of the media's representation of these ethnic groups. Then write a letter to one of your sources either complimenting its fairness or criticizing its distortions.

MEDIA MONTAGE

Create a collage or montage of pictures taken from current magazines and newspapers that illustrates the image portrayed in the media of one group of Americans. Choose portrayals of a single ethnic group, senior citizens, teenagers, women, men, or children as your focus. Write up an assessment of what you collected and present it to the class.

IMAGE MAKERS: GOOD OR BAD

Using details from three of the selections from this unit, write an essay that focuses on the idea of image makers as a positive and/or negative force.

Further Reading

These books deal with people of different cultural backgrounds and their attempts to function as real people rather than to fulfill the expectations of image makers.

Angelou, Maya. *Wouldn't Take Nothing for My Journey Now.* Random House, 1993. Brief essays provide distilled wisdom about being true to oneself and living according to one's own standards.

Bruchac, Joseph, ed. *Breaking Silence, An Anthology of Contemporary Asian American Poets.* Greenfield Review Press, 1983. Fifty poets who are recognized as new voices speak out to break the stereotypes of the past.

Dove, Rita. *Through the Ivory Gate.* Pantheon Books, 1992. In this novel, Virginia King, artist in residence at an elementary school in Ohio, is a young artist at a crossroads, examining issues of race, creativity, family ties, and culture to arrive at self-knowledge.

Major, Clarence, ed. *Calling the Wind: Twentieth Century African American Short Stories.* HarperCollins, 1993. This collection includes short stories from Reconstruction to the 1990s, along with biographical notes.

Ortiz, Simon, ed. *Earth Power Coming: Short Fiction in Native American Literature.* Navajo Community College Press, 1983. The collection includes a wide variety of styles, themes, and topics presented in the fiction of thirty authors.

Wright, Richard. *Black Boy.* Harper, 1945; HarperPerennial edition with notes, 1993. This autobiographical narrative of a young man's coming of age examines what it was like to be Southern, male, and African American in the United States between the world wars.

Many Ways to Learn

There are many ways to learn. Take a trip, assemble something, move to a new house, write a story, fall in love — each experience brings insights. And *you* can be a teacher too! Share your culture, your language, your family. Like Laurence Yep, we are all puzzles on our way to becoming puzzle solvers. Be alert for the pieces along the way.

ABOUT **RUDOLFO ANAYA**

Rudolfo A. Anaya, a second-generation New Mexican, traces his interest in writing back to the oral tradition of New Mexican folk tales — an influence especially evident in his first novel, *Bless Me, Ultima*. Published in 1972, the award-winning novel has become an essential work in Latino American fiction. Anaya has published several other novels, including *Heart of Aztlán, Tortuga,* and *Albuquerque;* a collection of short stories; and a volume of poetry. He is a full professor and teaches creative writing at the University of New Mexico, where he edits *Blue Mesa Review*. In addition, he works as a translator, playwright, and writer of children's books.

From Bless Me, Ultima

ON THE FIRST DAY of school I awoke with a sick feeling in my stomach. It did not hurt, it just made me feel weak. The sun did not sing as it came over the hill. Today I would take the goat path and trek into town for years and years of schooling. For the first time I would be away from the protection of my mother. I was excited and sad about it.

I heard my mother enter her kitchen, her realm in the castle the giants had built. I heard her make the fire grow and sing with the kindling she fed to it.

Then I heard my father groan. "¡Ay Dios, otro día! Another day and more miles of that cursed highway to patch! And for whom? For me that I might travel west! Ay no, that highway is not for the poor man, it is for the tourist—ay, María, we should have gone to California when we were young, when my sons were boys—"

He was sad. The breakfast dishes rattled.

"Today is Antonio's first day at school," she said.

"Huh! Another expense. In California, they say, the land flows with milk and honey—"

"Any land will flow with milk and honey if it is worked with honest hands!" my mother retorted. "Look at what my brothers have done with the bottomland of El Puerto—"

"Ay, mujer, always your brothers! On this hill only rocks grow!"

"Ay! And whose fault is it that we bought a worthless hill! No, you couldn't buy fertile land along the river, you had to buy this piece of, of—"

"Of the llano," my father finished.

"Yes!"

"It is beautiful," he said with satisfaction.

"It is worthless! Look how hard we worked on the garden all summer, and for what? Two baskets of chile and one of corn! Bah!"

"There is freedom here."

"Try putting that in the lunch pails of your children!"

"Tony goes to school today, huh?" he said.

"Yes. And you must talk to him."

"He will be all right."

"He must know the value of his education," she insisted. "He must know what he can become."

"A priest."

"Yes."

"For your brothers." His voice was cold.

"You leave my brothers out of this! They are honorable men. They have always treated you with respect. They were the first colonizers of the Llano Estacado. It was the Lunas who carried the charter from the Mexican government to settle the valley. That took courage—"

"Led by the priest," my father interrupted. I listened intently. I did not yet know the full story of the first Luna priest.

"What? What did you say? Do not dare to mention blasphemy where the children can hear, Gabriel Márez!"

She scolded him and chased him out of the kitchen. "Go feed the animals! Give Tony a few minutes extra sleep!" I heard him laugh as he went out.

"My poor baby," she whispered, and then I heard her praying. I heard Deborah and Theresa getting up. They were excited about school because they had already been there. They dressed and ran downstairs to wash.

✳

Spanish Words

mujer woman, wife, p.123

llano a grassy, treeless plain, p.124

Grande term of respect for a wise, older woman, p.125

I heard Ultima enter the kitchen. She said good morning to my mother and turned to help prepare breakfast. Her sound in the kitchen gave me the courage I needed to leap out of bed and into the freshly pressed clothes my mother had readied for me. The new shoes felt strange to feet that had run bare for almost seven years.

"Ay! My man of learning!" my mother smiled when I entered the kitchen. She swept me in her arms and before I knew it she was crying on my shoulder. "My baby will be gone today," she sobbed.

"He will be all right," Ultima said. "The sons must leave the sides of their mothers," she said almost sternly and pulled my mother gently.

"Yes, Grande," my mother nodded, "it's just that he is so small—the last one to leave me—" I thought she would cry all over again. "Go and wash, and comb," she said simply.

I scrubbed my face until it was red. I wet my black hair and combed it. I looked at my dark face in the mirror.

Jasón had said there were secrets in the letters. What did he mean?

"Antoniooooo! Come and eat."

"Tony goes to school, Tony goes to school!" Theresa cried.

"Hush! He shall be a scholar," my mother smiled and served me first. I tried to eat but the food stuck to the roof of my mouth.

"Remember you are a Luna—"

"And a Márez," my father interrupted her. He came in from feeding the animals.

Deborah and Theresa sat aside and divided the school supplies they had bought in town the day before. Each got a Red Chief tablet, crayons, and pencils. I got nothing. "We are ready, mamá!" they cried.

Jasón had said look at the letter carefully, draw it on the tablet, or on the sand of the playground. You will see, it has magic.

"You are to bring honor to your family," my mother cautioned. "Do nothing that will bring disrespect on our good name."

I looked at Ultima. Her magic. The magic of Jasón's Indian. They could not save me now.

"Go immediately to Miss Maestas. Tell her you are my boy. She knows my family. Hasn't she taught them all? Deborah, take him to Miss Maestas."

"Gosh, okay, let's go!"

"Ay! What good does an education do them," my father filled his coffee cup, "they only learn to speak like Indians. Gosh, okay, what kind of words are those?"

"An education will make him a scholar, like—like the old Luna priest."

"A scholar already, on his first day of school!"

"Yes!" my mother retorted. "You know the signs at his birth were good. You remember, Grande, you offered him all the objects of life when he was just a baby, and what did he choose, the pen and the paper—"

"True," Ultima agreed.

"¡Bueno! ¡Bueno!" my father gave in to them. "If that is what he is to be then it is so. A man cannot struggle against his own fate. In my own day we were given no schooling. Only the ricos could afford school. Me, my father gave me a saddle blanket and a wild pony when I was ten. There is your life, he said, and he pointed to the llano. So the llano was my school, it was my teacher, it was my first love—"

"It is time to go, mamá," Deborah interrupted.

"Ay, but those were beautiful years," my father continued.

"The llano was still virgin, there was grass as high as the stirrups of a grown horse, there was rain—and then the tejano came and built his fences, the railroad came, the roads—it was like a bad wave of the ocean covering all that was good—"

"Yes, it is time, Gabriel," my mother said, and I noticed she touched him gently.

✳

Spanish Words

¡Bueno! Good! p.126

ricos rich people, p.126

tejano Texan, p.126

suerte luck, p.127

En el nombre . . . Santo In the name of the Father, Son, and Holy Spirit, p.127

¡Madre de Dios! Mother of God, an exclamation, p.128

"Yes," my father answered, "so it is. Be respectful to your teachers," he said to us. "And you, Antonio," he smiled, "suerte." It made me feel good. Like a man.

"Wait!" My mother held Deborah and Theresa back, "we must have a blessing. Grande, please bless my children." She made us kneel with her in front of Ultima. "And especially bless my Antonio, that all may go well for him and that he may be a man of great learning—"

Even my father knelt for the blessing. Huddled in the kitchen we bowed our heads. There was no sound.

"En el nombre del Padre, del Hijo, y el Espíritu Santo—"

I felt Ultima's hand on my head and at the same time I felt a great force, like a whirlwind, swirl about me. I looked up in fright, thinking the wind would knock me off my knees. Ultima's bright eyes held me still.

In the summer the dust devils of the llano are numerous. They come from nowhere, made by the heat of hell they carry with them the evil spirit of a devil, they lift sand and papers in their path. It is bad luck to let one of these small whirlwinds strike you. But it is easy to ward off the dust devil, it is easy to make it change its path and skirt around you. The power of God is so great. All you have to do is to lift up your right hand and cross your right thumb over your first finger in the form of the cross. No evil can challenge that cross, and the swirling dust with the devil inside must turn away from you.

$\mathcal{O}$NCE I DID NOT make the sign of the cross on purpose. I challenged the wind to strike me. The twister struck with such force that it knocked me off my feet and left me trembling on the ground. I had never felt such fear before, because as the whirlwind blew its debris around me the gushing wind seemed to call my name:

Antoniooooooooooooooooo. . .

Then it was gone, and its evil was left imprinted on my soul.

"¡Antonio!"

"What?

"Do you feel well? Are you all right?" It was my mother speaking.

But how could the blessing of Ultima be like the whirlwind? Was the power of good and evil the same?

"You may stand up now." My mother helped me to my feet. Deborah and Theresa were already out the door. The blessing was done. I stumbled to my feet, picked up my sack lunch, and started towards the door.

"Tell me, Grande, please," my mother begged.

"María!" my father said sternly.

"Oh, please tell me what my son will be," my mother glanced anxiously from me to Ultima.

"He will be a man of learning," Ultima said sadly.

"¡Madre de Dios!" my mother cried and crossed herself. She turned to me and shouted, "Go! Go!"

I looked at the three of them standing there, and I felt that I was seeing them for the last time: Ultima in her wisdom, my mother in her dream, and my father in his rebellion.

"¡Adios!" I cried and ran out. I followed the two she-goats hopping up the path ahead of me. They sang and I brayed into the morning air, and the pebbles of the path rang as we raced with time towards the bridge. Behind me I heard my mother cry my name.

At the big juniper tree where the hill sloped to the bridge I heard Ultima's owl sing. I knew it was her owl because it was singing in daylight. High at the top by a clump of the ripe blue berries of the juniper I saw it. Its bright eyes looked down on me and it cried, whoooo, whoooo. I took confidence from its song, and wiping the tears from my eyes I raced towards the bridge, the link to town.

I was almost halfway across the bridge when someone called "Race!" I turned and saw a small, thin figure start racing towards me from the far end of the bridge. I recognized the Vitamin Kid.

Race? He was crazy! I was almost half way across. "Race!" I called, and ran. I found out that morning that no one had ever beaten the Vitamin Kid across the bridge, his bridge. I was a good runner and I ran as hard as I could, but just before I reached the other side the clatter of hoofbeats passed me by, the Kid smiled a "Hi Tony," and snorting and leaving a trail of saliva threads in the air, he was gone.

*N*O ONE KNEW the Vitamin Kid's real name, no one knew where he lived. He seemed older than the rest of the kids he went to school with. He never stopped long enough to talk, he was always on the run, a blur of speed.

I walked slowly after I crossed the bridge, partly because I was tired and partly because of the dread of school. I walked past Rosie's house, turned, and passed in front of the Longhorn Saloon. When I got to Main Street I was astounded. It seemed as if a million kids were shoutin-gruntingpushingcrying their way to school. For a long time I was held hypnotized by the thundering herd, then with a cry of resolution exploding from my throat I rushed into the melee.

Somehow I got to the schoolgrounds, but I was lost. The school was larger than I had expected. Its huge, yawning doors were menacing. I looked for Deborah and Theresa, but every face I saw was strange. I looked again at the doors of the sacred halls but I was too afraid to enter. My mother had said to go to Miss Maestas, but I did not know where to begin to find her. I had come to the town, and I had come to school, and I was very lost and afraid in the nervous, excited swarm of kids.

It was then that I felt a hand on my shoulder. I turned and looked into the eyes of a strange red-haired boy. He spoke English, a foreign tongue.

"First grade," was all I could answer. He smiled and took my hand, and with him I entered school. The building was cavernous and dark. It had strange, unfamiliar smells and sounds that seemed to gurgle from its belly. There was a big hall and many rooms, and many mothers with children passed in and out of the rooms.

I wished for my mother, but I put away the thought because I knew I was expected to become a man. A radiator snapped with steam and I jumped. The red-haired boy laughed and led me into one of the rooms. This room was brighter than the hall. So it was like this that I entered school.

Miss Maestas was a kind woman. She thanked the boy whose name was Red for bringing me in then asked my name. I told her I did not speak English.

"¿Cómo te llamas?" she asked.

"Antonio Márez," I replied. I told her my mother said I should see her, and that my mother sent her regards.

She smiled. "Anthony Márez," she wrote in a book. I drew closer to look at the letters formed by her pen. "Do you want to learn to write?" she asked.

"Yes," I answered.

"Good," she smiled.

I WANTED TO ASK HER immediately about the magic in the letters, but that would be rude and so I was quiet. I was fascinated by the black letters that formed on the paper and made my name. Miss Maestas gave me a crayon and some paper and I sat in the corner and worked at copying my name over and over. She was very busy the rest of the day with the other children that came to the room. Many cried when their mothers left, and one wet his pants. I sat in my corner alone and wrote. By noon I could write my name, and when Miss Maestas discovered that she was very pleased.

She took me to the front of the room and spoke to the other boys and girls. She pointed at me but I did not understand her. Then the other boys and girls laughed and pointed to me. I did not feel so good. Thereafter I kept away from the groups as much as I could and worked alone. I worked hard. I listened to the strange sounds. I learned new names, new words.

At noon we opened our lunches to eat. Miss Maestas left the room and a high school girl came and sat at the desk while we ate. My mother had packed a small jar of hot beans and some good, green chile wrapped in tortillas. When the other children saw my lunch they laughed and pointed again. Even the high school girl laughed. They showed me their sandwiches which were made of bread. Again I did not feel well.

I gathered my lunch and slipped out of the room. The strangeness of the school and the other children made me very sad. I did not understand them. I sneaked around the back of the school building, and standing against the wall I tried to eat. But I couldn't. A huge lump seemed to form in my throat and tears came to my eyes. I yearned for my mother, and at the same time I understood that she had sent me to this place where I was an outcast. I had tried hard to learn and they had laughed at me, I had opened my lunch to eat and again they had laughed and pointed at me.

The pain and sadness seemed to spread to my soul, and I felt for the first time what the grown-ups call, la tristeza de la vida. I wanted to run away, to hide, to run and never come back, never see anyone again. But I knew that if I did I would shame my family name, that my mother's dream would crumble. I knew I had to grow up and be a man, but oh it was so very hard.

But no, I was not alone. Down the wall near the corner I saw two other boys who had sneaked out of the room. They were George and Willy. They were big boys, I knew they were from the farms of Delia. We banded together and in our union found strength. We found a few others who were like us, different in language and custom, and a part of our loneliness was gone. When the winter set in we moved into the auditorium and there, although many a meal was eaten in complete silence, we felt we belonged. We struggled against the feeling of loneliness that gnawed at our souls and we overcame it; that feeling I never shared again with anyone, not even with Horse and Bones, or the Kid and Samuel, or Cico or Jasón.

RESPONDING

1. **Personal Response** If you were Antonio's teacher, how would you go about helping him to feel a part of the class? How would you prevent the other students from laughing and pointing at him?

2. **Literary Analysis** What effect does Anaya achieve by using *Spanish words* and phrases throughout the story?

3. **Multicultural Connection** According to Antonio, why do the "big boys" and a few others band together? Are groups in your school formed for similar reasons? Explain.

LANGUAGE WORKSHOP

Words from Spanish Look at the words in the Spanish Words boxes on pages 126 and 130. Even if you are not familiar with the Spanish language, you might be able to figure out some words because of similar words in English (*nombre/name, santo/saint* or *spirit*). Figure out the meaning of the following underlined words by using the Spanish words and meanings that follow.
1. It is vital that you eat fruit and vegetables. (*vida* meaning "life")
2. She was nominated for the role. (*nombre* meaning "name")
3. That is my maternal grandmother. (*madre* meaning "mother")

WRITER'S PORTFOLIO

Although Antonio's father and mother, from different backgrounds themselves, argue about the best kind of education for Antonio, they seem united in their high expectations for him. In your journal, describe what your family expects of you as far as education is concerned. Why do they feel as they do? Do you measure up to these expectations, or do you have your own plans?

LUCY TAPAHONSO  Luci Tapahonso, born in Shiprock, New Mexico, says she is as "Navajo as can be." A poet, storyteller, short story writer, and journalist, Tapahonso has published several books, including *One More Shiprock Night, Seasonal Woman,* and *Saanii Dahataal: The Women Are Singing,* in addition to teaching at the University of Kansas. Tapahonso writes about what she knows best — people who love and worry and drink coffee and sprinkle cornmeal.

GWENDOLYN BROOKS Growing up in Chicago, Gwendolyn Brooks dreamed of becoming a professional writer. By the time she was a teenager, she had written a notebook full of poems. For her second collection, *Annie Allen,* she received the Pulitzer Prize in poetry — the first African American woman so honored. Named Poet Laureate of Illinois in 1968, Consultant in Poetry to the Library of Congress in 1985, and Jefferson Lecturer in 1994, Brooks is also recognized as a dynamic teacher and speaker. She continues to write, to encourage young African American poets, and to inspire readers everywhere.

For Misty Starting School

LUCY TAPAHONSO

help her
my shiny-haired child
laboriously tying her shoes
she's a mere child of 4.

she starts school today
smiling shyly
pink heart-shaped earrings
long black hair

we pause outside the house and pray
a pinch of pollen for you starting school
and you, the older sister
and you, father of bright-eyed daughters.
with this pollen, we pray
you will learn easily
in this new place
you will laugh and share
loving people other than us.
guide her now. guide us now.
we tell her at school
sprinkle cornmeal here
by the door of your classroom.
she takes some and looks at me
then lets it fall to the threshold.
to help my teacher, mommy?
she asks

yes, to help your teacher
　　　　to help you
　　　　　　to help us as we leave her now.
　　oh, be gentle with her
　　feelings, thoughts and trust.

i tell them again:
remember now, my clear-eyed daughters
remember now, where this pollen
　　　　　　where this cornmeal is from
　　　　　　remember now, you are no different
see how it sparkles
feel this silky powder
it leaves a fine trail skyward
as it falls
blessing us
strengthening us.

remember now, you are no different
　　　　　　　　blessing us
　　　　　　　　leaving us.

✳

Culture Notes

pollen a yellow, powdery substance found in corn tassels, used in Native American prayer and rituals to symbolize life and renewal, p.134

cornmeal made from perfect ears of corn and considered sacred; sprinkled over objects and people to sanctify, bless, and protect, p.134

We Real Cool

GWENDOLYN BROOKS

The Pool Players,
Seven at the Golden Shovel.

We real cool. We
Left school. We

Lurk late. We
Strike straight. We

Sing sin. We
Thin gin. We

Jazz June. We
Die soon.

RESPONDING

1. Personal Response What is your attitude toward school? Compare and contrast it with the attitudes expressed in these poems.

2. Literary Analysis "We Real Cool" might seem more like a poem to you than does "For Misty Starting School." Look for poetic qualities such as *repetition*, *rhythm*, and *images* in Tapahonso's poem. Then explain whether or not you think it could just as well have been written as a prose paragraph.

3. Multicultural Connection Although we learn certain things in school (a formal setting), what do we also learn in our homes and communities (informal settings) that make us unique? Explain how the two kinds of settings can be at odds with one another.

LANGUAGE WORKSHOP

Compound Words Tapahonso uses compound words such as *cornmeal* and *shiny-haired*. Note that such words may be written as one word or hyphenated. When you are unsure how to write a compound word, consult a dictionary.

Write *cornmeal* and *shiny-haired* as labels for two columns. Then find five other compound words in "For Misty Starting School" and write them under the label that has the same structure.

WRITER'S PORTFOLIO

Imagine that you are a school counselor charged with writing a case study of Tapahonso's Misty, or one of Brooks's school dropouts. In your study, describe the character's special characteristics and needs as fully as you can. Conclude your study with specific recommendations designed to help the character in a school setting.

ABOUT **PAULETTE CHILDRESS WHITE**

A lifelong resident of Michigan, Paulette Childress White began her writing career in 1972. Since then she has seen her work represented in anthologies such as *Sturdy Black Bridges* and *Midnight Birds*. The author of two published works, *Love Poem to a Black Junkie* (1975) and *The Watermelon Dress: Portrait of a Woman* (1983), and a contributor to noted magazines, White frequently explores what could be considered the very ordinary events in the lives of quite ordinary women. Cast in a special light, however, her characters — African American women who struggle to overcome the realities of urban life — turn out to be extraordinary.

Getting the Facts of Life

THE AUGUST MORNING was ripening into a day that promised to be a burner. By the time we'd walked three blocks, dark patches were showing beneath Momma's arms, and inside tennis shoes thick with white polish, my feet were wet against the cushions. I was beginning to regret how quickly I'd volunteered to go.

"Dog. My feet are getting mushy," I complained.

"You should've wore socks," Momma said, without looking my way or slowing down.

I frowned. In 1961, nobody wore socks with tennis shoes. It was bare legs, Bermuda shorts and a sleeveless blouse. Period.

Momma was chubby but she could really walk. She walked the same way she washed clothes — up-and-down, up-and-down until she was done. She didn't believe in taking breaks.

This was my first time going to the welfare office with Momma. After breakfast, before we'd had time to scatter, she corralled everyone old enough to consider and announced in her serious-business voice that someone was going to the welfare office with her this morning. Cries went up.

Junior had his papers to do. Stella was going swimming at the high school. Dennis was already pulling the *Free Press* wagon across town every first Wednesday to get the surplus food — like that.

"You want clothes for school don't you?" That landed. School opened in two weeks.

"I'll go," I said.

"Who's going to baby-sit if Minerva goes?" Momma asked.

Stella smiled and lifted her golden nose. "I will," she said. "I'd rather baby-sit than do *that*."

That should have warned me. Anything that would make Stella offer to baby-sit had to be bad.

A small cheer probably went up among my younger brothers in the back rooms where I was not too secretly known as "The Witch" because of the criminal licks I'd learned to give on my rise to power. I was twelve, third oldest under Junior and Stella, but I had long established myself as first in command among the kids. I was chief baby-sitter, biscuit-maker and broom-wielder. Unlike Stella, who'd begun her development at ten, I still had my girl's body and wasn't anxious to have that changed. What would it mean but a loss of power? I liked things just the way they were. My interest in bras was even less than my interest in boys, and that was limited to keeping my brothers—who seemed destined for wildness—from taking over completely.

Even before we left, Stella had Little Stevie Wonder turned up on the radio in the living room, and suspicious jumping-bumping sounds were beginning in the back. They'll tear the house down, I thought, following Momma out the door.

We turned at Salliotte, the street that would take us straight up to Jefferson Avenue where the welfare office was. Momma's face was pinking in the heat, and I was huffing to keep up. From here, it was seven more blocks on the colored side, the railroad tracks, five blocks on the white side and there you were. We'd be cooked.

"Is the welfare office near the Harbor Show?" I asked. I knew the answer, I just wanted some talk.

"Across the street."

"Umm. Glad it's not way down Jefferson somewhere."

Nothing. Momma didn't talk much when she was outside. I knew that the reason she wanted one of us along when she had far to go was not for company but so she wouldn't have to walk by herself. I could understand that. To me, walking alone was like being naked or deformed—everyone seemed to look at you harder and longer. With Momma, the feeling was probably worse because you knew people were wondering if she were white, Indian maybe or really colored. Having one of us along, brown and clearly hers, probably helped define that. Still, it was like being a little parade, with Momma's pale skin and straight brown hair turning heads like the clang of cymbals. Especially on the colored side.

"Well," I said, "here we come to the bad part."

Momma gave a tiny laugh.

Most of Salliotte was a business street, with Old West-looking storefronts and some office places that never seemed to open. Ecorse, hinged onto southwest Detroit like a clothes closet, didn't seem to take itself seriously. There were lots of empty fields, some of which folks down the residential streets turned into vegetable gardens every summer. And there was this block where the Moonflower Hotel raised itself to three stories over the poolroom and Beaman's drugstore. Here, bad boys and drunks made their noise and did an occasional stabbing. Except for the cars that lined both sides of the block, only one side was busy — the other bordered a field of weeds. We walked on the safe side.

*T*F YOU WERE A WOMAN or a girl over twelve, walking this block—even on the safe side—could be painful. They usually hollered at you and never mind what they said. Today, because it was hot and early, we made it by with only one weak *Hey baby* from a drunk sitting in the poolroom door.

"Hey baby yourself," I said but not too loudly, pushing my flat chest out and stabbing my eyes in his direction.

"Minerva girl, you better watch your mouth with grown men like that," Momma said, her eyes catching me up in real warning though I could see that she was holding down a smile.

"Well, he can't do nothing to me when I'm with you, can he?" I asked, striving to match the rise and fall of her black pumps.

*S*HE SAID NOTHING. She just walked on, churning away under a sun that clearly meant to melt us. From here to the tracks it was mostly gardens. It felt like the Dixie Peach I'd used to help water-wave my hair was sliding down with the sweat on my face, and my throat was tight with thirst. Boy, did I want a pop. I looked at the last little store before we crossed the tracks without bothering to ask.

Across the tracks, there were no stores and no gardens. It was shady, and the grass was June green. Perfect-looking houses sat in unfenced spaces far back from the street. We walked these five blocks without a word. We just looked and hurried to get through it. I was beginning to worry about the welfare office in earnest. A fool could see that in this part of Ecorse, things got serious.

We had been on welfare for almost a year. I didn't have any strong feelings about it — my life went on pretty much the same. It just meant watching the mail for a check instead of Daddy getting paid, and occasional visits from a social worker that I'd always managed to miss. For Momma and whoever went with her, it meant this walk to the office and whatever went on there that made everyone hate to go. For Daddy, it seemed to bring the most change. For him, it meant staying away from home more than when he was working and a reason not to answer the phone.

At Jefferson, we turned left and there it was, halfway down the block. The Department of Social Services. I discovered some strong feelings. That fine name meant nothing. This was the welfare. The place for poor people. People who couldn't or wouldn't take care of themselves. Now I was going to face it, and suddenly I thought what I knew the others had thought, *What if I see someone I know?* I wanted to run back all those blocks to home.

I looked at Momma for comfort, but her face was closed and her mouth looked locked.

Inside, the place was gray. There were rows of long benches like church pews facing each other across a middle aisle that led to a central desk. Beyond the benches and the desk, four hallways led off to a maze of partitioned offices. In opposite corners, huge fans hung from the ceiling, humming from side to side, blowing the heavy air for a breeze.

Momma walked to the desk, answered some questions, was given a number and told to take a seat. I followed her through, trying not to see the waiting people—as though that would keep them from seeing me.

Gradually, as we waited, I took them all in. There was no one there that I knew, but somehow they all looked familiar. Or maybe I only thought they did, because when your eyes connected with someone's, they didn't quickly look away and they usually smiled. They were mostly women and children, and a few low-looking men. Some of them were white, which surprised me. I hadn't expected to see them in there.

Directly in front of the bench where we sat, a little girl with blond curls was trying to handle a bottle of Coke. Now and then, she'd manage to turn herself and the bottle around and watch me with big gray eyes that seemed to know quite well how badly I wanted a pop. I thought of asking Momma for fifteen cents so I could get one from the machine in the back but I was afraid she'd still say no so I just kept planning more and more convincing ways to ask. Besides, there was a water fountain near the door if I could make myself rise and walk to it.

*W*E WAITED THREE HOURS. White ladies dressed like secretaries kept coming out to call numbers, and people on the benches would get up and follow down a hall. Then more people came in to replace them. I drank water from the fountain three times and was ready to put my feet up on the bench before us—the little girl with the Coke and her momma got called—by the time we heard Momma's number.

"You wait here," Momma said as I rose with her.

I sat down with a plop.

The lady with the number looked at me. Her face reminded me of the librarian's at Bunch school. Looked like she never cracked a smile. "Let her come," she said.

"She can wait here," Momma repeated, weakly.

"It's OK. She can come in. Come on," the lady insisted at me.

I hesitated, knowing that Momma's face was telling me to sit.

"Come on," the woman said.

Momma said nothing.

*T*GOT UP and followed them into the maze. We came to a small room where there was a desk and three chairs. The woman sat behind the desk and we before it.

For a while, no one spoke. The woman studied a folder open before her, brows drawn together. On the wall behind her there was a calendar with one heavy black line drawn slantwise through each day of August, up to the twenty-first. That was today.

"Mrs. Blue, I have a notation here that Mr. Blue has not reported to the department on his efforts to obtain employment since the sixteenth of June. Before that, it was the tenth of April. You understand that department regulations require that he report monthly to this office, do you not?" Eyes brown as a wren's belly came up at Momma.

"Yes," Momma answered, sounding as small as I felt.

"Can you explain his failure to do so?"

Pause. "He's been looking. He says he's been looking."

"That may be. However, his failure to report those efforts here is my only concern."

Silence.

"We cannot continue with your case as it now stands if Mr. Blue refuses to comply with departmental regulations. He is still residing with the family, is he not?"

"Yes, he is. I've been reminding him to come in . . . he said he would."

"Well, he hasn't. Regulations are that any able-bodied man, head-of-household and receiving assistance who neglects to report to this office any effort to obtain work for a period of sixty days or more is to be cut off for a minimum of three months, at which time he may reapply. As of this date, Mr. Blue is over sixty days delinquent, and officially, I am obliged to close the case and direct you to other sources of aid."

"What is that?"

"Aid to Dependent Children would be the only source available to you. Then, of course, you would not be eligible unless it was verified that Mr. Blue was no longer residing with the family."

Another silence. I stared into the gray steel front of the desk, everything stopped but my heart.

"Well, can you keep the case open until Monday? If he comes in by Monday?"

"According to my records, Mr. Blue failed to come in May and such an agreement was made then. In all, we allowed him a period of seventy days. You must understand that what happens in such cases as this is not wholly my decision." She sighed and watched Momma with hopeless eyes, tapping the soft end of her pencil on the papers before her. "Mrs. Blue, I will speak to my superiors on your behalf. I can allow you until Monday next . . . that's the" — she swung around to the calendar—"twenty-sixth of August, to get him in here."

"Thank you. He'll be in," Momma breathed. "Will I be able to get the clothing order today?"

Hands and eyes searched in the folder for an answer before she cleared her throat and tilted her face at Momma. "We'll see what we can do," she said, finally.

My back touched the chair. Without turning my head, I moved my eyes down to Momma's dusty feet and wondered if she could still feel them; my own were numb. I felt bodyless—there was only my face, which wouldn't disappear, and behind it, one word pinging against another in a buzz that made no sense. At home, we'd have the house cleaned by now, and I'd be waiting for the daily appearance of my best friend, Bernadine, so we could comb each other's hair or talk about stuck-up Evelyn and Brenda. Maybe Bernadine was already there, and Stella was teaching her to dance the bop.

Then I heard our names and ages—all eight of them—being called off like items in a grocery list.

"Clifford, Junior, age fourteen." She waited.

"Yes."

"Born? Give me the month and year."

"October 1946," Momma answered, and I could hear in her voice that she'd been through these questions before.

"Stella, age thirteen."

"Yes."

"Born?"

"November 1947."

"Minerva, age twelve." She looked at me. "This is Minerva?"

"Yes."

No. I thought, no, this is not Minerva. You can write it down if you want to, but Minerva is not here.

"Born?"

"December 1948."

𝒯HE WOMAN WENT ON down the list, sounding more and more like Momma should be sorry or ashamed, and Momma's answers grew fainter and fainter. So this was welfare. I wondered how many times Momma had had to do this. Once before? Three times? Every time?

More questions. How many in school? Six. Who needs shoes? Everybody.

"Everybody needs shoes? The youngest two?"

"Well, they don't go to school . . . but they walk."

My head came up to look at Momma and the woman. The woman's mouth was left open. Momma didn't blink.

The brown eyes went down. "Our allowances are based on the median costs for moderately priced clothing at Sears, Roebuck." She figured on paper as she spoke. "That will mean thirty-four dollars for children over ten . . . thirty dollars for children under ten. It comes to one hundred ninety-eight dollars. I can allow eight dollars for two additional pairs of shoes.

"Thank you."

"You will present your clothing order to a salesperson at the store, who will be happy to assist you in your selections. Please be practical as further clothing requests will not be considered for a period of six months. In cases of necessity, however, requests for winter outerwear will be considered beginning November first."

Momma said nothing.

The woman rose and left the room.

*F*OR THE FIRST TIME, I shifted in the chair. Momma was looking into the calendar as though she could see through the pages to November first. Everybody needed a coat.

I'm never coming here again, I thought. If I do, I'll stay out front. Not coming back in here. Ever again.

She came back and sat behind her desk. "Mrs. Blue, I must make it clear that, regardless of my feelings, I will be forced to close your case if your husband does not report to this office by Monday, the twenty-sixth. Do you understand?"

"Yes. Thank you. He'll come. I'll see to it."

"Very well." She held a paper out to Momma.

We stood. Momma reached over and took the slip of paper. I moved toward the door.

"Excuse me, Mrs. Blue, but are you pregnant?"

"What?"

"I asked if you were expecting another child."

"Oh. No, I'm not," Momma answered, biting down on her lips.

"Well, I'm sure you'll want to be careful about a thing like that in your present situation."

"Yes."

I looked quickly to Momma's loose white blouse. We'd never known when another baby was coming until it was almost there.

"I suppose that eight children are enough for anyone," the woman said, and for the first time her face broke into a smile.

Momma didn't answer that. Somehow, we left the room and found our way out onto the street. We stood for a moment as though lost. My eyes followed Momma's up to where the sun was burning high. It was still there, blazing white against a cloudless blue. Slowly, Momma put the clothing order into her purse and snapped it shut. She looked around as if uncertain which way to go. I led the way to the corner. We turned. We walked the first five blocks.

I was thinking about how stupid I'd been a year ago, when Daddy lost his job. I'd been happy.

"You all better be thinking about moving to Indianapolis," he announced one day after work, looking like he didn't think much of it himself. He was a welder with the railroad company. He'd worked there for eleven years. But now, "Company's moving to Indianapolis," he said. "Gonna be gone by November. If I want to keep my job, we've got to move with it."

We didn't. Nobody wanted to move to Indianapolis— not even Daddy. Here, we had uncles, aunts and cousins on both sides. Friends. Everybody and everything we knew. Daddy could get another job. First came unemployment compensation. Then came welfare. Thank goodness for welfare, we said, while we waited and waited for that job that hadn't yet come.

*T*HE PROBLEM WAS that Daddy couldn't take it. If something got repossessed or somebody took sick or something was broken or another kid was coming, he'd carry on terribly until things got better—by which time things were always worse. He'd always been that way. So when the railroad left, he began to do everything wrong. Stayed out all hours. Drank and drank some more. When he was home, he was so grouchy we were afraid to squeak. Now when we saw him coming, we got lost. Even our friends ran for cover.

At the railroad tracks, we sped up. The tracks were as far across as a block was long. Silently, I counted the rails by the heat of the steel bars through my thin soles. On the other side, I felt something heavy rise up in my chest and I knew that I wanted to cry. I wanted to cry or run or kiss the dusty ground. The little houses with their sun scorched lawns and backyard gardens were mansions in my eyes. "Ohh, Ma . . . look at those collards!"

"Umm-hummm," she agreed, and I knew that she saw it too.

"Wonder how they grew so big?"

"Cow dung, probably. Big Poppa used to put cow dung out to fertilize the vegetable plots, and everything just grew like crazy. We used to get tomatoes this big"—she circled with her hands—"and don't talk about squash or melons."

"I bet y'all ate like rich people. Bet y'all had everything you could want."

"We sure did," she said. "We never wanted for anything when it came to food. And when the cash crops were sold, we could get whatever else that was needed. We never wanted for a thing."

"What about the time you and cousin Emma threw out the supper peas?"

"Oh! Did I tell you about that?" she asked. Then she told it all over again. I didn't listen. I watched her face and guarded her smile with a smile of my own.

We walked together, step for step. The sun was still burning, but we forgot to mind it. We talked about an Alabama girlhood in a time and place I'd never know. We talked about the wringer washer and how it could be fixed, because washing every day on a scrub-board was something Alabama could keep. We talked about how to get Daddy to the Department of Social Services.

Then we talked about having babies. She began to tell me things I'd never known, and the idea of womanhood blossomed in my mind like some kind of suffocating rose.

"Momma," I said, "I don't think I can be a woman."

"You can," she laughed, "and if you live, you will be. You gotta be some kind of woman."

"But it's hard," I said "sometimes it must be hard."

"Umm-humm," she said, "sometimes it is hard."

When we got to the bad block, we crossed to Beaman's drugstore for two orange crushes. Then we walked right through the groups of men standing in the shadows of the poolroom and the Moonflower Hotel. Not one of them said a word to us. I supposed they could see in the way we walked that we weren't afraid. We'd been to the welfare office and back again. And the facts of life, fixed in our mind like the sun in the sky, were no burning mysteries.

RESPONDING

1. **Personal Response** Do you think Minerva has a good relationship with her mother? Explain what for you constitutes a good parent-child relationship.

2. **Literary Analysis** What do you initially expect from a story with the *title* "Getting the Facts of Life"? What does Minerva actually learn about life, according to the last paragraph?

3. **Multicultural Connection** What does the color of one's skin have to do with the "facts of life," both physical and emotional, that Minerva learns during her trip to the welfare office? Will the lessons she learns help her in school when it commences in just two weeks? Explain.

LANGUAGE WORKSHOP

Mood Paulette Childress White creates a *mood* of intense heat and discomfort in this story with passages such as this: "It felt like the Dixie Peach I'd used to help water-wave my hair was sliding down with the sweat on my face, and my throat was tight with thirst." Find five other examples of words or phrases in the story that convey intense heat.

WRITER'S PORTFOLIO

As the supervisor of the woman who interviews Mrs. Blue, you are present for this interview. Now make a list of qualities you consider important for a welfare worker. You might consider efficiency, compassion, and professionalism, along with any other attributes. Then write a performance review that explains how the interviewer measures up. Remember that *your* job is to be positive when appropriate and to give constructive criticism when necessary.

ABOUT **HAKI R. MADHUBUTI**

Perhaps best known now as a critic and essayist, Haki R. Madhubuti was first recognized for his exceptional poetry. After the publication of his first two volumes, in 1967 and 1968, he decided to become a full-time writer and changed his given name, Don L. Lee, to a Swahili one in celebration of his African heritage. Although he has published widely and has served as poet-in-residence at several universities, Madhubuti devotes much of his time today to teaching and editing. A professor of English at Chicago State University and editor at the Third World Press, a company he founded to promote African American writers, he continues to be an influential voice in American letters — not only for the hip "street talk" of his poems but for the powerful messages of his prose.

Not Knowing and Not Wanting to Know

THE EDUCATION I RECEIVED in the Black community was entirely different—in content and context—from that of whites. Not only was my "training" not a challenge, it was discouraging. The major piece of information I absorbed after twelve years of public education was that I was a problem, inferior, ineducable and a victim. And, as a victim, I began to see the world through the eyes of a victim.

I'll never forget how hard my mother worked to make ends meet for my sister and me. Our material lives were impoverished; we didn't have a television, record player, car, telephone or too much food. We acquired much of our clothing from secondhand stores, and I learned to work the streets very early. My life began to change when I was introduced to other worlds.

One year on my birthday, my mother took me to a five-and-dime store to buy me a gift. She bought me a blue plastic airplane with blue wheels, a blue propeller and a blue string on the front of the plane so that one could pull it across the floor. I was happy. That following week she took me and my sister to Dearborn, Michigan where she occasionally did "day work." Day work, for the uninformed, means Black women cleaning up white folks' homes. Dearborn, Michigan is where many of the movers and shakers who controlled the automobile industry lived.

What I quickly noticed was that they lived differently. There were no five-and-dime stores in Dearborn at this time; there were craft shops. This is where the white mothers and fathers bought their children airplanes in boxes. In the boxes were wooden parts, directions for assembly, glue and small engines. Generally, the son would assemble the plane (which might take a day or two) and then take the plane outside and — guess what — it would fly.

This small slice of life is an example of the development — quite early — of two different consciousnesses. In my case and that of other poor youths, we would buy the plane already assembled, take it home and hope it rolled on the floor as if it was a car or truck rather than a plane. In Dearborn, the family would *invest* in a learning toy, and the child would put it together. Through this process, the child would learn work ethics and science and math principles. And, as a result of all that, the plane would *fly*. I was learning to be a consumer who depended on others to build the plane for me. The child in Dearborn made an investment, worked on it and, through his labor and brain power, produced a plane that flew. Translating this to the larger world, I was being taught to buy and to use my body from the neck down, while the white upper class boy was being taught, very early, to prepare himself to build things and run things, using the neck up. Two different worlds: my world — depending on and working for others, and his world — controlling his own destiny.

RESPONDING

1. **Personal Response** Madhubuti observes two kinds of education: that preparing kids to use their "bodies from the neck down" and that preparing them "to build things and run things, using the neck up." Give examples of both kinds of education that you have received. Do you think a student's color or economic status is likely to determine which kind of education he or she receives? Explain.

2. **Literary Analysis** Notice Madhubuti's *diction,* or choice of words. Why does he use the word *training* rather than *education* in the second sentence of this selection? What distinction does he make?

3. **Multicultural Connection** Do you think that public education has improved since Madhubuti graduated more than thirty years ago? Do you think that education in general prepares us to be consumers who depend on the brains and skills of others? Explain.

LANGUAGE WORKSHOP

Essay Structure Madhubuti states his *thesis* in an initial topic sentence, uses examples to illustrate his thesis, and concludes with a strong summary sentence. Make a brief outline of "Not Knowing and Not Wanting to Know" that shows this organization.

WRITER'S PORTFOLIO

Employed by a neighborhood preschool, you have been asked to design a brochure for parents. You include a list of activities that parents can use at home to prepare their children to "build things and run things, using the neck up." Develop three such activities that require materials found within the home (for example, a margarine tub and buttons or pennies for counting or sock puppets for role-playing or problem solving).

ABOUT **LAURENCE YEP**

Laurence Yep, a Chinese American writer who grew up in a predominantly African American neighborhood and attended a white high school, felt he had "no culture to call his own." Therefore, he decided to create one in his writing, publishing his first story, a science-fiction tale, when he was just eighteen. Five years later he published his first novel. Since then he has won numerous awards for his many children's and young adult novels. Of special note is Yep's acclaimed *Dragonwings*, about a Chinese American who built and flew his own "flying machine" in 1909. In addition to being a full-time writer (five of his works were published in 1991 alone), Yep teaches part-time and writes plays.

$\mathscr{P}$uzzle $\mathscr{S}$olving

$\mathscr{S}$T. IGNATIUS WAS A BOYS' HIGH school founded in 1855, which made it old for San Francisco. It was a hulking three-story building of stones that sat on the Stanyan Street hill. Down the slope lay the Haight-Ashbury, where flower power was being born in places like the coffeehouse called "The Blue Unicorn." But behind our high school's stone walls we were sheltered from most of those changes.

I'd had white friends when I was small—before the projects had been built and their families moved away. However, St. Ignatius High School was the first time I had ever been with so many whites.

My cousin Gregory, who was a year ahead of me, had trouble his first year. Seating was alphabetical so he had wound up sitting most of the time in front of a boy who hated Asians and who had tried to make Gregory's life miserable.

However, I was fortunate enough to be protected from much of that because I was put into an honors class my freshman year. We were all ambitious to some degree so good grades were a means of earning respect. Grades were also so important that my parents let me out of hated chores in the store during the school year; and I was eager to do well so I would not have to go back to putting cans of beer in the icebox. As a result, I received good grades.

I was also fortunate that most of us freshmen were about the same size. Though I couldn't dribble a basketball and catch a pop fly to save my life, I could play intramural football as a lineman — the really big bruisers went out for the frosh-soph team. Moreover, years of my father's instruction had taught me that even if you couldn't do something well you could at least "hustle" — an attitude that also stood me in good stead. (I gave up playing football the next fall when I found out that most of the intramural football players had grown another three inches and were twenty pounds heavier.)

While there were boys there who never managed to climb out of the pit their own prejudices had dug for them — like the one my cousin had encountered — most were willing to correct their impressions once they got to know me. In the first few weeks, a classmate by the name of Steel asked me, "How come you can talk English so good?"

It was clear that Steel was not in the honors class for his skills in English; and I had enough sense not to correct his grammar. As it turned out, my family had already been in America for several generations before Steel's family had come from Poland — and promptly changed their names to Steel.

Racism wasn't so easy to avoid when it was in a teacher. The coach of one of our sports teams had once been put in charge of our study period during which he entertained us with stories of killing "gooks" in Korea. It was about halfway through the period before I realized that a gook was either a Korean or a Chinese; and I cringed the rest of the session.

Fortunately, it was the last study period he supervised. It was the early 1960s when the civil rights marches were going on and the younger Jesuits were especially sensitive to racial issues. When there was a bombing of a black church down South, they made sure there was a good turnout from the school at a memorial mass in a black neighborhood; and

*

Culture Notes

flower power part of the "hippie" movement of the 1960s that originated in San Francisco and promoted, among other things, peace and freedom, p. 157

Jesuits the Society of Jesus, a Roman Catholic religious order, noted for teaching, founded by Ignatius of Loyola in 1534, p. 158

Taft-Hartley Act an Act of Congress (1947) that served as the basis for federal labor relations laws, p. 159

there were numerous other occasions when we were made aware of the larger issues.

My honors class, lacking the prestige that having a first-team varsity athlete gave a class, used to try to win the various school drives. Like all good Catholic schools, we had our chocolate wars; but we also had wars with everything else that could be used to raise money, including S & H Green stamps. (There was a period when stores gave out trading stamps when you purchased something. When you had enough stamps, you could use them to get various things from the stamp stores. In this case, though, it was musical instruments for the band.) It always seemed like every week there was some big roll of butcher paper in the school hallway with some kind of thermometer showing the progress of each class in that particular drive.

Each year we took a new nickname tied in to our class designation; and you were known by that name for the rest of the year either in intramural sports or drives or any other competition. Most other classes took names like 2C Cougars; but we also wound up with interesting names. In our junior year, we were the 3G Garbanzo Beans — the suggestion of a classmate who lobbied successfully for that name. At the time, none of us considered the fact that we would be identified throughout the year, on each drive chart and every intramural game, as "garbanzos."

My class was a group of funny, creative boys; and we had teachers to match. We learned American history from a Boston Irish who used to thunder at us rather than lecture — which was fine for stories about the Civil War but not for the intricacies of the Taft-Hartley Act.

Our history teacher had two pet peeves: President Franklin Delano Roosevelt and Coca-Cola. He suspected that President Roosevelt had died before his fourth term and that an actor had replaced him. Trying to prove he was wrong, I accepted his challenge and began to do library research that led to long, earnest discussions with Mr. Vincent the mortician concerning the preparation of corpses. While I was never able to prove or disprove my teacher's suspicions, it seemed at one time there had been a wide number of people who had shared his beliefs.

In any event, he was more concerned with the way that Coca-Cola was undermining the strength of America's youth and spoke against it at every opportunity in his deep growl. He told us of a B-24 bomber during World War II that had crash landed at the airfield. When the fire truck and ambulances had raced out to the wreck, they found that the plane had no bullet holes. Inside, the bomber crew was all dead without a mark on them, only empty bottles of Coca-Cola rolling around on the floor of the plane.

However, it was our science teachers who were especially memorable. I took physics from a priest who over the years had refined his science demonstrations down to the smallest detail; and they were presented with all the flair and precision of a Broadway show. His example of air pressure was especially memorable because he would place a marshmallow into a bell jar. Slowly he would pump out the air and the marshmallow, with less and less air pressing at its sides to help it hold its shape, would slowly begin to swell and expand. By the time most of the air had been taken out from the bell jar, the marshmallow looked as large as a rat. Then he would let in some air; and even that slight amount of air pressure was enough to make the marshmallow collapse into a gooey mess.

Among other scientific toys, he had a model rocket that whizzed across the physics lab. Rumor had it that when his assistant, who taught some of the other physics classes, broke the rocket, the good father locked the assistant out of the lab for the rest of the day.

However, like the good showman he was, he always saved the best for the climax, ending the final class with a bang. During the last day of instruction, he would set off a miniature replica of the atom bomb. There would be a bang and a flash of light and then a pillar of white dust would shoot up toward the ceiling where it spread out into the familiar mushroom shape.

Our lab reports had to be turned in on a special four-page cardboard form and in fountain pen ink. The report had to be thought out carefully in advance because it was impossible to erase any mistakes and no cross-outs were allowed. If you muffed the experiment itself, though, you could get a passing grade if you humbly wrote that you would have done better if you had followed his instructions. (However, that could be used as an excuse only once in the year so you still had to be careful in the lab. Like a "Get Out of Jail Free" card in Monopoly, you were wise to save that one for dire need.)

We also had an extraordinary chemistry teacher, a small, white-haired terrier of a man, who taught as a hobby rather than as a necessity. He had made a killing on the stock market with his knowledge of technology because he instantly grasped the money-making potential of a product. He had, I think, bought IBM and Xerox stock when they had first been offered and later invested in the Polaroid company. He only taught because he wanted to, not because he had to—which was just as well.

Our chemistry teacher was a smoker so it was hard on him that he could not smoke during school hours except in the teachers' room. As soon as the bell rang ending the last class, he would light up a cigarette. However, one day, early in his teaching career at St. Ignatius, he had poured that day's chemistry experiment down the drain and eagerly lit a cigarette. Without thinking, he tossed the match into the sink. The chemicals instantly caught fire and went racing through the school's plumbing. It was said that flames shot out of the basement toilets as if they were porcelain volcanoes—fortunately, they weren't occupied at the time of the eruptions. When the other teachers saw the flames coming out of the plumbing, they instinctively headed for the chemistry lab and our teacher.

His lectures were never dry, boring speeches because he always threw in stories of his adventures. As a young man, he had wandered up north where he had been an assayer—somebody who tests the purity of metals. Some days he had eaten whale blubber—which he said was delicious—because he had burned up so many calories that he needed to replace them quickly. However, almost every night he had slept on the bags of rock samples to make sure that no one made a switch.

In any event, I always looked forward to that particular class. He not only had a knack for making his lectures lively; but his demonstrations were equally entertaining.

When he was discussing liquid nitrogen, he put a half-dozen goldfish into a plastic bag and quick-froze them. To prove that they were frozen, he threw one against a wall where it shattered into a dozen little fish-bits that thawed into smelly pieces. The other, more fortunate, five were dropped into a goldfish bowl and allowed to thaw out there. I think three of them revived and were swimming around none the worse for wear.

Nor did he have trouble with discipline problems. If he thought we weren't paying enough attention, he would calmly step to the front of the lab, turn on a small electric fan to blow the fumes away from him and then set down a beaker with some chemical. Once, he used a type of acid which smells like vomit. Then he calmly went on lecturing while we began to gag. Since he had a regular arsenal of bad-smelling but harmless chemicals, he usually didn't have trouble with his classes.

From one of his favorite pranks in a restaurant, I learned how to make teaspoons that would dissolve in coffee—or anything else hot. I had to create a mold and then pour in a certain blend of metals with a low-boiling point. In his younger days, he used to like to switch his own spoon for the restaurant spoon, then stir it in the coffee which would melt the spoon. Then he would take a sip and spit it out, indignantly holding up the spoon and complaining in a loud voice to the rest of the restaurant that the coffee was too hot.

As a result, it was a pleasure to do extra credit work in chemistry. My own specialty was explosives. With a little practical chemistry, it's possible to make a bomb out of what you would find in most medicine cabinets. Among other things, he showed us how to make this marvelous paste which would not explode until it was dry. A bottle of it was dangerous; but a small amount was fun for practical jokes. It would go off with a bang like the smallest firecracker and perhaps sting the hand.

We smeared it all over the seat of this one classmate's desk and then waited expectantly. The victim strolled in without a worry on his mind and plopped down at his desk as he always did. There was a huge bang and he leapt out of his seat. At that point, we were still experimenting with the paste and making observations like good, budding scientists. We dutifully noted that we had used too much of the paste when we heard the loud BANG and the subject jumped up out of his seat. In fact, it hurt to sit down and he had to stand up for the rest of the class. Nor had anyone allowed for the fact that he would be wearing white jeans that were now stained a bright purple.

We became better at using the paste and also at defending ourselves. Once the paste had been set off, it wouldn't go off again so we soon learned to dust off desktops and seats and locker handles with our folders to set off any unexpected surprises. At the height of the madness, you could have seen a classroom of boys cautiously dusting off their desks like so many junior butlers.

However, like in any good Greek play, someone over-reached himself and put the paste on Father principal's doorknob. Father principal strolled down the hallway as he always did in his cassock and put his hand out to open his door as he did every day when it went off with a bang. Wringing his hand as if it had been slapped by a ruler, he knew immediately where to go—just as he had when the school toilets had caught fire. He stormed up the steps to the chem lab and informed our chemistry teacher that while it was fine to encourage young minds, he didn't have to encourage us *that* much and that particular set of experiments ended. However, I had done enough to win a science award when I graduated.

He also had a way of firing the imagination with the fortune waiting for the clever chemist. He was full of money-making ideas on a grand scale. A typical one was to develop a process to extract gold from the waters of the Pacific Ocean. Such a wild scheme might have made us laugh if it had come from someone else. However, we knew that his own futuristic vision had made him rich.

Because chemistry was not only profitable but fun, I fully intended to become a chemist as I headed into my senior year—a decision which pleased my father because he, too, had wanted to be a chemist before the Depression had forced him to drop out of junior college and take any job just to survive. I was going to be the one to learn how to skim gold from sea water.

Our school, however, was blessed with more than interesting science teachers; we also had excellent English teachers. In my senior year, we had Father Becker who taught us English by having us imitate the various writers and various forms. We had to write poems in the complicated rhyme scheme of the sestina; and we had to write scenes imitating Shakespeare. Our writing would never make anyone forget William or the other greats of English literature; but we learned the nuts and bolts of a style. To this day, I have to be careful what I read because I tend to imitate that writing.

Early in the semester, Father took some of us aside and said that if we wanted to get an "A" in his course, we would have to get something accepted by a national magazine. All of us were intimidated by the prospect; but in those days you didn't argue with a Jesuit priest—and you still don't. All of us tried. None of us got anything accepted; and he later retracted the threat and graded us by the same standards he used for the rest of the class. However, I got bitten by the bug and kept on trying.

I found that making up my own stories became as much fun as making explosives. Writing did not make a light bulb appear over my head. It did not make me scribble away in a frenzy as if I had just been zapped by an electric cattle prod. Nor was it a religious ecstasy. No symphony of cymbals crashed in climax when I reached the final paragraph.

Something else happened instead. Almost everyone I knew—whether they were white, yellow, or black—came from a single background. They were cut from one pattern of cloth. However, I was a bunch of different pieces that had been dumped together in a box by sheer circumstance.

I was the Chinese American raised in a black neighborhood, a child who had been too American to fit into Chinatown and too Chinese to fit in elsewhere. I was the clumsy son of the athletic family, the grandson of a Chinese grandmother who spoke more of West Virginia than of China.

When I wrote, I went from being a puzzle to a puzzle solver. I could reach into the box of rags that was my soul and begin stitching them together. Moreover, I could try out different combinations to see which one pleased me the most. I could take these different elements, each of which belonged to something else, and dip them into my imagination where they were melted down and cast into new shapes so that they became uniquely mine.

RESPONDING

1. **Personal Response** Yep says that "good grades were a means of earning respect" for him. What do good grades mean to you and your friends?

2. **Literary Analysis** Explain how Yep uses *figurative language* in the final paragraph to describe what writing has done for him.

3. **Multicultural Connection** Asian American students are often considered to be bright, ambitious academic achievers. Do you think this is a *stereotype*? Does young Laurence Yep seem to fit this image? Explain.

LANGUAGE WORKSHOP

Prefixes In Yep's chemistry class, mixtures *erupted*, *explosives* ignited, and metals were *extracted*. The *prefix ex-* (or *e-*) means "out of, from." Use a dictionary, if necessary, to tell what these three words mean. Then think of three other words with the prefix *ex-* or *e-* meaning "out of, from" and explain their meanings.

WRITER'S PORTFOLIO

Yep describes several of his teachers, some of whom are eccentric, demanding, and/or stimulating — but all effective and memorable. Write a thumbnail sketch of one of your teachers, using some of Yep's techniques.

Projects

GRADUATION CHECK LIST

With a partner, decide what students *should* know and be able to do by the time they graduate from high school. Then devise an exit review, a list of what graduates should know and be able to do both in *and* out of school. To help you in your task, consider intellectual, physical, social, and emotional development. For example, do you think changing a tire — or a baby — are necessary skills? programming a computer? doing fifty pushups? intelligently discussing a book? introducing yourself to an older person? speaking a second language? cooking a meal? playing an instrument? Share your list with the class and get its feedback.

PERSONALITY PUZZLE

Laurence Yep says that he was a "bunch of different pieces that had been dumped together in a box by sheer circumstance." Collect ten different objects or pictures of objects in a box that represent pieces of your own special puzzle. Write a paragraph telling why these items or pictures represent you. Present your personality puzzle to the class. (You might want to enlist your teacher's help and exchange "puzzles," trying to guess which classmate is being described.)

ESSAY ON KINDS OF EDUCATION

The selections in this unit demonstrate that there are many ways to learn. Some are formal or structured; others, informal and unstructured. Write an essay that explains the difference. To illustrate what you say, refer to specifics within the selections in this unit.

Further Reading

These books are about people who learn — both through formal and informal education.

Allen, Paula Gunn, ed. *Spider Woman's Granddaughters: Traditional Tales and Contemporary Writing by Native American Women.* Beacon Press, 1989. These storytellers follow in the tradition of Grandmother Spider by using their tales to educate as they reveal their connection to the tribal group's wisdom.

Anaya, Rudolfo. *Bless Me, Ultima.* TQS Publications, 1972. Antonio Márez comes of age as he learns to reconcile elements of the natural world with his Hispanic culture and religion — under the tutelage of his wise grandmother Ultima.

Comer, James. *Maggie's American Dream: The Life and Times of a Black Family.* New American Library, 1988. In this powerful oral history, Comer, an award-winning child psychologist and noted educator, provides a tribute to his mother, who saw education for her children as a means to attaining the American dream.

Yep, Laurence. *The Lost Garden.* Julian Messner, 1991. In this autobiography, Yep traces his development as a writer who arrived at his cultural identity through his craft.

Yezierska, Anzia. *How I Found America.* Persea Books, 1991. The collected stories of Yezierska provide keen insights into the immigrant experience.

The Crossroads of Culture

The United States is a multicultural crossroads, a place where cultures intersect. Whether these cultures collide or merge depends on what people do when they meet at these crossroads. As you read these selections, notice people who have guarded or lost their culture, or sought to devastate the culture of others. Notice others who have blended elements of their own culture with the cultures of others in order to enrich their lives and communities.

ABOUT **LESLIE SILKO**

Leslie Marmon Silko was raised in the Laguna Pueblo in New Mexico, where she was introduced to a rich oral tradition at an early age. Writing since the fifth grade, her career was launched in 1969, with the publication of her story, "The Man to Send Rain Clouds." Since then she has taught at the Navajo Community College and teaches presently at the University of Arizona. Her works include *Laguna Woman,* a collection of poems; and *Ceremony,* a highly acclaimed first novel about a dislocated World War II veteran. Richly informed by her Laguna heritage, Silko observes that in order to recognize "the power of what we share, we must understand how different we are, too."

The Man to Send Rain Clouds

ONE

THEY FOUND HIM under a big cotton-wood tree. His Levi jacket and pants were faded light-blue so that he had been easy to find. The big cottonwood tree stood apart from a small grove of winterbare cottonwoods which grew in the wide, sandy arroyo. He had been dead for a day or more, and the sheep had wandered and scattered up and down the arroyo. Leon and his brother-in-law, Ken, gathered the sheep and left them in the pen at the sheep camp before they returned to the cottonwood tree. Leon waited under the tree while Ken drove the truck through the deep sand to the edge of the arroyo. He squinted up at the sun and unzipped his jacket—it sure was hot for this time of year. But high and northwest the blue mountains were still deep in snow. Ken came sliding down the low, crumbling bank about fifty yards down, and he was bringing the red blanket.

Before they wrapped the old man, Leon took a piece of string out of his pocket and tied a small gray feather in the old man's long white hair. Ken gave him the paint. Across the brown wrinkled forehead he drew a streak of white and along the high cheekbones he drew a strip of blue paint. He paused and watched Ken throw pinches of corn meal and pollen into the wind that fluttered the small gray feather.

Culture Notes

corn meal and pollen
Meal and pollen are sprinkled over graves to help ensure spiritual blessing.
p.171

Angelus a bell, usually rung at morning, noon, and evening, that announces the daily prayer of the Roman Catholic Church, p.173

medicine bags small buckskin pouches filled with various sacred "power" or medicine objects to influence every undertaking in life, control sickness and death, and invoke the powers of the universe, p.173

Then Leon painted with yellow under the old man's broad nose, and finally, when he had painted green across the chin, he smiled.

"Send us rain clouds, Grandfather." They laid the bundle in the back of the pickup and covered it with a heavy tarp before they started back to the pueblo.

They turned off the highway onto the sandy pueblo road. Not long after they passed the store and post office they saw Father Paul's car coming toward them. When he recognized their faces he slowed his car and waved for them to stop. The young priest rolled down the car window.

"Did you find old Teofilo?" he asked loudly.

Leon stopped the truck. "Good morning, Father. We were just out to the sheep camp. Everything is O.K. now."

"Thank God for that. Teofilo is a very old man. You really shouldn't allow him to stay at the sheep camp alone."

"No, he won't do that any more now."

"Well, I'm glad you understand. I hope I'll be seeing you at Mass this week—we missed you last Sunday. See if you can get old Teofilo to come with you." The priest smiled and waved at them as they drove away.

TWO

LOUISE AND TERESA were waiting. The table was set for lunch and the coffee was boiling on the black iron stove. Leon looked at Louise and then at Teresa.

"We found him under a cottonwood tree in the big arroyo near sheep camp. I guess he sat down to rest in the shade and never got up again." Leon walked toward the old man's bed. The red plaid shawl had been shaken and spread carefully over the bed, and a new brown flannel shirt and pair of stiff new Levis were arranged neatly beside the pillow. Louise held the screen door open while Leon and Ken carried in the red blanket. He looked small and shriveled, and after they dressed him in the new shirt and pants he seemed more shrunken.

It was noontime now because the church bells rang the Angelus. They ate the beans with hot bread, and nobody said anything until after Teresa poured the coffee.

Ken stood up and put on his jacket. "I'll see about the gravediggers. Only the top layer of soil is frozen. I think it can be ready before dark."

Leon nodded his head and finished his coffee. After Ken had been gone for awhile, the neighbors and clanspeople came quietly to embrace Teofilo's family and to leave food on the table because the gravediggers would come to eat when they were finished.

THREE

THE SKY in the west was full of pale-yellow light. Louise stood outside with her hands in the pockets of Leon's green army jacket that was too big for her. The funeral was over, and the old men had taken their candles and medicine bags and were gone. She waited until the body was laid into the pickup before she said anything to Leon. She touched his arm, and he noticed that her hands were still dusty from the corn meal that she had sprinkled around the old man. When she spoke, Leon could not hear her.

"What did you say? I didn't hear you."

"I said that I had been thinking about something."

"About what?"

"About the priest sprinkling holy water for Grandpa. So he won't be thirsty."

Leon stared at the new moccasins that Teofilo had made for the ceremonial dances in the summer. They were nearly hidden by the red blanket. It was getting colder, and the wind pushed gray dust down the narrow pueblo road. The sun was approaching the long mesa where it disappeared during the winter. Louise stood there shivering and watching his face. Then he zipped up his jacket and opened the truck door. "I'll see if he's there."

FOUR

KEN STOPPED the pickup at the church, and Leon got out; and then Ken drove down the hill to the graveyard where people were waiting. Leon knocked at the old carved door with its symbols of the Lamb. While he waited he looked up at the twin bells from the King of Spain with the last sunlight pouring around them in their tower.

The priest opened the door and smiled when he saw who it was. "Come in! What brings you here this evening?"

The priest walked toward the kitchen, and Leon stood with his cap in his hand, playing with the earflaps and examining the living room — the brown sofa, the green armchair, and the brass lamp that hung down from the ceiling by links of chain. The priest dragged a chair out of the kitchen and offered it to Leon.

"No thank you, Father. I only came to ask you if you would bring your holy water to the graveyard."

The priest turned away from Leon and looked out the window at the patio full of shadows and the dining-room windows of the nuns' cloister across the patio. The curtains were heavy, and the light from within faintly penetrated; it was impossible to see the nuns inside eating supper. "Why didn't you tell me he was dead? I could have brought the Last Rites anyway."

Leon smiled. "It wasn't necessary, Father."

The priest stared down at his scuffed brown loafers and the worn hem of his cassock. "For a Christian burial it was necessary."

His voice was distant, and Leon thought that his blue eyes looked tired.

"It's O.K. Father, we just want him to have plenty of water."

The priest sank down into the green chair and picked up a glossy missionary magazine. He turned the colored pages full of lepers and pagans without looking at them.

"You know I can't do that, Leon. There should have been the Last Rites and a funeral Mass at the very least."

Leon put on his green cap and pulled the flaps down over his ears. "It's getting late, Father. I've got to go."

When Leon opened the door Father Paul stood up and said, "Wait." He left the room and came back wearing a long brown overcoat. He followed Leon out the door and across the dim churchyard to the adobe steps in front of the church. They both stooped to fit through the low adobe entrance. And when they started down the hill to the graveyard only half of the sun was visible above the mesa.

The priest approached the grave slowly, wondering how they had managed to dig into the frozen ground; and then he remembered that this was New Mexico, and saw the pile of cold loose sand beside the hole. The people stood close to each other with little clouds of steam puffing from their faces. The priest looked at them and saw a pile of jackets, gloves, and scarves in the yellow, dry tumbleweeds that grew in the graveyard. He looked at the red blanket, not sure that Teofilo was so small, wondering if it wasn't some perverse Indian trick — something they did in March to ensure a good harvest — wondering if maybe old Teofilo was actually at sheep camp corraling the sheep for the night. But there he was, facing into a cold dry wind and squinting at the last sunlight, ready to bury a red wool blanket while the faces of his parishioners were in shadow with the last warmth of the sun on their backs.

Culture Notes

Lamb another term for Christ, p.174

Last Rites a Catholic ritual for one who is sick or in danger of dying in which a priest anoints the person with holy oil and prays, p.174

Franciscan a priest belonging to a religious order founded in 1209 by St. Francis of Assisi, an Italian friar, p.176

His fingers were stiff, and it took him a long time to twist the lid off the holy water. Drops of water fell on the red blanket and soaked into dark icy spots. He sprinkled the grave and the water disappeared almost before it touched the dim, cold sand; it reminded him of something—he tried to remember what it was, because he thought if he could remember he might understand this. He sprinkled more water; he shook the container until it was empty, and the water fell through the light from sundown like August rain that fell while the sun was still shining, almost evaporating before it touched the wilted squash flowers.

The wind pulled at the priest's brown Franciscan robe and swirled away the corn meal and pollen that had been sprinkled on the blanket. They lowered the bundle into the ground, and they didn't bother to untie the stiff pieces of new rope that were tied around the ends of the blanket. The sun was gone, and over on the highway the eastbound lane was full of headlights. The priest walked away slowly. Leon watched him climb the hill, and when he had disappeared within the tall, thick walls, Leon turned to look up at the high blue mountains in the deep snow that reflected a faint red light from the west. He felt good because it was finished, and he was happy about the sprinkling of the holy water; now the old man could send them big thunderclouds for sure.

RESPONDING

1. **Personal Response** In this story, the death and burial of old Teofilo are treated matter-of-factly. Do you think this is a typical response to the death of a loved one? Would you tend to respond differently? Explain.

2. **Literary Analysis** What is the central *conflict* in this story? What details, especially about the priest, are relevant to the outcome of the conflict?

3. **Multicultural Connection** Although Silko mentions many of the pueblo rituals associated with the death of a

person, she does not include details of Teofilo's funeral itself. Make a list of those rituals. Why do you think Silko does not give specific details about the funeral?

LANGUAGE WORKSHOP

Direct Address In the third paragraph of Part One, Ken and Leon say, "Send us rain clouds, Grandfather." The comma is used to set off a noun of *direct address*. Use one comma if the noun is the first or last word in the sentence. Use two commas if the noun is in the middle: "If it happened, John, we would all be happy."

Punctuate the following sentences.
1. I wonder Suzanne if the weather will change.
2. I'm glad you understand Father.
3. Friends we will have to continue the ceremony later.

WRITER'S PORTFOLIO

Good writers know that references to color can help create desired moods and make descriptive passages more vivid. Study the way Silko uses different colors in her story. Then write a descriptive paragraph in which you convey the time of year (without mentioning the specific season) and a particular mood by making use of specific colors.

ABOUT **ALICE WALKER**

Alice Walker became a literary sensation with the publication of her Pulitzer Prize-winning novel, *The Color Purple*, in 1982. The eighth child of Georgia sharecroppers, Walker suffered a disfiguring eye injury when she was young — an injury that became a turning point. She started to devote her attention to writing poems, reading, and observing people — all beneficial in some way to her career as a writer. The valedictorian of her high school in 1961, Walker entered college on a scholarship, worked in the civil rights movement, and graduated from Sarah Lawrence College in 1965. Much of her work draws on her Southern background and deals with African American women who struggle to overcome the effects of poverty, racism, and male domination.

Everyday Use

for your grandmama

I WILL WAIT FOR HER in the yard that Maggie and I made so clean and wavy yesterday afternoon. A yard like this is more comfortable than most people know. It is not just a yard. It is like an extended living room. When the hard clay is swept clean as a floor and the fine sand around the edges lined with tiny, irregular grooves, anyone can come and sit and look up into the elm tree and wait for the breezes that never come inside the house.

Maggie will be nervous until after her sister goes: she will stand hopelessly in corners, homely and ashamed of the burn scars down her arms and legs, eying her sister with a mixture of envy and awe. She thinks her sister has held life always in the palm of one hand, that "no" is a word the world never learned to say to her.

You've no doubt seen those TV shows where the child who has "made it" is confronted, as a surprise, by her own mother and father, tottering in weakly from backstage. (A pleasant surprise, of course: What would they do if parent and child came on the show only to curse out and insult each other?) On TV mother and child embrace and smile into each other's faces. Sometimes the mother and father weep, the child wraps them in her arms and leans across the table to tell how she would not have made it without their help. I have seen these programs.

Sometimes I dream a dream in which Dee and I are suddenly brought together on a TV program of this sort. Out of a dark and softseated limousine I am ushered into a bright room filled with many people. There I meet a smiling, gray, sporty man like Johnny Carson who shakes my hand and tells me what a fine girl I have. Then we are on the stage and Dee is embracing me with tears in her eyes. She pins on my dress a large orchid, even though she had told me once that she thinks orchids are tacky flowers.

In real life I am a large, big-boned woman with rough, man-working hands. In the winter I wear flannel nightgowns to bed and overalls during the day. I can kill and clean a hog as mercilessly as a man. My fat keeps me hot in zero weather. I can work outside all day, breaking ice to get water for washing; I can eat pork liver cooked over the open fire minutes after it comes steaming from the hog. One winter I knocked a bull calf straight in the brain between the eyes with a sledge hammer and had the meat hung up to chill before nightfall. But of course all this does not show on television. I am the way my daughter would want me to be: a hundred pounds lighter, my skin like an uncooked barley pancake. My hair glistens in the hot bright lights. Johnny Carson has much to do to keep up with my quick and witty tongue.

But that is a mistake. I know even before I wake up. Who ever knew a Johnson with a quick tongue? Who can even imagine me looking a strange white man in the eye? It seems to me I have talked to them always with one foot raised in flight, with my head turned in whichever way is farthest from them. Dee, though. She would always look anyone in the eye. Hesitation was no part of her nature.

How do I look, Mama?" Maggie says, showing just enough of her thin body enveloped in pink skirt and red blouse for me to know she's there, almost hidden by the door.

"Come out into the yard," I say.

Have you ever seen a lame animal, perhaps a dog run over by some careless person rich enough to own a car, sidle up to someone who is ignorant enough to be kind to him? That is the way my Maggie walks. She had been like this, chin on chest, eyes on ground, feet in shuffle, ever since the fire that burned the other house to the ground.

Dee is lighter than Maggie, with nicer hair and a fuller figure. She's a woman now, though sometimes I forget. How long ago was it that the other house burned? Ten, twelve years? Sometimes I can still hear the flames and feel Maggie's arms sticking to me, her hair smoking and her dress falling off her in little black papery flakes. Her eyes seemed stretched open, blazed open by the flames reflected in them. And Dee. I see her standing off under the sweet gum tree she used to dig gum out of; a look of concentration on her face as she watched the last dingy gray board of the house fall in toward the red-hot brick chimney. Why don't you do a dance around the ashes? I'd wanted to ask her. She had hated the house that much.

I used to think she hated Maggie, too. But that was before we raised the money, the church and me, to send her to Augusta to school. She used to read to us without pity; forcing words, lies, other folks' habits, whole lives upon us two, sitting trapped and ignorant underneath her voice. She washed us in the river of make-believe, burned us with a lot of knowledge we didn't necessarily need to know. Pressed us to her with the serious way she read, to shove us away at just the moment, like dimwits, we seemed about to understand.

Dee wanted nice things. A yellow organdy dress to wear to her graduation from high school; black pumps to match a green suit she'd made from an old suit somebody gave me. She was determined to stare down any disaster in her efforts. Her eyelids would not flicker for minutes at a time. Often I fought off the temptation to shake her. At sixteen she had a style of her own: and knew what style was.

I never had education myself. After second grade the school was closed down. Don't ask me why: in 1927 colored asked fewer questions than they do now. Sometimes Maggie reads to me. She stumbles along good-naturedly but can't see well. She knows she is not bright. Like good looks and money, quickness passed her by. She will marry John Thomas (who has mossy teeth in an earnest face) and then I'll be free to sit here and I guess just sing church songs to myself. Although I never was a good singer. Never could carry a tune. I was always better at a man's job. I used to love to milk till I was hooked in the side in '49. Cows are soothing and slow and don't bother you, unless you try to milk them the wrong way.

I have deliberately turned my back on the house. It is three rooms, just like the one that burned, except the roof is tin; they don't make shingle roofs any more. There are no real windows, just some holes cut in the sides, like the port-holes in a ship, but not round and not square, with rawhide holding the shutters up on the outside. This house is in a pasture, too, like the other one. No doubt when Dee sees it she will want to tear it down. She wrote me once that no matter where we "choose" to live, she will manage to come see us. But she will never bring her friends. Maggie and I thought about this and Maggie asked me, "Mama, when did Dee ever *have* any friends?"

She had a few. Furtive boys in pink shirts hanging about on washday after school. Nervous girls who never laughed. Impressed with her they worshipped the well-turned phrase, the cute shape, the scalding humor that erupted like bubbles in lye. She read to them.

When she was courting Jimmy T she didn't have much time to pay to us, but turned all her fault-finding power on him. He *flew* to marry a cheap city girl from a family of ignorant flashy people. She hardly had time to recompose herself.

When she comes I will meet — but there they are!

Maggie attempts to make a dash for the house, in her shuffling way, but I stay her with my hand. "Come back here," I say. And she stops and tries to dig a well in the sand with her toe.

It is hard to see them clearly through the strong sun. But even the first glimpse of leg out of the car tells me it is Dee. Her feet were always neat-looking, as if God himself had shaped them with a certain style. From the other side of the car comes a short, stocky man. Hair is all over his head a foot long and hanging from his chin like a kinky mule tail. I hear Maggie suck in her breath. "Uhnnnh," is what it sounds like. Like when you see the wriggling end of a snake just in front of your foot on the road. "Uhnnnh."

Dee next. A dress down to the ground, in this hot weather. A dress so loud it hurts my eyes. There are yellows and oranges enough to throw back the light of the sun. I feel my whole face warming from the heat waves it throws out. Earrings gold, too, and hanging down to her shoulders. Bracelets dangling and making noises when she moves her arm up to shake the folds of the dress out of her armpits. The dress is loose and flows, and as she walks closer, I like it. I hear Maggie go "Uhnnnh" again. It is her sister's hair. It stands straight up like the wool on a sheep. It is black as night and around the edges are two long pigtails that rope about like small lizards disappearing behind her ears.

Culture Notes

Wa-su-zo-Tean-o
a greeting in one of the several Bantu languages of central and southern Africa, p.183

Asalamalakim
(ə sä′ləm ′ä lə ′kům)
Arabic for "Peace be with you," p.183

pork was unclean
Moslems are forbidden by their religion from eating pork. p.185

"Wa-su-zo-Tean-o!" she says, coming on in that gliding way the dress makes her move. The short, stocky fellow with the hair to his navel is all grinning and he follows up with "Asalamalakim, my mother and sister!" He moves to hug Maggie but she falls back, right up against the back of my chair. I feel her trembling there and when I look up I see the perspiration falling off her chin.

"Don't get up," says Dee. Since I am stout it takes something of a push. You can see me trying to move a second or two before I make it. She turns, showing white heels through her sandals, and goes back to the car. Out she peeks next with a Polaroid. She stoops down quickly and lines up picture after picture of me sitting there in front of the house with Maggie cowering behind me. She never takes a shot without making sure the house is included. When a cow comes nibbling around the edge of the yard she snaps it and me and Maggie *and* the house. Then she puts the Polaroid in the back seat of the car, and comes up and kisses me on the forehead.

MEANWHILE Asalamalakim is going through motions with Maggie's hand. Maggie's hand is as limp as a fish, and probably as cold, despite the sweat, and she keeps trying to pull it back. It looks like Asalamalakim wants to shake hands but wants to do it fancy. Or maybe he don't know how people shake hands. Anyhow, he soon gives up on Maggie.

"Well," I say. "Dee."

"No, Mama," She says. "Not 'Dee,' Wangero Leewanika Kemanjo!"

"What happened to 'Dee'?" I wanted to know.

"She's dead," Wangero said. "I couldn't bear it any longer, being named after the people who oppress me."

"You know as well as me you was named after your aunt Dicie," I said. Dicie is my sister. She named Dee. We called her "Big Dee" after Dee was born.

"But who was *she* named after?" asked Wangero.

"I guess after Grandma Dee," I said.

"And who was she named after?" asked Wangero.

"Her mother," I said, and saw Wangero was getting tired. "That's about as far back as I can trace it," I said. Though, in fact, I probably could have carried it back beyond the Civil War through the branches.

"Well," said Asalamalakim, "there you are."

"Uhnnnh," I heard Maggie say.

"There I was not," I said, "before 'Dicie' cropped up in our family, so why should I try to trace it that far back?"

He just stood there grinning, looking down on me like somebody inspecting a Model A car. Every once in a while he and Wangero sent eye signals over my head.

"How do you pronounce this name?" I asked.

"You don't have to call me by it if you don't want to," said Wangero.

"Why shouldn't I?" I asked. "If that's what you want us to call you, we'll call you."

"I know it might sound awkward at first," said Wangero.

"I'll get used to it," I said. "Ream it out again."

Well, soon we got the name out of the way. Asalamalakim had a name twice as long and three times as hard. After I tripped over it two or three times he told me to just call him Hakim-a-barber. I wanted to ask him was he a barber, but I didn't really think he was, so I didn't ask.

"You must belong to those beef-cattle peoples down the road," I said. They said "Asalamalakim" when they met you, too, but they didn't shake hands. Always too busy: feeding the cattle, fixing the fences, putting up salt-lick shelters, throwing down hay. When the white folks poisoned some of the herd the men stayed up all night with rifles in their hands. I walked a mile and a half just to see the sight.

Hakim-a-barber said, "I accept some of their doctrines, but farming and raising cattle is not my style." (They didn't tell me, and I didn't ask, whether Wangero (Dee) had really gone and married him.)

WE SAT DOWN to eat and right away he said he didn't eat collards and pork was unclean. Wangero, though, went on through the chitlins and corn bread, the greens and everything else. She talked a blue streak over the sweet potatoes. Everything delighted her. Even the fact that we still used the benches her daddy made for the table when we couldn't afford to buy chairs.

"Oh, Mama!" she cried. Then turned to Hakim-a-barber. "I never knew how lovely these benches are. You can feel the rump prints," she said, running her hands underneath her and along the bench. Then she gave a sigh and her hand closed over Grandma Dee's butter dish. "That's it!" she said. "I knew there was something I wanted to ask you if I could have." She jumped up from the table and went over in the corner where the churn stood, the milk in it clabber by now. She looked at the churn and looked at it.

"This churn top is what I need," she said. "Didn't Uncle Buddy whittle it out of a tree you all used to have?"

"Yes," I said.

"Uh huh," she said happily. "And I want the dasher, too."

"Uncle Buddy whittle that, too?" asked the barber.

Dee (Wangero) looked up at me.

"Aunt Dee's first husband whittled the dash," said Maggie so low you almost couldn't hear her. "His name was Henry, but they called him Stash."

"Maggie's brain is like an elephant's," Wangero said, laughing. "I can use the churn top as a centerpiece for the alcove table," she said, sliding a plate over the churn, "and I'll think of something artistic to do with the dasher."

When she finished wrapping the dasher the handle stuck out. I took it for a moment in my hands. You didn't even have to look close to see where hands pushing the dasher up and down to make butter had left a kind of sink in the wood. In fact, there were a lot of small sinks; you could see where thumbs and fingers had sunk into the wood. It was beautiful light yellow wood, from a tree that grew in the yard where Big Dee and Stash had lived.

AFTER DINNER Dee (Wangero) went to the trunk at the foot of my bed and started rifling through it. Maggie hung back in the kitchen over the dishpan. Out came Wangero with two quilts. They had been pieced by Grandma Dee and then Big Dee and me had hung them on the quilt frames on the front porch and quilted them. One was in the Lone Star pattern. The other was Walk Around the Mountain. In both of them were scraps of dresses Grandma Dee had worn fifty and more years ago. Bits and pieces of Grandpa Jarrell's paisley shirts. And one teeny faded blue piece, about the size of a penny matchbox, that was from Great Grandpa Ezra's uniform that he wore in the Civil War.

"Mama," Wangero said sweet as a bird. "Can I have these old quilts?"

I heard something fall in the kitchen, and a minute later the kitchen door slammed.

"Why don't you take one or two of the others?" I asked. "These old things was just done by me and Big Dee from some tops your grandma pieced before she died."

"No," said Wangero. "I don't want those. They are stitched around the borders by machine."

"That'll make them last better," I said.

"That's not the point," said Wangero. "These are all pieces of dresses Grandma used to wear. She did all this stitching by hand. Imagine!" She held the quilts securely in her arms, stroking them.

"Some of the pieces, like those lavender ones, come from old clothes her mother handed down to her," I said, moving up to touch the quilts. Dee (Wangero) moved back just enough so that I couldn't reach the quilts. They already belonged to her.

"Imagine!" she breathed again, clutching them closely to her bosom.

"The truth is," I said, "I promised to give them quilts to Maggie, for when she marries John Thomas."

She gasped like a bee had stung her.

"Maggie can't appreciate these quilts!" she said. "She'd probably be backward enough to put them to everyday use."

"I reckon she would," I said. "God knows I been saving 'em for long enough with nobody using 'em. I hope she will!" I didn't want to bring up how I had offered Dee (Wangero) a quilt when she went away to college. Then she had told me they were old-fashioned, out of style.

"But they're *priceless*!" she was saying now, furiously; for she had a temper. "Maggie would put them on the bed and in five years they'd be in rags. Less than that!"

"She can always make some more," I said. "Maggie knows how to quilt."

Dee (Wangero) looked at me with hatred. "You just will not understand. The point is these quilts, *these* quilts!"

"Well," I said, stumped. "What would *you* do with them?"

"Hang them," she said. As if that was the only thing you *could* do with quilts.

Maggie by now was standing in the door. I could almost hear the sound her feet made as they scraped over each other.

"She can have them, Mama," she said, like somebody used to never winning anything, or having anything reserved for her. "I can 'member Grandma Dee without the quilts."

I looked at her hard. She had filled her bottom lip with checkerberry snuff and it gave her face a kind of dopey, hangdog look. It was Grandma Dee and Big Dee who taught her how to quilt herself. She stood there with her scarred hands hidden in the folds of her skirt. She looked at her sister with something like fear but wasn't mad at her. This was Maggie's portion. This was the way she knew God to work.

When I looked at her like that something hit me in the top of my head and ran down to the soles of my feet. Just like when I'm in church and the spirit of God touches me and I get happy and shout. I did something I never had done before: hugged Maggie to me, then dragged her on into the room, snatched the quilts out of Miss Wangero's hands and dumped them into Maggie's lap. Maggie just sat there on my bed with her mouth open.

"Take one or two of the others," I said to Dee.

But she turned without a word and went out to Hakim-a-barber.

"You just don't understand," she said, as Maggie and I came out to the car.

"What don't I understand?" I wanted to know.

"Your heritage," she said. And then she turned to Maggie, kissed her, and said, "You ought to try to make something of yourself, too, Maggie. It's really a new day for us. But from the way you and Mama still live you'd never know it."

She put on some sunglasses that hid everything above the tip of her nose and her chin.

Maggie smiled; maybe at the sunglasses. But a real smile, not scared. After we watched the car dust settle I asked Maggie to bring me a dip of snuff. And then the two of us sat there just enjoying, until it was time to go in the house and go to bed.

RESPONDING

1. Personal Response Are there objects in your home that are packed away, covered, or set aside for special occasions or "show only" rather than reserved for "everyday use"? Do you feel more like Dee or like Mama about whether or not such things should be used?

2. Literary Analysis What details about the clothes and physical appearance of each female *character* provide clues to their personalities?

3. Multicultural Connection Describe Dee's understanding of her heritage in contrast to her mother and sister's understanding.

LANGUAGE WORKSHOP

Specialized Vocabulary Words and phrases such as *clabber, dasher,* and *hooked in the side,* reflect life in a rural setting. Match each word or phrase with one of the following meanings:
1. device for stirring the cream in a churn
2. injured by a cow's horn
3. thick, sour milk

WRITER'S PORTFOLIO

In this story, a mother imagines a *This is Your Life* episode. Write a short television scenario that celebrates the life of an older family member or friend. You may want to interview that person or some acquaintances of your subject, or go through a picture album for material.

ABOUT **GREGORY ORFALEA**

Born in Los Angeles, Gregory Orfalea graduated from Georgetown University in 1971 and the University of Alaska in 1974. He began his career as a reporter and teacher, but has held a number of positions associated with Arab American relations and the Middle East in Washington, D.C., since then. An editor as well as a writer, Orfalea co-edited *Grape Leaves: A Century of Arab American Poetry* (1988). As a "descendent of the first documented Arab immigrant family, a family that came to the United States in 1878," Orfalea speaks with uncommon conviction and insight about the difficulties encountered by those who face overwhelming problems in their homelands.

The Chandelier

MUKHLIS DRIVES up Asbury Street in Pasadena and brings his green Buick to an easy, slow stop underneath the largest flowering eucalyptus in southern California. The first door cracked is that of his wife, Wardi, who gets out as she has every week for the past forty years, as if she were with child. She has not been with child for many years, but her body at center is like the large burl of a cedar and her legs are bowed as an old chair's. Mukhlis emerges from the Buick. He looks left and right for cars—a short, searing look either way. And the sun tries to plant its white seed on the center of his bald head.

Mukhlis has made a small fortune in real estate. He has apartment complexes here and there in the city, and many of his tenants are black or brown. He himself is brown, or rather almond, and his eyes, like those of many Lebanese and Syrians, are blue. He owes this hue to the Crusaders. A continent man, Mukhlis' eyes are the last blue twinkle of a distant lust.

What words there are to say, Mukhlis rarely says. His eyes and body

> ### Culture Notes
>
> **Crusaders** men who participated in the military campaigns during the 11th, 12th, 13th centuries, undertaken by Christians to recover the Holy Land from the Muslims. The Crusades were often characterized by looting, pillage, and rape, p.191
>
> **continent man** a play on words; one who comes from the mainland of Europe (via his Crusader ancestors) or one who shows self-restraint, especially in sexual passion, p.191

speak—a body made to withstand. As he ascends the steps of his sister's home, the collar of his gray suit pulls taut around his neck. And his neck has the thickness of a foundation post; it welds his head to the shoulders. For years it has been bronzed by the sun. So tight is the tie and collar around his neck that his nape stands up in a welt of muscle. It is not a fat neck—nothing about the man is fat, save a slight bulge to his belly, brought on, no doubt, by forty years of Wardi's desserts, among the finest Arabic delights in Los Angeles. Mukhlis has learned it is useless to compliment her because Wardi (Rose, in English), like most Arabs, does not react to compliments; she prefers to go to great lengths to pay a compliment, instead. But not Mukhlis. He says not two crooked words about Wardi's *knafi*, the bird's nest whose wafer-like shell must be rolled with the patience of Job before it is filled with pistachios as green as Mukhlis' Buick—and probably greener—then topped with a spoon of rosewater syrup.

Mukhlis kisses his sister, Matile, and booms a greeting to the air behind her in a robust voice that speaks in simple sentences and laughs silently. His large head, sapphire eyes, and corded neck all shake with his laughter.

And if it is on a summer evening, with a large group of people chatting on Matile's porch, all will be aware of Mukhlis, though he will surely say the least, and when his hands come apart after having been clasped tightly on his belly for so long, people will take a drag on their cigarettes and turn in his direction.

"No one wants to work, and so the devil has his pick of the young people."

Wardi, who clasps her hands on a more bulbous belly, will nod and sip her coffee from the demitasse.

"Matile, do you have any cream?" Mukhlis asks his sister.

"Certainly, my honey," she sings. "Anything for you."

When Matile's voice sings it is to smooth over rough spots in conversation; her feigned joy or fright has saved many a wounded soul. But when Mukhlis sang—the fact that he once did sing is his most guarded secret—it was with the voice of the *hassoun*, the national bird of Lebanon, multicolored red, yellow, and black, prized for its rich warble, and fed marijuana seeds by children.

Sitting among immigrants from the First World War, Mukhlis was asked to fill the gaps in all hearts over the strange Atlantic, which in Arabic is called "The Sea of Darkness." Please, Mukhlis, sing the praise to the night! Sing of the moon and its white dress! Huddled on the stoops in Brooklyn, they asked for the song of two lovers separated by a river. The one of the nine months of pregnancy, in which Mukhlis stuffed a pillow under his shirt. Sing, cousin Mukhlis, for we are tired of the dress factories, we are tired of the fish market. Sing the Old Land on the Mediterranean!

And sing he did. His voice was effortless and sweet; it was made all the sweeter by the immense power everyone knew lay under it. Then one day this unschooled tenor, this voice dipped in rosewater, simply stopped. It stopped cold when Mukhlis' mother died in a little loft above a funeral parlor in Brooklyn. It died when he covered the four long white scars of her back, from the lashes of the Turks, for the last time. No one in California has ever heard him sing.

ALL OF THIS is whispered from time to time behind Mukhlis' back. None of it is spoken directly to his ears. He will not tolerate it. His usual response to any mention of the latest atrocity in Lebanon is: "How is your dog?" or "The apricots are too thick on the boughs this year. They need to be snapped off."

But today the large porch is empty, except for Matile herself and her oldest grandson, Mukhlis' great-nephew. This young man has been traveling for years. He is a restless soul, thinks Mukhlis, as they take their places on the porch—he on the legless couch, his wife on a white wrought-iron chair with a pillow of faded flowers made by Matile. The great-nephew takes to the old iron swing. What is it about this day? Mukhlis says to himself, noticing a vine in the yard. The wind is hurting the grape leaves.

Matile brings a tray of coffee and announces dinner is not too far off, and all must stay.

"It is never too far off with you, Matile," Mukhlis says, blowing over the coffee.

"You *must* stay," she sings. "I am making stuffed zucchini."

"Never mind," he says. "Have you got a *ghrabi?*"

"*Ghrabi?*" Matile stands so quickly she leaves her black shoes. And goes into a litany of food that lasts five minutes.

"No, no, no," Mukhlis punctuates each breathless pause in her list. "*Ghrabi*—just give me one."

"One!" she cries. "I have a hundred."

"One, please, is all I want."

SHE BRINGS A DISH piled high with the small hoops of butter, sugar, and dough, each with a mole or two of pistachio.

"Eat," she says.

Wardi takes one. Mukhlis shakes his head and breaks off half a *ghrabi*.

"Isn't that delicious?" Matile asks, preempting the compliment. Mukhlis chews. "You look real good today," she smiles with a brightened face, disregarding his nodding. Mukhlis turns to the young man.

"And so, what are you doing here?"

"Looking for work," says the great-nephew, a dark, slender fellow with broad shoulders. These eyes of his, Mukhlis thinks, have a dark sparkle. He's cried and laughed too much for his age; his laugh is a cry and his cry is a laugh.

"It's time for you to get serious and stop this wandering and get a good job in business," Mukhlis says rather loudly.

"You are playing with your life. When are you going to get married?"

Mukhlis gleams his crocodile smile and laughs silently. Then he becomes solemn, and touches the pistachio on a *ghrabi* with a thick forefinger, taps it several times, then removes it.

"Aren't you ever really hungry, Uncle Mukhlis?"

The old realtor looks out past the stanchions of the porch, past the thickened apricots.

"Boy, have you ever seen a person eat an orange peel?"

"I've eaten them myself. They're quite good."

"No, no, boy. I mean rotten orange peels, with mud and dung on them. Have you had that?"

The great-nephew purses his lips.

"Well, I want to tell you a story. I want to tell you about hunger, and I want to tell you about disgrace."

Matile gets up again, and lets out in her falsetto, "Don't go no further till I come back."

Mukhlis disregards her and squeezes a faded pillow on the legless couch, as if he were squeezing his brain. What is it about the breeze and the light today, the crystal light? Will he go on? He does not know. His great-nephew is too silent. Mukhlis does not like silence waiting for silence. He likes his silence to be hidden in a crowd. From the dome of his almond head, he takes some sweat and smells it. Wardi continues to eat.

"I was the oldest of us in Lebanon where we lived in the mountain, but when World War I started I was still a young boy. They cut off Beirut harbor in 1914. You see, the Germans were allied with the Turks who had hold over all the Arab lands. And so the Germans become our masters for a time. When it was all we could do to steer clear of the Turks! The Allies blockaded Beirut harbor, and for four years there was no food to be had in Mount Lebanon."

At this moment Matile puts a heap of grapes in front of him.

"Nothing like this purple grape, I can assure you! These were treacherous times of human brutality. People were hungry and hunger is the beginning of cruelty. The Turks themselves would tolerate no funny business. If people refused to cooperate with them they would take it out on the children. I saw them seize a small boy by the legs and literally rip him in half. I saw this happen with my own eyes; one half of the child flew into the fountain we had in Mheiti, which is near Bikfaya. The fountain was empty, but even after the War when it had water and the remains of the child were dried up no one would drink there."

"Yi! You tell them Mukhlis! You tell this to show what happen to us!" Matile's voice rises as she lays down a plate of goat's cheese and bread. "It was terrible."

"Food was so scarce people would pick up horse dung, wash it, and eat the grains of hay left. It was common to go days without eating or drinking, because the Nahr Ibrahim and Bardowni Rivers were contaminated by dead bodies. The Germans and the Turks would throw traitors into the river . . . then there was the chandelier."

Matile clicks her tongue, "I could tell you story, boy, I could tell you story."

"Did you know 'Lebanon' means 'snow'?" Mukhlis raises his pointer finger. "It means 'white as yogurt' because the mountains are covered with snow. It was very cold in the winter, and we had to stay in. Without food, it was colder."

"What about restaurants?" the great-nephew ventures.

"Restaurant? You are an idiot, young man, forgive me for saying. Any restaurant was destroyed in the first year, any market plundered by the soldiers. We had to find food for ourselves. Each day for four years was a battle for food."

"I could tell you story," Matile puts her eyes up to the stucco ceiling of the porch and shakes her hands. "*Thoobs!* A crust of bread was so rare it was like communion. My mother she had to go away for days to trade everything we had for food on the other side of the mountain—"

"Matile, I . . ."

"—she give us a slice of bread before she leaves and she shake her finger at us and say—Matile, Mukhlis, Milhem—you don't take this all at once. Each day you cut one piece of the bread. One piece! No more. And you cut this piece into four pieces—three for you, and then you break the last one for the infants. You understand? Like one cracker a day for each of us. Little Milhem and Leila, they cry all day. They want more. They too little to understand, and the baby . . . ah! Milhem hit us for the rest of the slice of bread. I hide it under my pillow one night. And that night

. . . oh, I could tell you story make your ears hurt!"

Mukhlis shifts in his seat and flings out his arms, "Now, when I went off in the snow . . ."

"The chandelier, you remember."

"Yes. Matile, of course I do."

"You remember, Wardi, you wouldn't believe it."

Wardi's eyes are large as a night creature behind her thick eyeglass lenses, and she nods.

MUKHLIS CLEARS HIS THROAT loudly. "My mother gave me the last piastres we had and told me to go through the snow over the mountain to the village in the dry land, to fetch milk and bread. I was not as strong as my mother but I was strong, and so I tried. But the first day out I was shot at by a highwayman, a robber. I hid behind a rock; still he found me and stripped off my jacket and took the piastres. I was glad he did not kill me. But what was I to do? I could not go home. I continued walking until I came to the monastery. I thought I would ask the monks for some milk. They were not there."

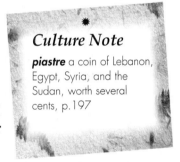

Culture Note

piastre a coin of Lebanon, Egypt, Syria, and the Sudan, worth several cents, p.197

"They die."

"Matile, please. They were not there. Perhaps they went to Greece. They were Greek monks. The place was empty. The door to the chapel opening with the wind that moved it back and forth. Inside the candles were snuffed. And the candlesticks were cold, and all the pews were covered with frost. It was winter, inside and out. Up above was a . . ."

"Chandelier!"

"Yes, Matile, a huge crystal chandelier. In all my life I have never seen one larger. Its branches were as far across as this couch, made of solid gold. Inlaid in the arms were rubies the size of your eyes, nephew! I remember standing in that chapel that day thinking how we had come to worship there with my father when I was a very young child; the chandelier was something I would worship. I would look up and its great shining light would say to me—God. This is your God. Mukhlis, here on Mount Lebanon. He brims with light and He will sit in your eyes, in your dreams. I had never thought of touching it. For one thing, it was too high. It was at least fifteen feet above my head. Well, so help the Almighty, I was hungry. And my mother was hungry. And so were my brothers . . . and my sisters. And we had not heard from our father, who was in America, for two years. Before God and man, I committed a sacrilege. The mosaics, you see, on the wall were shot out and in tatters. I crawled up the wall where the tile was gone. I crawled up that mosaic until I made it to the crossbeams of the ceiling. And I had to be very careful not to knock loose the mosaic where I was hanging—a mosaic of Our Lady it was, and who knows? Maybe my foot was in her mouth."

"How sad!" sighs Matile.

"But I hoisted myself onto the crossbeam and slid—like this, yes—slid across the beam. It was cold enough to hold my hands fast as I tried to balance. But finally I made it out over the nave of the chapel, to the chandelier."

"Yi!"

THE CHANDELIER was held to the ceiling with tall iron nails. Carefully, carefully I put my hands through the crystal teardrops, to latch onto the gold arms. And then you know what I did, young man? I became a monkey. I swung free on that chandelier! I pulled up and heaved down on it, trying to loosen it. I yanked and yanked with the crystal hitting my eyes and the rubies sweating in my hands. And I swung back and forth in the cold air. For a long time the chandelier would not loosen. It seemed like God Himself was holding onto the chandelier through the ceiling and saying to me: No you don't, Mukhlis! You do not take the chandelier from this church. This is mine, Mukhlis. This chandelier was given to the worship of the Almighty. And you—you are a puny human being who deserves to rot in hell for this.

"I am not talking about playing in the acacias. I am not talking about swinging about from those miserable apricot trees, which need to be cut back by the way, Matile."

"Anything you say, my honey."

"I am talking about a tree of crystal and gold. I am talking about food."

"Wardi, would you like more coffee, dear?"

"Matile, I am talking about food."

"So am I!"

Wardi's enlarged eyes close and her big bosom vibrates with mirth, like a dreaming horse.

"Oh it's useless. Why talk about it?" Mukhlis folds his hands, as if to tie up the story once and for all and leave everyone hanging on the chandelier.

Matile speaks with alarm: "Please, tell them, tell them. I won't get up no more. This is story you never heard the like of before. It can't be no worse!"

Mukhlis gets up, paces on the clay porch, and goes over to the apricot, breaking off a branch crowded with fruit.

"Here, Matile, here is your dessert," he spits and continues, still standing. "Finally, I heard it come loose. The plaster dust rained on my face and I heaved on this chandelier one more time. And then I fell."

Mukhlis raises his thick forearms and grips the air.

"It breaks, ah!"

"No, Matile, it does not break. Please, you are killing my story at every juncture."

She laughs and gets up for some rice pudding that is cooling in the refrigerator.

"I fall with it. I fall with it and I fall directly on my rump. This is why I walk slowly to this day, young man. Because of the chandelier. That chandelier had to become milk. It was going to save my life, our lives. What did my bones mean? Nothing. But I was a tough young fellow — not like you soft people today — and not one teardrop of that crystal was scratched. I got up, and my hip was partially cracked. But I got up. I carried the chandelier to the entrance of the church. No one was around. No one saw me do it."

"God finally let go?" the great-nephew asks, with a smirk.

"God never lets go. I yanked it out of His hands. But I could not carry the chandelier far—it weighed a ton. In the vestibule of the chapel was a small Oriental rug. I placed the chandelier on top of that, took the cord of chain, tied it around the branches of gold, and dragged the whole mess out into the snow. No, Matile, no rice pudding. For the next three days, I dragged the chandelier over the snow to get to the village over the mountain in the hot land of Bekaa. For three days I walked and pulled it behind me."

Mukhlis stops and wipes his brow. He is sweating heavily now, even though the California air is dry.

"I was exhausted by the end of the first day. I lay down in the snow by a cedar. I did not want to damage the chandelier, so I left it on the rug and tried to sleep on the snow with as much of my body as I could against the cedar. I was so tired and fell fast asleep."

"Did you dream?" asks the great-nephew, taking a spoonful of the sweet rice pudding.

I DON'T REMEMBER. No, I don't dream. Dreams are for soft times," Mukhlis grunts. "You've dropped some pudding." His listener takes up the white spot on the porch with a finger. For a while Mukhlis says nothing, and listens to them eating. His blue eyes stare out into the warm air past the apricots, past the flowering eucalyptus, to the cloudless sky.

"I awoke to the sound of licking in the dark. I felt warm breath near my face. I sat up. There were six eyes, six greenish eyes in the darkness. My blood went cold. Wolves. I got up fast, grabbed the chandelier and swung it around and around, turning inside it myself. It made a tinkling noise that was loud in the dead forest and the wolves howled and scattered back into the night. I was breathing so hard my heart felt like it would come out of me. I was much too awake now and decided to go on dragging the chandelier in the dark. All through the night the teardrops clinked against each other and the rug rubbed over the snow. My eyes have never been so wide as that night. I looked on all sides and hurried until dawn, then rested. I remember lying down by a boulder, hooking the chandelier with my arm. When it dawned, the sun sent it sparkling. It made rays of red all over the snow, and the rubies looked like drops of glistening blood. I rested a while, my eyes opening and closing, but I did not let them close completely. No, not again! The second day I met a family trudging in the snow — a mother, daughter, and two babies. The mother asked if I had any milk. I said I was going to get some for the chandelier. She shook her head and kissed me on the head. Her daughter's eyes were rimmed with blue and she was shaking. She had nothing on but a nightgown and thin sweater, and her toes showed through her leather shoes. They went on — they were going to Zahle, they said. I said I thought Zahle had no food, because my mother had been there and had bought the last scoop of flour in town. The mother asked where my family lived and I told her. They said they would try and go there. I said, Please do. The mother stared at me a while with her own blue-rimmed eyes. One baby had blue lips. The other was whimpering and breathing quickly in the daughter's arms. I went on. I went on and on, with the snow wedged in my socks and pants. That night I slept with my head inside the chandelier, my arms coiled in it, my legs twisted inside it so that if wolves came they would not want me, for they would think I was part of the chandelier. It worked. I was not bothered by wolves that night. The third day I descended from the mountain. I saw the dry lands in the distance — the rust-colored sand and rock of the Bekaa — and I broke out laughing, I was so happy. But I descended too quickly, and a thread of the rug snagged on a twig raised out of the snow. The chandelier slid off and down a smooth embankment of snow which the sun had turned into a plate of ice. I plunged down the cliff after the chandelier. But when it reached a ledge it fell. It fell about twenty feet. I cried out and rolled like a crazy dog down the snowbank and fell on my face in front of the chandelier. Luckily it had landed on snow that had not iced over, that had some shade from the ledge. I moved it slowly. One of the gold arms was bent and five or six teardrops of crystal were shattered. I turned it and stepped back. It did not look too bad if one looked from this perspective, with the broken part to the back. The rug was still above, so I fetched it and carefully laid the chandelier on it, like a wounded human being, and went on. Slow now, Mukhlis, slow now. I did not let myself be excited any more by the nearness of the Bekaa. I have never let myself be excited again because of that chandelier breaking over the

✳

Culture Note

Damascus the capital and largest city in Syria, located in the southwest part of the country, p. 202

ledge. That day, around four o'clock, I reached the small village my mother had told me about. The villagers there were healthy. They still had some fields producing corn and wheat and lentils, and the road to Damascus was open. When they saw me — a little runt dragging this chandelier on the dry, dusty road — they gathered around me, asking all sorts of questions. I was too tired to answer. I just said, 'Take me to a cow-farmer. Please, as soon as you can.' They led me to such a man. I said to him, 'Look, I have come from the mountain where it is very cold and no food is there. My family is starving. I will give you this chandelier for milk and anything else I can carry.' The farmer inspected the chandelier, God damn his soul. Our people! They will try to strike a deal no matter what. You may be flat on the ground, your legs chopped off, and they will throw dust in your eyes while they cheat at backgammon. This farmer held up the chandelier with the aid of another man and said, 'It is broken. It can't be worth much.' I said to him, 'Please, sir. It is made of gold and rubies and crystal.' 'Where did you get it from?' he asked. I said, 'I got it from the mountain.' He nodded. He did not want to ask me the next questions. 'I'm not sure,' he said. It was then that his wife, God save her soul, slapped him on the eyes. He pushed her away. 'All right,' he said, 'Two jugs of milk and we will put a pack of bread on your back. Can you carry all that?' I said, 'Yes, yes,

I can carry as much as you can give me.' And he gave me two lambskins of milk and hoisted the bread on my back. The wife put in two bags of dates and dried apricots when he wasn't looking. And she kissed me on the head.

"I stayed in that town to rest for the night. They fed me a good meal. It felt good to sleep, to sleep thoroughly. But by morning I was ready to go. I walked back up the mountain, rising from the warm air to the cold, walking back into the snow world and the dark forest. I walked steadily, though my back and pelvis were hurting. When I made it back to Mheiti in a few days, I found myself running through the worn path in the snow up to my little house — a house made of limestone blocks, a good, sturdy house in normal times. My mother spotted me through the window and came running. She shouted in a hoarse voice, 'Mukhlis! Oh Mukhlis, you've come!' "

MATILE IS STANDING RIGID. She does not speak, or offer food. She watches her brother's sapphire eyes melting in their own fire.

"My mother threw me above her — *ya rubi*, she was strong — and then carried me into the house before she even saw the milk. When she did, she nearly tore it off my neck. She gave some to Matile, to my brother Milhem, and to the baby Leila. But there was the infant to go — my brother Wadie. She frantically squeezed the lambskin's tip into his mouth as he lay in his crib. It was a wooden crib. A small wooden crib. I watched her force it on him. I saw that his eyes were stunned open as if he had seen a large rock toppling on top of him. She kept squeezing the lambskin of milk until half of it was dripping out of his mouth to the floor. 'Mother!' I called to her. 'Don't, don't! You're wasting it'. She wouldn't stop. I had to pull it from her hands. She squeezed the infant's cold cheeks and then took her nails directly to the wall and clawed it. She claws it, yes. After a while she put a sheet over the whole crib."

Mukhlis looks down, then far up to the ceiling of the porch. "I never knew him."

"Ach!" Mukhlis stands slowly. "Let's go, Wardi."

"No, no," Matile wakes from her trance. "You must stay for supper."

"We can't. I must go pick up a rent."

But Matile will not be swayed. She lifts her urgent voice, as if the food were gold and they were turning their backs on precious things. Mukhlis relents while shaking his head. All move into the dining room.

They sit under the chandelier, and pass the grape leaves, the stuffed zucchini, the swollen purple eggplant. They eat in silence, the unlit chandelier struck by the California sundown. It breaks into light above the food; it breaks in pieces of light on Mukhlis' almond head. When he finishes he stands, and ticks one of the crystal droplets with the thick nail of his finger, and does not speak.

"You hear what we went through?" Matile says after they are gone. "That was not all of it." She hugs her grandson, but not long. Even before she is through crying she had opened her mammoth horizontal freezer and said, "We need more bread, more bread."

RESPONDING

1. **Personal Response** Stories about the "olden times," such as the one Mukhlis tells and older members of your family recount, are often designed to teach important lessons. Share an "olden times" story you have heard and tell what lesson it contains.

2. **Literary Analysis** This story is a *narrative*, an account of a series of events that progress to a conclusion. There are, however, many interruptions in this narrative. What do Matile's interjections and offers of food add to the story?

3. **Multicultural Connection** Tell how the Crusades, World War I, and present-day events in Lebanon have affected Mukhlis.

LANGUAGE WORKSHOP

Words from Latin The following are Latin words from the story that are related to church or religion: *sacrilege, nave, vestibule, chapel.* Match each word with its definition.

1. the main part of a church or cathedral
2. a building for worship that is not as large as a church
3. an intentional injury to anything sacred
4. a passage or hall between the outer door and the inside of a building

WRITER'S WORKSHOP

Note the particular dishes or foods enjoyed by the Lebanese characters in this story. Then devise a menu for a dinner that reflects foods you have at family gatherings. Note any foods that maintain a cultural tradition and provide an explanation, if necessary. If possible, include a recipe and share with the class.

ABOUT **VICTOR VILLASEÑOR**

Victor Villaseñor (vē′ä sä nyôr′), born in Carlsbad, California, and raised on a ranch, first gained attention as a writer with *Macho!* (1973). This novel is about a young Tarascan Indian from Mexico who migrates illegally to California, is exploited there, and returns to Mexico only to find that he cannot accept some of his old traditions. This situation reflects both the Chicano's transcultural experience — and Villaseñor's own. On his way to becoming a writer, he was a school dropout and a field-worker, among other things, until he discovered books. In addition to writing novels and short stories, Villaseñor has contributed to *Aztlán* and many other peri-odicals. *Rain of Gold*, from which the following story is taken, focuses on Villaseñor's parents, who came to America on the eve of the Mexican Revolution in 1910.

From Rain of Gold

HIGH IN THE MOUNTAINS in northwest Mexico, an Indian named Espirito followed a doe and her fawn in search of water. The spring in the box canyon where Espirito and his tribe lived had dried up.

Following the deer through the brush and boulders, Espirito found a hidden spring on the other side of the box canyon at the base of a small cliff. Water dripped down the face of the cliff and the whole cliff glistened like a jewel in the bright mid-morning sunlight.

Once the deer were done drinking, Espirito approached the spring and drank, too. It was the sweetest water he'd ever tasted. Filling his gourd with water, Espirito pulled down a couple of loose rocks from the cliff and put them in his deerskin pouch. He knelt down, giving thanks to the Almighty Creator. He and his people weren't going to suffer the long, dry season, after all.

Then that winter came a torrent of rain and it got so cold that the raindrops froze and the mountaintops turned white. Espirito and his tribe grew cold and hungry. Desperately, Espirito went down to the lowlands to see if he could sell some of the sweet water that he'd found.

Walking into a small settlement alongside the great father river, El Rio Urique, Espirito told the store owner, Don Carlos Barrios, that he had the sweetest water in all the world to trade for food and clothing.

Laughing, Don Carlos said, "I'm sorry, but I can't trade for water, living here alongside a river. Do you have anything else to trade?"

"No," said Espirito, turning his purse inside out. "All I have are these little stones and this gourd of water."

Don Carlos's fat, grey eyebrows shot up. The stones were gold nuggets. Picking one up, Don Carlos put it to his teeth, marking it. "For these I can trade you all the food and clothing you want!" he screamed.

But Espirito was already going for the door. He'd never seen a man try to eat a stone before. It took all of Don Carlos's power to calm Espirito down and to come back into the store to trade.

Then, having traded, Espirito loaded the food and clothing into a sack, and he left the settlement as quickly as he could. He didn't want the crazy store owner to go back on their deal.

THE WINTER PASSED and Espirito made a dozen trips down the mountain to trade stones for food and clothing. Don Carlos made so much money from the gold nuggets that he quit attending to his store and began having great feasts every evening. He begged Espirito to sell him the place where he got the nuggets. He offered to send his fat son up the mountain with his two burros loaded with merchandise every week so Espirito wouldn't have to come down the mountain anymore.

"I can't do that," said Espirito. "I don't own the stones or the spring any more than I own the clouds or the birds in the sky. The stones belong to my people who use the spring."

"Well, then, talk to them," said Don Carlos excitedly. "And offer them my deal!"

"All right," said Espirito. He went back up into the mountains and he talked it over with his people. They agreed to Don Carlos's deal, but only on the condition that he'd never dig into the cliff itself and ruin the spring which held the sweetest water in all the world.

Coming down from the box canyon after delivering the first two burro-loads of merchandise, Don Carlos's fat son was beside himself with joy. "Papa," he said, "it's not just a pocket of gold. No, it's a whole cliff of gold raining down the mountainside!"

"How big a cliff?" asked Don Carlos, his eyes dancing with gold fever.

"As tall as twenty men standing on each other and twice as wide as our house."

Don Carlos bit his knuckles with anticipation. He began to send his fat son back up the mountain for more gold as soon as he'd come down.

Don Carlos's son lost all his soft flesh and grew as strong and slender as a deer. Espirito and his people came to like the boy and named him Ojos Puros because of his light blue eyes.

Years passed and all was going well in this enchanted box canyon of raining gold, until one day Ojos Puros came down the mountain and told his father that there wasn't any more gold.

"What do you mean no more gold?" demanded Don Carlos, who now wore fine clothes from Mexico City and boots from Spain.

"All the loose nuggets are gone," said Ojos Puros. "To get more gold, we'd need to dig at the cliff, and that would ruin their spring."

"So do it!" ordered Don Carlos.

"No," said Ojos Puros. "We gave our word not to ruin their spring, Papa."

The rage, the anger, that came to Don Carlos's face would have cowed Ojos Puros a few years before. But it didn't now. So Don Carlos slapped his son until his hand was covered with blood, but still his son never gave in nor did he hit him back. That night Don Carlos drank and ate with such rage that he came down with a terrible stomachache. He slept badly. He had nightmares. And in his sleep he saw an angel of God coming to kill him for having tried to go back on his word.

Three days later, Don Carlos awoke with a fever and he apologized to his son and wife for all the bad he'd done. Then he sold the gold mine to a local rancher who didn't know the meaning of the word "fear." This rancher's name was Bernardo Garcia. The next day Bernardo had a steer knocked down that Don Carlos still owed to the Indians and he had the animal skinned alive so he could keep the valuable hide. Then he forced the naked animal to run up the mountain to Espirito's encampment.

Seeing the naked animal come into their canyon, Espirito and his people were terrified. Bernardo himself cut the steer's throat in front of them, told the Indians that he'd bought the gold mine from Don Carlos, and he put a dozen men to work digging at the cliff. He ruined the spring and, when the Indians complained, he shot them and ran them out of their box canyon, even over Ojos Puros's protests.

Culture Notes

charro cowboy, p. 211

mestizos Mexican people of mixed Spanish and Native American heritage. Along with Native Americans in this story, they are rejected by those who consider themselves "pure" Spanish. p. 212

haciendas country estates, p. 212

In less than five years, Bernardo became a man so rich and powerful that he bought a home in Mexico City among the wealthiest of the world. He became a close friend of the great President Porfirio Diaz himself, and he took a second wife of European breeding, as Don Porfirio had done. Then, in 1903 he sold the mine to an American company from San Francisco, California, for unheard-of millions on Don Porfirio's advice of modernizing Mexico.

The American mining company came in with large equipment and dammed up the Urique River, put in a power plant, and built a road from the coast. The mine came to be officially known as La Lluvia de Oro, "The Rain of Gold," and thousands of poor Mexican people came to the box canyon hoping to get work.

Every six months the Americans loaded thirty-five mules with two sixty-pound bars of gold each and drove the mules out of the canyon and down the mountain to the railhead in El Fuerte. There, the Americans loaded the gold bars on trains and shipped them north to the United States.

THE YEARS PASSED, and the people who lived in the bottom of the box canyon made houses out of stone and lean-tos out of sticks and mud.

The American company prospered, grew, and built permanent buildings inside an enfenced area for their American engineers.

But then, in 1910, a huge meteorite came shooting out of the sky, exploding against the towering walls of the box canyon. The people who lived in the canyon thought it was the end of the world. They prayed and made love, asking God to spare them. And in the morning, when they saw the miracle of the new day, they knew God had, indeed, spared them. They thanked Him, refusing to go to work inside the darkness of the mine anymore.

The Americans became angry, but no matter how much they beat the people, they still could not get them to go back down into the darkness of the devil's domain. Finally, the Americans brought back Bernardo Garcia from Mexico City, and he threatened the people with God and the devil and got them back to work.

THAT SAME YEAR, President Porfirio Diaz used La Lluvia de Oro as one of his examples to show to foreign dignitaries — whom he'd invited to celebrate his eightieth birthday — of how foreign investors could make a profit in helping him modernize Mexico.

The celebration for Don Porfirio's birthday lasted one month, costing the Mexican people more then twenty million dollars in gold. Bernardo Garcia stood alongside Don Porfirio in gold-plated *charro* dress, welcoming the different foreign dignitaries with a present made of pure gold.

Both Don Porfirio and Bernardo wore white powder on their dark Indian faces so that they'd look white-European. No Indians were allowed in Mexico City during the celebration. No mestizos or poor, dark-skinned people. So for thirty days the foreign dignitaries were driven in gold-studded carriages up and down the boulevard of La Reforma in Mexico City, which had been specially built by Don Porfirio to be an exact replica of the main boulevard in Paris, and the foreign visitors only saw beautiful homes, prosperous factories, well-cared-for haciendas and well-to-do European-looking people.

This, then, was the last straw that broke the burro's back. And the poor, hungry people of Mexico rose up in arms by the tens of thousands, breaking Don Porfirio's thirty-year reign, and the Revolution of 1910 began.

Broken-hearted, Espirito and his people watched from the top of the towering cliffs as their beloved box canyon—in which they'd lived peacefully for hundreds of years—turned first into a settlement of electric fences, grey stone buildings and terrible noises, and now into a bloodbath for the soldiers of the Revolution.

Then, one cold, clear morning, Ojos Puros and his Indian wife—he'd married Espirito's youngest daughter—found the legendary Espirito dead up on the towering cliffs. It was said that Espirito had died of grief because he'd misled his people and brought them to ruin.

Ojos Puros and his wife buried Espirito where he'd died so that his soul could look down into their beloved box canyon for all eternity.

RESPONDING

1. **Personal Response** Espirito felt that he had "misled his people and brought them to ruin." Do you agree? Explain.

2. **Literary Analysis** Think about the point that Villaseñor is making in this account. Then explain the *theme*. Why does this seem a fitting introduction to the biography of his parents, who had fled to the United States to escape the horrors of the Mexican Revolution?

3. **Multicultural Connection** Although the American mining company plays a role in the destruction of Espirito's people, prejudice among the people who inhabit northwest Mexico and Mexico City also contributes to their downfall. How?

LANGUAGE WORKSHOP

Word Roots Knowing *word roots* can help you figure out meanings of words in a family. For example, in "Rain of Gold" we read that foreign *dignitaries* visit the box canyon. If you associate this word with others such as *dignity* ("worth, nobility") and *dignify* ("to make worthy") you can probably figure out that *dignitaries* are people of high worth or rank.

Think of one other word in the same family as each of the following italicized words; then try to arrive at the italicized word's meaning.
1. President Diaz *officiated* at his birthday celebration.
2. Miles away dynamite *activated* explosions on the mountainside.
3. It blasted apart a row of rocks at the canyon's *extremity*.

WRITER'S PORTFOLIO

According to an old saying, "Avarice is the root of all evil." In a short essay, explain this proverb. Use examples from this story and from your own experience to illustrate your explanation.

ABOUT **ELIZABETH WONG**

Elizabeth Wong, who grew up in California, majored in journalism at the University of Southern California. After working as a journalist, she earned a degree at the Tisch School of the Arts at New York University. Her first play, *Letters to a Student Revolutionary*, based on her exchange with a Chinese student involved in the demonstrations at Tiananmen Square in 1989, was produced by the Pan Asian Repertory Theater in New York in 1992. Another play, *Kimchee and Chitlins*, had its world premiere in Chicago in 1993. In addition to teaching, Wong moonlights as an editorial columnist for the *Los Angeles Times*. She lives in Los Angeles with her black cat Crusher.

The Struggle
to Be an
All-American Girl

IT'S STILL THERE, the Chinese school on Yale Street where my brother and I used to go. Despite the new coat of paint and the high wire fence, the school I knew 10 years ago remains remarkably, stoically the same.

Every day at 5 P.M., instead of playing with our fourth- and fifth-grade friends or sneaking out to the empty lot to hunt ghosts and animal bones, my brother and I had to go to Chinese school. No amount of kicking, screaming, or pleading could dissuade my mother, who was solidly determined to have us learn the language of our heritage.

Forcibly, she walked us the seven long, hilly blocks from our home to school, depositing our defiant tearful faces before the stern principal. My only memory of him is that he swayed on his heels like a palm tree, and he always clasped his impatient twitching hands behind his back. I recognized him as a repressed maniacal child killer, and knew that if we ever saw his hands we'd be in big trouble.

We all sat in little chairs in an empty auditorium. The room smelled like Chinese medicine, an imported faraway mustiness. Like ancient mothballs or dirty closets. I hated that smell. I favored crisp new scents. Like the soft French perfume that my American teacher wore in public school.

There was a stage far to the right, flanked by an American flag and the flag of the Nationalist Republic of China, which was also red, white and blue but not as pretty.

Although the emphasis at the school was mainly language—speaking, reading, writing—the lessons always began with an exercise in politeness. With the entrance of the teacher, the best student would tap a bell and everyone would get up, kowtow, and chant, "Sing san ho," the phonetic for "How are you, teacher?"

Being ten years old, I had better things to learn than ideographs copied painstakingly in lines that ran right to left from the tip of a *moc but,* a real ink pen that had to be held in an awkward way if blotches were to be avoided. After all, I could do the multiplication tables, name the satellites of Mars, and write reports on *Little Women* and *Black Beauty.* Nancy Drew, my favorite book heroine, never spoke Chinese.

The language was a source of embarrassment. More times than not, I had tried to disassociate myself from the nagging loud voice that followed me wherever I wandered in the nearby American supermarket outside Chinatown. The voice belonged to my grandmother, a fragile woman in her seventies who could outshout the best of the street vendors. Her humor was raunchy, her Chinese rhythmless, patternless. It was quick, it was loud, it was unbeautiful. It was not like the quiet, lilting romance of French or the gentle refinement of the American South. Chinese sounded pedestrian. Public.

In Chinatown, the comings and goings of hundreds of Chinese on their daily tasks sounded chaotic and frenzied. I did not want to be thought of as mad, as talking gibberish. When I spoke English, people nodded at me, smiled sweetly, said encouraging words. Even the people in my culture would cluck and say that I'd do well in life. "My, doesn't she move her lips fast," they would say, meaning that I'd be able to keep up with the world outside Chinatown.

Culture Notes

Nationalist Republic of China country consisting of Taiwan and adjacent islands; not to be confused with the mainland People's Republic of China whose capital is Beijing, p. 215

verb of being the complicated forms of the verb "to be" (I am, you are, he is, . . .) can cause learning difficulties for non-native speakers, p. 217

Cinco de Mayo May 5th, a Mexican national holiday in celebration of Mexico's independence from France, p. 217

My brother was even more fanatical than I about speaking English. He was especially hard on my mother, criticizing her, often cruelly, for her pidgin speech — smatterings of Chinese scattered like chop suey in her conversation. "It's not 'What it is,' Mom," he'd say in exasperation. "It's 'What *is* it, what *is* it, what *is* it!' " Sometimes Mom might leave out an occasional "the" or "a," or perhaps a verb of being. He would stop her in mid-sentence: "Say it again, Mom. Say it right." When he tripped over his own tongue, he'd blame it on her: "See, Mom, it's all your fault. You set a bad example."

What infuriated my mother most was when my brother cornered her on her consonants, especially "r." My father had played a cruel joke on Mom by assigning her an American name that her tongue wouldn't allow her to say. No matter how hard she tried, "Ruth" always ended up "Luth" or "Roof."

After two years of writing with a *moc but* and reciting words with multiples of meanings, I finally was granted a cultural divorce. I was permitted to stop Chinese school.

I thought of myself as multicultural. I preferred tacos to egg rolls; I enjoyed Cinco de Mayo more than Chinese New Year.

At last, I was one of you; I wasn't one of them.
Sadly, I still am.

RESPONDING

1. **Personal Response** How would you describe an "All-American Girl"? How does your description compare with Elizabeth Wong's?

2. **Literary Analysis** *Irony* is a contrast between what is said and what is actually meant. What is ironic about the title of this account?

3. **Multicultural Connection** What mixed messages about language does Wong receive from people in her Chinatown culture and her mother? Do you think speaking two languages can cause problems? Explain.

LANGUAGE WORKSHOP

Underlining *Underline* titles of books, foreign words, and words to be emphasized. In printed matter such as this book, these items are written in *italics*. Why are words italicized in the following sentences: "It's not 'What it is,' Mom," he'd say in exasperation. "It's 'What *is* it, what *is* it, what *is* it.' " Find examples of book titles and a foreign phrase italicized in this selection. Then underline the correct words in the sentences below.
1. Didn't you hear her say stop?
2. Their Eyes Were Watching God is read by many high school students.
3. They said shalom when they left.

WRITER'S PORTFOLIO

Wong says that she thought of herself as "multicultural." Apply this term to yourself in a short biographical sketch entitled "Multicultural Me." To help you focus, consider the language(s) you speak, the religion you practice, the nationalities of your ancestors, and the cultural customs or practices you have adopted from other cultures. Consider also words you use or clothes and music you like that reflect multicultural origins.

ABOUT VERN RUTSALA Vern Rutsala, born in Idaho and educated at Reed College and the State University of Iowa, has taught at Lewis and Clark College in Portland, Oregon, since 1961. The winner of several national awards and fellowships, he published his first volume of poems, *The Window: Poems*, in 1964, and has been writing ever since. In addition to contributing to a number of anthologies and periodicals, Rutsala has acted as editor of poetry publications. His volume, *Selected Poems* (1991), reveals one of his outstanding qualities — the ability to speak in an understated, quiet manner about matters of great significance.

ABOUT DIANE GLANCY Diane Glancy was born in Kansas City, Missouri, to an English-German mother and a father who was part Cherokee. She currently teaches Native American Literature and Creative Writing at Macalester College in St. Paul, Minnesota. Winner of many grants and writing awards, Glancy has published several volumes of poetry, stories, and essays, including *Offering: Poetry and Prose* (1988); *Iron Woman* (1990); and *Claiming Breath* (1992). Glancy says, "I keep thinking why bother with my Native American heritage. What does it matter? Let it go." But then she says that she hears "old footsteps of the ancestors in the leaves of autumn" and is reminded of "a heritage I feel everyday."

Becoming American

VERN RUTSALA

The Yankees needed ditch diggers,
sandhogs, fodder for the wild
hunger of their mills and sent out
invitations with no RSVPs.
My people came then, dimly knowing
they had to cut away the baggage
of the selves they brought with them.
The cutting was strangely easy
as they gaped at clerks smoothing
harsh corners off their names,
docking final vowels like tails.
Distance helped the cutting too—
the ocean roiling behind them
with all that danger and disease,
the old country already swallowed
by the horizon's bulging lead.
At most it was only a village,
a hut, the midden out back
all frozen in the endless winter
of the past. The new language
squeezed more color from that past,
making it shameful—starving winds
and nothingness. They tugged
the new words into their mouths
like odd-shaped and exotic food,
curiously spiced, hard to choke down.
They rolled its oddness on their
tongues, tried to suck the sense
from it and the new ran together
with the old like milk in coffee,
the color changing until the old
was mostly gone, half their lives
dropping off the edge of the world.
Though some—my grandmother, maybe yours—
spat out the venom of the new words

and hung suspended between two
languages, citizens of neither until
they lost both. Most learned the tricks
of getting by—how to count their pay,
the names of tools. Later they
prayed their children would have
no accents, knowing how their own
stubborn tongues kept them alien
and laughable, singsong and brogue
impossible to scrape away.
And then the generations forgot
their way across the muddy wilderness
threshing wheat, scraping coal
from the dark, laying ties, clearing
homesteads with their bare hands.
They clawed away all memories
of the Atlantic and finally reached
the third and fourth generations
where the crops turned ironic.
The old thought it was a kind
of madness. Everything that was so
expensively forgotten, the crumpled
sheets of the past now started singing
like a siren to the young and they
longed for all those lost places.
They wanted the amnesia reversed.
They wanted the erased words back
in their mouths. The destroyed huts,
every ditch and abandoned village
crooned to them, bright and dear
and hopelessly beyond their reach.

---

*

Culture Note

siren in Greek legends a sea nymph, part woman and
part bird, who lured mariners to destruction by seductive
singing, p. 221

Without Title

DIANE GLANCY

for my Father who lived without ceremony

It's hard you know without the buffalo,
the shaman, the arrow,
but my father went out each day to hunt
as though he had them.
He worked in the stockyards.
All his life he brought us meat.
No one marked his first kill,
no one sang his buffalo song.
Without a vision he had migrated to the city
and went to work in the packing house.
When he brought home his horns and hides
my mother said
get rid of them.
I remember the animal tracks of his car
backing out the drive in snow and mud,
the aerial on his old car waving
like a bow string.
I remember the silence of his lost power,
the red buffalo painted on his chest.
Oh, I couldn't see it
but it was there, and in the night I heard
his buffalo grunts like a snore.

✳ Culture Notes

shaman an intermediary to the spirit world, p. 222

buffalo song a song with spiritual and healing powers;
here, the song signals a coming of age associated with
a "first kill", p. 222

RESPONDING

1. **Personal Response** In "Becoming American," Rutsala says that people who immigrated to America "learned the tricks of getting by." What survival tricks have you used to get by in a new environment? Did you earn a place on a new team, make a special friend, retreat in a book, or use some other means of coping? Explain.

2. **Literary Analysis** A *simile* is a comparison between two unlike things, using the words *like* or *as*. Locate two similes in each poem and determine how effective each comparison is.

3. **Multicultural Connection** A sense of loss is apparent in both poems. What cultural losses occur? Is anything gained? Can the losses ever be recovered?

LANGUAGE WORKSHOP

Allusion An *allusion* is a reference to a historical or literary figure or event. It may refer to myth, religion, or to any other aspect of ancient or modern culture. If people called you a Judas, for example, they would be making a biblical allusion comparing you to a traitor. What would it mean if someone were to call you a Romeo? the next Michael Jordan?

Explain how the allusion to the siren in "Becoming American" (See Culture Note, page 221) relates to the young people mentioned in the poem.

WRITER'S PORTFOLIO

Interview someone who has moved to a new country, city, or neighborhood in the past few years. Ask the person to compare and contrast the old and the new settings and explain any adjustments that were made. What was gained and/or lost? Write up the interview as a feature article for a newspaper.

THE CROSSROADS OF CULTURE

Projects

CLASS CROSSROADS CHART

In a celebration of multiculturalism, design and mount a poster-sized Class Crossroads Chart that represents the members of your class. In each quadrant, labeled *National Origins, Languages, Religions,* and one other category of your choosing (for example, *Celebrations* or *Customs)*, indicate the distinctive contributions of your classmates to the cultural mix that is the United States. You will have to do an item inventory of class members, based on the labels you choose, before you fill in the specifics of each quadrant.

CULTURE CROSSROADS GAME

Make up a board game called "Culture Crossroads," to be played with 4 player markers, 32 cards, and a board. Squares on the board lead from a starting point to a destination of your choosing. Make up cards based on selections from the unit ("You have identified Cinco de Mayo. Advance 3 squares." "You have given away the family butter churn. Go back 2 squares." "If you can explain what a piastre is, advance 2 squares. If not, go back 2 squares.") Board squares may have traps and bonuses as well. Players in turn draw a card from the pile to determine their moves.

EXPLORING CONFLICT

One of the fundamental elements of all good writing is conflict, because "only trouble is interesting," as one critic points out. Using three of the selections from this unit, write an essay that explores the nature of the conflicts presented and how they are resolved.

Further Reading

These books all focus on the diverse collection of people living in the United States and on the conflicts and blendings that characterize multiculturalism.

Appleman, Deborah, et al. eds. *Braided Lives: An Anthology of Multicultural American Writing.* Minnesota Humanities Commission, 1991. This collection of works by over forty authors of different cultural backgrounds includes selections that represent the "multiplicity of American views, beliefs, and histories."

Blake, Sara M., and Madden-Simpson, Janet, eds. *Emerging Voices: A Cross-Cultural Reader.* Holt, Rinehart and Winston, 1990. This thematic collection, focusing on immigrant and ethnic experiences in the United States, is aimed at fostering "an awareness of the diverse forces at work in our society."

Brown, Wesley, and Ling, Amy, eds. *Imagining America: Stories from the Promised Land.* Persea Books, 1991. This multicultural anthology includes thirty-seven stories that span the century, depicting the diversity of Americans and the disparity between the realities and myths of America as the promised land.

Momaday, N. Scott. *House Made of Dawn.* Harper & Row, Publishers, 1968. Abel, a young Native American back from war, cannot find a place in white society nor in his ancestral surroundings.

Walker, Scott, ed. *Stories from the American Mosaic.* Graywolf Press, 1990. Fifteen great stories illustrate the interaction and intersecting of divergent cultures of the United States with the mainstream culture.

La Familia: Family Matters

Families come in many varieties — foster, extended, and single-parent, to name only a few. But one distinguishing feature of every family is that its members have some effect on one another. They give advice, support, criticism, and example. They share values, experiences, stories, clothes, food, pain, and joy. As one author in this unit says, families are one of the major forces "that give momentum to our lives."

ABOUT **JULIA ALVAREZ**

Julia Alvarez explains, "Although I was raised in the Dominican Republic by Dominican parents in an extended Dominican family, mine was an American childhood" — a unique combination resulting from her family's American political and educational ties. When her family fled to America in 1960 to escape Dominican political unrest, she felt that she was "coming home at last." Soon, however, she experienced feelings of homesickness and alienation. To help forget her pain, she turned to books and eventually to writing — activities that provided the basis for her career as a poet, fiction writer, and English professor. Alvarez's first volume of poems, *Homecoming,* appeared in 1984. She is best known for her award-winning *How the García Girls Lost Their Accents* (1991).

Daughter of Invention

OR A PERIOD after they arrived in this country, Laura García tried to invent something. Her ideas always came after the sightseeing visits she took with her daughters to department stores to see the wonders of this new country. On his free Sundays, Carlos carted the girls off to the Statue of Liberty or the Brooklyn Bridge or Rockefeller Center, but as far as Laura was concerned, these were men's wonders. Down in housewares were the true treasures women were after.

Laura and her daughters would take the escalator, marveling at the moving staircase, she teasing them that this might be the ladder Jacob saw with angels moving up and down to heaven. The moment they lingered by a display, a perky saleslady approached, no doubt thinking a young mother with four girls in tow fit the perfect profile for the new refrigerator with automatic defrost or the heavy duty washing machine with the prewash soak cycle. Laura paid close attention during the demonstrations, asking intelligent questions, but at the last minute saying she would talk it over with her husband. On the drive home, try as they might, her daughters could not engage their mother in conversation, for inspired by what she had just seen, Laura had begun inventing.

She never put anything actual on paper until she had settled her house down at night. On his side of the bed her husband would be conked out for an hour already, his Spanish newspapers draped over his chest, his glasses propped up on his bedside table, looking out eerily at the darkened room like a disembodied bodyguard. In her lighted corner, pillows propped behind her, Laura sat up inventing. On her lap lay one of those innumerable pads of paper her husband brought home from his office, compliments of some pharmaceutical company, advertising tranquilizers or antibiotics or skin cream. She would be working on a sketch of something familiar but drawn at such close range so she could attach a special nozzle or handier handle, the thing looked peculiar. Her daughters would giggle over the odd doodles they found in kitchen drawers or on the back shelf of the downstairs toilet. Once Yoyo was sure her mother had drawn a picture of a man's you-know-what; she showed her sisters her find, and with coy, posed faces they inquired of their mother what she was up to. *Ay,* that was one of her failures, she explained to them, a child's double-compartment drinking glass with an outsized, built-in straw.

Culture Notes

ladder Jacob saw . . . heaven a biblical reference to Jacob's vision of angels ascending and descending a ladder to heaven, p. 229

Bellevue a hospital in New York City associated with the treatment of mental and emotional problems, p. 231

Thomas Edison . . . Benjamin Franklin noted American inventors, p. 232

ER DAUGHTERS would seek her out at night when she seemed to have a moment to talk to them: they were having trouble at school or they wanted her to persuade their father to give them permission to go into the city or to a shopping mall or a movie — in broad daylight, Mami! Laura would wave them out of her room. "The problem with you girls . . ." The problem boiled down to the fact that they wanted to become Americans and their father — and their mother, too, at first — would have none of it.

"You girls are going to drive me crazy!" she threatened, if they kept nagging. "When I end up in Bellevue, you'll be safely sorry!"

She spoke in English when she argued with them. And her English was a mishmash of mixed-up idioms and sayings that showed she was "green behind the ears," as she called it.

If her husband insisted she speak in Spanish to the girls so they wouldn't forget their native tongue, she'd snap, "When in Rome, do unto the Romans."

Yoyo, the Big Mouth, had become the spokesman for her sisters, and she stood her ground in that bedroom. "We're not going to that school anymore, Mami!"

"You have to." Her eyes would widen with worry. "In this country, it is against the law not to go to school. You want us to get thrown out?"

"You want us to get killed? Those kids were throwing stones today!"

"Sticks and stones don't break bones," she chanted. Yoyo could tell, though, by the look on her face, it was as if one of those stones the kids had aimed at her daughters had hit her. But she always pretended they were at fault. "What did you do to provoke them? It takes two to tangle, you know."

"Thanks, thanks a lot, Mom!" Yoyo stormed out of that room and into her own. Her daughters never called her *Mom* except when they wanted her to feel how much she had failed them in this country. She was a good enough Mami, fussing and scolding and giving advice, but a terrible girlfriend parent, a real failure of a Mom.

Back she went to her pencil and pad, scribbling and tsking and tearing off sheets, finally giving up, and taking up her *New York Times*. Some nights, though, if she got a good idea, she rushed into Yoyo's room, a flushed look on her face, her tablet of paper in her hand, a cursory knock on the door she'd just thrown open. "Do I have something to show you, Cuquita!"

This was Yoyo's time to herself, after she finished her homework, while her sisters were still downstairs watching

TV in the basement. Hunched over her small desk, the overhead light turned off, her desk lamp poignantly lighting only her paper, the rest of the room in warm, soft, uncreated darkness, she wrote her secret poems in her new language.

"You're going to ruin your eyes!" Laura began, snapping on the overly bright overhead light, scaring off whatever shy passion Yoyo, with the blue thread of her writing, had just begun coaxing out of a labyrinth of feelings.

"Oh, Mami!" Yoyo cried out, her eyes blinking at her mother. "I'm writing."

"*Ay,* Cuquita." That was her communal pet name for whoever was in her favor. "Cuquita, when I make a million, I'll buy you your very own typewriter." (Yoyo had been nagging her mother for one just like the one her father had bought to do his order forms at home.) "Gravy on the turkey" was what she called it when someone was buttering her up. She buttered and poured. "I'll hire you your very own typist."

Down she plopped on the bed and held out her pad. "Take a guess, Cuquita?" Yoyo studied the rough sketch a moment. Soap sprayed from the nozzle head of a shower when you turned the knob a certain way? Instant coffee with creamer already mixed in? Time-released water capsules for your potted plants when you were away? A keychain with a timer that would go off when your parking meter was about to expire? (The ticking would help you find your keys easily if you mislaid them.) The famous one, famous only in hindsight, was the stick person dragging a square by a rope—a suitcase with wheels? "Oh, of course," Yoyo said, humoring her. "What every household needs: a shower like a car wash, keys ticking like a bomb, luggage on a leash!" By now, it had become something of a family joke, their Thomas Edison Mami, their Benjamin Franklin Mom.

Her face fell. "Come on now! Use your head." One more wrong guess, and she'd show Yoyo, pointing with her pencil to the different highlights of this incredible new wonder. "Remember that time we took the car to Bear Mountain, and we re-ah-lized that we had forgotten to pack an opener with our pick-a-nick?" (Her daughters kept correcting her, but she insisted this was how it should be said.) "When we were ready to eat we didn't have any way to open the refreshments cans?" (This before fliptop lids, which she claimed had crossed her mind.) "You know what this is now?" Yoyo shook her head. "Is a car bumper, but see this part is a removable can opener. So simple and yet so necessary, eh?"

"Yeah, Mami. You should patent it." Yoyo shrugged as her mother tore off the scratch paper and folded it, carefully, corner to corner, as if she were going to save it. But then, she tossed it in the wastebasket on her way out of the room and gave a little laugh like a disclaimer. "It's half of one or two dozen of another."

*N*ONE OF HER DAUGHTERS was very encouraging. They resented her spending time on those dumb inventions. Here they were trying to fit in America among Americans; they needed help figuring out who they were, why the Irish kids whose grandparents had been micks were calling them spics. Why had they come to this country in the first place? Important, crucial, final things, and here was their own mother, who didn't have a second to help them puzzle any of this out, inventing gadgets to make life easier for the American Moms.

Sometimes Yoyo challenged her. "Why, Mami? Why do it? You're never going to make money. The Americans have already thought of everything, you know that."

"Maybe not. Maybe, just maybe, there's something they've missed that's important. With patience and calm, even a burro can climb a palm." This last was one of her many Dominican sayings she had imported into her scrambled English.

"But what's the point?" Yoyo persisted.

"Point, point, does everything need a point? Why do you write poems?"

Yoyo had to admit it was her mother who had the point there. Still, in the hierarchy of things, a poem seemed much more important than a potty that played music when a toilet-training toddler went in its bowl.

They talked about it among themselves, the four girls, as they often did now about the many puzzling things in this new country.

"Better she reinvents the wheel than be on our cases all the time," the oldest, Carla, observed. In the close quarters of an American nuclear family, their mother's prodigious energy was becoming a real drain on their self-determination. Let her have a project. What harm could she do, and besides, she needed that acknowledgement. It had come to her automatically in the old country from being a de la Torre. "García de la Torre," Laura would enunciate carefully, giving her maiden as well as married name when they first arrived. But the blank smiles had never heard of her name. She would show them. She would prove to these Americans what a smart woman could do with a pencil and pad.

She had a near miss once. Every night, she liked to read *The New York Times* in bed before turning off her light, to see what the Americans were up to. One night, she let out a yelp to wake up her husband beside her. He sat bolt upright, reaching for his glasses which in his haste, he knocked across the room. "*¿Qué pasa? ¿Qué pasa?*" What is wrong? There was terror in his voice, the same fear she'd heard in the Dominican Republic before they left. They had been watched there; he was followed. They could not talk, of course, though they had whispered to each other in fear at night in the dark bed. Now in America, he was safe, a success even; his Centro de Medicina in the Bronx was thronged with the sick and the homesick yearning to go home again. But in dreams, he went back to those awful days and long nights, and his wife's screams confirmed his secret fear: they had not gotten away after all; the SIM had come for them at last.

"Ay, Cuco! Remember how I showed you that suitcase with little wheels so we should not have to carry those heavy bags when we traveled? Someone stole my idea and made a million!" She shook the paper in his face. "See, see! This man was no *bobo*! He didn't put all his pokers on a back burner. I kept telling you, one of these days my ship would pass me by in the night!" She wagged her finger at her husband and daughters, laughing all the while, one of those eerie laughs crazy people in movies laugh. The four girls had congregated in her room. They eyed their mother and each other. Perhaps they were all thinking the same thing, wouldn't it be weird and sad if Mami did end up in Bellevue?

"*¡Ya, ya!*" She waved them out of her room at last. "There is no use trying to drink spilt milk, that's for sure."

It was the suitcase rollers that stopped Laura's hand; she had weathervaned a minor brainstorm. And yet, this plagiarist had gotten all the credit, and the money. What use was it trying to compete with the Americans: they would always have the head start. It was their country, after all. Best stick close to home. She cast her sights about—her daughters ducked—and found her husband's office in need. Several days a week, dressed professionally in a white smock with a little name tag pinned on the lapel, a shopping bag full of cleaning materials and rags, she rode with her husband in his car to the Bronx. On the way, she organized the glove compartment or took off the address stickers from the magazines for the waiting room because she had read somewhere how by means of these stickers drug addict patients found out where doctors lived and burglarized their homes looking for syringes. At night, she did the books, filling in columns with how much money they had made that day. Who had time to be inventing silly things!

*S*HE DID take up her pencil and pad one last time. But it was to help one of her daughters out. In ninth grade, Yoyo was chosen by her English teacher, Sister Mary Joseph, to deliver the Teacher's Day address at the school assembly. Back in the Dominican Republic growing up, Yoyo had been a terrible student. No one could ever get her to sit down to a book. But in New York, she needed to settle somewhere, and since the natives were unfriendly, and the country inhospitable, she took root in the language.

By high school, the nuns were reading her stories and compositions out loud in English class.

But the spectre of delivering a speech brown-nosing the teachers jammed her imagination. At first she didn't want to and then she couldn't seem to write that speech. She should have thought of it as "a great honor," as her father called it. But she was mortified. She still had a slight accent, and she did not like to speak in public, subjecting herself to her classmates' ridicule. It also took no great figuring to see that to deliver a eulogy for a convent full of crazy, old, overweight nuns was no way to endear herself to her peers.

But she didn't know how to get out of it. Night after night, she sat at her desk, hoping to polish off some quick, noncommittal little speech. But she couldn't get anything down.

The weekend before the assembly Monday morning Yoyo went into a panic. Her mother would just have to call in tomorrow and say Yoyo was in the hospital, in a coma.

Laura tried to calm her down. "Just remember how Mister Lincoln couldn't think of anything to say at the Gettysburg, but then bang! *Four score and once upon a time ago,"* she began reciting. "Something is going to come if you just relax. You'll see, like the Americans say, *Necessity is the daughter of invention.* I'll help you."

That weekend, her mother turned all her energy towards helping Yoyo write her speech. "Please, Mami, just leave me alone, please," Yoyo pleaded with her. But Yoyo would get rid of the goose only to have to contend with the gander. Her father kept poking his head in the door just to see if Yoyo had "fulfilled your obligations," a phrase he had used when the girls were younger and he'd check to see whether they had gone to the bathroom before a car trip. Several times that weekend around the supper table, he recited his own high school valedictorian speech. He gave Yoyo pointers on delivery, notes on the great orators and their tricks. (Humbleness and praise and falling silent with great emotion were his favorites.)

Laura sat across the table, the only one who seemed to be listening to him. Yoyo and her sisters were forgetting a lot of their Spanish, and their father's formal, florid diction was hard to understand. But Laura smiled softly to herself, and turned the lazy Susan at the center of the table around and around as if it were the prime mover, the first gear of her attention.

*T*HAT SUNDAY EVENING, Yoyo was reading some poetry to get herself inspired: Whitman's poems in an old book with an engraved cover her father had picked up in a thrift shop next to his office. *I celebrate myself and sing myself. . . . He most honors my style who learns under it to destroy the teacher.* The poet's words shocked and thrilled her. She had gotten used to the nuns, a literature of appropriate sentiments, poems with a message, expurgated texts. But here was a flesh and blood man, belching and laughing and sweating in poems. *Who touches this book touches a man.*

That night, at last, she started to write, recklessly, three, five pages, looking up once only to see her father passing by the hall on tiptoe. When Yoyo was done, she read over her words, and her eyes filled. She finally sounded like herself in English!

As soon as she had finished that first draft, she called her mother to her room. Laura listened attentively while Yoyo read the speech out loud, and in the end, her eyes were glistening too. Her face was soft and warm and proud. "*Ay,* Yoyo, you are going to be the one to bring our name to the headlights in this country! That is a beautiful, beautiful speech. I want for your father to hear it before he goes to sleep. Then I will type it for you, all right?"

Down the hall they went, mother and daughter, faces flushed with accomplishment. Into the master bedroom where Carlos was propped up on his pillows, still awake,

> ✳
> ### *Culture Note*
> **Whitman's poems** Walt Whitman (1819–1892) is considered America's first modern poet for his introduction of free verse and his use of common people as poetic subjects. Whitman's words, "I celebrate . . . destroy the teacher," suggest that one who has truly absorbed knowledge has become self-sufficient, no longer needing an outside teacher. p. 237

reading the Dominican papers, already days old. Now that the dictatorship had been toppled, he had become interested in his country's fate again. The interim government was going to hold the first free elections in thirty years. History was in the making, freedom and hope were in the air again! There was still some question in his mind whether or not he might move his family back. But Laura had gotten used to the life here. She did not want to go back to the old country where, de la Torre or not, she was only a wife and a mother (and a failed one at that, since she had never provided the required son). Better an independent nobody than a high-class houseslave. She did not come straight out and disagree with her husband's plans. Instead, she fussed with him about reading the papers in bed, soiling their sheets with those poorly printed, foreign tabloids. "*The Times* is not that bad!" she'd claim if her husband tried to humor her by saying they shared the same dirty habit.

The minute Carlos saw his wife and daughter filing in, he put his paper down, and his face brightened as if at long last his wife had delivered the son, and that was the news she was bringing him. His teeth were already grinning from the glass of water next to his bedside lamp, so he lisped when he said "Eh-speech, eh-speech!"

"It is so beautiful, Cuco," Laura coached him, turning the sound on his TV off. She sat down at the foot of the bed. Yoyo stood before both of them, blocking their view of the soldiers in helicopters landing amid silenced gun reports and explosions. A few weeks ago it had been the shores of the Dominican Republic. Now it was the jungles of Southeast Asia they were saving. Her mother gave her the nod to begin reading.

Yoyo didn't need much encouragement. She put her nose to the fire, as her mother would have said, and read from start to finish without looking up. When she concluded, she was a little embarrassed at the pride she took in her own words. She pretended to quibble with a phrase or two, then looked questioningly to her mother. Laura's face was radiant. Yoyo turned to share her pride with her father.

The expression on his face shocked both mother and daughter. Carlos's toothless mouth had collapsed into a dark zero. His eyes bored into Yoyo, then shifted to Laura. In barely audible Spanish, as if secret microphones or informers were all about, he whispered to his wife, "You will permit her to read *that?*"

Laura's eyebrows shot up, her mouth fell open. In the old country, any whisper of a challenge to authority could bring the secret police in their black V.W.'s. But this was America. People could say what they thought. "What is wrong with her speech?" Laura questioned him.

"What ees wrrrong with her eh-speech?" Carlos wagged his head at her. His anger was always more frightening in his broken English. As if he had mutilated the language in his fury—and now there was nothing to stand between them and his raw, dumb anger. "What is wrong? I will tell you what is wrong. It show no gratitude. It is boastful. *I celebrate myself? The best student learns to destroy the teacher?*" He mocked Yoyo's plagiarized words. "That is insubordinate. It is improper. It is disrespecting of her teachers—" In his anger he had forgotten his fear of lurking spies: each wrong he voiced was a decibel higher than the last outrage. Finally, he shouted at Yoyo, "As your father, I forbid you to make that eh-speech!"

𝓛AURA LEAPT TO HER FEET, a sign that *she* was about to deliver her own speech. She was a small woman, and she spoke all her pronouncements standing up, either for more projection or as a carry-over from her girlhood in convent schools where one asked for, and literally, took the floor in order to speak. She stood by Yoyo's side, shoulder to shoulder. They looked down at Carlos. "That is no tone of voice—" she began.

But now, Carlos was truly furious. It was bad enough that his daughter was rebelling, but here was his own wife joining forces with her. Soon he would be surrounded by a houseful of independent American women. He too leapt from the bed, throwing off his covers. The Spanish newspapers flew across the room. He snatched the speech out of Yoyo's hands, held it before the girl's wide eyes, a vengeful, mad look in his own, and then once, twice, three, four, countless times, he tore the speech into shreds.

"Are you crazy?" Laura lunged at him. "Have you gone mad? That is her speech for tomorrow you have torn up!"

"Have *you* gone mad?" He shook her away. "You were going to let her read that . . . that insult to her teachers?"

"Insult to her teachers!" Laura's face had crumpled up like a piece of paper. On it was written a love note to her husband, an unhappy, haunted man. "This is America, Papi, America! You are not in a savage country anymore!"

Meanwhile, Yoyo was on her knees, weeping wildly, collecting all the little pieces of her speech, hoping that she could put it back together before the assembly tomorrow morning. But not even a sibyl could have made sense of those tiny scraps of paper. All hope was lost. "He broke it, he broke it," Yoyo moaned as she picked up a handful of pieces.

Probably, if she had thought a moment about it, she would not have done what she did next. She would have realized her father had lost brothers and friends to the dictator Trujillo. For the rest of his life, he would be haunted by blood in the streets and late night disappearances. Even after all these years, he cringed if a black Volkswagen passed him on the street. He feared anyone in uniform: the meter maid giving out parking tickets, a museum guard approaching to tell him not to get too close to his favorite Goya.

On her knees, Yoyo thought of the worst thing she could say to her father. She gathered a handful of scraps, stood up, and hurled them in his face. In a low, ugly whisper, she pronounced Trujillo's hated nickname: "Chapita! You're just another Chapita!"

It took Yoyo's father only a moment to register the loathsome nickname before he came after her. Down the halls they raced, but Yoyo was quicker than he and made it

into her room just in time to lock the door as her father threw his weight against it. He called down curses on her head, ordered her on his authority as her father to open that door! He throttled that doorknob, but all to no avail. Her mother's love of gadgets saved Yoyo's hide that night. Laura had hired a locksmith to install good locks on all the bedroom doors after the house had been broken into once while they were away. Now if burglars broke in again, and the family were at home, there would be a second round of locks for the thieves to contend with.

"Lolo," she said, trying to calm him down. "Don't you ruin my new locks."

Finally he did calm down, his anger spent. Yoyo heard their footsteps retreating down the hall. Their door clicked shut. Then, muffled voices, her mother's rising in anger, in persuasion, her father's deeper murmurs of explanation and self-defense. The house fell silent a moment, before Yoyo heard, far off, the gun blasts and explosions, the serious, self-important voices of newscasters reporting their TV war.

A little while later, there was a quiet knock at Yoyo's door, followed by a tentative attempt at the door knob. "Cuquita?" her mother whispered. "Open up, Cuquita."

"Go away," Yoyo wailed, but they both knew she was glad her mother was there, and needed only a moment's protest to save face.

Together they concocted a speech: two brief pages of stale compliments and the polite commonplaces on teachers, a speech wrought by necessity and without much invention by mother and daughter late into the night on one of the pads of paper Laura had once used for her own inventions. After it was drafted, Laura typed it up while Yoyo stood by, correcting her mother's misnomers and missayings.

Yoyo came home the next day with the success story of the assembly. The nuns had been flattered, the audience had stood up and given "our devoted teachers a standing ovation," what Laura had suggested they do at the end of the speech.

She clapped her hands together as Yoyo recreated the moment. "I stole that from your father's speech, remember? Remember how he put that in at the end?" She quoted him in Spanish, then translated for Yoyo into English.

That night, Yoyo watched him from the upstairs hall window, where she'd retreated the minute she heard his car pull up in front of the house. Slowly, her father came up the driveway, a grim expression on his face as he grappled with a large, heavy cardboard box. At the front door, he set the package down carefully and patted all his pockets for his house keys. (If only he'd had Laura's ticking key chain!) Yoyo heard the snapping open of locks downstairs. She listened as he struggled to maneuver the box through the narrow doorway. He called her name several times, but she did not answer him.

"My daughter, your father, he love you very much," he explained from the bottom of the stairs. "He just want to protect you." Finally, her mother came up and pleaded with Yoyo to go down and reconcile with him. "Your father did not mean to harm. You must pardon him. Always it is better to let bygones be forgotten, no?"

Downstairs, Yoyo found her father setting up a brand new electric typewriter on the kitchen table. It was even better than her mother's. He had outdone himself with all the extra features: a plastic carrying case with Yoyo's initials decaled below the handle, a brace to lift the paper upright while she typed, an erase cartridge, an automatic margin tab, a plastic hood like a toaster cover to keep the dust away. Not even her mother could have invented such a machine!

But Laura's inventing days were over just as Yoyo's were starting up with her school-wide success. Rather than the rolling suitcase everyone else in the family remembers, Yoyo thinks of the speech her mother wrote as her last invention. It was as if, after that, her mother had passed on to Yoyo her pencil and pad and said, "Okay, Cuquita, here's the buck. You give it a shot."

RESPONDING

1. **Personal Response** Parental involvement can be both a pain and a benefit, as this story reveals. Tell about a time when a parent or some other adult tried to help you with an assignment or project. Was this a help or a hindrance? Explain.

2. **Literary Analysis** The narrator refers to Laura García's odd expressions such as "green behind her ears" as "a mishmash of mixed-up idioms." What *idiom* is Laura misquoting? Find four other misquoted idioms and explain how Laura's mistakes help characterize her.

3. **Multicultural Connection** Both Mr. and Mrs. García exhibit certain fears, the product of their lives in the Dominican Republic. What do they fear? In what ways have they overcome their fears in America?

LANGUAGE WORKSHOP

Words as Different Parts of Speech Alvarez writes that Laura had "weathervaned a minor brainstorm." The word *weathervane,* which is usually used as a noun, has been transformed into a verb. There are many English words that can function as different parts of speech. For example, you can put out a *fire,* or *fire* an employee, or paint a *fire*-red sunset.

Write different sentences that use each of the following words as a noun, a verb, and an adjective: *feather, bear, water.*

WRITER'S PORTFOLIO

It's time for Teacher's Day, a day reserved to honor the teachers at your school. Write two short speeches — one that appeals to other students because it "sounds" like you and one designed to endear you to teachers. To help ensure a decided difference, pay attention to word choice, sentence length, and tone.

ABOUT JAMES BALDWIN

Considered one of the finest American writers of this century, James Baldwin had a brilliant career as a playwright, fiction writer, essayist, and social critic. Born and raised in Harlem, he displayed a passion for writing early in life, publishing his first short story at the age of twelve. With several successful books to his credit by the late 1950s, Baldwin's reputation was secure and his responsibility as an artist, "to try to change the world," made clear. Actively involved in the civil rights movement, Baldwin considered his mission "to make freedom real." While still a teenager, he briefly became a preacher, and it is the rhetoric of the pulpit that characterizes his style in "My Dungeon Shook."

My Dungeon Shook

DEAR JAMES:

I HAVE BEGUN this letter five times and torn it up five times. I keep seeing your face, which is also the face of your father and my brother. Like him, you are tough, dark, vulnerable, moody — with a very definite tendency to sound truculent because you want no one to think you are soft. You may be like your grandfather in this, I don't know, but certainly both you and your father resemble him very much physically. Well, he is dead, he never saw you, and he had a terrible life; he was defeated long before he died because, at the bottom of his heart, he really believed what white people said about him. This is one of the reasons that he became so holy. I am sure that your father has told you something about all that. Neither you nor your father exhibit any tendency towards holiness: you really *are* of another era, part of what happened when the Negro left the land and came into what the late E. Franklin Frazier called "the cities of destruction." You can only be destroyed by believing that you really are what the white world calls a *nigger*. I tell you this because I love you, and please don't you ever forget it.

I have known both of you all your lives, have carried your Daddy in my arms and on my shoulders, kissed and spanked him and watched him learn to walk. I don't know if you've known anybody from that far back; if you've loved anybody that long, first as an infant, then as a child, then as a man, you gain a strange perspective on time and human pain and effort. Other people cannot see what I see whenever I look into your father's face, for behind your father's face as it is today are all those other faces which were his. Let him laugh and I see a cellar your father does not remember and a house he does not remember and I hear in his present laughter his laughter as a child. Let him curse and I remember him falling down the cellar steps, and howling, and I remember, with pain, his tears, which my hand or your grandmother's so easily wiped away. But no one's hand can wipe away those tears he sheds invisibly today, which one hears in his laughter and in his speech and in his songs. I know what the world has done to my brother and how narrowly he has survived it. And I know, which is much worse, and this is the crime of which I accuse my country and my countrymen, and for which neither I nor time nor history will ever forgive them, that they have destroyed and are destroying hundreds of thousands of lives and do not know it and do not want to know it. One can be, indeed one must strive to become, tough and philosophical concerning destruction and death, for this is what most of mankind has been best at since we have heard of man. (But remember: *most* of mankind is not *all* of mankind.) But it is not permissible that the authors of devastation should also be innocent. It is innocence which constitutes the crime.

Now, my dear namesake, these innocent and well-meaning people, your countrymen, have caused you to be born under conditions not very far removed from those

✳

Culture Notes

E. Franklin Frazier African American sociologist, teacher, and author who was once appointed to investigate the Harlem riots during the Depression, the time alluded to in the first paragraph, p. 245

Charles Dickens English novelist who explored the terrible living conditions of the poor in 19th century London in his books, p. 247

Homer Greek poet thought to have composed the two great epic poems, *The Iliad* and *The Odyssey*, about 850 B.C., p. 249

described for us by Charles Dickens in the London of more than a hundred years ago. (I hear the chorus of the innocents screaming, "No! This is not true! How *bitter* you are!" — but I am writing this letter to *you*, to try to tell you something about how to handle *them,* for most of them do not yet really know that you exist. I *know* the conditions under which you were born, for I was there. Your countrymen were *not* there, and haven't made it yet. Your grandmother was also there, and no one has ever accused her of being bitter. I suggest that the innocents check with her. She isn't hard to find. Your countrymen don't know that *she* exists, either, though she has been working for them all their lives.)

WELL, YOU WERE BORN, here you came, something like fifteen years ago; and though your father and mother and grandmother, looking about the streets through which they were carrying you, staring at the walls into which they brought you, had every reason to be heavyhearted, yet they were not. For here you were. Big James, named for me — you were a big baby, I was not — here you were: to be loved. To be loved, baby, hard, at once, and forever, to strengthen you against the loveless world. Remember that: I know how black it looks today, for you. It looked bad that day, too, yes, we were trembling. We have not stopped trembling yet, but if we had not loved each other none of us would have survived. And now you must survive because we love you, and for the sake of your children and your children's children.

This innocent country set you down in a ghetto in which, in fact, it intended that you should perish. Let me spell out precisely what I mean by that, for the heart of the matter is here, and the root of my dispute with my country. You were born where you were born and faced the future that you faced because you were black and *for no other reason.* The limits of your ambition were, thus, expected to be set forever. You were born into a society which spelled out with brutal clarity, and in as many ways as possible, that you were a worthless human being. You were not expected to aspire to excellence: you were expected to make peace with mediocrity. Wherever you have turned, James, in your short time on this earth, you have been told where you could go and what you could do (and *how* you could do it) and where you could live and whom you could marry. I know your countrymen do not agree with me about this, and I hear them saying, "You exaggerate." They do not know Harlem, and I do. So do you. Take no one's word for anything, including mine—but trust your experience. Know whence you came. If you know whence you came, there is really no limit to where you can go. The details and symbols of your life have been deliberately constructed to make you believe what white people say about you. Please try to remember that what they believe, as well as what they do and cause you to endure, does not testify to your inferiority but to their inhumanity and fear. Please try to be clear, dear James, through the storm which rages about your youthful head today, about the reality which lies behind the words *acceptance* and *integration*. There is no reason for you to try to become like white people and there is no basis whatever for their impertinent assumption that *they* must accept *you*. The really terrible thing, old buddy, is that *you* must accept *them*. And I mean that very seriously. You must accept them and accept them with love. For these innocent people have no other hope. They are, in effect, still trapped in a history which they do not understand; and until they understand it, they cannot be released from it. They have had to believe for many years, and for innumerable reasons, that black men are inferior to white men. Many of them, indeed, know better, but, as you will discover, people find it very difficult to act on what they know. To act is to be committed, and to be committed is to be in danger. In this case, the danger, in the minds of most white Americans, is the loss of their identity. Try to imagine how you would feel if you woke up one morning to find the sun shining and all the stars aflame. You would be frightened because it is out of the order of nature. Any upheaval in the universe is terrifying because it so profoundly attacks one's sense of one's own reality. Well, the black man has functioned in the white man's world as a fixed star, as an immovable pillar: and as he moves out of his place, heaven and earth are shaken to their foundations. You, don't be afraid. I said that it was intended that you should perish in the ghetto, perish by never being allowed to go behind the white man's definitions, by never being allowed to spell your proper name. You have, and many of us have, defeated this intention; and, by a terrible law, a terrible paradox, those innocents who believed that your imprisonment made them safe are losing their grasp of reality. But these men are your brothers—your lost, younger brothers. And if the word *integration* means anything, this is what it means: that we, with love, shall force our brothers to see themselves as they are, to cease fleeing from reality and begin to change it. For this is your home, my friend, do not be driven from it; great men have done great things here, and will again, and we can make America what America must become. It will be hard, James, but you come from sturdy, peasant stock, men who picked cotton and dammed rivers and built railroads, and, in the teeth of the most terrifying odds, achieved an unassailable and monumental dignity. You come from a long line of great poets, some of the greatest poets since Homer. One of them said, *The very time I thought I was lost, My dungeon shook and my chains fell off.*

You know, and I know, that the country is celebrating one hundred years of freedom one hundred years too soon. We cannot be free until they are free. God bless you, James, and Godspeed.

YOUR UNCLE,

James

RESPONDING

1. **Personal Response** If you were Baldwin's nephew, what would you say in reply to his letter? Remember *he* thinks that you are tough, dark, vulnerable, and moody.

2. **Literary Analysis** What is the *connotation*—or interpretation of a word beyond its literal, dictionary meaning—of *innocent,* as it is used throughout the selection?

3. **Multicultural Connection** What evidence can you find that this letter, written in 1963 on the eve of the one-hundredth anniversary of the Emancipation Proclamation, is addressed to a wider audience than Baldwin's fifteen-year-old nephew?

LANGUAGE WORKSHOP

Adjectives One distinguishing feature of Baldwin's style is his effective use of *adjectives*—words that modify nouns and pronouns. For example, his nephew is characterized by the words *vulnerable* and *truculent.* If you do not know the meanings of these words, consult your glossary. Explain the meanings of the underlined adjectives in the sentences below, using your glossary, if necessary.

1. "You were born into a society which spelled out with <u>brutal</u> clarity . . . that you were a worthless human being."

2. ". . . there is no basis whatever for their <u>impertinent</u> assumption that *they* must accept *you*."

3. "They have had to believe for many years, and for <u>innumerable</u> reasons, that black men are inferior to white men."

4. "Well, the black man has functioned . . . as an <u>immovable</u> pillar. . . ."

5. ". . . you come from sturdy, peasant stock, men who picked cotton and dammed rivers and built railroads, and, in the teeth of the most terrifying odds, achieved an <u>unassailable</u> and <u>monumental</u> dignity."

WRITER'S PORTFOLIO

With two other students, plan an imaginary TV interview with James Baldwin on the topic, "What Freedom Really Means: Past, Present, and Future." One student can assume the role of a TV commentator/interviewer. Another can represent Baldwin, expressing ideas in keeping with those in this selection. The third should act as recorder, writing down the interviewer's questions and Baldwin's responses. If possible, perform the interview for the class.

ABOUT **JOHN OKADA**

John Okada's *No-No Boy* is considered the first authentic Japanese American novel. When it first appeared in 1957, however, it was not popular because it provided a grim reminder of the horrible experiences of Japanese Americans after Pearl Harbor. Born and raised in Seattle, Washington, Okada earned two undergraduate degrees from the University of Washington and a graduate degree in English from Columbia University. He also served as a sergeant in the Air Force during World War II, a time when Japanese Americans interned in relocation camps were forced to answer a "loyalty questionnaire." In 1971, Okada died in obscurity, believing that his work was unrecognized and rejected, even by Asian Americans. Shortly thereafter, however, *No-No Boy* began to earn the prominence it deserves.

From No-No Boy

HOME FOR KENJI was an old frame, two-story, seven-room house which the family rented for fifty dollars a month from a Japanese owner who had resettled in Chicago after the war and would probably never return to Seattle. It sat on the top of a steep, unpaved hill and commanded an uninspiring view of clean, gray concrete that was six lanes wide and an assortment of boxy, flat store buildings and spacious super gas-stations.

Kenji eased the car over into the left-turn lane and followed the blinking green arrow toward the hill. At its foot, he braked the car almost to a full stop before carefully starting up, for the sharp angle of the hill and the loose dirt necessitated skill and caution.

As he labored to the top, he saw his father sitting on the porch reading a newspaper. Before he could depress the horn ring, the man looked up and waved casually. He waved back and steered the Oldsmobile into the driveway.

When he walked around the side of the house and came up front, the father said "Hello, Ken" as matter-of-

About the Title

In 1943, a "loyalty questionnaire" administered to Japanese Americans confined in relocation camps asked if internees would: (1) be willing to serve in the American armed forces; (2) forswear allegiance to Japan. Most people responded yes to both questions. Ichiro, the main character of the novel, however, responded "No, No," thus refusing the draft.

factly as if he had seen his son a few hours previously, and returned his attention to the newspaper to finish the article he had been reading.

"Who's home, Pop?" he asked, holding out the bag.

"Nobody," said the father, taking the present and looking into the bag. It held two fifths of good blended whisky. He was a big man, almost six feet tall and strong. As a painter and paper hanger he had no equal, but he found it sufficient to work only a few days a week and held himself to it, for his children were all grown and he no longer saw the need to drive himself. He smiled warmly and gratefully: "Thank you."

"Sure, Pop. One of these days, I'll bring home a case."

"Last me two days. Better bring a truckful," he said, feigning seriousness.

*T*HEY LAUGHED together comfortably, the father because he loved his son and the son because he both loved and respected his father, who was a moderate and good man. They walked into the house, the father making the son precede him.

In the dining room the father deposited the two new bottles with a dozen others in the china cabinet. "I'm fixed for a long time," he said. "That's a good feeling."

"You're really getting stocked up," said Kenji.

"The trust and faith and love of my children," he said proudly. "You know I don't need clothes or shaving lotion in fancy jars or suitcases or pajamas, but whisky I can use. I'm happy."

"Are you, Pop?"

The father sat down opposite his son at the polished mahogany table and took in at a glance the new rugs and furniture and lamps and the big television set with the radio and phonograph all built into one impressive, blond console. "All I did was feed you and clothe you and spank you once in a while. All of a sudden, you're all grown up. The government gives you money, Hisa and Toyo are married to fine boys, Hana and Tom have splendid jobs, and

Eddie is in college and making more money in a part-time job than I did for all of us when your mother died. No longer do I have to work all the time, but only two or three days a week and I have more money than I can spend. Yes, Ken, I am happy and I wish your mother were here to see all this."

"I'm happy too, Pop." He shifted his legs to make himself comfortable and winced unwillingly.

Noticing, the father screwed his face as if the pain were in himself, for it was. Before the pain turned to sorrow, before the suffering for his son made his lips quiver as he held back the tears, he hastened into the kitchen and came back with two jigger-glasses.

"I am anxious to sample your present," he said jovially, but his movements were hurried as he got the bottle from the cabinet and fumbled impatiently with the seal.

Kenji downed his thankfully and watched his father take the other glass and sniff the whisky appreciatively before sipping it leisurely. He lifted the bottle toward his son.

"No more, Pop," refused Kenji. "That did it fine."

The father capped the bottle and put it back. He closed the cabinet door and let his hand linger on the knob as if ashamed of himself for having tried to be cheerful when he knew that the pain was again in his son and the thought of death hovered over them.

"Pop."

"Yes?" He turned slowly to face his son.

"Come on. Sit down. It'll be all right."

Sitting down, the father shook his head, saying: "I came to America to become a rich man so that I could go back to the village in Japan and be somebody. I was greedy and ambitious and proud. I was not a good man or an intelligent one, but a young fool. And you have paid for it."

"What kind of talk is that?" replied Kenji, genuinely grieved. "That's not true at all."

"That is what I think nevertheless. I am to blame."

"It'll be okay, Pop. Maybe they won't even operate."

"When do you go?"

"Tomorrow morning."

"I will go with you."

"No." He looked straight at this father.

In answer, the father merely nodded, acceding to his son's wish because his son was a man who had gone to war to fight for the abundance and happiness that pervaded a Japanese household in America and that was a thing he himself could never fully comprehend except to know that it was very dear. He had long forgotten when it was that he had discarded the notion of a return to Japan but remembered only that it was the time when this country which he had no intention of loving had suddenly begun to become a part of him because it was a part of his children and he saw and felt it in their speech and joys and sorrows and hopes and he was a part of them. And in the dying of the foolish dreams which he had brought to America, the richness of the life that was possible in this foreign country destroyed the longing for a past that really must not have been as precious as he imagined or else he would surely not have left it. Where else could a man, left alone with six small children, have found it possible to have had so much with so little? He had not begged or borrowed or gone to the city for welfare assistance. There had been times of hunger and despair and seeming hopelessness, but did it not mean something now that he could look around and feel the love of the men and women who were once only children?

And there was the one who sat before him, the one who had come to him and said calmly that he was going into the army. It could not be said then that it mattered not that he was a Japanese son of Japanese parents. It had mattered. It was because he was Japanese that the son had to come to his Japanese father and simply state that he had decided to volunteer for the army instead of being able to wait until such time as the army called him. It was because he was Japanese and, at the same time, had to prove to the world that he was not Japanese that the turmoil was in his soul and urged him to enlist. There was confusion, but, underneath it, a conviction that he loved America and would fight and die for it because he did not wish to live anyplace else. And the father, also confused, understood what the son had not said and gave his consent. It was not a time for clear thinking because the sense of loyalty had become dispersed and the shaken faith of an American interned in an American concentration camp was indeed a flimsy thing. So, on this steadfast bit of conviction that remained, and knowing not what the future held, this son had gone to war to prove that he deserved to enjoy those rights which should rightfully have been his.

$\mathscr{A}$ND HE REMEMBERED that a week after Kenji had gone to a camp in Mississippi, the neighbor's son, an American soldier since before Pearl Harbor, had come to see his family which was in a camp enclosed by wire fencing and had guards who were American soldiers like himself. And he had been present when the soldier bitterly spoke of how all he did was dump garbage and wash dishes and take care of the latrines. And the soldier swore and ranted and could hardly make himself speak of the time when the president named Roosevelt had come to the camp in Kansas and all the American soldiers in the camp who were Japanese had been herded into a warehouse and guarded by other American soldiers with machine guns until the president named Roosevelt had departed. And he had gone to his own cubicle with the seven steel cots and the potbellied stove and the canvas picnic-chairs from Sears Roebuck and cried for Kenji, who was now a soldier and would not merely turn bitter and swear if the army let him do only such things as the soldier had spoken of, but would be driven to protest more violently because he was the quiet one with the deep feelings whose anger was a terrible thing. But, with training over, Kenji had written that he was going to Europe, and the next letter was from Italy, where the Americans were fighting the Germans, and he found relief in the knowledge, partly because Kenji was fighting and he knew that was what his son wished and partly because the enemy was German and not Japanese.

He thought he remembered that he had not wanted Kenji to go into the army. But when he was asked, he had said yes. And so this son had come back after long months in a hospital with one good leg and another that was only a stick where the other good one had been. Had he done right? Should he not have forbidden him? Should he not have explained how it was not sensible for Japanese to fight a war against Japanese? If what he had done was wrong, how was it so and why?

"Would you," he said to his son, "have stayed out of the army if I had forbidden it?"

Kenji did not answer immediately, for the question came as a surprise to disturb the long, thought-filled silence. "I don't think so, Pop," he started out hesitantly. He paused, delving into his mind for an explanation, then said with great finality: "No, I would have gone anyway."

"Of course," said the father, finding some assurance in the answer.

Kenji pushed himself to a standing position and spoke gently: "You're not to blame, Pop. Every time we get to talking like this, I know you're blaming yourself. Don't do it. Nobody's to blame, nobody."

"To lose a leg is not the worst thing, but, to lose a part of it and then a little more and a little more again until . . . Well, I don't understand. You don't deserve it." He shrugged his shoulders wearily against the weight of his terrible anguish.

"I'm going up to take a nap." He walked a few steps and turned back to his father. "I'll go upstairs and lie down on the bed and I won't sleep right away because the leg will hurt a little and I'll be thinking. And I'll think that if things had been different, if you had been different, it might have been that I would also not have been the same and maybe you would have kept me from going into the war and I would have stayed out and had both my legs. But, you

About Japanese Americans

relocation center During World War II, Americans of Japanese descent were "relocated" into camps away from both coasts, ostensibly to protect the internees, but actually because the U.S. distrusted their loyalty. Their homes and possessions were confiscated and their civil rights violated. In recent years, the U.S. government has acknowledged the injustices of relocation and has made attempts to compensate survivors for some of their losses. p. 259

know, every time I think about it that way, I also have to think that, had such been the case, you and I would probably not be sitting down and having a drink together and talking or not talking as we wished. If my leg hurts, so what? We're buddies, aren't we? That counts. I don't worry about anything else."

Up in his room, he stretched out on his back on the bed and thought about what he had said to his father. It made a lot of sense. If, in the course of things, the pattern called for a stump of a leg that wouldn't stay healed, he wasn't going to decry the fact, for that would mean another pattern with attendant changes which might not be as perfectly desirable as the one he cherished. Things are as they should be, he assured himself, and, feeling greatly at peace, sleep came with surprising ease.

*A*FTER KENJI had left him, the father walked down the hill to the neighborhood Safeway and bought a large roasting chicken. It was a fat bird with bulging drumsticks and, as he headed back to the house with both arms supporting the ingredients of an ample family feast, he thought of the lean years and the six small ones and the pinched, hungry faces that had been taught not to ask for more but could not be taught how not to look hungry when they were in fact quite hungry. And it was during those years that it seemed as if they would never have enough.

But such a time had come. It had come with the war and the growing of the children and it had come with the return of the thoughtful son whose terrible wound paid no heed to the cessation of hostilities. Yet, the son had said he was happy and the father was happy also for, while one might grieve for the limb that was lost and the pain that endured, he chose to feel gratitude for the fact that the son had come back alive even if only for a brief while.

And he remembered what the young sociologist had said in halting, pained Japanese at one of the family-relations meetings he had attended while interned in the relocation center because it was someplace to go. The instructor was a recent college graduate who had later left the camp to do graduate work at a famous Eastern school. He, short fellow that he was, had stood on an orange crate so that he might be better heard and seen by the sea of elderly men and women who had been attracted to the mess hall because they too had nothing else to do and nowhere else to go. There had been many meetings, although it had early become evident that lecturer and audience were poles apart, and if anything had been accomplished it was that the meetings helped to pass the time, and so the instructor continued to blast away at the unyielding wall of indifference and the old people came to pass an hour or two. But it was on this particular night that the small sociologist, struggling for the words painstakingly and not always correctly selected from his meager knowledge of the Japanese language, had managed to impart a message of great truth. And this message was that the old Japanese , the fathers and mothers, who sat courteously attentive, did not know their own sons and daughters.

"How many of you are able to sit down with your own sons and own daughters and enjoy the companionship of conversation? How many, I ask? If I were to say none of you, I would not be far from the truth." He paused, for the grumbling was swollen with anger and indignation, and continued in a loud, shouting voice before it could engulf him: "You are not displeased because of what I said but because I have hit upon the truth. And I know it to be true because I am a Nisei and you old ones are like my own father and mother. If we are children of America and not the sons and daughters of our parents, it is because you have failed. It is because you have been stupid enough to think that growing rice in muddy fields is the same as growing a giant fir tree. Change, now, if you can, even if it may be too late, and become companions to your children. This is America, where you have lived and

✳
About Japanese Americans

Nisei (nē′sā′) person born in the United States or Canada whose parents were Japanese immigrants, p. 260. See also Language Workshop, p. 267.

worked and suffered for thirty and forty years. This is not Japan. I will tell you what it is like to be an American boy or girl. I will tell you what the relationship between parents and children is in an American family. As I speak, compare what I say with your own families." And so he had spoken and the old people had listened and, when the meeting was over, they got up and scattered over the camp toward their assigned cubicles. Some said they would attend no more lectures; others heaped hateful abuse upon the young fool who dared to have spoken with such disrespect; and then there was the elderly couple, the woman silently following the man, who stopped at another mess hall, where a dance was in progress, and peered into the dimly lit room and watched the young boys and girls gliding effortlessly around to the blaring music from a phonograph. Always before, they had found something to say about the decadent ways of an amoral nation, but, on this evening, they watched longer than usual and searched longingly to recognize their own daughter, whom they knew to be at the dance but who was only an unrecognizable shadow among the other shadows. . . .

Halting for a moment to shift the bag, Kenji's father started up the hill with a smile on his lips. He was glad that the market had had such a fine roasting chicken. There was nothing as satisfying as sitting at a well-laden table with one's family whether the occasion was a holiday or a birthday or a home-coming of some member or, yes, even if it meant someone was going away.

Please come back, Ken, he said to himself, please come back and I will have for you the biggest, fattest chicken that ever graced a table, American or otherwise.

HANAKO, who was chubby and pleasant and kept books for three doctors and a dentist in a downtown office, came home before Tom, who was big and husky like his father and had gone straight from high school into a drafting job at an aircraft plant. She had seen the car in the driveway and smelled the chicken in the oven and, smiling sympathetically with the father, put a clean cloth on the table and took out the little chest of Wm. & Rogers Silverplate.

While she was making the salad, Tom came home bearing a bakery pie in a flat, white box. "Hello, Pop, Sis," he said, putting the box on the table. "Where's Ken?"

"Taking a nap," said Hanako.

"Dinner about ready?" He sniffed appreciatively and rubbed his stomach in approval.

"Just about," smiled his sister.

"Psychic, that's what I am."

"What?"

"I say I'm psychic. I brought home a lemon meringue. Chicken and lemon meringue. Boy! Don't you think so?"

"What's that?"

"About my being psychic."

"You're always bringing home lemon meringue. Coincidence, that's all."

"How soon do we eat?"

"I just got through telling you — in a little while," she replied a bit impatiently.

"Good. I'm starved. I'll wash up and rouse the boy." He started to head for the stairs but turned back thoughtfully. "What's the occasion?" he asked.

"Ken has to go to the hospital again," said the father kindly. "Wash yourself at the sink and let him sleep a while longer. We will eat when he wakes up."

"Sure," said Tom, now sharing the unspoken sadness and terror which abided in the hearts of his father and sister. He went to the sink and, clearing it carefully of the pots and dishes, washed himself as quietly as possible.

It was a whole hour before Kenji came thumping down the stairs. It was the right leg, the good one, that made the thumps which followed the empty pauses when the false leg was gently lowered a step. When he saw the family sitting lazily around the table, he knew that they had waited for him.

"You shouldn't have waited," he said, a little embarrassed. "I slept longer than I intended."

"We're waiting for the chicken," lied the father. "Takes time to roast a big one."

Hanako agreed too hastily: "Oh, yes, I've never known a chicken to take so long. Ought to be just about ready now." She trotted into the kitchen and, a moment later, shouted back: "It's ready. Mmmm, can you smell it?"

"That's all I've been doing," Tom said with a famished grin. "Let's get it out here."

"Sorry I made you wait," smiled Kenji at his brother.

Tom, regretting his impatience, shook his head vigorously. "No, it's the bird, like Pop said. You know how he is. Always gets 'em big and tough. This one's made of cast iron." He followed Hanako to help bring the food from the kitchen.

*N*O ONE SAID MUCH during the first part of the dinner. Tom ate ravenously. Hanako seemed about to say something several times but couldn't bring herself to speak. The father kept looking at Kenji without having to say what it was that he felt for his son. Surprisingly, it was Tom who broached the subject which was on all their minds.

"What the hell's the matter with those damn doctors?" He slammed his fork angrily against the table.

"Tom, please," said Hanako, looking deeply concerned.

"No, no, no," he said, gesturing freely with his hands, "I won't please shut up. If they can't fix you up, why don't they get somebody who can? They're killing you. What do they do when you go down there? Give you aspirins?" Slumped in his chair, he glared furiously at the table.

The father grasped Tom's arm firmly. "If you can't talk sense, don't."

"It's okay, Tom. This'll be a short trip. I think it's just that the brace doesn't fit right."

"You mean that?" He looked hopefully at Kenji.

"Sure. That's probably what it is. I'll only be gone a few days. Doesn't really hurt so much, but I don't want to take any chances."

"Gee, I hope you're right."

"I ought to know. A few more trips and they'll make me head surgeon down there."

"Yeah," Tom smiled, not because of the joke, but because he was grateful for having a brother like Kenji.

"Eat," reminded the father, "baseball on television tonight, you know."

"I'll get the pie," Hanako said and hastened to the kitchen.

"Lemon meringue," said Tom hungrily, as he proceeded to clean up his plate.

The game was in its second inning when they turned the set on, and they had hardly gotten settled down when Hisa and Toyo came with their husbands and children.

Tom grumbled good naturedly and, giving the newcomers a hasty nod, pulled up closer to the set, preparing to watch the game under what would obviously be difficult conditions.

Hats and coats were shed and piled in the corner and everyone talked loudly and excitedly, as if they had not seen each other for a long time. Chairs were brought in from the dining room and, suddenly, the place was full and noisy and crowded and comfortable.

The father gave up trying to follow the game and bounced a year-old granddaughter on his knee while two young grandsons fought to conquer the other knee. The remaining three grandchildren were all girls, older, more well-behaved, and they huddled on the floor around Tom to watch the baseball game.

Hisa's husband sat beside Kenji and engaged him in conversation, mostly about fishing and about how he'd like to win a car in the Salmon Derby because his was getting old and a coupe wasn't too practical for a big family. He had the four girls and probably wouldn't stop until he hit a boy and things weren't so bad, but he couldn't see his way to acquiring a near-new used car for a while. And then he got up and went to tell the same thing to his father-in-law, who was something of a fisherman himself. No sooner had he moved across the room than Toyo's husband, who was soft-spoken and mild but had been a captain in the army and sold enough insurance to keep two cars in the double garage behind a large brick house in a pretty good neighborhood, slid into the empty space beside Kenji and asked him how he'd been and so on and talked about a lot of other things when he really wanted to talk to Kenji about the leg and didn't know how.

Then came the first lull when talk died down and the younger children were showing signs of drowsiness and everyone smiled thoughtfully and contentedly at one another. Hanako suggested refreshments, and when the coffee and milk and pop and cookies and ice cream were distributed, everyone got his second wind and immediately discovered a number of things which they had forgotten to discuss.

Kenji, for the moment alone, looked at all of them and said to himself: Now's as good a time as any to go. I won't wait until tomorrow. In another thirty minutes Hana and Toyo and the kids and their fathers will start stretching and heading for their hats and coats. Then someone will say "Well, Ken" in a kind of hesitant way and, immediately, they will all be struggling for something to say about my going to Portland because Hana called them and told them to come over because I'm going down there again and that's why they'll have to say something about it. If I had said to Pop that I was going the day after tomorrow, we would have had a big feast with everyone here for it tomorrow night. I don't want that. There's no need for it. I don't want Toyo to cry and Hana to dab at her eyes and I don't want everyone standing around trying to say goodbye and not being able to make themselves leave because maybe they won't see me again.

He started to get up and saw Hanako looking at him. "I'm just going to get a drink," he said.

"Stay, I'll get it," she replied.

"No. It'll give me a chance to stretch." He caught his father's eye and held it for a moment.

Without getting his drink, he slipped quietly out to the back porch and stood and waited and listened to the voices inside.

He heard Hisa's husband yell something to one of his girls and, the next minute, everyone was laughing amusedly. While he was wondering what cute deviltry the guilty one had done, his father came through the kitchen and out to stand beside him.

"You are going."

Kenji looked up and saw the big shoulders sagging wearily. "I got a good rest, Pop. This way, I'll be there in the morning and it's easier driving at night. Not so many cars, you know."

"It's pretty bad this time, isn't it?"

"Yes," he said truthfully, because he could not lie to his father, "it's not like before, Pop. It's different this time. The pain is heavier, deeper. Not sharp and raw like the other times. I don't know why. I'm scared."

"If . . . if . . ." Throwing his arm around his son's neck impulsively, the father hugged him close. "You call me every day. Every day, you understand?"

"Sure, Pop. Explain to everyone, will you?" He pulled himself free and looked at his father nodding, unable to speak.

Pausing halfway down the stairs, he listened once more for the voices in the house.

Hoarsely, in choked syllables, his father spoke to him: "Every day, Ken, don't forget. I will be home."

"Bye, Pop." Feeling his way along the dark drive with his cane, he limped to the car. Behind the wheel, he had to sit and wait until the heaviness had lifted from his chest and relieved the mistiness of his eyes. He started the motor and turned on the headlights and their brilliant glare caught fully the father standing ahead. Urged by an overwhelming desire to rush back to him and be with him for a few minutes longer, Kenji's hand fumbled for the door handle. At that moment, the father raised his arm once slowly in farewell. Quickly, he pulled back out of the driveway and was soon out of sight of father and home and family.

RESPONDING

1. **Personal Response** Do you think Kenji really had to join the army in order to prove himself? Why or why not? If you had a friend who planned to enlist for the same reasons, what would you say to that friend?

2. **Literary Analysis** In much of this story, Okada conveys the thoughts of Kenji and his father. Examine the paragraph that begins "And he remembered that . . ." (page 257). Then tell how the words, ideas, and *prose* rhythms imitate random thoughts.

3. **Multicultural Connection** Why does Kenji's father feel guilty? What are Kenji and his father's respective attitudes toward America? toward each other?

LANGUAGE WORKSHOP

Specialized Vocabulary People who migrate from Japan to the United States or Canada are *Issei* (ēs′sā′), or first generation. *Nisei* (nē′sā′), meaning second generation, are people born in the United States or Canada whose parents were Japanese immigrants. The children of *Nisei* are *Sansei* (sän′sā′), or third generation. What do you think *Yonsei* means? Which name applies to Kenji? to his father?

WRITER'S PORTFOLIO

The young sociologist in the relocation camp tells the old people that they must be companions to their children, understand them, and converse with them — as American parents do. Do you agree or disagree that American family members communicate and understand one another? Write an essay supporting your point of view, using personal observations.

ABOUT **CARMEN TAFOLLA**

Carmen Tafolla (**tä foi′yä**) was born and raised in San Antonio, Texas, and she credits the "magic" of her west-side barrio and the stories of elderly relatives for her own story-telling style. Her junior high school principal told her she had "potential to make it all the way to high school" if she'd just quit speaking Spanish. One Ph.D. (in bilingual education) later, she lives with her husband, her children Mari and Israel, her mother, three cats, a computer, and a houseful of books, wooden boxes, and herbs, along with the voices of all the people of her barrio, past and present. Tafolla has traveled through Europe and the U.S. performing her one-woman show in which she dramatizes an old lady, a high school student, a first-grader, a *pachuca* and other barrio characters from her writing.

Mi Familia

I KNOW when I began — or at least when I was born, on July 29th, 1951, at 8:41 P.M. — but that isn't really the whole story. My beginnings were somehow rooted in memories passed on to me through my grandmother's sayings and my father's songs, and my mother's stories, and in some mountains that I saw once from the highway, and in the thread of a dream below the voice and between the words of someone whose name I don't know but whose voice and dream I still carry.

The way I defined family was much like the old funerals I remember. In the front rows were the next of kin, the most greatly affected by the loss, behind them those close, behind them the friends, then the acquaintances, and always, somewhere, the people of whom no one knew the exact relationship to the departed, but that didn't matter — those people knew, and that was enough reason to be there. In fact, one's own internal reasons were the guiding law for anyone's presence, and no one had to make explanations at a time like that. Modern "family sections" later served to cut off, to make people separate off, who was family from who wasn't, who was "immediate family" from who was "distant." None of this was necessary in the old Mexicano funerals I remembered. The cousin (*prima hermana*, to emphasize how close the relationship really was) who'd spent eighty years of her life with the deceased didn't have to be turned away from the three skimpy rows of "Family

Section" just in order to allow room for younger siblings and spouse, nieces and nephews, who'd only spent twenty to sixty-some-odd years with the deceased. There was no having to judge "degree" of relationship, in competition with the others present. One merely found one's place according to one's own intuition.

Family was like that. There was the little boy in second grade that I was proud to claim as my "third step cousin-in-law" and there were the friends for whom no blood connection existed, but who counted in every way as cousins, to whom there was a life-long commitment and a life-long connection.

It was a big family. It seemed I had several dozen aunts and uncles, and at least fifty of the immediate cousins. It was a context that provided variety and contrast. "Somos como los frijoles pintos," my grandmother would say, "algunos güeros, algunos morenos, y algunos con pecas." (We're like pinto beans in this family — some light, some dark, and some with freckles.) I knew my grandmother so well, through all her sayings, but these had been told to me by my father, years after her death. I knew her through my father, even the details of her death, a death that happened shortly after my first birthday. Still, she guides me through many days, telling me "No hay sábado sin sol ni domingo sin misa." (There's no Saturday that doesn't have some sunshine, no Sunday that doesn't have a Mass.) Still, she warns me "Díme con quien andas y te diré quien eres." (Tell me who you hang around with, and I'll tell you who you are.)

She was from Mexico, a proud, quiet woman, who spoke little and said much, whose skirts always touched the ground, who never raised her voice or lowered her sense of dignity. Her high cheekbones were echoed in my father's face and in my own. I find it hard to imagine her as a noisy child, as a noisy anything.

My grandfather, on the other hand, lived by words, words were his tools, and he was a man who valued tools. "Cómprate un fierro con cada día de pago" (Buy yourself one tool every payday), he gave my father as *consejo*, and he taught his sons carpentry, plumbing, construction, and a hunger to build things. My father would later teach me, perhaps more randomly than he would have constructed the lessons for a boy, but still I knew how to use a hammer and a drill, how to putty the nail holes and clean a carburetor, and most importantly, how to hunger to build things. Had the training been less random, less riddled with gaps, I would have known *how* to build things. As it is, I sit with pen and paper today, and try to plan and guess how I could put together a table or a house, how to do it right, for it would not do to make one not solid, not "*macizo.*"

Yet my grandfather's main occupation in life was using words as tools. The preacher, teacher, leader, he was the first in the family (possibly in the whole barrio) to own a typewriter. I don't know how old he was when he got it, but it was still his, marked with his work and his determination, used solidly and squarely as any of his tools, the fountain of many letters, that somehow always looked as individual as if he'd marked them by fountain pen and fingerprint.

*H*IS NAME WAS MARIANO TAFOLLA. It was his grandfather's name, my father's name, and my father's oldest brother's name. Searching through the Santa Fe archives a few years ago, I found his grandfather's signature. It was almost a duplicate of my father's. I keep the name Tafolla, although my signature, perhaps even my personality, is far different. Perhaps it has something to do with words. With finding your place in the old Mexicano funerals, by internal guide, by intuition. This is who I am.

I have always considered my life one of great fortune, and the barrio was one of these points of fortune. It was a place rich in story and magic, warmth and wisdom. So magic it was that even the police would not come there, despite calls or complaints, unless they came in twos, with their car doors locked. We played baseball in the streets, shot off firecrackers on the Fourth of July, and raised our Easter chicks to fully grown (and temporarily spoiled) chickens.

When I was, years later, to hear about slums and ghettos, cultural deprivation, and poverty-warped childhoods — there was no identification in my mind with these. In our own view, we were wealthy — we had no deprivation of cultural experiences, but rather a double dose of *cultura*. Yes, my cousins from "up north" would come to visit, and they had so many more "facts" at hand, seemed to know so much and do so much in their schools. Our school had no interscholastic activities, no spelling bees or science fairs, no playground equipment, nor even a fence.

*T*HE MAIN THING the schools tried to teach us was not to speak Spanish. The main thing we learned was not to speak Spanish in front of the teachers, and not to lose Spanish within ourselves. Perhaps that is why so many good independent and critical minds came out of that time period. Or perhaps that is why so many good independent and critical minds dropped out of school. We learned — oh, did we learn, but it was not what the school district had planned for us to learn. It was much bigger than that.

We became filled with a hunger — I call it now, sometimes, Latino Hunger. A hunger to see ourselves, our families and friends, our values and lives and realities reflected in something other than our own minds. We wanted proof that we really existed — a proof documented in those many schoolbooks filled with Toms and Susans, and Dicks and Janes, but no Chuys or Guadalupes or Juanas, no Adelitas or Santos or Esperanzas. And we definitely needed Esperanzas, if we were to dream of anything at all beyond the sirens, the friskings, and the punishments for the sin of having spoken Spanish at school. There was a hunger and a place in our lives that needed to be filled with Esperanzas and Milagros.

So what we didn't see, we invented. Even the national anthem became our cultural playground: "Jo—o—sé, can you see—ee?" And we filled TV with our own *raza*, hidden between the lines and in the shadows of people's pasts.

My roots in New Mexico go back for centuries—*españoles* arriving in the 17th century to *indios parientes* already there. The move to Texas happened between 1848 and 1865 (a few wars got in the way, causing strange demographic reshuffles). My great-great-grandmother was already there, and had a seamstress shop in "downtown" San Antonio; my great-grandmother washed clothes in the San Antonio River; her *tío* had brought word in 1836 to Juan Segúin and the *tejanos* at the Alamo that Santa Ana's army was coming in great force. (They didn't listen.) She later married two (one at a time) Confederate veterans. Growing up, I teased that I had relatives on all sides of all wars.

The Tafollas' roots were in New Mexico, the Salinas' in San Antonio, the Sánchez' in Montemorelos, the Duartes' and Morenos' in Spain, but somehow it was San Antonio that won out. San Antonio is in my blood. Maybe that's because its earth was worn smooth by so many first-step baby feet kissed by mothers before my mother. Maybe because its air was charged by the anger and tension and passion of fights between family members and then warmed by the *abrazos* between them, healing their hearts. Maybe it's that the sunshine captured the laughter, or the river collected the tears from my own eyes and a thousand crying family eyes before me, and then returned the same life-moisture in rain to celebrate, and in honest sweat from good work done. Maybe it's the softness of the grass, the softness of the earth, that holds the softness

Spanish Words

consejo advice, p. 271

macizo sturdy, solid, p. 271

indios parientes relatives, p. 273

tío uncle, p. 273

tejanos Texans, p. 273

abrazos embraces, p. 273

vaqueros, rancheros, soldados cowboys, ranchers, soldiers, p. 274

of all those buried there by blood or heart related: my grandparents, my aunts, my father, my first-born child, and a thousand cousins and cousins of cousins for centuries held together by the warmth of *familia*.

From the *vaqueros, rancheros, soldados,* preachers, teachers and storytellers on my father's side and the metalworkers, maids, nursemaids, and servant people on my mother's side come the family members that sit by my side as I write today. So do the mesquite trees and *vacas,* coyotes and *ríos* of their lives, and the *molcajetes* and *gatos, libros* and computers, friends and strangers, races, telephones and headlines—of mine. They are all a part of my *familia,* that huge network of creatures in coexistence, sharing places and times and feelings, sharing commitment, sharing care about each other . . .

But that only tells part of the story. Because we don't *have* photographs or even mental images of most of the people that form our *familia*—we don't even know who they were, or who they will be. And everything and everyone I see out there, and the even more numerous ones I don't see, are all the *real* members of my *familia*. And when we speak of family, who can we really leave out?

RESPONDING

1. **Personal Response** Tafolla says that her father taught her to use a hammer and drill and clean a carburetor— just as her grandfather taught his sons. What tasks can you do that were once reserved for the opposite sex? How did you learn to do them?

2. **Literary Analysis** Tafolla once referred to her family and culture as a *caldo,* or soup, of many ingredients, all contributing to a special flavor. Judging from this selection, why do you think she chose this metaphor? Can you

think of another comparison that suggests things that are complementary yet diverse?

3. **Multicultural Connection** What does Tafolla mean by "Latino Hunger"? Do you think that students of diverse cultural groups see themselves reflected in schoolbooks today? Explain.

LANGUAGE WORKSHOP

Word Roots Knowing word roots can help you figure out meanings of related words. For example, the word *Familia* in the title has the same root as the word *family.* If you associate these words with others such as *familiar* and *familial,* you can probably figure out their meanings.

Think of one other word related to each of the following italicized words; then try to arrive at the italicized word's meaning.
1. "The cousin . . . spent eighty years of her life with the *deceased.* . . ."
2. ". . . its air was charged by the anger and the *tension* and passion of fights. . . ."
3. ". . . many good and *critical* minds came out of that time period."

WRITER'S PORTFOLIO

In three paragraphs, Tafolla tells about her "roots" by mentioning important places, dates, occupations, and objects. Study her example, which begins "My roots in New Mexico . . ." (page 273). Then write a short version of your own roots.

ABOUT **WALTER DEAN MYERS**

Since 1968, when he won first prize in a Council on Interracial Books for Children contest, Walter Dean Myers has published over twenty novels covering a wide range of subjects, including *Hoops* and *The Outside Shot* (basketball), *Scorpions* (a Harlem gang) and *Fallen Angels* (the Vietnam War and its consequences). His recent nonfiction works include a biography of Malcolm X and *Now Is Your Time*, a history of African Americans. He has also written a play, *Cages,* which examines the decisions a group of teens must make when confronted with the chance to decide their own destinies. Accolades for his work include the American Library Association's Best Books for Young Adults Award, three Coretta Scott King Awards, and the Newbery Honor Book Award. Myers lives with his family in Jersey City, New Jersey.

Cultural Substance: A Writer's Gift to Readers

WE NORMALLY THINK of memory as the process of bringing to the consciousness those things that we've either learned or experienced. But we have memories that are part of us, that we act upon, but that we seldom bring to our conscious mind. For a long time I thought that my earliest experience of self, of being me, was a reading experience. I remember being in Harlem and my mother working with me, teaching me to read. My foster parents weren't educated people. My mother often did Day's work, that is, working by the day for people who needed their houses cleaned.

When she wasn't working my mother would sit with me in the afternoons and read romance magazines to me. I still remember sitting in that sunny room. I was only allowed on the chair that didn't have doilies on it because I used to push my fingers through the doilies when I got excited. I wouldn't always understand what she was reading. I couldn't, for example, quite get the drift of heaving bosoms.

Those moments with my mother were so pleasant, so deeply ingrained in my memory, that I often thought of them as the beginning of my consciousness. But recently I attended a conference in which a speaker, Shirley Brice Heath, talked about the childhood experience of creating a world with the mind. The moment, the very moment, I began to think about this idea, I began to remember earlier

Culture Notes

Shirley Brice Heath noted educator, p. 277

Mojo and the Russians a novel by Myers about a gang's attempts to discover why Russian diplomats are visiting people in Harlem, p. 278

born with a veil over her face Those born with a caul — part of a membrane enclosing a child in the womb that sometimes clings to the head at birth — were considered lucky and protected against drowning. p. 278

experiences in my life. She had pushed back my experience of being me to an earlier time.

I lived in New York with my two sisters (my good sister and my bad sister), my foster parents and occasionally the father of my foster father. I didn't much like this old man. Especially I didn't like his scary stories. He told endless stories about the Garden of Eden, about Adam and Eve (I don't think he ever read the New Testament), and about the snake. Whatever I did, he had an Old Testament story for the particular occasion. The story I particularly hated was the story of Abraham and Isaac. Abraham took his son to the mountain and he had this knife with which he was going to sacrifice his son. Of course, being young, I saw myself as Isaac and I didn't even care if God showed up at the last minute, like a Saturday morning serial, to save Isaac. It was still a scary story.

*I*F I COMPLAINED about anything, I would get the entire story of Job. Sometimes I could avoid the stories but at other times I knew they were coming and there wasn't a thing I could do about it. For example, when my cousin Henrietta married an African man and the guy died, the whole family got together at my aunt's house and I knew the stories were coming. And they did. I went to my aunt's house (this is the same aunt that *Mojo and the Russians* was based on) and the stories came. Oh, there were stories about people coming back from the dead and knocking on your door in the middle of the night, or people that you could only see when you looked in the mirror. And, of course, I knew my aunt knew what she was talking about because everybody knew she was born with a veil over her face.

Right after the death of my cousin's husband, my father took me crabbing on the Hudson River. We lived on 122nd Street and went down to 125th Street to the old wooden piers. We had these crab baskets that you were supposed to let down into the water. The baskets had bait on the bottom and crabs were supposed to eat the bait. We'd pull the baskets up periodically to see if we had caught any crabs.

It was a very hot night and the entire pier was filled with people — Blacks, whites, Irish, Puerto Ricans — trying to escape the heat of the tenements. I asked my father for a dime for ice cream and he gave it to me. On the way back from the ice cream vendor I saw a man dressed in overalls, standing on the pier howling toward the heavens. People were standing around laughing at this crazy fool, and so I smiled, too. When I got back to my father he asked me what was going on and I told him. He said that you shouldn't laugh at people. Then he went back to his crabbing.

After a while there was another commotion on the pier and we looked to see what had happened. The man had jumped into the water. People looked over the side but the man quickly disappeared into the dark waters. The police came and after a while they recovered the man's lifeless body.

I KNEW HE WAS coming back. I knew he would be coming back and be mad at me because I smiled at him. I went home with my father, and I tried to get this guy out of my mind. I went to bed and said a prayer. "Lord, don't let this man come and get me." I knew he was there, though. What I was afraid of was that when I pulled down the covers he would be sitting on the chair next to my bed. Maybe he wasn't there, maybe he was. In the morning, it took me a long time to get my head out from under the covers to discover that the drowned man wasn't there. Thank God!

I hoped that my father would not tell my grandfather about the drowned man. He did. Furthermore, my father and mother were leaving for the evening. Also, my good sister was leaving. I knew she was because I could smell the hair grease that she used to do her hair. That would leave me home with just my bad sister (the one that once lost me on 125th Street even though Mama had told her to keep an eye on me) and my grandfather.

I tried to stall the coming story by going to the window. I used my mother's window pillow. My mother had a special pillow she used to lean on when she looked out of the window. If you were poor you took a pillow from the bed, but if you had a few dollars you had a special window pillow. I leaned on that pillow and watched the world go by until it was time to go to bed. Did I tell you I had a bad bed?

*I*T WASN'T SO MUCH a bad bed as it was a spooky bed. It was spooky because I had this quilt on the bed that this woman named Goldy, who had died of sugar diabetes, had given my mother. I had avoided my grandfather's stories, at least for that night.

I didn't like my grandfather because of his stories and sometimes I didn't like my father because of his stories. When I told my mother that I was afraid of the drowned guy coming back, my father pulled me aside and told me not to worry. The guy was probably not coming back, he said. I didn't have to worry unless I heard a certain kind of rap on the wall. And then he rapped on the wall and jumped up from his chair.

"Oh, my God, here he comes now!" he yelled as he ran down the hall.

I ran after him, screaming. My mother was furious.

I didn't like my grandfather's stories. But what my grandfather was doing, besides scaring me, was passing down the cultural substance of our lives. The idea of the Old Testament, of moral being and moral judgment, that was cultural substance. He passed it down to my father and then to me. The fear of God, too, was part of that cultural substance.

My grandfather told stories, and that storytelling is part of the cultural substance of my life, and of my people.

The smell of the grease that my sister used to groom her hair, and the quilt that Goldy gave my mother, my father taking me crabbing — all these things set me apart from the world and join me with a people who understand and find value in the same experiences.

My name is Walter Milton Myers, but I go by the name of Walter Dean Myers. The Dean family raised me, and that family, what African-Americans call the extended family, is a special part of my heritage, a part created by my people to cope with our families being split during the long night of our captivity.

What does the writer bring to the writing experience? What should I bring as an African-American? What does the Irish-American writer bring? We should bring a history of those experiences and values that identify us, that is a part of both the individual memory of the writer and the collective memory of his cultural being.

For a recent book, *Now Is Your Time,* I traced an African-American family from Norfolk, Virginia, to colonization in Liberia, to Cape Cod. The family, once it reached Cape Cod, was isolated from other people of color. After a rather lengthy interview with a member of the family, I was ready to leave when he asked me to stay a moment longer.

"You know what many people miss in their lives?" he asked.

Of course I didn't know. He went on to tell me how my brief history of his family reminded him of one of the major uses of the family concept, the transmittal of values through culture. I knew what he meant. Long before the reading experience, before we begin to make all of those defining decisions about who we are and who we want to be, there are forces that give momentum to our lives and which influence our every action and even our ability to learn.

I believe that what I have to bring to young people is the cultural substance of my experience and to recognize that experience as a celebration of African-American life. Very often young people don't even know that they are part of a culture. I must tell them that they are.

RESPONDING

1. **Personal Response** Think of two questions you would like to ask Walter Dean Myers, based on the selection or his biography.

2. **Literary Analysis** Myers's piece was delivered as a *speech*. Select a paragraph to deliver orally, using emphasis, pauses, and changes in tone when appropriate to hold a listener's attention.

3. **Multicultural Connection** Myers reminds readers that they are part of a culture. What story, possession, or artifact would you share with your grandchildren to let them know what your world was like in the 1990s? Explain what this item reveals about your culture.

LANGUAGE WORKSHOP

Euphemisms Myers refers to slavery as "the long night of our captivity." A mild or indirect word or phrase used instead of one that is more direct or harsh or that may have unpleasant connotations is called a *euphemism*.

Substitute a direct expression for the following italicized euphemisms.
1. My great uncle has *departed from this earth.*
2. Those *pre-owned* clothes are *a good buy.*
3. That large corporation has *downsized* 20% of its management team.

WRITER'S PORTFOLIO

You are making a time capsule, based on your personal response to item 3 under Responding. In a paragraph or two, explain what the item you have chosen to present two generations from now reveals about you and your world.

LUIS J. RODRIGUEZ Luis J. Rodriguez recounts in his autobiography, *Always Running,* how his childhood was filled with poverty and violence. A survivor who profited from contact with the Chicano movement of the 1960s, Rodriguez eventually turned his life around, partly by writing poetry. His collections, *Poems Across the Pavement* and *The Concrete River,* depict life in the barrio. Presently, he is working as a peace arbitrator with gangs in Los Angeles and elsewhere, as well as running Tía Chucha Press and conducting poetry workshops in homeless shelters in Chicago.

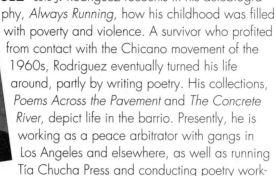

TINA KOYAMA Tina Koyama, whose first poems appeared in *Breaking Silence: An Anthology of Contemporary Asian American Poets,* is a native of Seattle, Washington. Koyama says, "Whether it's a poem, story, or journal entry—and sometimes even a letter, note, or E-mail message—I write primarily to understand my life." She says that writing "Fishhook" long after the real-life event occurred helped her articulate feelings she didn't understand at the time—about herself, her father, and their relationship.

SIMON ORTIZ Simon Ortiz's writing reveals a respect for the earth and his Native American past, a belief in the importance of words and language, and an unremitting hope for harmony among all people. Ortiz, an Acoma, grew up in New Mexico, worked in uranium mines and processing plants, served in the military, and graduated from the University of New Mexico and the University of Iowa. His poetry collections include *Going for the Rain, After and Before the Lightning,* and *Woven Stone.* He also writes stories and children's works, and edits anthologies.

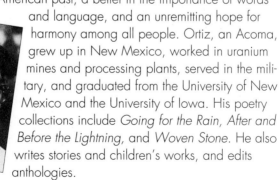

Speaking with Hands

LUIS J. RODRIGUEZ

There were no markets in Watts.
There were these small corner stores
we called *marketas*
who charged more money
for cheaper goods than what existed
in other parts of town.
The owners were often thieves in white coats
who talked to you like animals,
who knew you had no options;
who knew Watts was the preferred landfill
of the city.

One time, Mama started an argument
at the cash register.
In her broken English,
speaking with her hands,
she had us children stand around her
as she fought with the grocer
on prices & quality & dignity.

Mama became a woman swept
by a sobering madness;
she must have been what Moses saw
in the burning bush,
a pillar of fire,

Culture Note

Watts a poverty-stricken area in East Los Angeles; scene
of the 1960s riots for civil rights (and of later riots in
1992), p. 284

consuming the still air
that reeked of overripe fruit
and bad meat from the frozen food
section.

She refused to leave
until the owner called the police.
The police came and argued too,
but Mama wouldn't stop.
They pulled her into the parking lot,
called her crazy . . .
and then Mama showed them crazy!

They didn't know what to do
but let her go, and Mama took us children
back toward home, tired of being tired.

✳
Biblical Notes

Moses Hebrew leader, prophet, and lawgiver, p. 284

burning bush God appeared to Moses in a burning
bush and counsels him about freeing his people from
bondage in Egypt, p. 284

ishhook

TINA KOYAMA

First he tried to cut it free himself,
then held out to me his pocketknife
and hand, the fishhook deep in my father's thumb.

A little sheepish and amazed, he pointed
where I wouldn't have to cut
very far to free the barb. He wasn't bleeding
much; I felt my face turn white.

I couldn't remember holding his hand before,
not as a child, nor as I did then
with the awkward tenderness
we both ignored.

Stalling, I cleaned his knife
with the flame of a match. "Hurry,"
he said, getting stern.
I could have used the moment
to remind him of the only time

We caught shiners together from a dock.
I was nine. I watched how quickly
he baited tiny hooks as the green smell of ocean
wet the wind. How easily he tore
them from the mouths of fish
as they struggled.

If I were brave, I would have held
my breath and cut quickly through
his skin. More familiar than callouses,

the palms full of lines, was their smell—
always his hands have smelled of turpentine,
metal and fish. The simple ingenuity
of fishhooks would have struck me
then, how they cannot be removed
without first hurting deeper.

But I am not brave, and he told me so
as I drove him to Emergency instead.
It's the blood, I told myself,
I'm afraid of. With his other hand,
he lit his pipe, tried
the radio for news.

Father, if I were brave,
I would have asked you why
I'd never held your hand before,
why it took a fishhook in your thumb
to remind me of the waterfront, the shiny fish,
the sting of briny wind in my face.

My Father's Song

SIMON ORTIZ

Wanting to say things,
I miss my father tonight.
His voice, the slight catch,
the depth from his thin chest,
the tremble of emotion
in something he has just said
to his son, his song:

We planted corn one Spring at Acu —
we planted several times
but this one particular time
I remember the soft damp sand
in my hand.

My father had stopped at one point
to show me an overturned furrow;
the plowshare had unearthed
the burrow nest of a mouse
in the soft moist sand.

Very gently, he scooped tiny pink animals
into the palm of his hand
and told me to touch them.
We took them to the edge
of the field and put them in the shade
of a sand moist clod.

I remember the very softness
of cool and warm sand and tiny alive mice
and my father saying things.

Culture Note

Acu Ortiz's home in New Mexico, p. 288

RESPONDING

1. **Personal Response** If you were involved in a misunder-standing at school and could take one of the parents in these poems to school to speak on your behalf, whom would you choose? Why?

2. **Literary Analysis** These poets, who are relating per-sonal anecdotes, do not use *rhyme* at the ends of lines. Speculate on how rhyme would change their poems.

3. **Multicultural Connection** What cultural clues can you find in these poems about the lives of the speakers?

LANGUAGE WORKSHOP

Assonance The repetition of vowel sounds followed by different consonant sounds in words is called *assonance*. (". . . remind him of the only time we caught shiners"). Assonance can contribute to the meaning of a work, to its musical quality, and to its unity. What sound is repeated in each of the following items from the poems in this group?
1. "I remember . . . tiny, alive mice."
2. "I remember the soft damp sand in my hand."

WRITER'S PORTFOLIO

Now it's your turn to write a poem! Describe something you find memorable about a family member. It might be a saying, a mannerism, a skill, or something else. Jot down your impressions and any words that come to mind. Now try to shape your ideas into a poem, using anything you have read in these three poems as models.

LA FAMILIA: FAMILY MATTERS

Projects

FAMILY CALENDAR

You can make a family calendar for immediate and extended family members. First, conduct interviews to find out their birth dates and the dates of events important to them. Then collect or take photographs (or draw pictures) of each family member. Then:

• Make a calendar grid by hand or by computer. Allow one month per sheet, making sure boxes are large enough for writing.

• Mount the pictures of family members whose birthdays fall in the same month around the borders of the appropriate page.

• Print family names in the birth date boxes.

• Print important events on dates they occur.

• Photocopy pages and distribute to family members.

FAMILY DINNER

You have been invited to have dinner with one of the families portrayed in this unit. Choose a family and brainstorm with a small group some ideas that would make you a welcome guest. For example, what small gift could you bring? What could you ask the family at the dinner table? What kinds of questions could you anticipate they might ask you? Whom would you like to sit next to? What would you say in a thank-you note?

FAMILY MATTERS: AN ESSAY

The selections in this unit show that family matters in every culture. Write an essay on this topic using three selections from this unit and one of your own experiences to illustrate what you say.

Further Reading

The following books show how diverse American families can be.

Alvarez, Julia. *How the García Girls Lost Their Accents.* Penguin Books, 1991. Comprised of fifteen interconnected stories, this novel recounts the adjustments the García family makes when they move to New York City from the Dominican Republic.

Barrio, Raymond. *The Plum Plum Pickers.* Bilingual Press, 1985. This novel focuses on the members of a Mexican American family who live the life of migrant workers.

Cleaver, Vera and Bill. *Where the Lilies Bloom.* Harper-Collins, 1969. Mary Call Luther struggles to keep her siblings together and to honor promises to her recently deceased father in this novel set against the backdrop of the Great Smoky Mountains.

Dorris, Michael. *A Yellow Raft in Blue Water.* Holt, 1987. Three generations of Native American women bound together by secrets, hardships, and kinship tell family history from their own unique perspectives in this memorable novel.

Uchida, Yoshiko. *The Invisible Thread.* Messner, 1992. Uchida's autobiography describes her family history and experiences in a relocation camp.

Washington, Mary H. ed. *Memory of Kin.* Doubleday, 1991. These stories by African American writers focus on families.

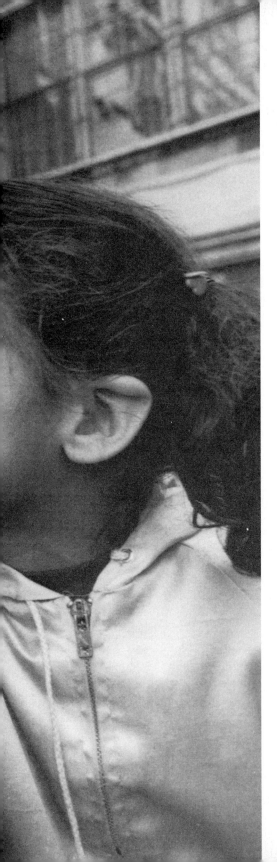

Scenes from Childhood

Have you ever looked through someone's photo album and seen strangers posing, flirting, and playing in settings unfamiliar to you? But look again! Haven't *you* blown out birthday candles, or swung a bat, or dressed up for a party in much the same way? The following unit includes "literary snapshots" capturing scenes from childhood. Although these selections are about other people, they deal with universals that may call up scenes from your own life.

ABOUT **AMY TAN**

Amy Tan was born in California, shortly after her parents emigrated from China, and more than one hundred years after the first wave of Chinese immigrants came to America. After her father's death when she was fifteen, Tan moved with her mother to Europe and graduated from high school in Switzerland. After returning to the United States and earning a master's degree in English, (her mother had wanted her to be a neurosurgeon — and a concert pianist on the side), Tan worked as a technical writer before she began writing books full time. Tan's works include the acclaimed *Joy Luck Club, The Kitchen God's Wife,* and *The Moon Lady,* a storybook for children.

Two Kinds

My MOTHER BELIEVED you could be anything you wanted to be in America. You could open a restaurant. You could work for the government and get good retirement. You could buy a house with almost no money down. You could become rich. You could become instantly famous.

"Of course you can be prodigy, too," my mother told me when I was nine. "You can be best anything. What does Auntie Lindo know? Her daughter, she is only best tricky."

America was where all my mother's hopes lay. She had come here in 1949 after losing everything in China: her mother and father, her family home, her first husband, and two daughters, twin baby girls. But she never looked back with regret. There were so many ways for things to get better.

We didn't immediately pick the right kind of prodigy. At first my mother thought I could be a Chinese Shirley Temple. We'd watch Shirley's old movies on TV as though they were training films. My mother would poke my arm and say, "*Ni kan*"—You watch. And I would see Shirley tapping her feet, or singing a sailor song, or pursing her lips into a very round O while saying, "Oh my goodness."

"*Ni kan*," said my mother as Shirley's eyes flooded with tears. "You already know how. Don't need talent for crying!"

Soon after my mother got this idea about Shirley Temple, she took me to a beauty training school in the Mission district and put me in the hands of a student who could barely hold the scissors without shaking. Instead of getting big fat curls, I emerged with an uneven mass of crinkly black fuzz. My mother dragged me off to the bathroom and tried to wet down my hair.

"You look like Negro Chinese," she lamented, as if I had done this on purpose.

The instructor of the beauty training school had to lop off these soggy clumps to make my hair even again. "Peter Pan is very popular these days," the instructor assured my mother. I now had hair the length of a boy's, with straight-across bangs that hung at a slant two inches above my eyebrows. I liked the haircut and it made me actually look forward to my future fame.

In fact, in the beginning, I was just as excited as my mother, maybe even more so. I pictured this prodigy part of me as many different images, trying each one on for size. I was a dainty ballerina girl standing by the curtains, waiting to hear the right music that would send me floating on my tiptoes. I was like the Christ child lifted out of the straw manger, crying with holy indignity. I was Cinderella stepping from her pumpkin carriage with sparkly cartoon music filling the air.

In all of my imaginings, I was filled with a sense that I would soon become *perfect*. My mother and father would adore me. I would be beyond reproach. I would never feel the need to sulk for anything.

But sometimes the prodigy in me became impatient. "If you don't hurry up and get me out of here, I'm disappearing for good," it warned. "And then you'll always be nothing."

EVERY NIGHT after dinner, my mother and I would sit at the Formica kitchen table. She would present new tests, taking her examples from stories of amazing children she had read in *Ripley's Believe It or Not*, or *Good Housekeeping*, *Reader's Digest*, and a dozen other magazines she kept in a pile in our bathroom. My mother got these magazines from people whose houses she cleaned. And since she cleaned many houses each week, we had a great assortment. She would look through them all, searching for stories about remarkable children.

The first night she brought out a story about a three-year-old boy who knew the capitals of all the states and even most of the European countries. A teacher was quoted as saying the little boy could also pronounce the names of the foreign cities correctly.

"What's the capital of Finland?" my mother asked me, looking at the magazine story.

All I knew was the capital of California, because Sacramento was the name of the street we lived on in Chinatown. "Nairobi!" I guessed, saying the most foreign word I could think of. She checked to see if that was possibly one way to pronounce "Helsinki" before showing me the answer.

The tests got harder — multiplying numbers in my head, finding the queen of hearts in a deck of cards, trying to stand on my head without using my hands, predicting the daily temperatures in Los Angeles, New York, and London.

One night I had to look at a page from the Bible for three minutes and then report everything I could remember. "Now Jehoshaphat had riches and honor in abundance and . . . that's all I remember, Ma," I said.

And after seeing my mother's disappointed face once again, something inside of me began to die. I hated the tests, the raised hopes and failed expectations. Before going to bed that night, I looked in the mirror above the bathroom sink and when I saw only my face staring back — and that it would always be this ordinary face — I began to cry. Such a sad, ugly girl! I made high-pitched noises like a crazed animal, trying to scratch out the face in the mirror.

And then I saw what seemed to be the prodigy side of me — because I had never seen that face before. I looked at my reflection, blinking so I could see more clearly. The girl staring back at me was angry, powerful. This girl and I were the same. I had new thoughts, willful thoughts, or rather thoughts filled with lots of won'ts. I won't let her change me, I promised myself. I won't be what I'm not.

So now on nights when my mother presented her tests, I performed listlessly, my head propped on one arm. I pretended to be bored. And I was. I got so bored I started counting the bellows of the foghorns out on the bay while my mother drilled me in other areas. The sound was comforting and reminded me of the cow jumping over the moon. And the next day, I played a game with myself, seeing if my mother would give up on me before eight bellows. After a while I usually counted only one, maybe two bellows at most. At last she was beginning to give up hope.

Two or three months had gone by without any mention of my being a prodigy again. And then one day my mother was watching *The Ed Sullivan Show* on TV. The TV was old and the sound kept shorting out. Every time my mother got halfway up from the sofa to adjust the set, the sound would go back on and Ed would be talking. As soon as she sat down, Ed would go silent again. She got up, the TV broke into loud piano music. She sat down. Silence. Up and down, back and forth, quiet and loud. It was like a stiff embraceless dance between her and the TV set. Finally she stood by the set with her hand on the sound dial.

She seemed entranced by the music, a little frenzied piano piece with this mesmerizing quality, sort of quick passages and then teasing lilting ones before it returned to the quick playful parts.

"*Ni kan*," my mother said, calling me over with hurried hand gestures. "Look here."

I could see why my mother was fascinated by the music. It was being pounded out by a little Chinese girl, about nine years old, with a Peter Pan haircut. The girl had the sauciness of a Shirley Temple. She was proudly modest like a proper Chinese child. And she also did this fancy sweep of a curtsy, so that the fluffy skirt of her white dress cascaded slowly to the floor like the petals of a large carnation.

In spite of these warning signs, I wasn't worried. Our family had no piano and we couldn't afford to buy one, let alone reams of sheet music and piano lessons. So I could be generous in my comments when my mother bad-mouthed the little girl on TV.

"Play note right, but doesn't sound good! No singing sound," complained my mother.

"What are you picking on her for?" I said carelessly. "She's pretty good. Maybe she's not the best, but she's trying hard." I knew almost immediately I would be sorry I said that.

"Just like you," she said. "Not the best. Because you not trying." She gave a little huff as she let go of the sound dial and sat down on the sofa.

The little Chinese girl sat down also to play an encore of "Anitra's Dance" by Grieg. I remember the song, because later on I had to learn how to play it.

THREE DAYS after watching *The Ed Sullivan Show*, my mother told me what my schedule would be for piano lessons and piano practice. She had talked to Mr. Chong, who lived on the first floor of our apartment building. Mr. Chong was a retired piano teacher and my mother had traded housecleaning services for weekly lessons and a piano for me to practice on every day, two hours a day, from four until six.

When my mother told me this, I felt as though I had been sent to hell. I whined and then kicked my foot a little when I couldn't stand it anymore.

"Why don't you like me the way I am? I'm *not* a genius! I can't play the piano. And even if I could, I wouldn't go on TV if you paid me a million dollars!" I cried.

My mother slapped me. "Who ask you be genius?" she shouted. "Only ask you be your best. For you sake. You think I want you be genius? Hnnh! What for! Who ask you!"

"So ungrateful," I heard her mutter in Chinese. "If she had as much talent as she has temper, she would be famous now."

Mr. Chong, whom I secretly nicknamed Old Chong, was very strange. always tapping his fingers to the silent music of an invisible orchestra. He looked ancient in my eyes. He had lost most of the hair on top of his head and he wore thick glasses and had eyes that always looked tired and sleepy. But he must have been younger than I thought, since he lived with his mother and was not yet married.

I met Old Lady Chong once and that was enough. She had this peculiar smell like a baby that had done something in its pants. And her fingers felt like a dead person's, like an old peach I once found in the back of the refrigerator; the skin just slid off the meat when I picked it up.

I soon found out why Old Chong had retired from teaching piano. He was deaf. "Like Beethoven!" he shouted to me. "We're both listening only in our head!" And he would start to conduct his frantic silent sonatas.

Our lessons went like this. He would open the book and point to different things, explaining their purpose: "Key! Treble! Bass! No sharps or flats! So this is C major! Listen now and play after me!"

And then he would play the C scale a few times, a simple chord, and then, as if inspired by an old, unreachable itch, he gradually added more notes and running trills and a pounding bass until the music was really something quite grand.

I would play after him, the simple scale, the simple chord, and then I just played some nonsense that sounded like a cat running up and down on top of garbage cans. Old Chong smiled and applauded and then said, "Very good! But now you must learn to keep time!"

So that's how I discovered that Old Chong's eyes were too slow to keep up with the wrong notes I was playing. He went through the motions in half-time. To help me keep rhythm, he stood behind me, pushing down on my right

✳
Famous Composers

Grieg Edvard Grieg, a Norwegian composer (1843–1907), p. 299

Beethoven Ludwig van Beethoven, a German composer (1770–1827), p. 300

Schumann Robert Schumann, a German composer (1810–1856), p. 302

shoulder for every beat. He balanced pennies on top of my wrists so I would keep them still as I slowly played scales and arpeggios. He had me curve my hand around an apple and keep that shape when playing chords. He marched stiffly to show me how to make each finger dance up and down, staccato like an obedient little soldier.

He taught me all these things, and that was how I also learned I could be lazy and get away with mistakes, lots of mistakes. If I hit the wrong notes because I hadn't practiced enough, I never corrected myself. I just kept playing in rhythm. And Old Chong kept conducting his own private reverie.

So maybe I never really gave myself a fair chance. I did pick up the basics pretty quickly, and I might have become a good pianist at that young age. But I was so determined not to try, not to be anybody different that I learned to play only the most ear-splitting preludes, the most discordant hymns.

Over the next year, I practiced like this, dutifully in my own way. And then one day I heard my mother and her friend Lindo Jong both talking in a loud bragging tone of voice so others could hear. It was after church, and I was leaning against the brick wall wearing a dress with stiff white petticoats. Auntie Lindo's daughter, Waverly, who was about my age, was standing farther down the wall about five feet away. We had grown up together and shared all the closeness of two sisters squabbling over crayons and dolls. In other words, for the most part, we hated each other. I thought she was snotty. Waverly Jong had gained a certain amount of fame as "Chinatown's Littlest Chinese Chess Champion."

"She bring home too many trophy," lamented Auntie Lindo that Sunday. "All day she play chess. All day I have no time to do nothing but dust off her winnings." She threw a scolding look at Waverly, who pretended not to see her.

"You lucky you don't have this problem," said Auntie Lindo with a sigh to my mother.

And my mother squared her shoulders and bragged: "Our problem worser than yours. If we ask Jing-mei wash dish, she hear nothing but music. It's like you can't stop this natural talent."

And right then, I was determined to put a stop to her foolish pride.

A FEW WEEKS later, Old Chong and my mother conspired to have me play in a talent show which would be held in the church hall. By then, my parents had saved up enough to buy me a secondhand piano, a black Wurlitzer spinet with a scarred bench. It was the showpiece of our living room.

For the talent show, I was to play a piece called "Pleading Child" from Schumann's *Scenes from Childhood*. It was a simple, moody piece that sounded more difficult than it was. I was supposed to memorize the whole thing, playing the repeat parts twice to make the piece sound longer. But I dawdled over it, playing a few bars and then cheating, looking up to see what notes followed. I never really listened to what I was playing. I daydreamed about being somewhere else, about being someone else.

The part I liked to practice best was the fancy curtsy: right foot out, touch the rose on the carpet with a pointed foot, sweep to the side, left leg bends, look up and smile.

My parents invited all the couples from the Joy Luck Club to witness my debut. Auntie Lindo and Uncle Tin were there. Waverly and her two older brothers had also come. The first two rows were filled with children both younger and older than I was. The littlest ones got to go first. They recited simple nursery rhymes, squawked out tunes on miniature violins, twirled Hula Hoops, pranced in pink ballet tutus, and when they bowed or curtsied, the audience would sigh in unison, "Awww," and then clap enthusiastically.

When my turn came, I was very confident. I remember my childish excitement. It was as if I knew, without a doubt,

Culture Note

Joy Luck Club Members of this club, established by the narrator's mother, played mah-jongg, feasted, told stories, and hoped for good fortune. p.302

that the prodigy side of me really did exist. I had no fear whatsoever, no nervousness. I remember thinking to myself, This is it! This is it! I looked out over the audience, at my mother's blank face, my father's yawn, Auntie Lindo's stiff-lipped smile, Waverly's sulky expression. I had on a white dress layered with sheets of lace, and a pink bow in my Peter Pan haircut. As I sat down I envisioned people jumping to their feet and Ed Sullivan rushing up to introduce me to everyone on TV.

And I started to play. It was so beautiful. I was so caught up in how lovely I looked that at first I didn't worry how I would sound. So it was a surprise to me when I hit the first wrong note and I realized something didn't sound quite right. And then I hit another and another followed that. A chill started at the top of my head and began to trickle down. Yet I couldn't stop playing, as though my hands were bewitched. I kept thinking my fingers would adjust themselves back, like a train switching to the right track. I played this strange jumble through two repeats, the sour notes staying with me all the way to the end.

When I stood up, I discovered my legs were shaking. Maybe I had just been nervous and the audience, like Old Chong, had seen me go through the right motions and had not heard anything wrong at all. I swept my right foot out, went down on my knee, looked up and smiled. The room was quiet, except for Old Chong, who was beaming and shouting, "Bravo! Bravo! Well done!" But then I saw my mother's face, her stricken face. The audience clapped weakly, and as I walked back to my chair, with my whole face quivering as I tried not to cry, I heard a little boy whisper loudly to his mother, "That was awful," and the mother whispered back, "Well, she certainly tried."

And now I realized how many people were in the audience, the whole world it seemed. I was aware of eyes burning into my back. I felt the shame of my mother and father as they sat stiffly throughout the rest of the show.

We could have escaped during intermission. Pride and some strange sense of honor must have anchored my parents to their chairs. And so we watched it all: the eighteen-year-old boy with a fake mustache who did a magic show and juggled flaming hoops while riding a unicycle. The breasted girl with white makeup who sang from *Madama Butterfly* and got honorable mention. And the eleven-year-old boy who won first prize playing a tricky violin song that sounded like a busy bee.

After the show, the Hsus, the Jongs, and the St. Clairs from the Joy Luck Club came up to my mother and father.

"Lots of talented kids," Auntie Lindo said vaguely, smiling broadly.

"That was somethin' else," said my father, and I wondered if he was referring to me in a humorous way, or whether he even remembered what I had done.

Waverly looked at me and shrugged her shoulders. "You aren't a genius like me," she said matter-of-factly. And if I hadn't felt so bad, I would have pulled her braids and punched her stomach.

But my mother's expression was what devastated me: a quiet, blank look that said she had lost everything. I felt the same way, and it seemed as if everybody were now coming up, like gawkers at the scene of an accident, to see what parts were actually missing. When we got on the bus to go home, my father was humming the busy-bee tune and my mother was silent. I kept thinking she wanted to wait until we got home before shouting at me. But when my father unlocked the door to our apartment, my mother walked in and then went to the back, into the bedroom. No accusations. No blame. And in a way, I felt disappointed. I had been waiting for her to start shouting, so I could shout back and cry and blame her for all my misery.

I ASSUMED my talent-show fiasco meant I never had to play the piano again. But two days later, after school, my mother came out of the kitchen and saw me watching TV.

"Four clock," she reminded me as if it were any other day. I was stunned, as though she were asking me to go through the talent-show torture again. I wedged myself more tightly in front of the TV.

"Turn off TV," she called from the kitchen five minutes later.

I didn't budge. And then I decided. I didn't have to do what my mother said anymore. I wasn't her slave. This wasn't China. I had listened to her before and look what happened. She was the stupid one.

She came out from the kitchen and stood in the arched entryway of the living room. "Four clock," she said once again, louder.

"I'm not going to play anymore," I said nonchalantly. "Why should I? I'm not a genius."

She walked over and stood in front of the TV. I saw her chest was heaving up and down in an angry way.

"No!" I said, and I now felt stronger, as if my true self had finally emerged. So this was what had been inside me all along.

"No! I won't!" I screamed.

She yanked me by the arm, pulled me off the floor, snapped off the TV. She was frighteningly strong, half pulling, half carrying me toward the piano as I kicked the throw rugs under my feet. She lifted me up and onto the hard bench. I was sobbing by now, looking at her bitterly. Her chest was heaving even more and her mouth was open, smiling crazily as if she were pleased I was crying.

"You want me to be someone that I'm not!" I sobbed. "I'll never be the kind of daughter you want me to be!"

"Only two kinds of daughters," she shouted in Chinese. "Those who are obedient and those who follow their own mind! Only one kind of daughter can live in this house. Obedient daughter!"

"Then I wish I wasn't your daughter. I wish you weren't my mother," I shouted. As I said these things I got scared. It felt like worms and toads and slimy things crawling out of my chest, but it also felt good, as if this awful side of me had surfaced, at last.

"Too late change this," said my mother shrilly.

And I could sense her anger rising to its breaking point. I wanted to see it spill over. And that's when I remembered the babies she had lost in China, the ones we never talked about. "Then I wish I'd never been born!" I shouted. "I wish I were dead! Like them."

It was as if I had said the magic words. Alakazam!— and her face went blank, her mouth closed, her arms went slack, and she backed out of the room, stunned, as if she were blowing away like a small brown leaf, thin, brittle, lifeless.

It was not the only disappointment my mother felt in me. In the years that followed, I failed her so many times, each time asserting my own will, my right to fall short of expectations. I didn't get straight As. I didn't become class president. I didn't get into Stanford. I dropped out of college.

For unlike my mother, I did not believe I could be anything I wanted to be. I could only be me.

And for all those years, we never talked about the disaster at the recital or my terrible accusations afterward at the piano bench. All that remained unchecked, like a betrayal that was now unspeakable. So I never found a way to ask her why she had hoped for something so large that failure was inevitable.

And even worse, I never asked her what frightened me the most: Why had she given up hope?

For after our struggle at the piano, she never mentioned my playing again. The lessons stopped. The lid to the piano was closed, shutting out the dust, my misery, and her dreams.

So she surprised me. A few years ago, she offered to give me the piano, for my thirtieth birthday. I had not played in all those years. I saw the offer as a sign of forgiveness, a tremendous burden removed.

"Are you sure?" I asked shyly. "I mean, won't you and Dad miss it?"

"No, this your piano," she said firmly. "Always your piano. You only one can play."

"Well, I probably can't play anymore," I said. "It's been years."

"You pick up fast," said my mother, as if she knew this was certain. "You have natural talent. You could been genius if you want to."

"No I couldn't."

"You just not trying," said my mother. And she was neither angry nor sad. She said it as if to announce a fact that could never be disproved. "Take it," she said.

But I didn't at first. It was enough that she had offered it to me. And after that, every time I saw it in my parents' living room, standing in front of the bay windows, it made me feel proud, as if it were a shiny trophy I had won back.

LAST WEEK I sent a tuner over to my parents' apartment and had the piano reconditioned, for purely sentimental reasons. My mother had died a few months before and I had been getting things in order for my father, a little bit at a time. I put the jewelry in special silk pouches. The sweaters she had knitted in yellow, pink, bright orange — all the colors I hated — I put those in mothproof boxes. I found some old Chinese silk dresses, the kind with little slits up the sides. I rubbed the old silk against my skin, then wrapped them in tissue and decided to take them home with me.

After I had the piano tuned, I opened the lid and touched the keys. It sounded even richer than I remembered. Really, it was a very good piano. Inside the bench were the same exercise notes with handwritten scales, the same secondhand music books with their covers held together with yellow tape.

I opened up the Schumann book to the dark little piece I had played at the recital. It was on the left-hand side of the page, "Pleading Child." It looked more difficult than I remembered. I played a few bars, surprised at how easily the notes came back to me.

And for the first time, or so it seemed, I noticed the piece on the right-hand side. It was called "Perfectly Contented." I tried to play this one as well. It had a lighter melody but the same flowing rhythm and turned out to be quite easy. "Pleading Child" was shorter but slower; "Perfectly Contented" was longer, but faster. And after I played them both a few times, I realized they were two halves of the same song.

RESPONDING

1. **Personal Response** Describe a time when a parent or teacher held high expectations for you and how you reacted. How was your reaction like or unlike Jing-mei's?

2. **Literary Analysis** What do you learn about Jing-mei's mother from her first words, "Of course you can be prodigy too"? from her *dialogue* with Auntie Lindo that begins at the bottom of page 301?

3. **Multicultural Connection** According to the narrator, "America was where all my mother's hopes lay." Why do you think this country appears to be the land of dreams for so many immigrants?

LANGUAGE WORKSHOP

Simile A figure of speech using the word *like* or *as* to compare essentially unlike things is called a *simile*. The narrator in "Two Kinds" says that she "played some nonsense that sounded like a cat running up and down on top of garbage cans." What is being compared here? Find five other similes in this selection.

WRITER'S PORTFOLIO

Write a dialogue between a parent and child that reflects their different goals. Begin in the middle of an argument, and fill in details about how they arrived at these goals.

NIKKI GIOVANNI Born in Tennessee, Nikki Giovanni grew up in a predominantly African American community in Lincoln Heights, Ohio, the child of middle class professionals. As a student at Fisk University in Nashville, Tennessee, she became involved in the civil rights activities of the 1960s. Known as an editor and author of children's books as well as a poet, Giovanni writes poems that are conversational in tone and informed by rhythm and blues music. Early poetry collections such as *Ego-Tripping and Other Poems* still enjoy popularity.

RITA DOVE Rita Dove admits to being a daydreamer and recognizes this activity as an essential springboard for writing poetry. As a child, she loved math — "the neatness of fractions, all those pies sliced into ever-diminishing wedges." But drilling with flash cards frightened her, reminding her of "the numbing repetitions of daily existence — taking out the garbage, doing the dishes, washing laundry." After daydreaming about the subject, she came up with the poem "Flash Cards."

JAMES MASAO MITSUI James Masao Mitsui, who earned eleven letters in high school sports and was designated the outstanding graduate of his college ROTC class, is fond of Persian cats, cooking paella, and rooting for the Seattle SuperSonics. *Mitsui* translated into English means "Three Wells." Fittingly, Mitsui claims an affinity for water, and has lived most of his life in Seattle, Washington. A high school English teacher, he received his M.A. in English at the University of Washington. His first book of poems, *Journal of the Sun,* received the Pacific NW Booksellers' Award. His other books are *Crossing the Phantom River* and *After the Long Train.*

Nikki–Rosa

NIKKI GIOVANNI

childhood remembrances are always a drag
if you're Black
you always remember things like living in
    Woodlawn
with no inside toilet
and if you become famous or something
they never talk about how happy you were to have
    your mother
all to yourself and
how good the water felt when you got your bath
    from one of those
big tubs that folk in chicago barbecue in
and somehow when you talk about home
it never gets across how much you
understood their feelings
as the whole family attended meetings about
    Hollydale
and even though you remember
your biographers never understand
your father's pain as he sells his stock
and another dream goes
and though you're poor it isn't poverty that
concerns you
and though they fought a lot
it isn't your father's drinking that makes any
    difference
but only that everybody is together and you
and your sister have happy birthdays and very
    good christmasses

and I really hope no white person ever has cause to
write about me
because they never understand Black love is Black
wealth and they'll
probably talk about my hard childhood and never
understand that
all the while I was quite happy

Flash Cards

RITA DOVE

In math I was the whiz kid, keeper
of oranges and apples. *What you don't understand,
master,* my father said; the faster
I answered, the faster they came.

I could see one bud on the teacher's geranium,
one clear bee sputtering at the wet pane.
The tulip trees always dragged after heavy rain
so I tucked my head as my boots slapped home.

My father put up his feet after work
and relaxed with a highball and *The Life of Lincoln.*
After supper we drilled and I climbed the dark

before sleep, before a thin voice hissed
numbers as I spun on a wheel. I had to guess.
Ten, I kept saying, *I'm only ten.*

When Father Came Home for Lunch

JAMES MASAO MITSUI

I listen to my parents' language,
watch my father eat his separate meal,
the railroad motor car
cooling off & waiting
on the siding by the section house.
He sits with his back to the burning
woodstove in a captain's chair.
and eats the family left-overs,
a bowl of rice balanced in his hand,
chopsticks flicking
around to the bowls & dishes
arranged in front of him.

Mother adds fried onions, an egg
and potatoes to his main bowl.
He adds catsup, shoyu
and mixes it with the white radish,
egg plant and cold chicken.
He works around to the mustard caked bowl
before each mouth of rice,
sauce hanging from his moustache.
Hot coffee, heavy with sugar & cream,
steams from a china mug.
Half-an-hour of noisy manners
and he's gone, back to work
in oily bib overalls.
I can still smell sweat
soaking his long-sleeved workshirt.

RESPONDING

1. Personal Response What parts of childhood described in these poems appeal to you? What parts don't? Why?

2. Literary Analysis Explain whether you agree or disagree with the *speaker* in "Nikki-Rosa" that childhood remembrances can be a drag.

3. Multicultural Connection Find references in two of the poems to a specific culture and traditions. Do those references enhance or detract from their universal appeal? Explain.

LANGUAGE WORKSHOP

Images The *images* in "When Father Came Home for Lunch" and "Flash Cards" make a strong appeal to all of the senses. Under the headings *Touch, Taste, Sight, Hearing,* and *Smell,* list as many words and phrases as you can find.

WRITER'S PORTFOLIO

Assume that the speaker in Nikki-Rosa is Nikki Giovanni herself. Write a new biography for her, using details from her poem and disproving that "biographers never understand."

ABOUT **ALBERTO ALVARO RÍOS**

Alberto Alvaro Ríos was born in the border town of Nogales, Arizona, to a Mexican father and an English mother. Fluent in Spanish, Ríos draws heavily on his Mexican/Chicano background and conveys both the familiar and foreign in his poetry and prose. Since 1982 he has been a professor of English at Arizona State University and presents frequent poetry readings, lectures, and workshops. The recipient of many awards and grants, Ríos enjoys an enviable record as a contributor of poetry,

fiction, and drama to many anthologies and periodicals. In addition, he has published a number of collections of prose and poetry. Among them are *The Iguana Killer, Five*  *Indiscretions, Whispering to Fool the Wind,* and *Teodoro Luna's Two Kisses.*

The Secret Lion

I WAS TWELVE and in junior high school and something happened that we didn't have a name for, but it was there nonetheless like a lion, and roaring, roaring that way the biggest things do. Everything changed. Just like that. Like the rug, the one that gets pulled — or better, like the tablecloth those magicians pull where the stuff on the table stays the same but the gasp! from the audience makes the staying-the-same part not matter. Like that.

What happened was there were teachers now, not just one teacher, teach-erz, and we felt personally abandoned somehow. When a person had all these teachers now, he didn't get taken care of the same way, even though six was more than one. Arithmetic went out the door when we walked in. And we saw girls now, but they weren't the same girls we used to know because we couldn't talk to them anymore, not the same way we used to, certainly not to Sandy, even though she was my neighbor, too. Not even to her. She just played the piano all the time. And there were words, oh there were words in junior high school, and we wanted to know what they were, and how a person did them — that's what school was supposed to be for. Only, in junior high school, school wasn't school, everything was backward-like. If you went up to a teacher and said the word to try and find out what it meant you got in trouble for saying it. So we didn't. And we figured it must have been that way about other stuff, too, so we never said anything about anything — we weren't stupid.

But my friend Sergio and I, we solved junior high school. We would come home from school on the bus, put our books away, change shoes, and go across the highway to the arroyo. It was the one place we were not supposed to go. So we did. This was, after all, what junior high had at least shown us. It was our river, though, our personal Mississippi, our friend from long back, and it was full of stories and all the branch forts we had built in it when we were still the Vikings of America, with our own symbol, which we had carved everywhere, even in the sand, which let the water take it. That was good, we had decided; whoever was at the end of this river would know about us.

At the very very top of our growing lungs, what we would do down there was shout every dirty word we could think of, in every combination we could come up with, and we would yell about girls, and all the things we wanted to do with them, as loud as we could — we didn't know what we wanted to do with them, just things — and we would yell about teachers, and how we loved some of them, like Miss Crevelone, and how we wanted to dissect some of them, making signs of the cross, like priests, and we would yell this stuff over and over because it felt good, we couldn't explain why, it just felt good and for the first time in our lives there was nobody to tell us we couldn't. So we did.

One Thursday we were walking along shouting this way, and the railroad, the Southern Pacific, which ran above and along the far side of the arroyo, had dropped a grinding ball down there, which was, we found out later, a cannonball thing used in mining. A bunch of them were put in a big vat which turned around and crushed the ore. One had been dropped, or thrown — what do caboose men do when they get bored — but it got down there regardless and as we were walking along yelling about one girl or another, a particular Claudia, we found it, one of these things, looked at it, picked it up, and got very very excited, and held it and passed it back and forth, and we were saying "Guythisis, this is, geeGuythis . . .": we had this perception about nature then, that nature is imperfect and that round things are perfect: we said "GuyGodthis is perfect, thisisthis is perfect, it's round, round and heavy, it'sit's the best thing we'veeverseen. Whatisit?" We didn't know. We just knew it was great. We just, whatever, we played with it, held it some more.

And then we had to decide what to do with it. We knew, because of a lot of things, that if we were going to take this and show it to anybody, this discovery, this best thing, was going to be taken away from us. That's the way it works with little kids, like all the polished quartz, the tons of it we had collected piece by piece over the years. Junior high kids too. If we took it home, my mother, we knew, was going to look at it and say "throw that dirty thing in the, get rid of it." Simple like, like that. "But ma it's the best thing I" "Getridofit." Simple.

So we didn't. Take it home. Instead, we came up with the answer. We dug a hole and we buried it. And we marked it secretly. Lots of secret signs. And came back the next week to dig it up and, we didn't know, pass it around some more or something, but we didn't find it. We dug up that whole bank, and we never found it again. We tried.

Sergio and I talked about that ball or whatever it was when we couldn't find it. All we used were small words, neat, good. Kid words. What we were really saying, but didn't know the words, was how much that ball was like that place, that whole arroyo: couldn't tell anybody about it, didn't understand what it was, didn't have a name for it. It just felt good. It was just perfect in the way it was that place, that whole going to that place, that whole junior high school lion. It was just iron-heavy, it had no name, it felt good or not, we couldn't take it home to show our mothers, and once we buried it, it was gone forever.

The ball was gone, like the first reasons we had come to that arroyo years earlier, like the first time we had seen the arroyo, it was gone like everything else that had been taken away. This was not our first lesson. We stopped going to the arroyo after not finding the thing, the same way we had stopped going there years earlier and headed for the mountains. Nature seemed to keep pushing us around one way or another, teaching us the same thing every place we ended up. Nature's gang was tough that way, teaching us stuff.

When we were young we moved away from town, me and my family. Sergio's was already out there. Out in the wilds. Or at least the new place seemed like the wilds since everything looks bigger the smaller a man is. I was five, I guess, and we had moved three miles north of Nogales where we had lived, three miles north of the Mexican border. We looked across the highway in one direction and there was the arroyo; hills stood up in the other direction. Mountains, for a small man.

When the first summer came the very first place we went to was of course the one place we weren't supposed to go, the arroyo. We went down in there and found water running, summer rain water mostly, and we went swimming. But every third or fourth or fifth day, the sewage treatment plant that was, we found out, upstream, would release whatever it was that it released, and we would never know exactly what day that was, and a person really couldn't tell right off by looking at the water, not every time, not so a person could get out in time. So, we went swimming that summer and some days we had a lot of fun. Some days we didn't. We found a thousand ways to explain what happened on those other days, constructing elaborate stories about the neighborhood dogs, and hadn't she, my mother, miscalculated her step before, too? But she knew something was up because we'd come running into the house those days, wanting to take a shower, even — if this can be imagined — in the middle of the day.

That was the first time we stopped going to the arroyo. It taught us to look the other way. We decided, as the second side of summer came, we wanted to go into the mountains. They were still mountains then. We went running in one summer Thursday morning, my friend Sergio and I, into my mother's kitchen, and said, well, what'zin, what'zin those hills over there — we used her word so she'd understand us — and she said nothingdon'tworryaboutit. So we went out, and we weren't dumb, we thought with our eyes to each other, ohhoshe'stryingtokeepsomethingfromus. We knew adult.

We had read the books, after all; we knew about bridges and castles and wildtreacherousraging alligatormouth rivers. We wanted them. So we were going to go out and get them. We went back that morning into that kitchen and we said, "We're going out there, we're going into the hills, we're going away for three days, don't worry." She said, "All right."

"You know," I said to Sergio, "if we're going to go away for three days, well, we ought to at least pack a lunch."

But we were two young boys with no patience for what we thought at the time was mom-stuff: making sa-and-wiches. My mother didn't offer. So we got our little kid knapsacks that my mother had sewn for us, and into them we put the jar of mustard. A loaf of bread. Knivesforksplates, bottles of Coke, a can opener. This was lunch for the two of us. And we were weighed down, humped over to be strong enough to carry this stuff. But we started walking, anyway, into the hills. We were going to eat berries and stuff otherwise. "Goodbye." My mom said that.

After the first hill we were dead. But we walked. My mother could still see us. And we kept walking. We walked until we got to where the sun is straight overhead, noon. That place. Where that is doesn't matter; it's time to eat. The truth is we weren't anywhere close to that place. We just agreed that the sun was overhead and that it was time to eat, and by tilting our heads a little we could make that the truth.

"We really ought to start looking for a place to eat."

"Yeah. Let's look for a good place to eat." We went back and forth saying that for fifteen minutes, making it lunchtime because that's what we always said back and forth before lunchtimes at home. "Yeah, I'm hungry all right." I nodded my head. "Yeah, I'm hungry all right too. I'm hungry." He nodded his head. I nodded my head back. After a good deal more nodding, we were ready, just as we came over a little hill. We hadn't found the mountains yet. This was a little hill.

And on the other side of this hill we found heaven.

It was just what we thought it would be.

Perfect. Heaven was green, like nothing else in Arizona. And it wasn't a cemetery or like that because we had seen cemeteries and they had gravestones and stuff and this didn't. This was perfect, had trees, lots of trees, had birds, like we had never seen before. It was like "The Wizard of Oz," like when they got to Oz and everything was so green, so emerald, they had to wear those glasses, and we ran just like them, laughing, laughing that way we did that moment, and we went running down to this clearing in it all, hitting each other that good way we did.

We got down there, we kept laughing, we kept hitting each other, we unpacked our stuff, and we started acting "rich." We knew all about how to do that, like blowing on our nails, then rubbing them on our chests for the shine. We made our sandwiches, opened our Cokes, got out the rest of the stuff, the salt and pepper shakers. I found this particular hole and I put my Coke right into it, a perfect fit, and I called it my Coke-holder. I got down next to it on my back, because everyone knows that rich people eat lying down, and I got my sandwich in one hand and put my other arm around the Coke in its holder. When I wanted a drink, I lifted my neck a little, put out my lips, and tipped my Coke a little with the crook of my elbow. Ah.

We were there, lying down, eating our sandwiches, laughing, throwing bread at each other and out for the birds. This was heaven. We were laughing and we couldn't believe it. My mother *was* keeping something from us, ah ha, but we had found her out. We even found water over at the side of the clearing to wash our plates with—we had brought plates. Sergio started washing his plates when he was done, and I was being rich with my Coke, and this day in summer was right.

When suddenly these two men came, from around a corner of trees and the tallest grass we had ever seen. They had bags on their backs, leather bags, bags and sticks.

We didn't know what clubs were, but I learned later, like I learned about the grinding balls. The two men yelled at us. Most specifically, one wanted me to take my Coke out of my Coke-holder so he could sink his golf ball into it.

Something got taken away from us that moment. Heaven. We grew up a little bit, and couldn't go backward. We learned. No one had ever told us about golf. They had told us about heaven. And it went away. We got golf in exchange.

We went back to the arroyo for the rest of that summer, and tried to have fun the best we could. We learned to be ready for finding the grinding ball. We loved it, and when we buried it we knew what would happen. The truth is, we didn't look so hard for it. We were two boys and twelve summers then, and not stupid. Things get taken away.

We buried it because it was perfect. We didn't tell my mother, but together it was all we talked about, till we forgot. It was the lion.

RESPONDING

1. **Personal Response** The narrator says, "We grew up a little bit, and couldn't go backward." Describe an incident that made you feel the same way.

2. **Literary Analysis** How would you explain the *title*, "The Secret Lion"?

3. **Multicultural Connection** Imagine that this story took place in a locale or country other than the southwestern United States. Substitute a new locale and suggest a few changes that would have to be made.

LANGUAGE WORKSHOP

Style The manner in which writers use words and sentences to fit their ideas is called *style*. Ríos writes: ". . . it'sit's the best thing we'veeverseen. Whatisit?"

1. Break Ríos's words apart to determine what the narrator is saying.
2. Why might Ríos have squeezed these words together to express a boy's speech on discovering something?

WRITER'S PORTFOLIO

Victor Hugo, a French writer, said: "No one ever keeps a secret so well as a child." Do you agree or disagree? In your journal, explain your position, using personal experiences to support your ideas.

ABOUT **LORENE CARY**

Lorene Cary was born in Philadelphia with several advantages: a supportive family, a mother totally committed to seeing that her daughter receive the best education possible, and Cary's own willingness to become part of "that mammoth enterprise — the integration, the moral transformation, no less, of America." After attending an integrated showcase public grade school, she attended St. Paul's, an exclusive prep school in New Hampshire. After graduating, Cary earned degrees from both the University of Pennsylvania and the University of Sussex.

Later she returned to teach at St. Paul's and is now a trustee. The impetus for *Black Ice*, a memoir, came from an idea to do a factual report on St. Paul's, in keeping with her experience as a reporter and magazine writer.

From Black Ice

I HAD NEVER heard of St. Paul's School until Mrs. Evans rang to tell me about it one fall night in 1971. I had just come home from Woolworth's, where I worked at the cheap-and-greasy fountain on Friday nights and Saturdays in a town my friends and I called "Tacky" Darby. I smelled as if I had scrubbed the grill with my uniform. My face shone with hamburger fat, and my Earth Shoes were spattered. At fourteen years old, I felt irritable and entitled to it, as adults seemed to be when they finished their work for the day.

Mrs. Evans's voice brimmed with excitement and fun. She was our next-door neighbor, a retired kindergarten teacher married to a newspaper reporter who had been the first black man on staff at the Philadelphia *Bulletin*. Three years before, when I was eleven, he had given me my first typewriter, a straight-back, black Underwood. Mrs. Evans was witty and down-to-earth, firm but easygoing with children. Her eyesight was poor; she had a recurring tickle that caused her to clear her throat nearly to gagging; under her shiny skin her knuckles were gnarled—yet she glowed with health. My father said that she had better legs than most thirty-year-olds, and my mother asked her advice. My sister, Carole, ran away to the brick house where a plaster Venus arose from her seashell and dolphins leapt at half-moons in the cream-colored ceiling molding. It was a fairy-tale house, and Mrs. Evans was a fairy godmother to us, distant and charming. I forgot that at first. Instead, I cradled the receiver on my shoulder and counted my tips while she talked, laying the coins silently on the kitchen counter.

$\textrm{M}$RS. EVANS had been told about St. Paul's School by a "lovely woman"—I took that to mean someone white, but trustworthy. This "very exclusive boarding school" had recently gone coed, and they were interested in finding black girls, too, so they'd put out the word with alumni and friends. Mrs. Evans had never visited the school, but she knew that the campus would be beautiful, that there would be music and languages and the arts.

✳
Culture Note

Dickensian (di ken′zē ən) an adjective referring to Charles Dickens, a nineteenth-century British writer who wrote novels of social protest, many of them with scenes taking place in lawyers' chambers. p. 324

She also knew that scholarships—generous scholarships—were available. Mrs. Evans gave me the phone number of an alumnus, a judge, to call for more information. I wrote it down, thanked her for thinking of me, and went upstairs. I didn't need another school, I thought. I needed a bath.

Later that night, despite my adolescent defiance, I could not help but think about what Mrs. Evans had said. This education was more than knowledge; it could mean credentials, self-confidence, power. I imagined living away from home, making a precocious launch into the wide world of competition.

On Monday after school, I hurried home to call the judge, but when I got there, all I could do was stand next to the telephone preparing statements. My mother watched me as she cooked dinner. "Did Mrs. Evans give you the number to his home or his chambers?" she asked.

I hadn't thought about "chambers." Did "chambers" have telephones? I imagined a Dickensian suite of rooms, wood-paneled and dark, and in the middle a big, florid man draped in black robes, pondering important papers, a man who was not used to being interrupted by phone calls from strange fourteen-year-old black girls who wanted to go to his alma mater.

My mother laughed at me as I stood by the telephone in the kitchen staring at the number. "Just call him," she said.

Whenever I rang, the judge did not answer. A woman took the message and said that he would get back to me. We got on with dinner preparation. Our TV blared. Pots crackled, and dishes clattered; my parents talked over the TV; my eight-year-old sister talked over my parents; I talked over my sister. Then the telephone rang.

By the time I had motioned wildly for silence, the conversation was nearly finished. The judge said that he was pleased to hear of my interest. Then he gave me the name and address of another alumnus who would be hosting a meeting, and urged me to attend.

THE MEETING took place within a couple weeks. We drove through West Philadelphia, past the squat row houses where I had been raised, past the city center and then north where Wissahickon Creek falls away from the road, and woods rise up behind it. We were headed toward Chestnut Hill, more a place name than a place for me until then, a symbol of money and social exclusiveness. My father steered us through Germantown, where wet leaves lay in treacherous layers over trolley tracks and cobblestones. Cars slipped on and off the rails and then swerved to avoid each other, making rubbery squeals and muffled thuds.

By the time we pulled into the stone driveway, I felt as if we were a long way away from our home in the west end of Yeadon, an enclave of black professionals, paraprofessionals, wish-they-was-, look-like-, and might-as-well-be professionals, as we called ourselves. We were far away from the black suburb that, as a West Philly transplant, I disliked for its self-satisfied smugness. When we'd moved from our city apartment — from the living room with a convertible couch where my parents slept, from the bedroom where my sister and I slept (which was transformed into a dining room at Christmas), and from the kitchen where we normally ate, and where my mother pressed and curled women's hair in the evenings — Yeadon had impressed me with its leafy green grandeur and insularity. But now, as we stood in the Chestnut Hill driveway, I saw how modest our Tudors were, our semidetached Dutch colonials, our muddy driveways and the cyclone fences that held in our dogs. I saw it then, with eyes made keen by years of witnessing our merciless self-criticism: "What's wrong with the colored race? I'll tell you what's wrong with the colored race. We don't *think*. That's what. And we do not stick together. And money? Forget it. Invest? Get outta here. Now you take a look at the Jews. Or you take the Chinese. . . . " I saw how consumed we'd been with ambition, and how modest had been our goals.

Inside the stone house, in a large living room, we joined a few other black people who had also come to learn about the School. A boy who was younger than I sat next to his mother. When I said hello, he did not turn his head to look at me, but only peeped out of the corner of his eyes and nodded, as if we might bolt out of the house together and go howling into the Chestnut Hill woods if we were to look too hard at each other. His mother, her hair done up like Coretta Scott King's, sat still like her son. She looked as dignified as a picture on the back of a church fan, and just as inanimate. If she kept any unauthorized verb forms from flying out from between her lips, she also held in any sign of life.

Jeremy Price (this name and a few others have been changed), a black teacher from St. Paul's, tried a few times to make small talk, but he was a Brahmin from another planet: cool, ironic, aloof. He was in his thirties, tweed-jacketed and bearded, with a round belly. He touched his body lightly with his fingers, as if he were not used to his own girth. In every other way he appeared absolutely smooth and easy to my adolescent eye, and assured to the point of arrogance.

Mr. Price made quick judgments of us; they showed in his eyes. Clearly, the pillar-of-the-church lady with the Southern coif (and Southern diffidence in the presence of white folks) wasn't his type. Mr. Price seemed about to say something brutal to her. My father stepped in to ask if he could join them. The look she gave Daddy went beyond grateful to adoring.

WOMEN LOOKED at my father that way. Their attention seemed to affect him as naturally as sunshine—and he never talked too much. "Still water runs deep," my great-grandmother had said about him when he came courting; she said so until she died. Men saw more ripples on the pond, which those of us who lived with him knew positively were caused by undertows.

For one thing, when men exchanged the inevitable sports conversation they discovered, as Mr. Price did, that my father was a student of judo. He'd spent three nights a week since his twenty-eighth birthday at the dojo. He had progressed from white belt to brown to black. We'd gone to competitions throughout the mid-Atlantic region, and I'd watched three-minute dramas on the mat. Each time he had to beat or be beaten. In contest after contest he was a light-middleweight whose feet made the sound of rushing as they swept the dry mat and whose face turned purple when the last man, the one he finally could not beat, held him down, cutting into his windpipe with his bleached white *gi*. In those moments, when I prayed that he would not be killed in some fluke throw, I saw in his eyes a concentration and force that made life with us in the sparkling three-room apartment seem like some errant choice. He was, above all, a physical being, a wiry man who

> ✳
> ### Culture Notes
> **dojo** a training school or workout studio for judo, p. 327
>
> **gi** (gē) judo uniform, p. 327

once tied our deluxe-size refrigerator to his back to move it, and would probably not object to being remembered that way. We three, two girls and a woman, surrounded him with doll babies and crisscross curtains. It was like watching a carnivore sit down to porridge each night.

Dad had first seen judo practiced in a 1945 film, *Blood on the Sun*, with James Cagney. Intended as anti-Japanese propaganda, the film showed an expansionist culture, arrogant and absolute. Daddy loved it. Judo: there was a vision of power—mental, physical, spiritual—beneath a placid exterior. It was nearly twenty years before my father stepped onto a mat. Now, he only needed to mention the word. People looked at him as if he had jumped out of a Samurai movie. Even Mr. Price lost his frost when the subject came up. As I watched the two of them chat, my fear of Mr. Price dissipated, but not my wariness. He did not quite seem one of us.

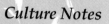

Culture Notes

James Cagney movie actor famous for his "tough guy" roles, p. 328

Samurai members of the warrior class in feudal Japan, p. 328

Sidney Poitier actor and director, p. 328

Mike Russell did. He was a St. Paul's School senior recruiting black candidates as an independent-study project, and he had more poise than I'd ever seen in a teenager. His skin was chocolatey and fine-pored, and his bottom lip pouted like Sidney Poitier's. He was sleek and articulate. He paid attention to me.

I crossed my legs with what I hoped was lithe grace and stretched my neck until I nearly pitched forward onto the floor. I wanted to know the things he must know: about science and literature and language, living away from home, New England, white people, money, power, himself. I suppose that the other black students at St. Paul's must have had Russell's sophistication and charm, his commitment to black progress.

I had to be part of that. With the force of religious conversion, the great God of education moved within me, an

African Methodist God with a voice that boomed like thunder. It took all my strength to hold myself inside my skin. This school — why, this was what I had been raised for, only I hadn't known it. They closed the curtains and turned off the lights for the slide show. I hoped that my face had not betrayed me.

Russell narrated the slide show. He told us about the Old Chapel, a steepled red-brick church, and towering behind it on the green lawn, the Chapel of St. Peter and St. Paul, built in 1886 to accommodate a larger student body, and enlarged in 1927. The New Chapel was massive. Its brick and stone walls were heavy and stolid; and yet its stained-glass windows seemed infinitely light, as if they could almost float up to the heavens.

We saw other buildings as well: the Schoolhouse, student houses (in keeping with the school's family-centered lexicon, they were not to be called dormitories), the Rectory, the funny circular post office, and special academic buildings for science, math, and art. The gray granite library with its white columns had been built by somebody famous. It sat at the edge of yet another pond, casting a wavering, silvery reflection on the water.

OVER AND OVER again we saw these buildings, draped with scenic young people, alone or in small groups, talking, laughing, bending their heads toward one another or running together on a green field in some pantomime of benevolent competition. I saw black boys. I saw girls, a few of them black, too. And I saw them all in a brilliant medley of New Hampshire seasons. At one point in the slide show, Russell flashed through the carousel to find a misplaced slide, creating an intoxicating display of colors — autumn red and gold, winter snowy blue-white, spring green and pink and blue — so sharp and bright that they seemed to originate not on the screen, but from deep inside my head, like music.

Mr. Price's voice, clear and insouciant, brought me back to myself. He was asking for someone to open the drapes.

My mother began with a question about the progress of coeducation. First there were tea dances, Mr. Price said, begun in the nineteenth century and carried forward into the 1960s as dance weekends. Girls were bused in, talked to, danced with, and then bused out again. He looked at Mike Russell and asked ironically, "How were they?"

Russell shook his head and laughed. "They were awful!"

Mr. Price went on. In 1969 and 1970, girls came, like foreigners, to participate in a winter-term exchange. The next winter, the first nineteen came to stay.

What was a tea dance? I wondered. Tea meant little girls with clean hands and faces sipping out of china cups, eating butter cookies with raspberry jam. Teas belonged in church or in childhood. A dance, to the contrary, meant teenagers in a basement: black lights, red bulbs, music jamming its way through our shoes and up into our feet. It meant arms in the air, whistles, a soul train down the middle of the room, whipping out new steps nice and casual as if we hadn't spent all week practicing. It meant sweat steaming out of the tops of our heads, shrinking Afros worthy of Angela Davis down to dreaded TWAs (teeny weeny Afros). A dance meant watching sharp so that no amorous brother spoiled our hot pants.

❋
Culture Note

Angela Davis Davis, who was prominent as a radical in the 1960s, is now a social activist and educator. p. 330

Tea had nothing to do with it.

Mr. Price acted as cultural interpreter for us, as if a bank of white and black computers stood on either side of him, bleeping away in incompatible languages. When my mother asked about the grading system, I heard her asking whether white teachers four hundred miles away would give her kid a fair grade. Hanging in the air was our fear that they'd let us survive, but never excel. Mr. Price answered by describing the system: High Honors for work that was truly outstanding; Honors for work that was very, very good; High Pass—he laughed and shook his head— was a great, gray, muddy area between the very good and the OK; Pass was just acceptable; and Unsatisfactory was "self-explanatory." Then he estimated how many students received which grades, and quite directly — said it right out in this white alumnus's house with the costly furnishings — told us how the black students were doing. He said most of them were working hard, but some were not, frankly, getting what the school had to offer. He did not answer the black mothers' fear of their children's powerlessness, their vulnerability to white adults who might equate sharpness of the mind with sharpness of features.

Mr. Price encouraged Russell to comment. Mike told a few stories about himself, portraying St. Paul's as a place where well-meaning, well-trained teachers tried hard to live up to their calling. Some, he added meaningfully, were more sensitive than others.

Then my mother told a story about a science award I had won in third grade. She started with the winning — the long, white staircase in the auditorium of the Franklin Institute, and how the announcer called my name twice because we were way at the back and it took me so long to get down those steps.

MAMA'S EYES GLOWED. She was a born raconteur, able to increase the intensity of her own presence and fill the room. She was also a woman who seldom found new audiences for her anecdotes, so she made herself happy, she insisted, with us children, her mother, her sisters, her grandparents — an entire clan of storytellers competing for a turn on the family stage. This time all eyes were on my mother. Her body, brown and plump and smooth, was shot through with energy. This time the story had a purpose.

She told them how my science experiment almost did not get considered in the citywide competition. My third-grade teacher, angry that I'd forgotten to bring a large box for displaying and storing the experiment, made me pack it up to take home. (Our teacher had told us that the boxes were needed to carry the experiments from our class to the exhibition room, and she'd emphasized that she would not be responsible for finding thirty boxes on the day of the fair. Without a box, the experiment would have to go home. Other kids, white kids, had forgotten boxes during the week. They'd brought boxes the next day. I asked for the same dispensation, but was denied. The next day was the fair, she said. That was different.)

I came out of school carrying the pieces of the experiment my father had picked out for me from a textbook. This was a simple buoyancy experiment where I weighed each object in the air and then in water, to prove that they weighed less in water. I had with me the scale, a brick, a piece of wood, a bucket, and a carefully lettered poster.

W ELL, MY MOTHER marched me and my armload of buoyant materials right back into school and caught the teacher before she left. The box was the only problem? Just the box? Nothing wrong with the experiment? An excited eight-year-old had forgotten a lousy, stinking box that you get from the supermarket, and for that, she was out of the running? The teacher said I had to learn to follow directions. My mother argued that I had followed directions by doing the experiment by myself, which was more than you could say for third graders who'd brought in dry-cell batteries that lit light bulbs and papier-mâché volcanoes that belched colored lava.

"Don't you ever put me in a position like that again," Mama said when we were out of earshot of the classroom. "You never know who is just waiting for an excuse to shut us out."

We got the box; my experiment went into the fair; I won the prize at school. I won third prize for my age group in the city.

My ears began to burn. I could not help but believe that they would see through this transparent plug, and before I had even laid hands on an application. They'd think we were forward and pushy. I forgot, for the moment, how relieved I'd felt when Mama had stood in front of that teacher defending me with a blinding righteousness, letting the teacher know that I was not as small and black and alone as I seemed, that I came from somewhere, and where I came from, she'd better believe, somebody was home.

The other mothers nodded approvingly. My father gave me a wide, clever-girl smile. Mr. Price and Russell looked at me deadpan. They seemed amused by my embarrassment.

The story was an answer, part rebuke and part condolence, to Mike Russell's stories, where no parents figured at all. It was a message to Mr. Price about her maternal concerns, and a way to prove that racism was not some vanquished enemy, but a real, live person, up in your face, ready, for no apparent reason, to mess with your kid. When I was in third grade, and her marriage to my father had looked like forever, when Martin Luther King was alive preaching love, and white flight had not yet sunk the real-estate values in West Philly, Mama could do her maternal duty, and face down a white teacher who would have deprived me of my award. Who at St. Paul's School would stand up for her child in her stead?

Mr. Price did not answer my mother's story. Instead he invited a few more questions. The Mama's boy asked about food and mosquitoes and telephones. He looked appalled to hear that there were no phones in the rooms, only public phone booths outside, and only a handful at that. I doubted that I'd see that child again.

If we wanted to be considered for candidacy, we were to write for an application, our own letters, composed in our own hand, and register to take standardized tests. In addition, Mr. Price said, it would be worth our while to visit the school in person.

Our host, Ralph Starr, who had slipped out of the room during the discussion, had slipped back in. Mr. Price thanked him for the use of his house. Mr. Starr took exception. He was glad to be able to help in the good work that Mr. Price and Mike were doing. In fact he thanked *us* for coming. The adults appeared pleased. They chatted with each other; I talked to Mike, and the session ended.

As we drove away, my mother could not get over how Mrs. Starr had given her barefoot toddler a spoonful of peanut butter to lick before she was spirited upstairs. Mama didn't feed us peanut butter. It wasn't proper good food, she said. It was what PWTs—poor white trash—gave their kids. For my lunch, Mom packed baked chicken on toast with lettuce and mayonnaise, ham, tuna, sliced tongue, or cheese.

I was as jolted by the sight as my mother, and not just the peanut butter, but the whole family scene. I had thought that rich white people would have been quieter, their children more tidy, their mothers less vibrant. I didn't like it that my mother, too, had been surprised. It made me nervous.

A week later, however, I did not think of the background kid-babble in Chestnut Hill, but of the wide drawing room and the slides. Mr. Price wrote promptly to inform us that he had indeed scheduled the visit we'd said we wanted to make to the school.

"They don't play, do they?" My parents took turns asking each other and answering back.

"Those people do not play."

RESPONDING

1. **Personal Response** During her visit to Chestnut Hill, a "symbol of money and social exclusiveness," Cary has mixed feelings. Explain how you would have felt in this setting.

2. **Literary Analysis** Cary uses *details* in her narrative to make events and people appear realistic and vivid. Find such details in the first two paragraphs.

3. **Multicultural Connection** Why does Cary's mother ask the questions she does about co-education and the grading system of St. Paul's?

LANGUAGE WORKSHOP

Proper Nouns and Adjectives This selection contains many *proper nouns* — words that name a particular person (Sidney Poitier), place (St. Paul's School), or thing (High Honors), as well as *adjectives* that can be based on these nouns (Chestnut Hill driveway). Such words are always capitalized. Find ten other proper nouns or adjectives in the selection.

WRITER'S PORTFOLIO

You are the narrator, writing a letter thanking one of the following: (1) Mrs. Evans; (2) Jeremy Price; (3) Mike Russell; (4) Mr. and Mrs. Ralph Starr. Adapt your tone to the audience you have chosen.

ABOUT **VIRGIL SUÁREZ**

Born in Havana, Cuba, Virgil Suárez emigrated with his parents to Madrid, Spain, before moving to America in 1974 and settling in Los Angeles. Currently a teacher at Louisiana State University, Suárez has published three books about the Cuban American experience. His first novel, *Latin Jazz,* deals with the problems faced by an immigrant family that leaves Cuba after Fidel Castro's rise to power. His other works include *The Cutter* and *Welcome to the Oasis and Other Stories.* Concerned with the issues of identity and cultural heritage, Suárez has helped promote other Latino writers. Recently he co-edited *Iguana Dreams: New Latino Fiction,* a volume intended to unite the distinct cultures that speak a common language and share a common need for cultural survival.

A Perfect Hotspot

THIS IDEA of selling ice cream during the summer seems ridiculous, pointless. I'd much rather be close to water. The waves. Where I can hear them tumble in and then roll out, and see the tiny bubbles left behind on the sand pop one by one. Or feel the undercurrents warm this time of year. Swimming. Watching the girls in bikinis with stand stuck to the backs of their thighs walk up and down the boardwalk. At this time of the morning, the surfers are out riding the waves.

Instead I'm inside an ice cream truck with my father, selling, cruising the streets. The pumps suck oil out of the ground rapidly with the creaking sounds of iron biting iron in a fenced lot at the end of the street. They look like giant rocking horses. Father turns at the corner, then, suddenly, he points to another ice cream truck.

"There's the competition," he says. "If the economy doesn't improve soon, these streets'll be full of them."

He's smoking, and the smoke floats back my way and chokes me. I can't stand it. Some of the guys on the swim team smoke. I don't understand how they can smoke and do their best when it's time for competition. I wouldn't smoke. To do so would be like cheating myself out of winning.

All morning he's been instructing me on how to sell ice cream.

"Tonio," he says now, "come empty your pockets."

I walk to the front of the truck, stick my hands deep into my pockets and grab a handful of coins — what we've made in change all morning. The coins fall, overlap and multiply against the sides of the grease-smudged change box. I turn my pockets inside-out until the last coin falls. He picks out the pieces of lint and paper from the coins.

When he begins to explain the truck's quirks, "the little problems," as he calls the water leaks, burning oil, and dirty carburetor, I return to the back of the truck and sit down on top of the wood counter next to the window.

"Be always on the lookout for babies," Father says. "The ones in pampers. They pop out of nowhere. Check your mirrors all the time."

A CAUTION CHILDREN cardboard sign hangs from the rearview mirror. Running over children is a deep fear that seems to haunt him.

All I need, I keep reminding myself, is to pass the CPR course, get certified, and look for a job as a beach lifeguard.

"Stop!" a kid screams, slamming the screen door of his house open. He runs to the grassy part next to the sidewalk. Father stops the truck. The kid's hand comes up over the edge of the window with a dollar bill forked between his little fingers.

"What do you want?" I say.

"A Froze Toe," he says, jumping up and down, dirt rings visible on his neck. He wets the corners of his mouth with his cherry, Kool-aid-stained tongue. I reach inside the freezer and bring out a bar. On its wrapper is the picture of an orange foot with a blue bubble gum ball on the big toe.

"See what else he wants," Father says. "Make sure they always leave the dollar."

The kid takes his ice cream, and he smiles.

"What else?" I ask him.

He shrugs his shoulders, shakes his head, and bites the wrapper off. The piece of paper falls on the grass. I give him his change; he walks back to his house.

"Should always make sure they leave all the money they bring," Father says. "They get it to spend it. That's the only way you'll make a profit. Don't steal their money, but exchange it for merchandise." His ears stick out from underneath his L.A. Dodgers cap. The short hair on the back of his head stands out.

I grin up at the rearview mirror, but he isn't looking.

"Want to split a Pepsi, Tonio?" he says.

"I'm not thirsty."

"Get me some water then."

The cold mist inside the freezer crawls up my hand. After he drinks and returns the bottle, I place it back with the ice cream.

"Close the freezer," he says, "before all the cold gets out and they melt."

If the cold were out I'd be at the natatorium doing laps.

O N ANOTHER STREET, a group of kids jumps and skips around a short man. The smallest of the kids hangs from the man's thigh. The man signals my father to stop, then walks up to the window. The kids scream excitedly.

"Want this one, daddy," one of the girls says.

"This one!" a boy says.

The smallest kid jumps, pointing his finger at the display my father has made with all the toys and candies.

"No, José," the man says, taking the kid by the wrist. "No candy."

The kid turns to look up at his father, not fully understanding, and then looks at me. His little lips tremble.

"Give me six Popsicles," the man says.

"I don't want no Pop—"

"Popsicles or nothing. I don't have money to buy you what you want."

"A Blue Ghost. I want a Blue Ghost."

"No, I said."

The smallest kid cries.

"Be quiet, José, or I'm going to tell the man to go away."

I put the six Popsicles on the counter.

"How much?" the man asks. The skin around his eyes is a darker brown than that of his nose and cheeks.

"A dollar-fifty," I say.

He digs inside his pockets and produces two wrinkled green balls which he throws on the counter. The two dollar bills roll. I unfold the bills, smooth them, and give them to Father, who returns the man his change through the front window.

The man gives each kid a Popsicle, then walks away with his hands in his pockets. José, still crying, grabs his as he follows his father back to their house.

"He doesn't want to spend his beer money," Father says, driving away from the curb.

AFTER THAT, we have no more customers for hours. Ever since he brought the truck home two years ago, Father has changed. Ice creams have become his world. According to Father, appearance and cleanliness isn't important as long as the truck passes the Health Department inspection in order to obtain the sales license. The inside of the truck is a mess: paint flakes off, rust hides between crevices, the freezer lids hold layer upon layer of dirt and melted ice cream. Here I'll have to spend the rest of my summer, I think, among the strewn Doritos, Munchos, and the rest of the merchandise.

The outside of the truck had been painted by Father's friend Gaspar, before mother died. I remember how Gaspar drank beer after beer while he painted the crown over the K in KING OF ICE CREAM and assured mother, who never missed one of my swim meets and who always encouraged me to become the best swimmer I could be, that I was going to make it all right in the end.

Father lives this way, I know, out of loneliness. He misses mother as much as I do.

I count the passing of time by how many ice creams I sell. It isn't anything like swimming laps. Doing laps involves the idea of setting and breaking new limits.

"How much do you think we have?" my father asks. The visor of his cap tilts upward.

"I don't know." I hate the metallic smell money leaves on my fingers.

"Any idea?"

"No."

"A couple of months on your own and you'll be able to guess approximately how much you make."

A couple of months, I think, and I'll be back in high school. Captain of the varsity swim team. A customer waits down the street.

"Make the kill fast," Father says.

A barefooted woman holding a child to her breast comes to the window. She has dirty fingernails, short and uneven, as if she bites them all the time. Make the kill fast, I think.

Ice creams on the counter, I tell her, "Two dollars."

She removes the money out of her brassiere and hands it to me, then she walks away. She has yellow blisters on the back of each heel.

After that, he begins to tell me the story of the wild dog. When he was a kid, a wild bitch came down from the hills and started killing my grandfather's chickens. "Seeing the scattered feathers," Father says. "made your grandfather so angry I thought his face would burst because it'd turned so red."

"Anyway," he continues, "the wild dog kept on killing chickens."

Not only my grandfather's, but other farmers' as well. The other farmers were scared because they thought the wild dog was a witch. One morning, my grandfather got my father out of bed early and took him up to the hills behind the house with a jar of poison. A farmer had found the bitch's litter. My grandfather left my father in charge of anointing the poison all over the puppies' fur so that when the mother came back, if he hadn't shot it by then, she'd die the minute she licked her young. My father didn't want to do it, but my grandfather left him in command while he went after the wild dog to shoot it. The dog disappeared and the puppies licked each other to death.

When he finishes telling me the story, Father looks at the rearview mirror and grins, then he drives on. He turns up the volume of the music box and now *Raindrops Keep Falling on My Head* blares out of the speakers. The old people'll complain, he says, because the loud music hurts their eardrums, but the louder the music, the more people'll hear it, and more ice creams'll get sold.

Farther ahead, another kid stops us. The kid has his tongue out. His eyes seem to be too small for his big face. Though he seems old, he still drools. He claps his small hands quickly.

"Does he have money?" Father asks.

"Can't see."

The kid walks over to the truck and hangs from the edge of the window.

"Get him away from the truck," Father says, then to the kid, "Hey, move away!"

"Come on," I tell the kid. "you might fall and hurt yourself."

"Wan icleam," the kid says.

"We'll be back in a little while," Father tells him.

"Wan icleam!" He doesn't let go. "Wan icleam!"

"Move back!" Father shouts. "Tonio, get him away from the truck."

I try to unstick the kid's pudgy fingers from the metal edge of the window, but he won't let go. His saliva falls on my hands.

"Wan icleam!"

I reach over to one of the shelves to get a penny candy for him so that I can bait him into letting go, but Father catches me.

"Don't you dare," he says.

He opens the door and comes around the back to the kid, pulling him away from the truck to the sidewalk where he sets the kid down, and returns.

"Can't give your merchandise away," he says. "You can't make a profit that way, Tonio."

The kid runs after us shouting, waving his arms. I grab a handful of candies and throw them out the window to the sidewalk, where they fall on the grass and scatter.

The sun sets slowly, and, descending, it spreads Popsicle orange on the sky. Darkness creeps on the other side of the city.

If I don't get a job as a lifeguard, I think, I'm going to travel southeast and visit the islands.

"How are the ice creams doing?" Father asks. "Are they softening?"

I check by squeezing a bar and say, "I think we should call it a day."

"Tonio," he says. He turns off the music, makes a left turn to the main street, and heads home. "Why didn't you help me with that kid? You could have moved him. What will happen when you're here by yourself?"

"Couldn't do it."

"Here," he says, giving me the change box. "Take it inside when we get home."

"I'll get it when we get there."

HE PUTS the blue box back down on top of the stand he built over the motor. Cars speed by. The air smells heavy with exhaust and chemical fumes. In the distance, columns of smoke rise from factory smokestacks.

He turns into the driveway, drives the truck all the way to the front of the garage, and parks underneath the long branches of the avocado tree.

"Take the box inside," he says, turning off the motor. He steps down from the truck and connects the freezer to the extension cord coming out of the kitchen window.

I want to tell him that I won't come out tomorrow.

"Come on, Tonio. Bring the box in."

"You do it," I say.

"What's the matter, son?"

"I'd rather you do it."

"Like you'd rather throw all my merchandise out of the window," he says, growing red in the face. "I saw you."

He walks toward me, and I sense another argument coming. Father stops in front of me and gives me a wry smile. "Dreamers like you," he says, "learn the hard way."

He turns around, picks up the change box, and says, "I'm putting the truck up for sale. From now on you're on your own, you hear. I'm not forcing you to do something you don't want to."

I don't like the expressionless look on his face when usually, whenever he got angry at me, his face would get red and sweaty.

He unlocks the kitchen door and enters the house.

I jump out of the truck, lock the door, and walk around our clapboard house to the patio. Any moment now, I think, Father'll start slamming doors inside and throwing things around. He'll curse. I lean against the wall and feel the glass of the window behind me when it starts to tremble.

RESPONDING

1. **Personal Response** Tell about a job (paid or unpaid) that you disliked as much as Tonio dislikes his. How did you handle your obligation and what was the final outcome?

2. **Literary Analysis** Part of the vividness of this story depends on its *imagery*, word pictures that appeal to the senses. Point out words or phrases related to each of the five senses.

3. **Multicultural Connection** What clues does the story provide about the economic state of Tonio's father? about his neighborhood? How do these influence his father's attitude toward his business? his son's future?

LANGUAGE WORKSHOP

Apostrophe An *apostrophe* is used to indicate a possessive noun and to show the omission of one or more letters in contractions. Tonio says of his father, "He's smoking. . . . I can't stand it." Explain why the apostrophes appear here. Now place apostrophes where they belong in the following sentences.
1. Tonios father guards his merchandise closely.
2. Hes afraid someone will carry off the days earnings.
3. Tonio sees the look on a boys face and decides hes hungry.
4. Several fathers decide its time to give their kids a treat.
5. Tonios afraid his fatherll start slamming doors.

WRITER'S PORTFOLIO

The King of Ice Cream truck is dirty and unappealing, service is poor, and business is bad. Tonio decides to present his father with a plan to improve all three. If his father agrees to the plan, Tonio will take care of the business for the rest of the summer. Design his improvement plan, complete with approximate costs (which should be kept as low as possible).

ABOUT **TONI MORRISON**

Toni Morrison was awarded the 1993
Nobel Prize for Literature — the first African
American woman to be so honored. Beginning
with *The Bluest Eye* in 1970, she has published
a steady stream of award-winning novels,
including *Sula, Song of Solomon, Tar Baby,
Beloved,* and *Jazz.* Born in Lorain, Ohio,
Morrison graduated from Howard and Cornell
Universities. From 1955 to 1964, she was a
college teacher; from 1965 to the early '80s
when she returned to teaching, she acted as
an editor for a major publishing company.
Although she has also written drama, essays,
and reviews, Morrison is known
primarily for her
novels — all of which
are revered for their
poetic use of language,
mythic vision, and fresh
view of African
American life.

From The Bluest Eye

MY DADDY'S FACE is a study. Winter moves into it and presides there. His eyes become a cliff of snow threatening to avalanche; his eyebrows bend like black limbs of leafless trees. His skin takes on the pale, cheerless yellow of winter sun; for a jaw he has the edges of a snowbound field dotted with stubble; his high forehead is the frozen sweep of the Erie, hiding currents of gelid thoughts that eddy in darkness. Wolf killer turned hawk fighter, he worked night and day to keep one from the door and the other from under the windowsills. A Vulcan guarding the flames, he gives us instructions about which doors to keep closed or opened for proper distribution of heat, lays kindling by, discusses qualities of coal, and teaches us how to rake, feed, and bank the fire. And he will not unrazor his lips until spring.

> ### Culture Notes
>
> **Erie** Lake Erie, one of the five Great Lakes, p. 347
>
> **Vulcan** ancient Roman god of fire and metal working, p. 347

Winter tightened our heads with a band of cold and melted our eyes. We put pepper in the feet of our stockings, Vaseline on our faces, and stared through dark icebox mornings at four stewed prunes, slippery lumps of oatmeal, and cocoa with a roof of skin.

But mostly we waited for spring, when there could be gardens.

By the time this winter had stiffened itself into a hateful knot that nothing could loosen, something did loosen it, or rather someone. A someone who splintered the knot into silver threads that tangled us, netted us, made us long for the dull chafe of the previous boredom.

This disrupter of seasons was a new girl in school named Maureen Peal. A high-yellow dream child with long brown hair braided into two lynch ropes that hung down her back. She was rich, at least by our standards, as rich as the richest of the white girls, swaddled in comfort and care. The quality of her clothes threatened to derange Frieda and me. Patent-leather shoes with buckles, a cheaper version of which we got only at Easter and which had disintegrated by the end of May. Fluffy sweaters the color of lemon drops tucked into the skirts with pleats so orderly they astounded us. Brightly colored knee socks with white borders, a brown velvet coat trimmed in white rabbit fur, and a matching muff. There was a hint of spring in her aloe green eyes, something summery in her complexion, and a rich autumn ripeness in her walk.

SHE ENCHANTED the entire school. When teachers called on her, they smiled encouragingly. Black boys didn't trip her in the halls, white boys didn't stone her, white girls didn't suck their teeth when she was assigned to be their work partners; black girls stepped aside when she wanted to use the sink in the girls' toilet, and their eyes genuflected under sliding lids. She never had to search for anybody to eat with in the cafeteria—they flocked to the table of her choice, where she opened fastidious lunches, shaming our jelly-stained bread with egg-salad sandwiches cut into four dainty squares, pink-frosted cupcakes, stocks of celery and carrots, proud, dark apples. She even bought and liked white milk.

Frieda and I were bemused, irritated, and fascinated by her. We looked hard for flaws to restore our equilibrium, but had to be content at first with uglying up her name, changing Maureen Peal to Meringue Pie. Later a minor epiphany was ours when we discovered that she had a dog tooth—a charming one to be sure—but a dog tooth nonetheless. And when we found out that she had been born with six fingers on each hand and that there was a little bump where each extra one had been removed, we smiled. They were small triumphs, but we took what we could get—snickering behind her back and calling her Six-finger-dog-tooth-meringue-pie. But we had to do it alone, for none of the other girls would cooperate with our hostility. They adored her.

WHEN SHE WAS ASSIGNED a locker next to mine, I could indulge my jealousy four times a day. My sister and I both suspected that we were secretly prepared to be her friend, if she would let us, but I knew it would be a dangerous friendship, for when my eye traced the white border patterns of those Kelly-green knee socks, and felt the pull and slack of my brown stockings, I wanted to kick her. And when I thought of the unearned haughtiness in her eyes, I plotted accidental slammings of locker doors on her hand.

As locker friends, however, we got to know each other a little, and I was even able to hold a sensible conversation with her without visualizing her fall off a cliff, or giggling my way into what I thought was a clever insult.

One day, while I waited at the locker for Frieda, she joined me.

"Hi."

"Hi."

"Waiting for your sister?"

"Uh-huh."

"Which way do you go home?"

"Down Twenty-first Street to Broadway."

"Why don't you go down Twenty-second Street?"

" 'Cause I live on Twenty-first Street."

"Oh. I can walk that way, I guess. Partly, anyway."

"Free country."

Frieda came toward us, her brown stockings straining at the knees because she had tucked the toe under to hide a hole in the foot.

"Maureen's gonna walk part way with us."

Frieda and I exchanged glances, her eyes begging my restraint, mine promising nothing.

It was a false spring day, which, like Maureen, had pierced the shell of a deadening winter. There were puddles, mud, and an inviting warmth that deluded us. The kind of day on which we draped our coats over our heads, left our galoshes in school, and came down with croup the following day. We always responded to the slightest change in weather, the most minute shifts in time of day. Long before seeds were stirring, Frieda and I were scuffing and poking at the earth, swallowing air, drinking rain. . . .

As WE EMERGED from the school with Maureen, we began to moult immediately. We put our head scarves in our coat pockets, and our coats on our heads. I was wondering how to maneuver Maureen's fur muff into a gutter when a commotion in the playground distracted us. A group of boys was circling and holding at bay a victim, Pecola Breedlove.

Bay Boy, Woodrow Cain, Buddy Wilson, Junie Bug— like a necklace of semiprecious stones they surrounded her. Heady with the smell of their own musk, thrilled by the easy power of a majority, they gaily harassed her.

"Black e mo. Black e mo. Yadaddsleepsnekked. Black e mo black e mo ya dadd sleeps nekked. Black e mo. . . ."

They had extemporized a verse made up of two insults about matters over which the victim had no control: the color of her skin and speculations on the sleeping habits of an adult, wildly fitting in its incoherence. That they themselves were black, or that their own father had similarly relaxed habits was irrelevant. It was their contempt for their own blackness that gave the first insult its teeth. They seemed to have taken all of their smoothly cultivated ignorance, their exquisitely learned self-hatred, their elaborately designed hopelessness and sucked it all up into a fiery cone of scorn that had burned for ages in the hollows of their minds—cooled—and spilled over lips of outrage, consuming whatever was in its path. They danced a macabre ballet around the victim, whom, for their own sake, they were prepared to sacrifice to the flaming pit.

> Black e mo Black e mo Ya daddy sleeps nekked.
> Stch ta ta stch ta ta
> stach ta ta ta ta ta

Pecola edged around the circle crying. She had dropped her notebook, and covered her eyes with her hands.

We WATCHED, afraid they might notice us and turn their energies our way. Then Frieda, with set lips and Mama's eyes, snatched her coat from her head and threw it on the ground. She ran toward them and brought her books down on Woodrow Cain's head. The circle broke. Woodrow Cain grabbed his head.

"Hey, girl!"

"You cut that out, you hear?" I had never heard Frieda's voice so loud and clear.

Maybe because Frieda was taller than he was, maybe because he saw her eyes, maybe because he had lost interest in the game, or maybe because he had a crush on Frieda, in any case Woodrow looked frightened just long enough to give her more courage.

"Leave her 'lone, or I'm gone tell everybody what you did!"

Woodrow did not answer; he just walled his eyes.

Bay Boy piped up, "Go on, gal! Ain't nobody bothering you."

"You shut up, Bullet Head." I had found my tongue.

"Who you calling Bullet Head?"

"I'm calling you Bullet Head, Bullet Head."

Frieda took Pecola's hand. "Come on."

"You want a fat lip?" Bay Boy drew back his fist at me.

"Yeah. Gimme one of yours."

"You gone get one."

Maureen appeared at my elbow, and the boys seemed reluctant to continue under her springtime eyes so wide with interest. They buckled in confusion, not willing to beat up three girls under her watchful gaze. So they listened to a budding male instinct that told them to pretend we were unworthy of their attention.

"Come on, man."

"Yeah. Come on. We ain't got time to fool with them."

Grumbling a few disinterested epithets, they moved away.

I picked up Pecola's notebook and Frieda's coat, and the four of us left the playground.

"Old Bullet Head, he's always picking on girls."

Frieda agreed with me. "Miss Forrester said he was incorrigival."

"Really?" I didn't know what that meant, but it had enough of a doom sound in it to be true of Bay Boy.

WHILE FRIEDA and I clucked on about the near fight, Maureen, suddenly animated, put her velvet-sleeved arm through Pecola's and began to behave as though they were the closest of friends.

"I just moved here. My name is Maureen Peal. What's yours?"

"Pecola."

"Pecola? Wasn't that the name of the girl in *Imitation of Life?*"

"I don't know. What is that?"

"The picture show, you know. Where this mulatto girl hates her mother 'cause she is black and ugly but then cries at the funeral. It was real sad. Everybody cries in it. Claudette Colbert too."

"Oh." Pecola's voice was no more than a sigh.

"Anyway, her name was Pecola too. She was so pretty. When it comes back, I'm going to see it again. My mother has seen it four times."

Frieda and I walked behind them, surprised at Maureen's friendliness to Pecola, but pleased. Maybe she wasn't so bad, after all. Frieda had put her coat back on her head, and the two of us, so draped, trotted along enjoying the warm breeze and Frieda's heroics.

"You're in my gym class, aren't you?" Maureen asked Pecola.

"Yes."

"Miss Erkmeister's legs sure are bow. I bet she thinks they're cute. How come she gets to wear real shorts, and we have to wear those old bloomers? I want to die every time I put them on."

Pecola smiled but did not look at Maureen.

"Hey." Maureen stopped short. "There's an Isaley's. Want some ice cream? I have money."

She unzipped a hidden pocket in her muff and pulled out a multifolded dollar bill. I forgave her those knee socks.

"My uncle sued Isaley's," Maureen said to the three of us. "He sued the Isaley's in Akron. They said he was disorderly and that that was why they wouldn't serve him, but a friend of his, a policeman, came in and beared the witness, so the suit went through."

"What's a suit?"

"It's when you can beat them up if you want to and won't anybody do nothing. Our family does it all the time. We believe in suits."

At the entrance to Isaley's Maureen turned to Frieda and me, asking, "You all going to buy some ice cream?"

We looked at each other. "No," Frieda said.

Maureen disappeared into the store with Pecola.

Frieda looked placidly down the street; I opened my mouth, but quickly closed it. It was extremely important

> ## Culture Notes
>
> **incorrigival** mispronunciation of incorrigible, meaning "too bad to change," p. 352
>
> **Claudette Colbert** actress of the 1940s, p. 352
>
> **bow:** bowed; curved or bent, p. 353
>
> **beared [bore] the witness** testified on someone's behalf, p. 353

that the world not know that I fully expected Maureen to buy us some ice cream, that for the past 120 seconds I had been selecting the flavor, that I had begun to like Maureen, and that neither of us had a penny.

We supposed Maureen was being nice to Pecola because of the boys, and were embarrassed to be caught — even by each other — thinking that she would treat us, or that we deserved it as much as Pecola did.

RESPONDING

1. **Personal Response** In this story, a new girl in school creates quite a stir. Describe your own reactions to a new student or your own experience as a new student.

2. **Literary Analysis** Find examples of *figurative language* in the first paragraph and explain them. Try describing the narrator's daddy using literal language. What does Morrison's description add?

3. **Multicultural Connection** How do the various characters in this selection respond to shades of "blackness"? Why?

LANGUAGE WORKSHOP

Dash As a means of punctuation, a *dash* is stronger than a comma, more relaxed than parentheses, and less formal than a colon. The dash can signal an explanation or set off an interruption. What purpose does the dash serve in the following passage from the selection: ". . .we discovered that she had a dog tooth — a charming one to be sure — but a dog tooth nonetheless"? Find three other passages in which Morrison uses a dash. Try substituting a colon, comma, or parentheses, and see if you like the results as well.

WRITER'S PORTFOLIO

Both Maureen and Pecola are victims of name-calling by contemporaries. Draw up three short lists of recommendations (addressed to students, teachers, and administrators) designed to reduce or eliminate the use of name-calling in your school. Combine your efforts with those of other class members, present a master list to your administrator, and volunteer to help implement the recommendations.

SCENES FROM CHILDHOOD

Projects

DRAMATIC SCENE

With a partner, act out a dramatic scene between two characters in one of the selections. You will need to make some changes when dialogue is provided or invent dialogue when little or none is given. Also think of a way to conclude before you present your scene to the class.

CHARACTERS' SCRAPBOOK

With a partner, assemble a brief scrapbook of items that portray "scenes from childhood" of several characters in this unit. Find pictures or create facsimiles. Along with items mentioned in the selections, you might add others that are in keeping with the characters (for example, a waitress badge or a record album popular around 1971 for the narrator in the excerpt from *Black Ice*).

REFLECTION ON CHILDHOOD

Nikki Giovanni says in the first line of her poem that "childhood remembrances are always a drag." Write your own poem (or a short prose memoir) that reveals both the positive and negative events of your childhood. If you need a starter, use a variation of Giovanni's line.

Further Reading

These books about coming-of-age reinforce the theme of growing up, presenting various scenes from childhood.

Augenbraum, Harold and Ilan Stavans, eds. *Growing Up Latino: Memoirs and Stories.* Houghton Mifflin, 1993. This excellent collection contains twenty-five pieces by well-known authors.

Hale, Janet Campbell. *Owl's Song.* Avon, 1975. This novel describes the problems a Native American boy faces growing up on a reservation and in the city.

Ione, Carole. *Pride of Family.* Summit Books, 1991. This autobiography traces four generations of African American women, including a high-kicking dancer in the 1920s, a doctor/ social reformer, and a writer.

Kincaid, Jamaica. *Annie John.* Penguin Books, 1983. The title character in this novel is a headstrong and rebellious adolescent growing up in Antigua.

Lee, Gus. *China Boy.* Signet, 1992. In this novel, an over-protected Chinese American boy learns, with the aid of an African American friend and his mentors in the YMCA boxing program, to cope with neighborhood bullies.

Lee, Harper. *To Kill a Mockingbird.* Warner Books, 1993 (first published in 1960). The narrator of this novel, Scout Finch, describes growing up under unusual circumstances during the Great Depression of the 1930s in a tiny Alabama town.

Looking for Love

Love has been compared to everything — from flowers and warfare to baseball, measles, and vegetables. People have praised it, blamed it, pursued it, and taken pains to avoid it. It's been called infinite and blind, heartless and kind. It can appear as a nudge, a bump, or an earthquake. Despite its different shapes, love seems to be everywhere — from greeting cards, songs, and graffiti to this very book. Read on to see if any of the following characters feel about love as you do.

ABOUT **ZORA NEALE HURSTON**

When Zora Neale Hurston died in a
Florida welfare home in 1960, she was
buried in an unmarked grave in a segregated
cemetery. A decade later, however, she was
rediscovered and is honored today as one of
America's most important writers and the spiritual godmother to many contemporary African
American women writers. Born in Eatonville,
Florida, Hurston went to live with various relatives at age nine when her mother died. Later,
she worked as a domestic, a wardrobe girl,
and a maid. She attended Howard University,

Barnard College, and
eventually Columbia
University, where she
studied anthropology.
Determined to be a
writer, she went back to
the South to mine the
rich lode of African
American tales, songs,
and folkways. Her works
include *Mules and Men*, *Their Eyes Were
Watching God*, and *Dust Tracks on a Road*.

From *Their Eyes Were Watching God*

*J*ANIE SAW HER LIFE like a great tree in leaf with the things suffered, things enjoyed, things done and undone. Dawn and doom was in the branches.

"Ah know exactly what Ah got to tell yuh, but it's hard to know where to start at.

"Ah ain't never seen my papa. And Ah didn't know 'im if Ah did. Mah mama neither. She was gone from round dere long before Ah wuz big enough tuh know. Mah grandma raised me. Mah grandma and de white folks she worked wid. She had a house out in de backyard and dat's where Ah wuz born. They was quality white folks up dere in West Florida. Named Washburn. She had four gran'chillun on de place and all of us played together and dat's how come Ah never called mah grandma nothin' but Nanny, 'cause dat's what everybody on de place called her. Nanny used to ketch us in our devilment and lick every youngun on de place and Mis' Washburn did de same. Ah reckon dey never hit us uh lick amiss 'cause dem three boys and us two girls wuz pretty aggravatin', Ah speck.

"Ah was wid dem white chillun so much till Ah didn't know Ah wuzn't white till Ah was round six years old. Wouldn't have found it out then, but a man come long takin' pictures and without askin' anybody, Shelby, dat was de oldest boy, he told him to take us. Round a week later de man brought de picture for Mis' Washburn to see and pay him which she did, then give us all a good lickin'.

"So when we looked at de picture and everybody got pointed out there wasn't nobody left except a real dark little girl with long hair standing by Eleanor. Dat's where Ah wuz s'posed to be, but Ah couldn't recognize dat dark chile as me. So Ah ast, 'where is me? Ah don't see me.'

"Everybody laughed, even Mr. Washburn. Miss Nellie, de Mama of de chillun who come back home after her husband dead, she pointed to de dark one and said, 'Dat's you, Alphabet, don't you know yo' ownself?'

"Dey all useter call me Alphabet 'cause so many people had done named me different names. Ah looked at de picture a long time and seen it was mah dress and mah hair so Ah said:

" 'Aw, aw! Ah'm, colored!'

"Den dey all laughed real hard. But before Ah seen de picture Ah thought Ah wuz just like de rest.

"Us lived dere havin' fun till de chillun at school got to teasin' me 'bout livin' in de white folks backyard. Dere wuz uh knotty head gal name Mayrella dat useter git mad every time she look at me. Mis' Washburn useter dress me up in all de clothes her gran'chillun didn't need no mo' which still wuz better'n whut de rest uh de colored chillun had. And then she useter put hair ribbon on mah head fuh me tuh wear. Dat useter rile Mayrella uh lot. So she would pick at me all de time and put some others up tuh do de same. They'd push me 'way from de ring plays and make out they couldn't play wid nobody dat lived on premises. Den they'd tell me not to be takin' on over mah looks 'cause they mama told 'em 'bout de hound dawgs huntin' mah papa all night long. 'Bout Mr. Washburn and de sheriff puttin' de bloodhounds on de trail tuh ketch mah papa for whut he done tuh mah mama. Dey didn't tell about how he wuz seen tryin' tuh git in touch wid mah mama later on so he could marry her. Naw, dey didn't talk dat part of it atall. Dey made it sound real bad so as tuh crumple mah feathers.

✱

Characters Offstage

Pheoby Janie's friend; the person she is addressing in this story, p. 363

Leafy Nanny's daughter and Janie's mother, p. 371

None of 'em didn't even remember whut his name wuz, but dey all knowed de bloodhound part by heart. Nanny didn't love tuh see me wid mah head hung down, so she figgered it would be mo' better fuh me if us had uh house. She got de land and everything and then Mis' Washburn helped out uh whole heap wid things."

Pheoby's hungry listening helped Janie to tell her story. So she went on thinking back to her young years and explaining them to her friend in soft, easy phrases while all around the house, the night time put on flesh and blackness.

She thought awhile and decided that her conscious life had commenced at Nanny's gate. On a late afternoon Nanny had called her to come inside the house because she had spied Janie letting Johnny Taylor kiss her over the gatepost.

*I*T WAS A SPRING AFTERNOON in West Florida. Janie had spent most of the day under a blossoming pear tree in the back-yard. She had been spending every minute that she could steal from her chores under that tree for the last three days. That was to say, ever since the first tiny bloom had opened. It had called her to come and gaze on a mystery. From barren brown stems to glistening leaf-buds; from the leaf-buds to snowy virginity of bloom. It stirred her tremendously. How? Why? It was like a flute song forgotten in another existence and remembered again. What? How? Why? This singing she heard that had nothing to do with her ears. The rose of the world was breathing out smell. It followed her through all her waking moments and caressed her in her sleep. It connected itself with other vaguely felt matters that had struck her outside observation and buried themselves in her flesh. Now they emerged and quested about her consciousness.

She was stretched on her back beneath the pear tree soaking in the alto chant of the visiting bees, the gold of the sun and the panting breath of the breeze when the inaudible voice of it all came to her. She saw a dust-bearing bee sink into the sanctum of a bloom; the thousand sister-calyxes arch to meet the love embrace and the ecstatic shiver of the tree from root to tiniest branch creaming in every blossom and frothing with delight. So this was a marriage! She had been summoned to behold a revelation. Then Janie felt a pain remorseless sweet that left her limp and languid.

After a while she got up from where she was and went over the little garden field entire. She was seeking confirmation of the voice and vision, and everywhere she found and acknowledged answers. A personal answer for all other creations except herself. She felt an answer seeking her, but where? When? How? She found herself at the kitchen door and stumbled inside. In the air of the room were flies tumbling and singing, marrying and giving in marriage. When she reached the narrow hallway she was reminded that her grandmother was home with a sick headache. She was lying across the bed asleep so Janie tipped on out of the front door. Oh to be a pear tree–*any* tree in bloom! With kissing bees singing of the beginning of the world! She was sixteen. She had glossy leaves and bursting buds and she wanted to struggle with life but it seemed to elude her. Where were the singing bees for her? Nothing on the place nor in her grandma's house answered her. She searched as much of the world as she could from the top of the front steps and then went on down to the front gate and leaned over to gaze up and down the road. Looking, waiting, breathing short with impatience. Waiting for the world to be made.

Through pollinated air she saw a glorious being coming up the road. In her former blindness she had known him as shiftless Johnny Taylor, tall and lean. That was before the golden dust of pollen had beglamored his rags and her eyes.

In the last stages of Nanny's sleep, she dreamed of voices. Voices far-off but persistent, and gradually coming nearer. Janie's voice. Janie talking in whispery snatches with a male voice she couldn't quite place. That brought her wide awake. She bolted upright and peered out of the window and saw Johnny Taylor lacerating her Janie with a kiss.

"Janie!"

The old woman's voice was so lacking in command and reproof, so full of crumbling dissolution,—that Janie half believed that Nanny had not seen her. So she extended herself outside of her dream and went inside of the house. That was the end of her childhood.

*N*ANNY'S HEAD and face looked like the standing roots of some old tree that had been torn away by storm. Foundation of ancient power that no longer mattered. The cooling palma christi leaves that Janie had bound about her grandma's head with a white rag had wilted down and become part and parcel of the woman. Her eyes didn't bore and pierce. They diffused and melted Janie, the room and the world into one comprehension.

"Janie, youse uh 'oman, now, so—"

"Naw, Nanny, naw Ah ain't no real 'oman yet."

The thought was too new and heavy for Janie. She fought it away.

Nanny closed her eyes and nodded a slow, weary affirmation many times before she gave it voice.

"Yeah, Janie, youse got yo' womanhood on yuh. So Ah mout ez well tell yuh whut Ah been savin' up for uh spell. Ah wants to see you married right away."

"Me, married? Naw, Nanny, no ma'am! Whut Ah know 'bout uh husband?"

"Whut Ah seen just now is plenty for me, honey, Ah don't want no trashy nigger, no breath-and-britches, lak Johnny Taylor usin' yo' body to wipe his foots on."

Nanny's words made Janie's kiss across the gatepost seem like a manure pile after a rain.

"Look at me, Janie. Don't set dere wid yo' head hung down. Look at yo' ole grandma!" Her voice began snagging on the prongs of her feelings. "Ah don't want to be talkin' to you lak dis. Fact is Ah done been on mah knees to mah Maker many's de time askin' *please*—for Him not to make de burden too heavy for me to bear."

"Nanny, Ah just — Ah didn't mean nothin' bad."

"Dat's what makes me skeered. You don't mean no harm. You don't even know where harm is at. Ah'm ole now. Ah can't be always guidin' yo' feet from harm and danger. Ah wants to see you married right away."

"Who Ah'm goin' tuh marry off-hand lak dat? Ah don't know nobody."

"De Lawd will provide. He know Ah done bore de burden in de heat uh de day. Somebody done spoke to me 'bout you long time ago. Ah ain't said nothin' 'cause dat wasn't de way Ah placed you. Ah wanted yuh to school out and pick from a higher bush and a sweeter berry. But dat ain't yo' idea, Ah see."

"Nanny, who — who dat been askin' you for me?"

"Brother Logan Killicks. He's a good man, too."

"Naw, Nanny, no ma'am! Is dat whut he been hangin' around here for? He look like some ole skullhead in de grave yard."

The older woman sat bolt upright and put her feet to the floor, and thrust back the leaves from her face.

"So you don't want to marry off decent like, do yuh? You just wants to hug and kiss and feel around with first one man and then another, huh? You wants to make me suck de same sorrow yo' mama did, eh? Mah ole head ain't gray enough. Mah back ain't bowed enough to suit you!"

The vision of Logan Killicks was desecrating the pear tree, but Janie didn't know how to tell Nanny that. She merely hunched over and pouted at the floor.

"Janie."

"Yes, ma'am."

"You answer me when Ah speak. Don't you set dere poutin' wid me after all Ah done went through for you!"

*S*HE SLAPPED the girl's face violently, and forced her head back so that their eyes met in struggle. With her hand uplifted for the second blow she saw the huge tear that welled up from Janie's heart and stood in each eye. She saw the terrible agony and the lips tightened down to hold back the cry and desisted. Instead she brushed back the heavy hair from Janie's face and stood there suffering and loving and weeping internally for both of them.

"Come to yo' grandma, honey. Set in her lap lak yo' use tuh. Yo' Nanny wouldn't harm a hair uh yo' head. She don't want nobody else to do it neither if she kin help it. Honey, de white man is de ruler of everything as fur as Ah been able tuh find out. Maybe it's some place way off in de ocean where de black man is in power, but we don't know nothin' but what we see. So de white man throw down de load and tell de nigger man tuh pick it up. He pick it up because he have to, but he don't tote it. He hand it to his womenfolks. De nigger woman is de mule uh de world so fur as Ah can see. Ah been prayin' fuh it tuh be different wid you. Lawd, Lawd, Lawd!"

For a long time she sat rocking with the girl held tightly to her sunken breast. Janie's long legs dangled over one arm of the chair and the long braids of her hair swung low on the other side. Nanny half sung, half sobbed a running chant-prayer over the head of the weeping girl.

"Lawd have mercy! It was a long time on de way but Ah reckon it had to come. Oh Jesus! Do, Jesus! Ah done de best Ah could."

Finally, they both grew calm.

"Janie, how long you been 'lowin' Johnny Taylor to kiss you?"

"Only dis one time, Nanny. Ah don't love him at all. Whut made me do it is — oh, Ah don't know."

"Thank you, Massa Jesus."

"Ah ain't gointuh do it no mo', Nanny. Please don't make me marry Mr. Killicks."

" 'Tain't Logan Killicks Ah wants you to have, baby, it's protection. Ah ain't gittin' ole, honey. Ah'm *done* ole. One mornin' soon, now, de angel wid de sword is gointuh stop by here. De day and de hour is hid from me, but it won't be long. Ah ast de Lawd when you was uh infant in mah arms to let me stay here till you got grown. He done spared me to see de day. Mah daily prayer now is tuh let dese golden moments rolls on a few days longer till Ah see you safe in life."

"Lemme wait, Nanny, please, jus' a lil bit mo'."

"Don't think Ah don't feel wid you, Janie, 'cause Ah do. Ah couldn't love yuh no more if Ah had uh felt yo' birth pains mahself. Fact ud de matter, Ah loves yuh a whole heap more'n Ah do yo' mama, de one Ah did birth. But you got to take in consideration you ain't no everyday chile like most of 'em. You ain't got no papa, you might jus' as well as say no mama, for de good she do yuh. You ain't got nobody but me. And mah head is ole and tilted towards de grave. Neither can you stand along by yo'self. De thought uh you bein' kicked around from pillar tuh post is uh hurtin' thing. Every tear you drop squeezes a cup uh blood outa mah heart. Ah got tuh try and do for you befo' mah head is cold."

A sobbing sigh burst out of Janie. The old woman answered her with little soothing pats of the hand.

"You know, honey, us colored folks is branches without roots and that makes things come round in queer ways. You in particular. Ah was born back dere in slavery so it wasn't for me to fulfill my dreams of whut a woman oughta be and do. Dat's one of de hold-backs of slavery. But nothing can't stop you from wishing'. You can't beat nobody down so low till you can rob 'em of they will. Ah didn't want to be used for a work-ox and a brood-sow and Ah didn't want mah daughter used dat way neither. It sho wasn't mah will for things to happen lak they did. Ah even hated de way you was born. But, all de same Ah said thank God, Ah got another chance. Ah wanted to preach a great sermon about colored women sittin' on high, but they wasn't no pulpit for me. Freedom found me wid a baby daughter in mah arms, so Ah said Ah'd take a broom and a cook-pot and throw up a highway through de wilderness for her. She would expound what Ah felt. But somehow she got lost offa de highway and next thing Ah knowed here you was in de world. So whilst Ah was tendin' you of nights Ah said Ah'd save de text for you. Ah been waitin' a long time, Janie, but nothin' Ah been through ain't too much if you just take a stand on high ground lak Ah dreamed."

OLD NANNY SAT THERE rocking Janie like an infant and thinking back and back. Mind-pictures brought feelings, and feelings dragged out dramas from the hollows of her heart.

"Dat mornin' on de big plantation close to Savannah, a rider come in a gallop tellin' 'bout Sherman takin' Atlanta. Marse Robert's son had done been kilt at Chickamauga. So he grabbed his gun and straddled his best horse and went off wid de rest of de gray-headed men and young boys to drive de Yankees back into Tennessee.

"They was all cheerin' and cryin' and shoutin' for de men dat was ridin' off. Ah couldn't see nothin' cause yo' mama wasn't but a week old, and Ah was flat uh my back. But pretty soon he let on he forgot somethin' and run into mah cabin and made me let down mah hair for de last time. He sorta wropped his hand in it, pulled mah big toe, lak he always done, and was gone after de rest lak lightnin'. Ah heard 'em give one last whoop for him. Then de big house and de quarters got sober and silent.

"It was de cool of de evenin' when Mistis come walkin' in mah door. She throwed de door wide open and stood dere lookin' at me outa her eyes and her face look lak she been livin' through uh hundred years in January without one day of spring. She come stood over me in de bed.

" 'Nanny, Ah come to see that baby uh yourn.'

"Ah tried not to feel de breeze off her face, but it got so cold in dere dat Ah was freezin' to death under the kivvers. So Ah couldn't move right away lak Ah aimed to. But Ah knowed Ah had to make haste and do it.

Civil War Notes

Sherman William Tecumseh Sherman (1820–91), the Union general responsible for the burning of Atlanta and the destructive 285-mile march through Georgia and South Carolina, p. 369

Chickamauga site of a famous 1863 Civil War battle in northwest Georgia, p. 369

" 'You better git dat kivver offa dat youngun and dat quick!' she clashed at me. 'Look lak you don't know who is Mistis on dis plantation, Madam. But Ah aims to show you.'

"By dat time I had done managed tuh unkivver mah baby enough for her to see de head and face.

" 'Nigger, whut's yo' baby doin' wid gray eyes and yaller hair? She begin tuh slap mah jaws ever which a'way. Ah never felt the fust ones 'cause Ah wuz too busy gittin' de kivver back over mah chile. But dem last lick burnt me lak fire. Ah had too many feelin's tuh tell which one tuh follow so Ah didn't cry and Ah didn't do nothin' else. But then she kept on askin' me how come mah baby look white. She asted me dat maybe twenty-five or thirty times, lak she got tuh sayin' dat and couldn't help herself. So Ah told her, 'Ah don't know nothin' but what Ah'm told tuh do, 'cause Ah ain't nothin' but uh nigger and uh slave.'

"Instead of pacifyin' her lak Ah thought, look lak she got madder. But Ah reckon she was tired and wore out 'cause she didn't hit me no more. She went to de foot of de bed and wiped her hands on her hand-ksher. 'Ah wouldn't dirty mah hands on yuh. But first thing in de mornin' de overseer will take you to de whippin' post and tie you down on yo' knees and cut de hide offa yo' yaller back. One hundred lashes wid a raw-hide on yo' bare back. Ah'll have you whipped till de blood run down to yo' heels! Ah mean to count de licks mahself. And if it kills you Ah'll stand de loss. Anyhow, as soon as dat brat is a month old Ah'm going to sell it offa dis place.'

"She flounced on off and left her winter time wid me. Ah knowed mah body wasn't healed, but Ah couldn't consider dat. In de black dark Ah wrapped mah baby de best Ah knowed how and made it to de swamp by de river. Ah knowed de place was full uh moccasins and other bitin' snakes, but Ah was more skeered uh whut was behind me. Ah hide in dere day and night and suckled de baby ever time she start to cry, for fear somebody might hear her and Ah'd git found. Ah ain't sayin' uh friend or two didn't feel mah care. And den de Good Lawd seen to it dat Ah wasn't taken. Ah don't see how come mah milk didn't kill mah chile, wid me so skeered and worried all de time. De noise uh de owls skeered me; de limbs of dem cypress trees took to crawlin' and movin' round after dark, and two three times Ah heered panthers prowlin' round. But nothin' never hurt me 'cause de Lawd knowed how it was.

$\mathcal{D}$EN, ONE NIGHT Ah heard de big guns boomin' lak thunder. It kept up all night long. And de next mornin' Ah could see uh big ship at a distance and a great stirrin' round. So Ah wrapped Leafy up in moss and fixed her good in a tree and picked mah way on down to de landin'. The men was all in blue, and Ah heard people say Sherman was comin' to meet de boats in Savannah, and all of us slaves was free. So Ah run got mah baby and got in quotation wid people and found a place Ah could stay.

"But it was a long time after dat befo' de Big Surrender at Richmond. Den de big bell ring in Atlanta and all de men in gray uniforms had to go to Moultrie, and bury their swords in de ground to show they was never to fight about slavery no mo'. So den we knowed we was free.

"Ah wouldn't marry nobody, though Ah could have uh heap uh times, cause Ah didn't want nobody mistreating mah baby. So Ah got with some good white people and come down here in West Florida to work and make de sunshine on both sides of de street for Leafy.

"Mah Madam help me wid her just lak she been doin' wid you. Ah put her in school when it got so it was a school to put her in. Ah was 'spectin' to make a school teacher outa her.

"But one day she didn't come home at de usual time and Ah waited and waited, but she never come all dat night. Ah took a lantern and went round askin' everybody but

> ✳
> ## Civil War Notes
>
> **Savannah** east Georgia city where Sherman's March to the Sea culminated, p. 371
>
> **Richmond** Confederate capital located in Virginia whose evacuation was followed by the "Big Surrender" at Appomattox Court House on April 9, p. 371
>
> **Moultrie** a town in southern Georgia, p. 371

nobody ain't seen her. De next mornin' she come crawlin' in on her hands and knees. A sight to see. Dat school teacher had done hid her in de woods all night long, and he had done raped mah baby and run on off just before day.

"She was only seventeen, and somethin' lak dat to happen! Lawd a'mussy! Look lak Ah kin see it all over again. It was a long time before she was well, and by dat time we knowed you was on de way. And after you was born she took to drinkin' likker and stayin' out nights. Couldn't git her to stay here and nowhere else. Lawd knows where she is right now. She ain't dead, 'cause Ah'd know it by mah feelings, but sometimes Ah wish she was at rest.

"And, Janie, maybe it wasn't much, but Ah done de best Ah kin by you. Ah raked and scraped and bought dis lil piece uh land so you wouldn't have to stay in de white folks' yard and tuck yo' head befo' other chillun at school. Dat was all right when you was little. But when you got big enough to understand things, Ah wanted you to look upon yo'self. Ah don't want yo' feathers always crumpled by folks throwin' up things in yo' face. And Ah can't die easy thinkin' maybe de menfolks white or black is makin' a spit cup outa you: Have some sympathy fuh me. Put me down easy, Janie, Ah'm a cracked plate."

RESPONDING

1. **Personal Response** Do you think Nanny's decision to have Janie marry Logan Killicks was the best way of protecting her? Why or why not?

2. **Literary Analysis** What does the blossoming pear tree, the central *metaphor* of this selection, represent? Why does Janie's vision of Logan Killicks "desecrate the pear tree"?

3. **Multicultural Connection** What indications can you find that Nanny is a very independent woman, despite the restrictions society imposes on her?

LANGUAGE WORKSHOP

Personification When a nonhuman or inanimate object, quality, or idea is given lifelike characteristics or powers, a figure of speech called *personification* is created. For example, Zora Neale Hurston writes that a breeze *pants*, the pear tree bloom *calls*, a tree *shivers*, and the limbs of trees *crawl*.

Now its *your* turn. Personify each of the following qualities, objects, and ideas in a sentence: *freedom, hair, love, rain.*

WRITER'S PORTFOLIO

At the end of her life, Nanny sees herself as a "cracked plate," but details of her life prove her to be an incredibly strong, loving woman. After analyzing events in her life, write a character sketch of Nanny. If you prefer, write a character sketch of an older person you know.

ABOUT **SANDRA CISNEROS**

Sandra Cisneros (**sēs ne′rōs**) says she writes about "those ghosts inside that haunt me, that will not let me sleep. . . ." Her "ghosts" turn out to be part of a cultural gold mine — one she discovered as a graduate student in a creative writing program. Born in Chicago in 1954, Cisneros fantasized that she and her family would someday be able to live like affluent families on television. Her first work of fiction, *The House on Mango Street,* earned the American Book Award in 1985. It was followed by *Woman Hollering Creek and Other Stories.* Cisneros's collection of poems, *My Wicked Wicked Ways,* shows the poet's development over time in a number of cities, nations, and barrios. These poems reveal both the inside self and the outside world in episodic flashes, a technique she uses often in her prose as well.

*S*ire

I DON'T REMEMBER when I first noticed him looking at me — Sire. But I knew he was looking. Every time. All the time I walked past his house. Him and his friends sitting on their bikes in front of the house, pitching pennies. They didn't scare me. They did, but I wouldn't let them know. I don't cross the street like other girls. Straight ahead, straight eyes. I walked past. I knew he was looking. I had to prove to me I wasn't scared of nobody's eyes, not even his. I had to look back hard, just once, like he was glass. And I did. I did once. But I looked too long when he rode his bike past me. I looked because I wanted to be brave, straight into the dusty cat fur of his eyes and the bike stopped and he bumped into a parked car, bumped, and I walked fast. It made your blood freeze to have somebody look at you like that. Somebody looked at me. Somebody looked. But his kind, his ways. He is a punk, Papa says, and Mama says not to talk to him.

And then his girlfriend came. Lois I heard him call her. She is tiny and pretty and smells like baby's skin. I see her sometimes running to the store for him. And once when she was standing next to me at Mr. Benny's grocery she was barefoot, and I saw her barefoot baby toenails all painted pale pale pink, like little pink seashells, and she smells pink like babies do. She's got big girl hands, and her bones are long like ladies' bones, and she wears make-up too. But she doesn't know how to tie her shoes. I do.

$\mathscr{S}$OMETIMES I HEAR THEM laughing late, beer cans and cats and the trees talking to themselves: wait, wait, wait. Sire lets Lois ride his bike around the block, or they take walks together. I watch them. She holds his hand, and he stops sometimes to tie her shoes. But Mama says those kinds of girls, those girls are the ones that go into alleys. Lois who can't tie her shoes. Where does he take her?

Everything is holding its breath inside me. Everything is waiting to explode like Christmas. I want to be all new and shiny. I want to sit out bad at night, a boy around my neck and the wind under my skirt. Not this way, every evening talking to the trees, leaning out my window, imagining what I can't see.

A boy held me once so hard, I swear, I felt the grip and weight of his arms, but it was a dream.

Sire. How did you hold her? Was it? Like this? And when you kissed her? Like this?

RESPONDING

1. **Personal Response** Try to remember a time when you were attracted to someone. Was your experience the same as the narrator's in "Sire" or was it different? Explain.

2. **Literary Analysis** Cisneros's stories are sometimes described as *prose poems*. How does this selection fit that description of her style?

3. **Multicultural Connection** What is the narrator's parents' attitude toward their daughter? toward the other young people in the barrio? Given details in the story, do you think their judgment of Sire and Lois is fair?

LANGUAGE WORKSHOP

Sentence Fragments A *sentence fragment* is a group of words that is punctuated like a sentence but lacks a subject or a verb, or in some other way fails to express a complete thought. Sometimes writers deliberately use fragments for effect. Rewrite the first paragraph of "Sire," changing all the fragments to complete sentences. What is lost or gained?

WRITER'S PORTFOLIO

It appears that Lois and Sire have a great deal of freedom and little supervision, while the narrator is subject to parental constraints. Given these facts, imagine how all three will turn out in the future. Write a separate diary entry for each of these characters, written three years after the story takes place, that reveals their hopes and aspirations, fears and problems.

ABOUT **YOSHIKO UCHIDA**

Yoshiko Uchida (yō shē′kō yü chē′də) was born in California and relocated with her family during World War II, first to a horse stall at Tanforan Racetrack and then to a barracks at Topaz in the Utah desert. After surviving the horrors of camp life, Uchida earned her master's degree from Smith College in Massachusetts and held various jobs — as a teacher in Philadelphia and a secretary for the Lawrence Radiation Laboratory in California and for the United Student Christian Council in New York City. Her first book, *Dancing Kettles and Other Japanese Folk Tales,* was published in 1949. In the years that followed, she produced children's fiction and nonfiction, mythology, folklore, and novels. *Journey to Topaz* and *Picture Bride* are among Uchida's best known works. Her autobiography, *The Invisible Thread,* was published in 1991, the year before her death.

Tears of Autumn

HANA OMIYA STOOD at the railing of the small ship that shuddered toward America in a turbulent November sea. She shivered as she pulled the folds of her silk kimono close to her throat and tightened the wool shawl about her shoulders.

She was thin and small, her dark eyes shadowed in her pale face, her black hair piled high in a pompadour that seemed too heavy for so slight a woman. She clung to the moist rail and breathed the damp salt air deep into her lungs. Her body seemed leaden and lifeless, as though it were simply the vehicle transporting her soul to a strange new life, and she longed with childlike intensity to be home again in Oka Village.

She longed to see the bright persimmon dotting the barren trees beside the thatched roofs, to see the fields of golden rice stretching to the mountains where only last fall she had gathered plum white mushrooms, and to see once more the maple trees lacing their flaming colors through the green pine. If only she could see a familiar face, eat a meal without retching, walk on solid ground and stretch out at night on a *tatami* mat instead of in a hard narrow bunk. She thought now of seeking the warm shelter of her bunk but could not bear to face the relentless smell of fish that penetrated the lower decks.

Why did I ever leave Japan, she wondered bitterly. Why did I ever listen to my uncle? And yet she knew it was she herself who had begun the chain of events that placed her on this heaving ship. It was she who had first planted in her uncle's mind the thought that she would make a good wife for Taro Takeda, the lonely man who had gone to America to make his fortune in Oakland, California.

It all began one day when her uncle had come to visit her mother.

"I must find a nice young bride," he had said, startling Hana with this blunt talk of marriage in her presence. She blushed and was ready to leave the room when her uncle quickly added, "My good friend Takeda has a son in America. I must find someone willing to travel to that far land."

This last remark was intended to indicate to Hana and her mother that he didn't consider this a suitable prospect for Hana who was the youngest daughter of what once had been a fine family. Her father, until his death fifteen years ago, had been the largest landholder of the village and one of its last *samurai*. They had once had many servants and field hands, but now all that was changed. Their money was gone. Hana's older sisters had made good marriages, and the eldest remained in their home with her husband to carry on the Omiya name and perpetuate the homestead. Her other sisters had married merchants in Osaka and Nagoya and were living comfortably.

*N*OW THAT HANA was twenty-one, finding a proper husband for her had taken on an urgency that produced an embarrassing secretive air over the entire matter. Usually, her mother didn't speak of it until they were lying side by side on their quilts at night. Then, under the protective cover of darkness, she would suggest one name and then another, hoping that Hana would indicate an interest in one of them.

Her uncle spoke freely of Taro Takeda only because he was so sure Hana would never consider him. "He is a conscientious, hard-working man who has been in the United

States for almost ten years. He is thirty-one, operates a small shop and rents some rooms above the shop where he lives." Her uncle rubbed his chin thoughtfully. "He could provide well for a wife," he added.

"Ah," Hana's mother said softly.

"You say he is successful in this business?" Hana's sister inquired.

"His father tells me he sells many things in his shop—clothing, stockings, needles, thread and buttons—such things as that. He also sells bean paste, pickled radish, bean cake and soy sauce. A wife of his would not go cold or hungry."

They all nodded, each of them picturing this merchant in varying degrees of success and affluence. There were many Japanese emigrating to America these days, and Hana had heard of the picture brides who went with nothing more than an exchange of photographs to bind them to a strange man.

"Taro San is lonely," her uncle continued, "I want to find for him a fine young woman who is strong and brave enough to cross the ocean alone."

"It would certainly be a different kind of life," Hana's sister ventured, and for a moment, Hana thought she glimpsed a longing ordinarily concealed behind her quiet, obedient face. In that same instant, Hana knew she wanted more for herself than her sisters had in their proper, arranged and loveless marriages. She wanted to escape the smothering strictures of life in her village. She certainly was not going to marry a farmer and spend her life working beside him planting, weeding and harvesting in the rice paddies until her back became bent from too many years of stooping and her skin turned to brown leather by the sun and wind. Neither did she particularly relish the idea of marrying a merchant in a big city as her two sisters had done. Since her mother objected to her going to Tokyo to seek employment as a teacher, perhaps she would consent to a flight to America for what seemed a proper and respectable marriage.

Almost before she realized what she was doing, she spoke to her uncle. "Oji San, perhaps I should go to America to make this lonely man a good wife."

"You, Hana Chan?" Her uncle observed her with startled curiosity. "You would go all alone to a foreign land so far away from your mother and family?"

"I would not allow it." Her mother spoke fiercely. Hana was her youngest and she had lavished upon her the attention and latitude that often befall the last child. How could she permit her to travel so far, even to marry the son of Takeda who was known to her brother.

But now, a notion that had seemed quite impossible a moment before was lodged in his receptive mind, and Hana's uncle grasped it with the pleasure that comes from an unexpected discovery.

"You know," he said looking at Hana, "it might be a very good life in America."

Hana felt a faint fluttering in her heart. Perhaps this lonely man in America was her means of escaping both the village and the encirclement of her family.

Her uncle spoke with increasing enthusiasm of sending Hana to become Taro's wife. And the husband of Hana's sister, who was head of their household, spoke with equal eagerness. Although he never said so, Hana guessed he would be pleased to be rid of her, the spirited younger sister who stirred up his placid life with what he considered radical ideas about life and the role of women. He often claimed that Hana had too much schooling for a girl. She had graduated from Women's High School in Kyoto which gave her five more years of schooling than her older sister.

"It has addled her brain—all that learning from those books," he said when he tired of arguing with Hana.

A man's word carried much weight for Hana's mother. Pressed by the two men, she consulted her other daughters and their husbands. She discussed the matter carefully with her brother and asked the village priest. Finally, she agreed to an exchange of family histories and an investigation was begun into Taro Takeda's family, his education and his health, so they would be assured there was no insanity or tuberculosis or police records concealed in his family's past. Soon Hana's uncle was devoting his energies entirely to serving as go-between for Hana's mother and Taro Takeda's father.

When at last an agreement to the marriage was almost reached, Taro wrote his first letter to Hana. It was brief and proper and gave no more clue to his character than the stiff formal portrait taken at his graduation from Middle School. Hana's uncle had given her the picture with apologies from his parents because it was the only photo they had of him and it was not a flattering likeness.

Hana hid the letter and photograph in the sleeve of her kimono and took them to the outhouse to study in private. Squinting in the dim light and trying to ignore the foul odor, she read and reread Taro's letter, trying to find the real man somewhere in the sparse unbending prose.

By the time he sent her money for her steamship tickets, she had received ten more letters, but none revealed much more of the man than the first. In none did he disclose his loneliness or his need, but Hana understood this. In fact, she would have recoiled from a man who bared his intimate thoughts to her so soon. After all, they would have a lifetime together to get to know one another.

*S*O IT WAS that Hana had left her family and sailed alone to America with a small hope trembling inside of her. Tomorrow, at last, the ship would dock in San Francisco and she would meet face to face the man she was soon to marry. Hana was overcome with excitement at the thought of being in America and terrified of the meeting about to take place. What would she say to Taro Takeda when they first met, and for all the days and years after?

Hana wondered about the flat above the shop. Perhaps it would be luxuriously furnished with the finest of brocades and lacquers, and perhaps there would be a servant, although he had not mentioned it. She worried whether she would be able to manage on the meager English she had learned at Women's High School. The overwhelming anxiety for the day to come and the violent rolling of the ship were more than Hana could bear. Shuddering in the face of the wind, she leaned over the railing and became violently and wretchedly ill.

By five the next morning, Hana was up and dressed in her finest purple silk kimono and coat. She could not eat the bean soup and rice that appeared for breakfast and took only a few bites of the yellow pickled radish. Her bags, which had scarcely been touched since she boarded the ship, were easily packed for all they contained were her kimonos and some of her favorite books. The large willow basket, tightly secured by a rope, remained under the bunk, untouched since her uncle had placed it there.

She had not befriended the other women in her cabin, for they had lain in their bunks for most of the voyage, too sick to be company to anyone. Each morning Hana had fled the closeness of the sleeping quarters and spent most of the day huddled in a corner of the deck, listening to the lonely songs of some Russians also traveling to an alien land.

As the ship approached land, Hana hurried up to the deck to look out at the gray expanse of ocean and sky, eager for a first glimpse of her new homeland.

"We won't be docking until almost noon," one of the deck hands told her.

Hana nodded. "I can wait," she answered, but the last hours seemed the longest.

*W*HEN SHE SET FOOT on American soil at last, it was not in the city of San Francisco as she had expected, but on Angel Island, where all third-class passengers were taken. She spent two miserable days and nights waiting, as the immigrants were questioned by officials, examined for trachoma and tuberculosis and tested for hookworm by a woman who collected their stools on tin pie plates. Hana was relieved she could produce her own, not having to borrow a little from someone else, as some of the women had to do. It was a bewildering, degrading beginning, and Hana was sick with anxiety, wondering if she would ever be released.

On the third day, a Japanese messenger from San Francisco appeared with a letter for her from Taro. He had written it the day of her arrival, but it had not reached her for two days.

Taro welcomed her to America and told her that the bearer of the letter would inform Taro when she was to be released so he could be at the pier to meet her.

The letter eased her anxiety for a while, but as soon as she was released and boarded the launch for San Francisco, new fears rose up to smother her with a feeling almost of dread.

The early morning mist had become a light chilling rain, and on the pier, black umbrellas bobbed here and there, making the task of recognition even harder. Hana searched desperately for a face that resembled the photo she had studied so long and hard. Suppose he hadn't come. What would she do then?

Hana took a deep breath, lifted her head and walked slowly from the launch. The moment she was on the pier, a man in a black coat, wearing a derby and carrying an umbrella, came quickly to her side. He was of slight build, not much taller than she, and his face was sallow and pale. He bowed stiffly and murmured, "You have had a long trip, Miss Omiya. I hope you are well."

Hana caught her breath. "You are Takeda San?" she asked.

He removed his hat and Hana was further startled to see that he was already turning bald.

"You are Takeda San?" she asked again. He looked older than thirty-one.

"I am afraid I no longer resemble the early photo my parents gave you. I am sorry."

Hana had not meant to begin like this. It was not going well.

"No, no," she said quickly. "It is just that I . . . that is, I am terribly nervous . . ." Hana stopped abruptly, too flustered to go on.

"I understand," Taro said gently. "You will feel better when you meet my friends and have some tea. Mr. and Mrs. Toda are expecting you in Oakland. You will be staying with them until . . ." He couldn't bring himself to mention the marriage just yet and Hana was grateful he hadn't.

He quickly made arrangements to have her baggage sent to Oakland and then led her carefully along the rain slick pier toward the street car that would take them to the ferry.

Hana shuddered at the sight of another boat, and as they climbed to its upper deck she felt a queasy tightening of her stomach.

"I hope it will not rock too much," she said anxiously. "Is it many hours to your city?"

Taro laughed for the first time since their meeting, revealing the gold fillings of this teeth. "Oakland is just across the bay," he explained. "We will be there in twenty minutes."

Raising a hand to cover her mouth, Hana laughed with him and suddenly felt better. I am in America now, she thought, and this is the man I came to marry. Then she sat down carefully beside Taro, so no part of their clothing touched.

RESPONDING

1. **Personal Response** Do you think Hana was wise to enter into an arranged marriage? Explain.

2. **Literary Analysis** The circumstances that brought Hana Omiya to America are revealed in a *flashback*, beginning at the top of page 380. From what is she escaping?

3. **Multicultural Connection** What connections can you make between the age-old practice of arranging marriages through picture brides and modern dating services?

LANGUAGE WORKSHOP

Cause and Effect There are many things that contribute
to Hana's decision to come to America as a picture
bride. One such *cause-effect relationship* is the death of
her father, which results in a loss of money and makes
it difficult for her to make a "good marriage" in Japan.

Explain how each of the following leads to Hana's decision to come to America: her sisters' "proper, arranged,
and loveless marriages"; the fact that Taro owns a small
shop in California; the "smothering strictures" of life
with her family in the small village.

WRITER'S PORTFOLIO

Given what you know about Hana and Taro, what
predictions would you make for their future? Write
a conclusion to this story based on your predictions.

ABOUT **HARRY MARK PETRAKIS**

Novelist Kurt Vonnegut, Jr., observed
that the characters of Harry Mark Petrakis
(**pe trä⁄kis**) would make a "wonderful basketball team . . . Every one of them is at least
fourteen feet tall." A creator of mythic, large-
scale characters, Petrakis was born in St. Louis
in 1923 of Greek immigrant parents. He
spent most of his life in Chicago and
captured the lives and locale of the Greek
American community there in many of his
writings. His works include *A Dream of Kings,
Pericles on 31st Street,* and *Ghost of the Sun.*

Although he now lives in
Chesterton, Indiana,
Petrakis "came home" in
1994, when *Greek
Streets,* three one-act
plays based on his
short stories (including
"The Wooing of
Ariadne"), was per-
formed at the Royal
George Theatre in Chicago.

The Wooing of Ariadne

I KNEW FROM THE BEGINNING she must accept my love—put aside foolish female protestations. It is the distinction of the male to be the aggressor and the cloak of the female to lend grace to the pursuit. Aha! I am wise to these wiles.

I first saw Ariadne at a dance given by the Spartan brotherhood in the Legion Hall on Laramie Street. The usual assemblage of prune-faced and banana-bodied women smelling of virtuous anemia. They were an outrage to a man such as myself.

Then I saw her! A tall stately woman, perhaps in her early thirties. She had firm and slender arms bare to the shoulder and a graceful neck. Her hair was black and thick and piled in a great bun at the back of her head. That grand abundance of hair attracted me at once. This modern aberration women have of chopping their hair close to the scalp and leaving it in fantastic disarray I find revolting.

I went at once to my friend Vasili, the baker, and asked him who she was.

"Ariadne Langos," he said. "Her father is Janco Langos, the grocer."

389

"Is she engaged or married?"

"No," he said slyly. "They say she frightens off the young men. They say she is very spirited."

"Excellent," I said and marveled at my good fortune in finding her unpledged. "Introduce me at once."

"Marko," Vasili said with some apprehension. "Do not commit anything rash."

I pushed the little man forward. "Do not worry, little friend," I said. "I am a man suddenly possessed by a vision. I must meet her at once."

We walked together across the dance floor to where my beloved stood. The closer we came the more impressive was the majestic swell of her breasts and the fine great sweep of her thighs. She towered over the insignificant apple-core women around her. Her eyes, dark and thoughtful, seemed to be restlessly searching the room.

Be patient, my dove! Marko is coming.

"Miss Ariadne," Vasili said. "This is Mr. Marko Palamas. He desires to have the honor of your acquaintance."

*S*HE LOOKED AT ME for a long and piercing moment. I imagined her gauging my mighty strength by the width of my shoulders and the circumference of my arms. I felt the tips of my mustache bristle with pleasure. Finally she nodded with the barest minimum of courtesy. I was not discouraged.

"Miss Ariadne," I said, "may I have the pleasure of this dance?"

She stared at me again with her fiery eyes. I could imagine more timid men shriveling before her fierce gaze. My heart flamed at the passion her rigid exterior concealed.

"I think not," she said.

"Don't you dance?"

Vasili gasped beside me. An old prune-face standing nearby clucked her toothless gums.

"Yes, I dance," Ariadne said coolly. "I do not wish to dance with you."

"Why?" I asked courteously.

"I do not think you heard me," she said. "I do not wish to dance with you."

Oh, the sly and lovely darling. Her subterfuge so apparent. Trying to conceal her pleasure at my interest.

"Why?" I asked again.

"I am not sure," she said. "It could be your appearance, which bears considerable resemblance to a gorilla, or your manner, which would suggest closer alliance to a pig."

"Now that you have met my family," I said engagingly, "let us dance."

"Not now," she said, and her voice rose. "Not this dance or the one after. Not tonight or tomorrow night or next month or next year. Is that clear?"

Sweet, sweet Ariadne. Ancient and eternal game of retreat and pursuit. My pulse beat more quickly.

Vasili pulled at my sleeve. He was my friend, but without the courage of a goat. I shook him off and spoke to Ariadne.

"There is a joy like fire that consumes a man's heart when he first sets eyes on his beloved," I said. "This I felt when I first saw you." My voice trembled under a mighty passion. "I swear before God from this moment that I love you."

She stared shocked out of her deep dark eyes and, beside her, old prune-face staggered as if she had been kicked. Then my beloved did something which proved indisputably that her passion was as intense as mine.

She doubled up her fist and struck me in the eye. A stout blow for a woman that brought a haze to my vision, but I shook my head and moved a step closer.

"I would not care," I said, "if you struck out both my eyes. I would cherish the memory of your beauty forever."

By this time the music had stopped, and the dancers formed a circle of idiot faces about us. I paid them no attention and ignored Vasili, who kept whining and pulling at my sleeve.

"You are crazy!" she said. "You must be mad! Remove yourself from my presence or I will tear out both your eyes and your tongue besides!"

You see! Another woman would have cried, or been frightened into silence. But my Ariadne, worthy and venerable, hurled her spirit into my teeth.

"I would like to call on your father tomorrow," I said. From the assembled dancers who watched there rose a few vagrant whispers and some rude laughter. I stared at them carefully and they hushed at once. My temper and strength of arm were well known.

Ariadne did not speak again, but in a magnificent spirit stamped from the floor. The music began, and men and women began again to dance. I permitted Vasili to pull me to a corner.

✸

Culture Note

like a Turk a comparison that refers to the hostility between the Greeks and Turks during the Ottoman (Turkish) Empire, which flourished during the 1500s, p. 392

"You are insane!" he said. He wrung his withered fingers in anguish. "You assaulted her like a Turk! Her relatives will cut out your heart!"

"My intentions were honorable," I said. "I saw her and loved her and told her so." At this point I struck my fist against my chest. Poor Vasili jumped.

"But you do not court a woman that way," he said.

"*You* don't, my anemic friend," I said. "Nor do the rest of these sheep. But I court a woman that way!"

He looked to heaven and helplessly shook his head. I waved good-by and started for my hat and coat.

"Where are you going?" he asked.

"To prepare for tomorrow," I said. "In the morning I will speak to her father."

$\mathscr{I}$ LEFT THE HALL and in the street felt the night wind cold on my flushed cheeks. My blood was inflamed. The memory of her loveliness fed fuel to the fire. For the first time I understood with a terrible clarity the driven heroes of the past performing mighty deeds in love. Paris stealing Helen in passion, and Menelaus pursuing with a great fleet. In that moment if I knew the whole world would be plunged into conflict I would have followed Ariadne to Hades.

I went to my rooms above my tavern. I could not sleep. All night I tossed in restless frenzy. I touched my eye that she had struck with her spirited hand.

Ariadne! Ariadne! my soul cried out.

In the morning I bathed and dressed carefully. I confirmed the address of Langos, the grocer, and started to his store. It was a bright cold November morning, but I walked with spring in my step.

When I opened the door of the Langos grocery, a tiny bell rang shrilly. I stepped into the store piled with fruits and vegetables and smelling of cabbages and greens.

A stooped little old man with white bushy hair and owlish eyes came toward me. He looked as if his veins contained vegetable juice instead of blood, and if he were, in truth, the father of my beloved I marveled at how he could have produced such a paragon of women.

"Are you Mr. Langos?"

"I am," he said and he came closer. "I am."

"I met your daughter last night," I said. "Did she mention I was going to call?"

He shook his head somberly.

"My daughter mentioned you," he said. "In thirty years I have never seen her in such a state of agitation. She was possessed."

"The effect on me was the same," I said. "We met for the first time last night, and I fell passionately in love."

"Incredible," the old man said.

About Mythology

Paris . . . Helen . . . Menelaus In Greek legend, Paris kidnapped Helen, the young wife of Menelaus, an incident that led to the Trojan War. p. 392

Hades in classical mythology, the underworld inhabited by departed souls, p. 392

Penelope . . . Ulysses In Greek mythology, Ulysses fought in the Trojan War; during his absence, his wife Penelope remained faithful to him in spite of many suitors. p. 398

"You wish to know something about me," I said. "My name is Marko Palamas. I am a Spartan emigrated to this country eleven years ago. I am forty-one years old. I have been a wrestler and a sailor and fought with the resistance movement in Greece in the war. For this service I was decorated by the king. I own a small but profitable tavern on Dart Street. I attend church regularly. I love your daughter."

As I finished he stepped back and bumped a rack of fruit. An orange rolled off to the floor. I bent and retrieved it to hand it to him, and he cringed as if he thought I might bounce it off his old head.

"She is a bad-tempered girl," he said. "Stubborn, impatient and spoiled. She has been the cause of considerable concern to me. All the eligible young men have been driven away by her temper and disposition."

"Poor girl," I said. "Subjected to the courting of calves and goats."

The old man blinked his owlish eyes. The front door opened and a battleship of a woman sailed in.

"Three pounds of tomatoes, Mr. Langos," she said. "I am in a hurry. Please to give me good ones. Last week two spoiled before I had a chance to put them into Demetri's salad."

"I am very sorry," Mr. Langos said. He turned to me. "Excuse me, Mr. Poulmas."

"Palamas," I said. "Marko Palamas."

*H*E NODDED NERVOUSLY. He went to wait on the battleship, and I spent a moment examining the store. Neat and small. I would not imagine he did more than hold his own. In the rear of the store there were stairs leading to what appeared to be an apartment above. My heart beat faster.

When he had bagged the tomatoes and given change, he returned to me and said, "She is also a terrible cook. She cannot fry an egg without burning it." His voice shook with woe. "She cannot make pilaf or lamb with squash." He paused. "You like pilaf and lamb with squash?"

"Certainly."

"You see?" he said in triumph. "She is useless in the kitchen. She is thirty years old, and I am resigned she will remain an old maid. In a way I am glad because I know she would drive some poor man to drink."

"Do not deride her to discourage me," I said. "You need have no fear that I will mistreat her or cause her unhappiness. When she is married to me she will cease being a problem to you." I paused. "It is true that I am not pretty by the foppish standards that prevail today. But I am a man. I wrestled Zahundos and pinned him two straight falls in Baltimore. A giant of a man. Afterward he conceded he had met his master. This from Zahundos was a mighty compliment."

"I am sure," the old man said without enthusiasm. "I am sure."

He looked toward the front door as if hoping for another customer.

"Is your daughter upstairs?"

He looked startled and tugged at his apron. "Yes," he said. "I don't know. Maybe she has gone out."

"May I speak to her? Would you kindly tell her I wish to speak to her."

"You are making a mistake," the old man said. "A terrible mistake."

"No mistake," I said firmly.

The old man shuffled toward the stairs. He climbed them slowly. At the top he paused and turned the knob of the door. He rattled it again.

"It is locked," he called down. "It has never been locked before. She has locked the door."

"Knock," I said. "Knock to let her know I am here."

"I think she knows," the old man said. "I think she knows."

He knocked gently.

"Knock harder," I suggested. "Perhaps she does not hear."

"I think she hears," the old man said. "I think she hears."

"Knock again," I said. "Shall I come up and knock for you?"

"No, no," the old man said quickly. He gave the door a sound kick. Then he groaned as if he might have hurt his foot.

"She does not answer," he said in a quavering voice. "I am very sorry she does not answer."

"The coy darling," I said and laughed. "If that is her game." I started for the front door of the store.

I went out and stood on the sidewalk before the store. Above the grocery were the front windows of their apartment. I cupped my hands about my mouth.

"Ariadne!" I shouted. "Ariadne!"

The old man came out the door running disjointedly. He looked frantically down the street.

"Are you mad?" he asked shrilly. "You will cause a riot. The police will come. You must be mad!"

"Ariadne!" I shouted. "Beloved!"

A window slammed open, and the face of Ariadne appeared above me. Her dark hair tumbled about her ears.

"Go away!" she shrieked. "Will you go away!"

"Ariadne," I said loudly. "I have come as I promised. I have spoken to your father. I wish to call on you."

"Go away!" she shrieked. "Madman! Imbecile! Go away!"

By this time a small group of people had assembled around the store and were watching curiously. The old man stood wringing his hands and uttering what sounded like small groans.

"Ariadne," I said. "I wish to call on you. Stop this nonsense and let me in."

She pushed farther out the window and showed me her teeth.

"Be careful, beloved," I said. "You might fall."

She drew her head in quickly, and I turned then to the assembled crowd.

"A misunderstanding," I said. "Please move on."

Suddenly old Mr. Langos shrieked. A moment later something broke on the sidewalk a foot from where I stood.

✳
Culture Notes

Pindar a Greek lyrical poet (522–448 B.C.?) known for his praise of military events, p. 397

Twelve Apostles the twelve disciples of Christ, chosen to preach the gospel, p. 400

A vase or a plate. I looked up, and Ariadne was preparing to hurl what appeared to be a water pitcher.

"Ariadne!" I shouted. "Stop that!"

The water pitcher landed closer than the vase, the fragments of glass struck my shoes. The crowd scattered, and the old man raised his hands and wailed to heaven.

Ariadne slammed down the window.

*T*HE CROWD moved in again a little closer, and somewhere among them I heard laughter. I fixed them with a cold stare and waited for some one of them to say something offensive. I would have tossed him around like sardines, but they slowly dispersed and moved on. In another moment the old man and I were alone.

I followed him into the store. He walked an awkward dance of agitation. He shut the door and peered out through the glass.

"A disgrace," he wailed. "A disgrace. The whole street will know by nightfall. A disgrace."

"A girl of heroic spirit," I said. "Will you speak to her for me? Assure her of the sincerity of my feelings. Tell her I pledge eternal love and devotion."

The old man sat down on an orange crate and weakly made his cross.

"I had hoped to see her myself," I said. "But if you promise to speak to her, I will return this evening."

"That soon?" the old man said.

"If I stayed now," I said, "it would be sooner."

"This evening," the old man said and shook his head in resignation. "This evening."

I went to my tavern for a while and set up the glasses for the evening trade. I made arrangements for Pavlakis to tend bar in my place. Afterward I sat alone in my apartment and read a little of majestic Pindar to ease the agitation of my heart.

Once in the mountains of Greece when I fought with the guerrillas in the last year of the great war, I suffered a wound from which it seemed I would die. For days high fever raged in my body. My friends brought a priest at night secretly from one of the captive villages to read the last rites. I accepted the coming of death and was grateful for many things. For the gentleness and wisdom of my old grandfather, the loyalty of my companions in war, the years I sailed between the wild ports of the seven seas, and the strength that flowed to me from the Spartan earth. For one thing only did I weep when it seemed I would leave life, that I had never set ablaze the world with a burning song of passion for one woman. Women I had known, pockets of pleasure that I tumbled for quick joy, but I had been denied mighty love for one woman. For that I wept.

*I*N ARIADNE I swore before God I had found my woman. I knew by the storm-lashed hurricane that swept within my body. A woman whose majesty was in harmony with the earth, who would be faithful and beloved to me as Penelope had been to Ulysses.

That evening near seven I returned to the grocery. Deep twilight had fallen across the street, and the lights in the window of the store had been dimmed. The apples and oranges and pears had been covered with brown paper for the night.

I tried the door and found it locked. I knocked on the glass, and a moment later the old man came shuffling out of the shadows and let me in.

"Good evening, Mr. Langos."

He muttered some greeting in answer. "Ariadne is not here," he said. "She is at the church. Father Marlas wishes to speak with you."

"A fine young priest," I said. "Let us go at once."

I waited on the sidewalk while the old man locked the store. We started the short walk to the church.

"A clear and ringing night," I said. "Does it not make you feel the wonder and glory of being alive?"

The old man uttered what sounded like a groan, but a truck passed on the street at that moment and I could not be sure.

At the church we entered by a side door leading to the office of Father Marlas. I knocked on the door, and when he called to us to enter we walked in.

Young Father Marlas was sitting at his desk in his black cassock and with his black goatee trim and imposing beneath his clean-shaven cheeks. Beside the desk, in a dark blue dress sat Ariadne, looking somber and beautiful. A bald-headed, big-nosed old man with flint and fire in his eyes sat in a chair beside her.

"Good evening, Marko," Father Marlas said and smiled.

"Good evening, Father," I said.

"Mr. Langos and his daughter you have met," he said and he cleared his throat. "This is Uncle Paul Langos."

"Good evening, Uncle Paul," I said. He glared at me and did not answer. I smiled warmly at Ariadne in greeting, but she was watching the priest.

"Sit down," Father Marlas said.

I sat down across from Ariadne, and old Mr. Langos took a chair beside Uncle Paul. In this way we were arrayed in battle order as if we were opposing armies.

A long silence prevailed during which Father Marlas cleared his throat several times. I observed Ariadne closely. There were grace and poise even in the way her slim-fingered hands rested in her lap. She was a dark and lovely flower, and my pulse beat more quickly at her nearness.

"Marko," Father Marlas said finally. "Marko, I have known you well for the three years since I assumed duties in this parish. You are most regular in your devotions and very generous at the time of the Christmas and Easter offerings. Therefore, I find it hard to believe this complaint against you."

"My family are not liars!" Uncle Paul said, and he had a voice like a hunk of dry hard cheese being grated.

"Of course not," Father Marlas said quickly. He smiled benevolently at Ariadne. "I only mean to say—"

"Tell him to stay away from my niece," Uncle Paul burst out.

"Excuse me, Uncle Paul," I said very politely. "Will you kindly keep out of what is not your business."

Uncle Paul looked shocked. "Not my business?" He looked from Ariadne to Father Marlas and then to his brother. "Not my business?"

"This matter concerns Ariadne and me," I said. "With outside interference it becomes more difficult."

"Not my business!" Uncle Paul said. He couldn't seem to get that through his head.

"Marko," Father Marlas said, and his composure was slightly shaken. "The family feels you are forcing your attention upon this girl. They are concerned."

"I understand, Father," I said. "It is natural for them to be concerned. I respect their concern. It is also natural for me to speak of love to a woman I have chosen for my wife."

"Not my business!" Uncle Paul said again, and shook his head violently.

"My daughter does not wish to become your wife," Mr. Langos said in a squeaky voice.

"That is for your daughter to say," I said courteously.

Ariadne made a sound in her throat, and we all looked at her. Her eyes were deep and cold, and she spoke slowly and carefully as if weighing each word on a scale in her father's grocery.

"I would not marry this madman if he were one of the Twelve Apostles," she said.

"See!" Mr. Langos said in triumph.

"Not my business!" Uncle Paul snarled.

"Marko," Father Marlas said. "Try to understand."

"We will call the police!" Uncle Paul raised his voice.

"Put this hoodlum under a bond!"

"Please!" Father Marlas said. "Please!"

"Today he stood on the street outside the store," Mr. Langos said excitedly. "He made me a laughingstock."

"If I were a younger man," Uncle Paul growled, "I would settle this without the police. Zi-ip!" He drew a callused finger violently across his throat.

"Please," Father Marlas said.

"A disgrace!" Mr. Langos said.

"An outrage!" Uncle Paul said.

"He must leave Ariadne alone!" Mr. Langos said.

"We will call the police!" Uncle Paul said.

"Silence!" Father Marlas said loudly.

With everything suddenly quiet he turned to me. His tone softened.

"Marko," he said and he seemed to be pleading a little. "Marko, you must understand."

Suddenly a great bitterness assailed me, and anger at myself, and a terrible sadness that flowed like night through my body because I could not make them understand.

"Father," I said quietly, "I am not a fool. I am Marko Palamas and once I pinned the mighty Zahundos in Baltimore. But this battle, more important to me by far, I have lost. That which has not the grace of God is better far in silence."

I turned to leave and it would have ended there.

"Hoodlum!" Uncle Paul said. "It is time you were silent!"

I SWEAR in that moment if he had been a younger man I would have flung him to the dome of the church. Instead I turned and spoke to them all in fire and fury.

"Listen," I said. "I feel no shame for the violence of my feelings. I am a man bred of the Spartan earth and my emotions are violent. Let those who squeak of life feel shame. Nor do I feel shame because I saw this flower and loved her. Or because I spoke at once of my love."

No one moved or made a sound.

"We live in a dark age," I said. "An age where men say one thing and mean another. A time of dwarfs afraid of life. The days are gone when mighty Pindar sang his radiant blossoms of song. When the noble passions of men set ablaze cities, and the heroic deeds of men rang like thunder to every corner of the earth."

I spoke my final words to Ariadne. "I saw you and loved you," I said gently. "I told you of my love. This is my way—the only way I know. If this way has proved offensive to you I apologize to you alone. But understand clearly that for none of this do I feel shame."

I turned then and started to the door. I felt my heart weeping as if waves were breaking within my body.

"Marko Palamas," Ariadne said. I turned slowly. I looked at her. For the first time the warmth I was sure dwelt in her body radiated within the circles of her face. For the first time she did not look at me with her eyes like glaciers.

"Marko Palamas," she said and there was a strange moving softness in the way she spoke my name. "You may call on me tomorrow."

Uncle Paul shot out of his chair. "She is mad too!" he shouted. "He has bewitched her!"

"A disgrace!" Mr. Langos said.

"Call the police!" Uncle Paul shouted. "I'll show him if it's my business!"

"My poor daughter!" Mr. Langos wailed.

"Turk!" Uncle Paul shouted. "Robber!"

"Please!" Father Marlas said. "Please!"

I ignored them all. In that winged and zestful moment I had eyes only for my beloved, for Ariadne, blossom of my heart and black-eyed flower of my soul!

RESPONDING

1. **Personal Response** What do you understand the terms *courting* and *wooing* to mean? What do you think of the courting techniques of Marko Palamas? Describe some contemporary methods of courting.

2. **Literary Analysis** What statement of Ariadne's indicates a turning point in the *plot*?

3. **Multicultural Connection** How do *allusions* to Greek history and culture in the story contribute to Marko's sense of self-importance?

LANGUAGE WORKSHOP

Suffixes A *suffix* is an addition at the end of a root word to make another word (bad*ly*, good*ness*). In this story, an aggressive male is an *aggressor,* a group of women who assemble at the Legion Hall become an *assemblage,* and a man who resembles a gorilla is said to bear a *resemblance* to it. Use the glossary, if necessary, to tell what these words mean. Then think of three other words that end with *-or, -age,* or *-ance.*

WRITER'S PORTFOLIO

You have been asked to respond to Marko's comment, "It is the distinction of the male to be the aggressor and the cloak of the female to lend grace to the pursuit." Take a stand for or against this comment, backing up your opinion with examples from life.

N. SCOTT MOMADAY   Navarre Scott Momaday was born to a Kiowa father and part-Cherokee mother in Lawton, Oklahoma, in 1934. He spent most of his early years on the Navajo, San Carlos, and Jemez Pueblo reservations where his parents were employed as teachers. After college, he taught one year on the Jicarilla Reservation and began to write. Among his best known prose works are *House Made of Dawn, The Way to Rainy Mountain, The Names: A Memoir,* and *The Ancient Child.* He has also published several volumes of poetry, including *Angle of Geese* and *The Gourd Dancers. In the Presence of the Sun: A Gathering of Shields,* a collection of Plains shields that tell individual stories, reveals Momaday's talent as a visual artist.

GARY SOTO   Gary Soto was born in Fresno, California, in 1952. After graduating from California State University, he studied creative writing and began publishing poems that often drew on his childhood memories of the conditions of rural farm laborers and urban factory workers and his dreams of a better life. He became a college lecturer and professor at the University of California, Berkeley. A celebrated prose writer as well as a poet, Soto's collections bearing on his experience as a Chicano include *The Elements of San Joaquin, Living Up the Street, Black Hair, Baseball in April,* and *Taking Sides.*

Four Notions of Love and Marriage

N. SCOTT MOMADAY

for Judith and Richardson Morse, their wedding

1.
Formerly I thought of you twice,
as it were.
Presently I think of you once
and for all.

2.
I wish you well:
that you are the runners of a wild vine,
that you are the roan and russet of dusk,
that you are a hawk and the hawk's shadow,
that you are grown old in love and delight,
I wish you well.

3.
Be still, lovers.
When the moon falls away westward,
there is your story in the stars.

4.
In my regalia,
in moccasins,
with gourd and eagle-feather fan,
in my regalia
imagine me;
imagine that I sing
and dance at your wedding.

That Girl

GARY SOTO

The public library was saying things
In so many books,
And I, Catholic boy
In a green sweater,
Was reading the same page
A hundred times.
A girl was in my way,
Protestant or Jew.
And she was at the other end
Of the oak table,
Her hands like doves
On the encyclopedia, E–G.
England, I thought,
Germany before the war?
She'll copy from that book,
Cursive like waves
Riding to the shore,
And tomorrow walk across lawns
In a public school dress
With no guilt pulling at an ear.
And me? I'll kick
My Catholic shoes through
Leaves, stand in the
Cloakroom and eat
A friend's lunch. My work
Was never finished.
My maps were half-colored,
History a stab in the dark,
And fractions the inside
Of a pocket watch
Spilled on my desk.
I was no good. And who do I
Blame? That girl.
When she scribbled a pink
Eraser and her pony

Tails bounced like skirts,
I looked up, gazed for what
My mother and sister could not
Offer, then returned to
The same sentence: *The Nile*
Is the longest river in the world.
A pencil rolled from the
Table when she clicked open
Her binder. I looked up,
Gazed, looked back down:
The Nile is the longest river . . .

RESPONDING

1. Personal Response If you were Gary Soto's friend, what tips could you give him about meeting and impressing "that girl"?

2. Literary Analysis These poems present very different aspects of the *theme* of love. Briefly tell what each poem reveals about love.

3. Multicultural Connection How are Soto's Catholic background and Momaday's observance of Native American traditions reflected in their poems?

LANGUAGE WORKSHOP

Tone *Tone* is an author's attitude toward a subject (for example, serious, playful, or joyous). Choose a word to describe the tone of each poem and explain what things help achieve this tone.

WRITER'S PORTFOLIO

Here's your chance to write a love poem for a greeting card. Your audience can be anyone you love (a parent, friend, relative, or someone else). Your tone can be serious or humorous—or something in between. You might want to illustrate your poem and send it.

LOOKING FOR LOVE

Projects

ADVERTISEMENT

Many of the selections in this unit feature characters who are searching for love. Choose two such characters and write an ad for each that could appear in a "Love Wanted" column, presenting their qualifications and their needs.

LOVE MOBILE

Prepare a mobile featuring different aspects of love. Include pictures, small objects, cards, captions, song titles, items you have made yourself—and anything else that suggests a facet of love. Add several items suggested by the selections in this unit. Present your mobile to the class. You might want to use appropriate background music for your presentation.

INTERVIEW ON HOW THEY MET

Interview a couple who has been together since before you were born. Ask them how they met, how they felt about each other at the beginning, how they decided to get together permanently, and what advice they might have for a young couple just starting out. Write the results of your interview in the form of a sketch. Use dialogue and punctuate it correctly.

Further Reading

The following books depict love in its many guises.

Angelou, Maya. *I Know Why the Caged Bird Sings.* Bantam, 1983. The first of five autobiographical books chronicles Angelou's life up to the age of sixteen, portraying, among other things, her special devotion to her grandmother.

Chavez, Denise. *The Last of the Menu Girls.* Arte Público, 1987. In this semi-autobiographical collection of stories, Chavez relates the joys and sorrows of the narrator's steps towards maturity.

Crew, Linda. *Children of the River.* Dell/Bantam, 1991. This novel, an ALA Best Book for Young Adults winner, is about a teenage girl who flees war-torn Cambodia and struggles to be accepted and to maintain her own culture—a conflict made sharper when she and a fellow classmate develop a close relationship.

Hurston, Zora Neale. *Their Eyes Were Watching God.* Harper & Row, Perennial Library, 1990 (first published in 1937). This is the story of Janie Crawford's evolving selfhood through three marriages, the final one with Tea Cake, a man who engages her heart and spirit.

McCullough, Frances. *Love Is Like the Lion's Tooth.* HarperCollins, 1984. This international collection of love poems from many cultures and eras for teenagers runs the gamut from romance, jealousy, and pain, to ecstasy.

Dreams and Realities

Having a dream is one thing; *acting upon* a dream is quite another. When you try to make your dreams come true, reality may get in the way. Meet the people in this unit, who try to reconcile their dreams with life's realities. Notice how they pursue their dreams in different ways, with varying degrees of success. Their pursuits require courage, perseverance, and even a bit of magic.

ABOUT **TOMÁS RIVERA**

Author, scholar, and university administrator, Tomás Rivera was born in Crystal City, Texas, in 1935, to parents who were migrant workers. In spite of having to alternate school with migrant labor, Rivera graduated from high school and went on to college to become a teacher. After teaching high school English and Spanish, he earned a Ph.D. in Spanish literature, taught at the university level, and ultimately served as Chancellor of the University of California, Riverside, until 1984, when he suffered a fatal heart attack. Poet, fiction writer, and critic, Rivera published works that deal with the suffering, strength, and perseverance of migrant workers. His award-winning novel, . . . y no se lo tragó la tierra (And the Earth Did Not Devour Him), documents a proud people's search for a better future.

The Portrait

As soon as the people returned from up north the portrait salesmen began arriving from San Antonio. They would come to rake in. They knew that the workers had money and that was why, as Dad used to say, they would flock in. They carried suitcases packed with samples and always wore white shirts and ties; that way they looked more important and the people believed everything they would tell them and invite them into their homes without giving it much thought. I think that down deep they even longed for their children to one day be like them. In any event, they would arrive and make their way down the dusty streets, going house to house carrying suitcases full of samples.

I remember once I was at the house of one of my father's friends when one of these salesmen arrived. I also remember that that particular one seemed a little frightened and timid. Don Mateo asked him to come in because he wanted to do business.

"Good afternoon, traveler. I would like to tell you about something new that we're offering this year."

"Well, let's see, let's see . . ."

"Well, sir, see, you give us a picture, any picture you may have, and we will not only enlarge it for you but we'll also set it in a wooden frame like this one and we'll shape the image a little, like this — three dimensional, as they say."

"And what for?"

"So that it will look real. That way . . . look, let me show you . . . see? Doesn't he look real, like he's alive?"

"Man, he sure does. Look, vieja. This looks great. Well,

you know, we wanted to send some pictures to be enlarged . . . but now, this must cost a lot, right?"

"No, I'll tell you, it costs about the same. Of course, it takes more time."

"Well, tell me, how much?"

"For as little as thirty dollars we'll deliver it to you done with inlays just like this, one this size."

"Boy, that's expensive! Didn't you say it didn't cost a lot more? Do you take installments?"

"Well, I'll tell you, we have a new manager and he wants everything in cash. It's very fine work. We'll make it look like real. Shaped like that, with inlays . . . take a look. What do you think? Some fine work, wouldn't you say? We can have it all finished for you in a month. You just tell us what color you want the clothes to be and we'll come by with it all finished one day when you least expect, framed and all. Yes, sir, a month at the longest. But like I say, this man, who's the new manager, he wants the full payment in cash. He's very demanding, even with us."

"Yes, but it's much too expensive."

"Well, yes. But the thing is, this is very fine work. You can't say you've ever seen portraits done like this, with wood inlays."

"No, well, that's true. What do you think, vieja?"

"Well, I like it a lot. Why don't we order one? And if it turns out good . . . my Chuy . . . may he rest in peace. It's the only picture we have of him. We took it right before he left for Korea. Poor m'ijo, we never saw him again. See . . . this is his picture. Do you think you can make it like that, make it look like he's alive?"

"Sure, we can. You know, we've done a lot of them in soldier's uniforms and shaped it, like you see in this sample, with inlays. Why, it's more than just a portrait. Sure. You just tell me what size you want and whether you want a round or square frame. What do you say? How should I write it down?"

"What do you say, vieja, should we have it done like this one?"

"Well, I've already told you what I think. I would like to have m'ijo's picture fixed up like that and in color."

"All right, go ahead and write it down. But you take good care of that picture for us because it's the only one we have of our son grown up. He was going to send us one all dressed up in uniform with the American and Mexican flags crossed over his head, but he no sooner got there when a letter arrived telling us that he was lost in action. So you take good care of it."

"Don't you worry. We're responsible people. And we understand the sacrifices that you people make. Don't worry. And you just wait and see, when we bring it, you'll see how pretty it's gonna look. What do you say, should we make the uniform navy blue?"

✱

Spanish Words

Don Spanish title of respect used before masculine Christian names, p. 413

vieja "old woman," a traditional Spanish term for a wife, p. 414

m'ijo a contraction of mi hijo (my son), p. 414

"But he's not wearing a uniform in that picture."

"No, but that's just a matter of fixing it up with some wood fiber overlays. Look at these. This one, he didn't have a uniform on but we put one on him. So what do you say? Should we make it navy blue?"

"All right."

"Don't you worry about the picture."

And that was how they spent the entire day, going house to house, street by street, their suitcases stuffed with pictures. As it turned out, a whole lot of people had ordered enlargements of that kind.

"They should be delivering those portraits soon, don't you think?"

"I think so, it's delicate work and takes more time. That's some fine work those people do. Did you see how real those pictures looked?"

"Yeah, sure. They do some fine work. You can't deny that. But it's already been over a month since they passed by here."

"Yes, but from here they went on through all the towns picking up pictures . . . all the way to San Antonio for sure. So it'll probably take a little longer."

"That's true, that's true."

And two more weeks had passed by the time they made the discovery. Some very heavy rains had come and some children, who were playing in one of the tunnels leading to the dump, found a sack full of pictures, all worm-eaten and soaking wet. The only reason that they could tell that these were pictures was because there were a lot of them and most of them the same size and with faces that could just barely be made out. Everybody caught on right away. Don Mateo was so angry that he took off to San Antonio to find the so and so who had swindled them.

"Well, you know, I stayed in Esteban's house. And every day I went with him to the market to sell produce. I helped him with everything. I had faith that I would run into that son of a gun some day soon. Then, after I'd been there for a few days, I started going out to the different barrios and I found out a lot that way. It wasn't so much the money that upset me. It was my poor vieja, crying and all because we'd lost the only picture we had of Chuy. We found it in the sack with all the other pictures but it was already ruined, you know."

"I see, but tell me, how did you find him?"

"Well, you see, to make a long story short, he came by the stand at the market one day. He stood right in front of us and bought some vegetables. It was like he was trying to remember who I was. Of course, I recognized him right off. Because when you're angry enough, you don't forget a face. I just grabbed him right then and there. Poor guy couldn't even talk. He was all scared. And I told him that I wanted that portrait of my son and that I wanted it three dimensional and that he'd best get it for me or I'd let him have it. And I went with him to where he lived. And I put him to work right then and there. The poor guy didn't know where to begin. He had to do it all from memory."

"And how did he do it?"

"I don't know. I suppose if you're scared enough, you're capable of doing anything. Three days later he brought me the portrait all finished, just like you see it there on that table by the Virgin. Now tell me, how do you like the way my boy looks?"

"Well, to be honest, I don't remember too well how Chuy looked. But he was beginning to look more and more like you, isn't that so?"

"Yes, I would say so. That's what everybody tells me now. That Chuy's a chip off the old block and that he was already looking like me. There's the portrait. Like they say, one and the same."

RESPONDING

1. **Personal Response** Do you think the story has a happy ending? Explain why or why not.

2. **Literary Analysis** How does the *theme* of this story relate to more than just one family's experience?

3. **Multicultural Connection** Why is the setting, a barrio of migrant workers after the Korean conflict, important?

LANGUAGE WORKSHOP

Words Often Confused Do not confuse *homonyms*, words that sound alike or similar but have different meanings. This story is about a *picture*, not a *pitcher*.

Choose the correct word in each sentence below.
1. Children found a sack full of (worn, warn) pictures.
2. Don Mateo's (principal, principle) regret was that the (reins, rains) had destroyed the picture.
3. Don Mateo and his wife didn't (loose, lose) hope when (their, they're, there) only picture was destroyed.

WRITER'S PORTFOLIO

Write a public service announcement to be aired on the radio warning people about unscrupulous salespeople who are going door-to-door in Don Mateo's community.

ABOUT **THE INDIANS OF ALCATRAZ**

On November 9, 1969, fourteen Native American college students staged a takeover of Alcatraz, an island in San Francisco Bay and the site of an abandoned federal prison. Led by Adam Nordwall, a Chippewa, and Russell Oakes, a Mohawk, the group claimed the island as a center for Native American culture. They laid claim to the island under the mistaken belief that they were allowed by treaty to claim abandoned federal property. Soon joined by other Native Americans, the group occupied the island for nearly two years. The occupation of Alcatraz drew national attention as a protest against reservation conditions and an affirmation of Native American pride.

Proclamation of the Indians of Alcatraz

Proclamation:
To the Great White Father and All His People

WE, THE NATIVE AMERICANS, reclaim the land known as Alcatraz Island in the name of all American Indians by right of discovery.

We wish to be fair and honorable in our dealings with the Caucasian inhabitants of this land, and hereby offer the following treaty:

We will purchase said Alcatraz Island for twenty-four dollars ($24) in glass beads and red cloth, a precedent set by the white man's purchase of a similar island about 300 years ago. We know that $24 in trade goods for these 16 acres is more than was paid when Manhattan Island was sold, but we know that land values have risen over the years. Our offer of $1.24 per acre is greater than the 47¢ per acre that the white men are now paying the California Indians for their land.

We will give to the inhabitants of this island a portion of that land for their own, to be held in trust by the American Indian Affairs and by the bureau of Caucasian Affairs to hold in perpetuity, for as long as the sun shall rise and the rivers go down to the sea. We will further guide the inhabitants in the proper way of living. We will offer them our religion, our education, our life-ways, in order to help them achieve our level of civilization and thus raise them and all their white brothers up from their savage and unhappy state. We offer this treaty in good faith and wish to be fair and honorable in our dealings with all white men.

We feel that this so-called Alcatraz Island is more than suitable for an Indian Reservation, as determined by the white man's own standards. By this we mean that this place resembles most Indian reservations in that:

1. It is isolated from modern facilities, and without adequate means of transportation.
2. It has no fresh running water.
3. It has inadequate sanitation facilities.
4. There are no oil or mineral rights.
5. There is no industry and so unemployment is very great.
6. There are no health care facilities.
7. The soil is rocky and non-productive; and the land does not support game.
8. There are no educational facilities.
9. The population has always exceeded the land base.
10. The population has always been held as prisoners and kept dependent upon others.

Culture Note

Golden Gate strait between San Francisco Bay and the Pacific Ocean, p. 420

Further, it would be fitting and symbolic that ships from all over the world, entering the Golden Gate, would first see Indian land, and thus be reminded of the true history of this nation. This tiny island would be a symbol of the great lands once ruled by free and noble Indians.

RESPONDING

1. **Personal Response** Do you think the Native Americans had a right to take over the island of Alcatraz? Why or why not?

2. **Literary Analysis** What does this proclamation ridicule? Would you say that this *satire* is intended to entertain readers or to bring about a change? Explain.

3. **Multicultural Connection** Reread the list that explains why Alcatraz would make a good Indian Reservation. What does the list indicate about actual reservation conditions?

LANGUAGE WORKSHOP

Fact and Opinion A *fact* can be proven; an *opinion* is someone's belief, which is not provable. That fourteen Native Americans staged a takeover of Alcatraz in 1969 is a fact; that this takeover was a bad idea is an opinion. Based on this selection, determine whether each of the following is fact or opinion.
1. Alcatraz is an island.
2. Alcatraz had no fresh running water.
3. White brothers must be saved from their savage and unhappy state.

WRITER'S PORTFOLIO

Write a short satire protesting some condition, rule, or practice in your school or community. Remember that your job is to get people to recognize the problem and to do something about it. Feel free to use humor, exaggeration, or irony to make your point.

LANGSTON HUGHES Elected class poet of his Lincoln, Illinois, elementary school at age thirteen, Langston Hughes promptly wrote

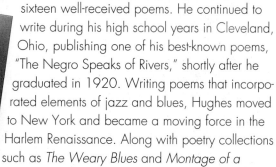

sixteen well-received poems. He continued to write during his high school years in Cleveland, Ohio, publishing one of his best-known poems, "The Negro Speaks of Rivers," shortly after he graduated in 1920. Writing poems that incorporated elements of jazz and blues, Hughes moved to New York and became a moving force in the Harlem Renaissance. Along with poetry collections such as *The Weary Blues* and *Montage of a Dream Deferred*, he published stories and plays and edited numerous anthologies. In addition to his poetry, Hughes is perhaps best known for his "Simple" stories about a shrewd though seemingly naive African American resident of Harlem.

WENDY ROSE The daughter of a Hopi father and an Anglo-Miwok mother, Wendy Rose was born in Oakland, California, and spent

her early life feeling, in her words, "out of balance." Rose dropped out of high school but eventually entered college and became a college teacher. An artist, editor, and anthropologist, Rose says her early experiences provided the original sources of her poetry. Since 1973, she has published ten highly regarded poetry collections and an anthropological study, and her work has appeared in numerous anthologies. Among her poetry volumes are *Hopi Roadrunner Dancing*, *Lost Copper*, and *The Halfbreed Chronicles*. Today, part of Rose's "balance" comes from serious attention to her Native American heritage — from a personal and an anthropological point of view.

Dream Deferred

LANGSTON HUGHES

What happens to a dream deferred?

    Does it dry up
    like a raisin in the sun?
    Or fester like a sore—
    And then run?
    Does it stink like rotten meat?
    Or crust and sugar over—
    like a syrupy sweet?

    Maybe it just sags
    like a heavy load.

    Or does it explode?

The Dream Keeper

LANGSTON HUGHES

Bring me all of your dreams,
You dreamers,
Bring me all of your
Heart melodies
That I may wrap them
In a blue cloud-cloth
Away from the too-rough fingers
Of the world.

To some few Hopi ancestors

WENDY ROSE

No longer the drifting
and falling of wind
your songs have changed;
they have become
thin willow whispers
that take us by the ankle
and tangle us up
with red mesa stone,
that keep us turned
to the round sky,
that follow us down
to Winslow, to Sherman,
to Oakland, to all the spokes
that have left earth's middle.
You have engraved yourself
with holy signs, encased yourself
in pumice, hammered on my bones
till you could no longer hear
the howl of the missions
slipping screams through
your silence, dropping dreams
from your wings.

> Is this why
> you made me
> sing and weep
> for you?

Like butterflies
made to grow another way
this woman is chiseled
on the face of your world.

Culture Notes

Winslow, Sherman, Oakland cities in Arizona, Texas, and California, respectively. Radiating from the "earth's middle," they are like spokes on a wheel.

earth's middle In a Hopi myth, tribal ancestors climbed up through three cave worlds, emerging from the Grand Canyon into a fourth world — Earth. Hopi ancestors migrated from various locations to settle near the Grand Canyon.

this woman is chiseled
on the face of your world.
The badger-claw of her father
shows slightly in the stone
burrowed from her sight,
facing west from home.

RESPONDING

1. **Personal Response** Which one of the poems in this unit do you like best? What do you find appealing about it?

2. **Literary Analysis** Find examples of *alliteration* — the repetition of similar consonant sounds (for example, fickle fortune) to create melody, mood, or dramatic effect — in both Hughes's and Rose's poems. Explain what effects are achieved.

3. **Multicultural Connection** How is Rose's Native American heritage reflected in her poem?

LANGUAGE WORKSHOP

Prefixes Wendy Rose uses the words *engraved* and *encased* in her poem. The prefix *-en* can mean "to make" or "to cause to be." One meaning of *grave* is "to carve." What does *engrave* mean? What does *encase* mean? Figure out the meanings of the following words: *enfeeble, enthrone, enable, enliven.*

WRITER'S PORTFOLIO

These poems express not only personal dreams, but dreams for an entire culture and for humanity in general. Write a brief poem to the world at large about *your* dreams. If you need a launch, consider using Martin Luther King, Jr.'s, phrase, "I have a dream."

ABOUT **DENISE CHÁVEZ**

Born in Las Cruces, New Mexico, in 1948, Denise Chávez grew up sensitive to the harshness and beauty of the desert Southwest. Her early experiences in a culturally diverse community (both Hispanic and Anglo), her ear for the nuances of language, and her appreciation of ordinary people all directed her toward a writing career. Since graduating from college with degrees in drama and creative writing, Chávez has written more than twenty plays and numerous stories. She has toured the United States in a one-woman show based on diverse characters she has created — from a savvy, smart-mouthed adolescent to a *curandera,* or healer. *The Last of the Menu Girls,* a collection of semi-autobiographical stories, features a young girl's coming of age. Central to her work are the family, the neighborhood, and the role of women.

The Flying Tortilla Man

CHARACTERS

Carlos *age twelve*
Bennie *age fourteen*
Elias *age thirteen*
Oscar *age eighteen*
Tudi *age twenty*
Nora *early thirties*

Neno *age twelve*
Hermano Gil *age forty-five*
Bertina *early fifties*
Cotil *age fifteen*
Fatty Campbell *age fifty-five*
The Birds/Old Women

The Tortilla Man *ageless*

SCENE 1

It is late evening on a hot summer night in Cuchillo, New Mexico. The heat permeates the walls of an aluminum building that houses a small but prosperous tortilla factory. The odor of cooked maize hangs heavy in the air. The building seems collapsible, barely grounded to the earth. The factory is in full swing preparing for the day's orders. A screen door is held in place by two long wooden planks.

The radio jumps to a lively Mexican station, XELO, *and casts a lyrical spell over the grinding, pulsating machines. Several teen-age boys are at their posts, silhouetted against machines in an eerie, yellow-maize darkness that creeps inside the factory and finds relief in the midst of activity.*

Carlos carries a pan of maize from a large metal trough to a machine that rinses the corn. He is a thin yet muscular boy of unspoiled character, gentle and filled with a natural goodness, a dreamer. Carlos *stands not far from* Elias, *who supervises the maize in the grinding machine and changes the pans of crushed corn that go to the cutter as a finished masa.* Elias *is a mischievous adolescent with thick burnt red hair and fair skin, appropriately named* "El Güero." *Next to* Elias *stands* Neno, *guarding the cutting machines. He is about the same age as* Carlos, *somewhat tired and sickly-looking, with a dark chinless face. Not far from* Neno *stands* Bennie, *who pushes the dough through the cutting machine roller. He is silent and shy, lean and greyhoundlike. At the end of the cooking conveyor belt sit* Oscar *and* Nora, *taking turns counting out a dozen tortillas and spreading them, fanlike, on the metal shelf where they are packaged by the roving* Bennie. Oscar *is fat, jolly and toothy.* Nora *is a cheerful woman, who is somewhat simple-minded, yet she works with amazing speed and agility.*

At the far end of the factory stands the office, a tucked-away bastion of power amid the heat and sweat. Inside is a large metal desk covered with orders and business papers. Beside the desk stands a counter full of frozen products from the factory: flour and corn tortillas, taco shells, tamales. At the desk, behind the closed and forbidding door, sits Tudi, *who oversees the factory with a hard, anxious eye. He is a good-looking, somewhat morose young man. He is not the actual boss but simply manages the factory in the owner's stead. The radio plays . . . all are intense and involved in the swinging, swaying creation of the tortillas.*

Neno. It's hot!

Oscar. So, why don't you work in an ice plant?

Elias. Quiet, you guys, this is my favorite song!

Oscar *(laughing to himself).* This one, ese, are you kidding me?

[*All are momentarily caught up in the dramatically sad tune coming from the radio: another song about lost love.*]

Spanish Words

masa dough, p. 428

El Güero term referring to a male with fair skin and light hair, p. 428

ese a slang expression comparable to "hey man," p. 428

metate a stone used for grinding grain, p. 429

ruca slang for girlfriend, p. 430

Hijole exclamation meaning "wow," p. 430

Neno. What am I doing here? I can't think . . . I can't breathe . . . it's so hot!

Oscar. You're not paid to think, man; you're paid to sweat!

Neno. I gotta get out of here . . . my head is on fire. Trade with me, Elias . . .

Elias. Heck no, Neno. I got my own work to do. You start doing it once, and you'll want to do it all the time.

Carlos. I'll trade, Neno.

Elias. They play this song to me this one night and you guys won't shut up.

Oscar. What's so special about tonight? It don't feel so special to me.

Elias. It's a special request from my girl!

Oscar. You have a girl, Güero? Who would want a pale worm like you?

Elias. None of your business, horsemouth!

Oscar. You called in the song yourself tonight, corn face, before you came in to work. Isn't that right, Nora? Doesn't have a girl at all, unless it's Nora here. Are you sweethearts with La Nica, Elias? NicaNora, NicaNora, NicaNora, old metate face. (Oscar *sings to* Nora, *who is first oblivious to him and then joins in, clapping her hands and humming, in a strange and haunting way.* Neno *is beginning to look progressively worse, and* Elias *makes ugly scowling faces at* Oscar, *who encourages* Bennie *to join him in his crazed chanting.*) NicaNora, NicaNora, NicaNora, old metate face! Laugh, Nica, laugh!

Elias. You're jealous!

Oscar. Of La Nica? Heck, man, I see her every day — that's enough for me.

Nora. Funny, Oscar, funny! (Nora *continues to clap her hands.*)

Oscar. Be quiet, Nora, and get back to work! The Boss gonna get on our case. We got lots of work to do . . .

[Nora hums.]

Carlos. Nora hasn't done anything to you, Oscar; leave her alone!

Oscar. You leave *me* alone, Mr. Corn Lifter. I was only making fun.

Elias. You tell him, Carlos . . . trying to make believe that La Nica is my girlfriend. That old hag, I'd rather drown in the irrigation ditch!

Carlos. Leave her alone, Elias!

Oscar. But she's his ruca, ese . . .

Elias. If you're such a good boy, Carlos, be quiet . . . shut your mouth, okay?

Carlos. Where's Tudi? He's been gone a long time. I'm worried about Neno.

Nora. Tudi? Tudi?

Oscar. Shut up and get to work!

Carlos. Don't talk to her that way, Oscar. Show some respect!

Oscar. To a crazy woman?

Elias. You think you're so good, Carlos . . . well, you're the one that's crazy! That's what happens when you don't have real parents. When you're an orphan! And when you live with people that ain't your kin, in a house full of strangers!

Carlos. I have parents!

Elias. You call those two — the stringbean and the squash — your parents? Heck, man, they have a house-ful of kids, like rabbits, over there at that place.

Carlos. They're good to me.

Elias. It's because they feel sorry.

Nora. Carlitos, good boy!

Elias. See, even La Nica feels sorry.

Oscar. Go on Elias; you're finally showing a little nerve. Nica might fall in love with your strength!

Bennie. You guys better be still. Tudi might come back!

Oscar. Let him come back. I'll show him who OSCAR SALCEDO is!

Elias. Híjole, Oscar, you couldn't whip a mouse!

Oscar. Be careful, you bleached earthworm!

Elias. You're going to get it one of these days, you fat hyena!

Bennie. Be quiet! Be quiet, or we'll get in trouble! Tudi's in his office!

Oscar. So El Tudi is in the office, huh? I don't trust that guy. He always looks like a dog who wants to bark. Too much power. Wooo! What do you say, Nica?

Nora. Where's Tudi? Tudi is a nice man.

Carlos. Her name is Nora.

Oscar (*referring to* Nora *as he counts tortillas*). So what does she know anyway? All she can do is count to twelve. Ay, this heat! It gets into your blood and drives you crazy. After so many years, you start counting all the time. Stupid things you start counting for nothing. All this heat . . . it affects your brain. It starts suddenly, like with Neno, until one day you're as dry in the head as Nica, right, Nenito? Where'd he go?

Carlos. He's at the washer.

Bennie. Don't let Tudi see you, Neno; it'll go rough for us!

Elias. So who cares! You've all got baked corn for brains, anyway!

Neno. I don't feel good. I'm going outside. (Neno *starts for the door and suddenly faints.* Carlos, Elias, *and* Bennie *run to him, followed by* Nora. Oscar *remains behind.*)

Oscar (*paying no attention to the others, he continues talking*). You just keep counting, that's all . . .

Carlos. What's wrong, Neno?

Bennie. He's sick!

Elias. You're really a smart one, Bennie. Is that why you work here?

Bennie. What about you, Güero? The light too bright for you out there in the world? You need to be in this cave, eh?

Oscar (*still oblivious to the others,* Oscar *continues to count tortillas*). Ten . . . eleven . . . twelve . . .

Carlos. Help me take him outside. He needs some fresh air.

Oscar. He's got the rot. It just happens.

Elias. You must be an advanced case.

Oscar. Sooner or later . . .

Elias. Would you shut up?

Oscar. It gets you.

Elias. Is that why you're still here after all these years?

[The boys carry Neno *outside and lean him up against the steps.* Nora *has gone to the water trough near the maize bags and dips her apron in and returns to the steps. She uses her apron as a towel on* Neno's *forehead.* Neno *is in a daze.]*
Carlos. Thank you, Nora.
Nora *(in a soothing voice).* Neno, Nenito. Good boy, Nenito.

*[*Neno *unsteadily gets to his feet with the help of* Nora *and* Carlos.]*

Elias. Oh, he's okay.
[Bennie, Elias, Carlos, Nora and Neno file back inside the building.]
Bennie. We'd better get back to work!
Oscar. Since when have you worked around here, Bennie? And you, Nica. Where have you been, you lazy good-for-nothing? Who do you think you are, wiping people's foreheads? And who does Neno think he is? Hey, I already did more than my share of work, so where is everybody?

*[*Nora *runs back, confused. Her movements are pointed and jittery.]*

Nora. Sorry, Nora so sorry. Oscar not mad with Nora. She's sorry.
Oscar. Back to work, back to work! They can hear you in the other room, the bosses, the big shots. They can hear you out here like rats in the night. Isn't that right, Nica, like rats?
Nora *(making a ratlike face).* Like rats, like rats.
Carlos. Leave her alone, Oscar . . . she hasn't done any-thing to you. She was only trying to help Neno out.
Oscar. It'll go bad for us all, Carlos. You get back to work.
Carlos. He's sick!
Oscar. He's got the corn rot and the fever that comes nights working at a place like this. It starts flowing in your blood.
Elias *(sarcastically).* What are you anyway, a doctor?
Oscar. And you're the nurse!

Carlos. I can't leave him alone. He's sick!

Oscar. Oh, that's right . . . you're the one who doesn't have anyone to take care of you, so you take care of the world.

Tudi *(coming in and looking around suspiciously).* What's going on? Why aren't you working?

Neno. I'll be okay in a few minutes.

Bennie. Didn't I tell you guys?

Tudi. Get to work! All of you!

Carlos. Neno isn't feeling well, Tudi, I . . .

Tudi. Get to work, Carlos. We have orders to fill. It's late. The night's almost over and we're behind. Go on, all of you!

Carlos. Neno is sick. He needs to rest. Maybe he should go home.

Tudi. We can't have this, Carlos. We have orders to fill. This isn't the first time someone has played a trick, pretending to be sick . . .

Carlos. Feel his head . . .

Tudi. Huerfanito, you, Carlos . . . help Neno get back to his job. He'll make it, all right. Now, boys, I've been in the office, thinking. *(Oscar snickers.)* And I've come up with a new set of rules.

Oscar. Not again!

Tudi. Quiet! Number one: one break every three hours, depending how far behind we are. Number two: no eating or drinking on the job. Number three: no visiting of an extended nature.

Oscar. Number four: No breathing! Visiting, man, are you joking me? Who's there to visit en esta maldita cueva?

Tudi. Number four: more than one absence constitutes dismissal. Number five: we will all work together as a happy, united working force, producing as best as we can, without strife and dissension.

Bennie. Dissension, what's dissension?

Tudi. Quiet! Now then, I'll be available to talk to you guys any time. Remember that I'm the boss in place of our

BOSS, who is gone. I am the absolute head in this place, and I demand respect and will treat you accordingly. Come on, boys, let's be friends!

Oscar. After all that . . . man, are you pulling my leg? It's a joke, Tudi.

Carlos. I'm taking Neno home, Tudi.

Elias. Let them go, let them go. . . they're nothing but trouble.

Oscar. Those two didn't do a thing all night.

Nora. Nice boys, Tudi, they're my friends.

Tudi. La Nica's very talkative tonight. She seems to be on your side, Carlos. Why are you helping Neno anyway? You know none of them would ever lift a finger for you. You could die right here on the job.

Oscar. Carlos was just standing around doing nothing, Tudi.

Carlos. I was helping my friend. I'm taking him home.

Tudi. If you do that, you might not have a job when you get back.

Carlos. You just can't *not* help someone. Especially a friend, someone you work with. Look at him, Tudi . . . he looks bad. Friendship is more than just standing by while someone is sick. Neno and I are friends.

Tudi. Go on, Carlos. Get outta here. Just try and come back. You're always getting in my way. Take your friend home. Just take him home. He's worthless!

Neno. I'm feeling better; really, I am. I can go to work, Carlos. I can go . . . *(He appears ready to faint and then recovers a bit.)* I can go home alone, Carlos; you stay here. Let me go alone.

Carlos. I'm taking you home! I care more about you than all the tortillas in the world!

Elias. Ah, they'll be back, begging for a job!

Tudi. Just you wait and see what happens, Carlos. Go on with you! Don't come back!

Nora. Goodbye. Goodbye, my friends. See you soon.

Oscar. You make me laugh, Nica. You really make me laugh! *(He starts laughing. They all join in.* Carlos *and* Neno *exit.)*

[It is a rainy, windy night. The lightning crackles the breeze, and the boys look small and helpless against the sky. They don't have too far to go to Neno's *but they make their way slowly and cautiously, pausing under the archways and porches, huddling together against the fury of the oncoming storm.* Carlos *knocks at* Neno's *door. A woman answers and takes* Neno *in, then closes the door.* Carlos *stands there long after they have gone in, unsure of what to do. He then dashes out of the doorway and runs madly to the next shelter. A delicate-looking man of above-average height with a fine, smooth face and warm, small eyes is standing there, also seeking shelter. They look at one another for a few seconds, the boy and the man, both dreamers.]*

Tortilla Man. Where are you, boy?

*[*Carlos *is not sure he heard the old gentlemen correctly. He is taken aback by the seemingly strange question. Often* The Tortilla Man *will ask questions that seem to make no sense whatsoever, and yet they really do.]*

Carlos *(in an uncertain voice).* Where am I going, sir?
Tortilla Man. Where are you?
Carlos. I don't understand.
Tortilla Man. That's what's wrong with everyone. They're out of touch; they don't know where they are, especially in the middle of a storm. They're lost, going from one place to another, from one thing to another.
Carlos. WHO are you?
Tortilla Man. You don't know me?
Carlos *(suddenly wary).* What do you want?
Tortilla Man. What makes you think I want anything?
Carlos. If you'll excuse me, sir, I'll have to leave you and get back to work.
Tortilla Man. If I were you, I'd stay around and talk awhile. It's too early to be running off, and besides, your Boss hasn't decided to take you back yet. Wait up, boy; talk to an old man . . . tell him where you are.
Carlos. Who are you? You seem to know a lot. You're not from here, are you?

Tortilla Man. I remember Cuchillo when there was nothing out here but rocks and weeds and the bare sky to wear as a hat . . . when you blessed yourself for another day in this wilderness and prayed for rain . . .

Carlos. You don't look *that* old . . .

Tortilla Man. No impudence, boy, just listen to me. For he who teaches you for one day is your father for life. I read that in a book.

Carlos. I can barely read, and I don't have a father.

Tortilla Man. You do now, boy. We're in the same line of work.

Carlos. Tortillas?

Tortilla Man. Well, yes and no. Mostly yes.

Carlos. I don't have a job now. I've been fired. I don't know whether I should go back and beg—they said I would—or whether I should go home . . . I mean, where I live. My parents, Hermano Gil and Bertina, they'll be mad at me. I finally got this job and now it's gone!

Tortilla Man. You'll go back to the factory, of course. No one should ever avoid what needs to be done.

Carlos. Yes, I thought so, too. How did you know?

Tortilla Man. We do the same work.

Carlos. You make tortillas, too?

Tortilla Man. In a way, yes, but we'll come to that later. We both make things grow, come alive.

Carlos. We do?

Tortilla Man. We do, Carlos!

Carlos. You know my name!

Tortilla Man. Boy, you look like a Carlos—long, gangly, a real weed, a Carlos who is growing.

Carlos. You talk funny!

Tortilla Man. Boy, you look funny, all wet and long!
[They both laugh.]

Carlos. Who are you?

Tortilla Man. I'm The Flying Tortilla Man.

Carlos. The Tortilla Man? You run a factory, like our boss? He's never there, so Tudi takes his place. I never have seen the boss; I don't even know who he is . . .

Carlos *(realizing* The Tortilla Man *might be his boss).* You aren't . . .

Tortilla Man. I make things grow.

Carlos. But tortillas don't grow! They're a dead thing . . . they're just corn that becomes bread and that's eaten and is gone . . .

Tortilla Man. But, Carlos, tortillas are more than that . . . they're life to so many people. They're magic offerings; they're alive as the land, and as flat!

Carlos. They are, huh? What's your real name?

Tortilla Man. Juan.

Carlos. You're Mr. Juan, The Tortilla Man; pleased to meet you.

Tortilla Man. Enchanted. We are enchanted to meet you.

Carlos. Who's we?

Tortilla Man. Why, the Magic Tortilla, of course.

Carlos *(looking around).* Where is it?

Tortilla Man *(putting his arm around* Carlos's *shoulder and speaking confidentially).* I couldn't bring it out in this rain, could I?

Carlos *(disappointed).* I guess not.

Tortilla Man. Now . . . back to work . . . they're waiting for you.

Carlos. They are?

Tortilla Man. Don't be impudent, boy . . . don't you trust me?

Carlos. Yes . . . yes, I do! But I know I don't have a job anymore.

Tortilla Man. Who says? You just wait and see. Carlos, you just wait and see. You just can't stop something from growing.

Carlos. I'll try . . . I'll try . . .

Tortilla Man. Grow, boy. Let them see you grow, in front of their eyes! *(He laughs an infectious, clear laugh that is warm and comforting.)* You'll see. It's waiting there to grow . . . they can't stop you. They can't stop you . . . they'll try . . . Now, goodbye, think of me, and run, run . . .

[Carlos *runs into the darkness of a now-clear night. He is full of energy. He suddenly stops to say something to* The Tortilla Man, *who has vanished.*]

Carlos. THANK YOU! Sir . . . Mr. Juan . . . goodbye . . . he says he makes things grow, but how? Magic tortillas? And he says the sky is a hat . . .

[Carlos *runs back to the factory and walks in. Everyone is working noisily. The radio competes with the tortilla machine for dominance.*]

Tudi (*seeing* Carlos, *he signals for him to come closer*). It's about time . . . what took you so long?
Carlos. I was getting some fresh air; it's too hot in here . . .
Oscar. There, what'd I tell you . . . the rot . . . it starts nights . . .
Elias. Shut up!!
Tudi. Well get back to work! We have orders to fill and the night is half over, and we've just begun!
Oscar. You're lucky, man . . . you're just lucky. Isn't that right, Nica?
Nora. Hello, Carlitos. Hello. How's your Mama?
Oscar. What a memory!
Nora. Lucky boy, lucky boy.
Carlos (*back at his post, he rinses out the maize*). I'm fine, Nora . . . I'm just fine! How are you?

[Blackout. End of scene one.]

SCENE 2

The orphanage where Carlos *lives with his foster parents,* Hermano Gil *and* Bertina. *It is a large, rambling house with about twenty-five children and teenagers and two frazzled adults. The orphans are not juvenile delinquents, merely displaced and disoriented people.* Carlos's *room is set off from the main house. It is a small junk-filled closet/shed that serves as a storage area and utility room, as well as* Carlos's *room. Spread about the room are boxes full of cloth remnants, paper, old toys, and empty lug-*

gage; up against the wall, near Carlos's *bed, are some old picture frames, an old hoe, and some posters, as well as a beat-up, much-used vacuum cleaner. Nonetheless, despite its disarray, the room has a certain personal coziness, as if someone has tried his best to make a living space of his own and half succeeded. There is a small night table next to the bed and a chest of drawers nearby. On the table is an old decorated cigar box, with* CARLOS *written on the outside. It is* Carlos's *private property and personal joy. Inside the box are an old dried feather, a small fossil, a large rubber band tied into a series of amazing knots, a soft red handkerchief, two glass marbles, and a picture of a sickly old woman in black. It is a picture of Isa,* Carlos's *guardian after the death of his mother, whom he hardly knew.* Carlos *is sleeping. It is about six A.M. He has not been in bed very long. A man is singing. It is* Hermano Gil. *He is a short, smallish man who works in the kitchen of a Mexican restaurant. He is energetic and sprightly despite the hour and his obvious inebriation. He has a dark complexion that seems even darker in the half-light.*

The house is asleep for the most part, and the lights have a dim, early-morning quality. Carlos *sleeps in a twisted position. Suddenly, the door opens to his room, and his foster father,* Hermano Gil, *wanders in, looking for something in the dark room. He accidentally falls against the sleeping* Carlos. Hermano Gil *gets up and continues his search for a suitcase of his that is somewhere in the room.*

Hermano Gil. This is the last time I'll bother you, any one of you . . . this time I'm leaving for good! I'll take a job as a singer. (*He sings a few bars from a Mexican love ballad in Spanish.*) I'll come up in the world at last. Half my life spent in someone else's kitchen, cleaning up. That's no kind of life. Then I have to come home to a house full of strangers. I told Bertina, "Don't do it, Bert." I said, "I can't take it." She didn't listen. "I can't be a father to the entire world; we have a daughter of our own. Isn't that enough, woman? I'm leaving . . . I'm leaving . . ."

Carlos (*he has awakened and is sitting up on the bed, listening*). Papa, wait, don't leave!

Hermano Gil. I'm not your Papa . . . let me pack.

Carlos (*in a tired and sleepy voice*). We'll miss you, Papa!

Hermano Gil. I have to leave. I can't go on living in a hallway in a house full of lost children. What am I talking about? I just work in a kitchen. (*looking at* Carlos) You're nothing to me!

Carlos. Don't say that, Papa. We love you!

Hermano Gil. All my life in a kitchen . . . for what? To run a house of stray dogs and cats . . . all my money going to feed twenty-five hungry mouths . . . as if Bertina and Cotil and I didn't have our own problems.

[Hermano Gil *sits down on the edge of the bed. He puts his hand on the side of his head and sighs. He is holding a ragged suitcase. As* Hermano Gil *is bemoaning his fate, he accidentally knocks over* Carlos's *cigar box, and the contents fall to the floor.* Carlos *scrambles to retrieve the objects, but* Hermano Gil *has swooped them up and holds them in his dark and unsteady hands.*]

Carlos. Papa!

Hermano Gil. So why do you keep this junk? Isn't there enough here already to crowd into your life?

Carlos. These are *my* things — they mean something to *me*! They remind me of people and places and times I've loved. They're alive to me.

Hermano Gil. This seashell is dead, son. There was a life here once, but where is it now? Show me, if you can. Can it talk to you? Can it tell you how it feels to be buried in the sand and come up to the sky as a rock, a hardened thing, an outline of something that was once alive? No, son, these are dead things — they have no use. You keep them because you are a silly dreamer like I used to be and because you make up stories to pass away your silly time. Like how you are going to be a singer and come up in the world . . . (*Referring to his own broken life,* Hermano Gil *breaks down and cries.* Carlos *comforts him.* Hermano Gil *wipes his eyes and looks at the knots in the rubber band.*) This game of knots, this game of glass. Of what use is it? (*He cries a bit more and then looks at the picture.*) Who is this old pan face? She has the skin of an old wrinkled prune . . . This is what I mean, Carlitos! Your name is Carlos; I forget with all the names. I forget, son, so many people pass through here and go away with not so much as a thank you for the food. They leave their mugres—stuff, son, stuff—behind for us to collect and store in this room. *(He looks at the feather and the rock.)* What is this? What does this mean? This dirty old bird feather and this rock?

Carlos. It's not a rock, Papa; it's a fossil.

Hermano Gil. It's a dirty old rock and this is a chicken feather! Like the ones whose necks I used to wring when I was a boy . . . *(He imitates the wringing of a chicken's neck.)* Squawk!

Carlos. It's a seashell.

Hermano Gil. So it is, Juanito.

Carlos. Carlos, Papa . . . Let me have my things, please, Papa . . . please.

Hermano Gil *(referring to the photograph).* This is the deadest thing of all, in black, like a spider.

Carlos. That's Isa, my mother's aunt. She took care of me when Mama died.

Hermano Gil *(touched).* Here, son . . . *(He puts the objects on the bed.)* Keep your treasures. You may be a fool, but you have a heart, and no man—not even the worst of us—can go against that. Keep your treasures. You'll need them out there in the world. Keep your feathers, your rocks, and your old lady's knotted life. *(He gets up.)* I don't want anything to do with strangers anymore. You've worn me out. I'm tired of trying to feed and clothe the world.

[Carlos *takes his things and puts them back in the box. Then he goes to the chest of drawers and puts the box on top of it, under some clothing, just as* Cotil *comes in.* Cotil *is a conniving young lady of fifteen, who besides being prone to fits of unthinking and unsolicited malice, is a chubby romantic.*]

Cotil. Hiding things again, lazy boy?

Carlos. Good morning, Cotil.

Cotil. Papa, Mama wants you to get ready for work.

Hermano Gil. I told you, I'm leaving. This is it, Cotil. You're the only flesh and blood of mine in this infernal household. Why should I remain the father of this faceless screaming brood? Tell me!

Cotil. Mama wants you to come and eat, or the atole will get cold.

Hermano Gil. EAT? Child, how can I eat the fruit of my labor with a mouth full of sand? Let the maggots take it!

Cotil. Papa, you better go before Mama comes to get you. And you, lazy boy, get up. You've already slept long enough.

Hermano Gil. Leave him alone.

Cotil. If I do, Papa, he'll sleep all day.

Hermano Gil. He's one of the few people that works around here. Let him rest! Go away!

Cotil. I'll tell Mama!

Hermano Gil. Tell her . . . tell her!

Cotil. You'd better get up, Carlos. I'll tell Mama you steal and hide things. I'll show her where you put them.

Hermano Gil. Out, out!

Cotil. He's got you believing him, Papa!

Hermano Gil. Flesh of my flesh, blood of my blood . . . (Cotil *exits with a wicked smile.* Hermano Gil *rises and gets ready to go to breakfast.*) Can you put away the suitcase, Carlitos? I am a bit hungry, now that I think about it. Carlos, you and me, we'll go away someday, just the two of us, just the two of us old fossils and we'll never come back . . .

Bertina (*yelling from the kitchen*). Gil, honey, come on. Come and have breakfast, or you'll be late for work.

Hermano Gil (*speaking to* Carlos). We'll have to make a few plans before we can leave . . . I'm coming . . . I'm coming, Bert!

Carlos. I'm sorry, Papa; I'll help you. I'll go away and become rich, and I'll send you lots of money. I'll make you happy.

Hermano Gil. Ha! Go back to bed and dream some more, son. Rub your magic things together and pray for someone to show you the way. Ask for money first, then loaves of bread and fish. Pray for rain, boy. This is New Mexico and our souls are dry! No, boy, go back to bed, but first put up the suitcase, so I'll know where to find it the next time . . . Thanks, son . . . (Hermano Gil *pauses in the doorway.*) It's so nice, so nice to believe in miracles . . . so keep your dried-out turkey feathers, who knows . . . who really knows . . .

[Bertina *is at the door, with* Cotil *beside her.* Bertina *is in her early fifties, a plump, kindly woman who is gracious and tactful.*]

Cotil. I told you, Mama. I told you they were talking and plotting, making all kinds of plans. Carlos is a trouble-maker, Mama. I've always told you that.

Hermano Gil. Hello, Bert. Good morning to my dear and beloved wife and darling daughter.

Cotil. Carlos is a snake, Mama!

Hermano Gil. Shut up, my darling girl. Now go run and sharpen your tongue while your Mama and I eat breakfast.

Bertina. Go on, Cotil; your father is hungry.

Cotil. But MAMA!

Bertina. I only say things once. You know that. What would you like for breakfast, Gilito?

Hermano Gil. I thought you decided already. You take care of things like that, Bert. You always do.

Bertina. We'll start with a little atole . . . chile . . .

Cotil. What about Carlos? He's still in bed, Mama!

Hermano Gil. Let the world sleep! I'm going to have my atolito. You have all day to run your mother ragged, Cotil. I don't know how she does it. I don't know how you do it, Bert. A house full of children, both young and old.

Bertina. I love them as I love you, Gilito . . . that's all. We're all God's children . . .

Hermano Gil. But twenty-five!!

Cotil (*standing at the door to* Carlos's *room*). I saw you hide that box, Carlitos Warlitos. Such a good boy wouldn't have secrets.

Carlos. I don't!

Cotil. Then show me what's in the box!

Carlos. They're personal things.

Cotil. Nothing is personal in this house.

Carlos. Let me sleep!

Cotil. You're a lazy orphan, and my Mama and Papa don't really love you. They only put up with you because you don't have parents or a house.

Carlos. Leave me alone . . . please, Cotil.

Cotil. I'll never leave you alone — never!

Carlos. You hate me, don't you?

Cotil. Yes! You orphan!

Carlos (*sitting on the bed*). Why? Why? I haven't done anything to you!

Cotil. You think you're better than us.

Carlos. No, I don't!

Cotil. You have secrets!

Carlos. Why do you hate me so much, Cotil? (*It is a tense, electric moment.*)

Cotil. I don't know . . . but I do! (*She slams the door and leaves. She thinks twice about it and returns.*) Get up, you lazy, yawning nobody, or I'll tell Mama about your secrets!

[Cotil *exits and leaves* Carlos *very hurt and stunned.*]

Carlos. What have I done that everyone hates me! I'm quiet and I work hard and all they do is yell at me. Get to work! Get to work! You better straighten up and show respect! I don't understand. Who can tell me what's going wrong? (Carlos *goes to the chest of drawers and removes the box from underneath the clothing. He looks at the photograph and then at the fossil.*) Hello, Isa. What can you tell me today? Gone to see some friends? And you, Carlos, do you have any friends? (*Thinking aloud,* Carlos *remembers* Mr. Juan.) Where are you now, Mr. Juan?

(remembering The Tortilla Man's words) He said they'll try and stop you. They'll try but they can't . . . because for some reason, a person wants to keep growing . . .
(Carlos goes back to sleep.)

SCENE 3

[Early the next evening, outside the factory. The workers have not yet arrived. We can hear whispers in the distance.]

Elias. I'm here behind the building. To the right. Did you have any trouble?

Cotil. I had to sneak out of the house.

Elias. Will you get into trouble?

Cotil. Oh, no! I can do just about anything and my Mama won't care. She likes me. I'm the favorite.

Elias. What about your Papa?

Cotil. What about him? He does what my Mama says.

Elias (coming closer to Cotil, he puts his arms around her). Cotil, how are you?

Cotil (moving away). We don't have much time. Is everything ready?

Elias. Yes, Cotil. Oscar and I have gone over the plans many times. There's no doubt that we'll get Carlos — and good this time. Who does he think he is, walking all over Oscar and me like we were rocks under his feet?

Cotil. He's that way. He needs to be taught a lesson. He strolls through our house like he owns it, like he was my own true brother.

Elias. I'm glad I'm not your brother! Why don't you stay awhile?

Cotil. I have to go or Mama will get suspicious. You see, lucky for us, Carlos left the house to do an errand for Papa, and I snuck into his room and got this . . . (She brings Carlos's cigar box from behind her back and shows it to Elias.) See, it says CARLOS on it. That way, when the robbery is reported, everyone will figure he stole the stuff.

Elias. I'm glad you came, my dove, my little sunshine.

Cotil. Let's get on with it, okay?

Elias. Okay, okay. This is the plan: after work we stick around, Oscar and I. He opens the locks — he's real good at that — then we go into the office and fool around the safe. We mess up the room and leave. When Tudi comes in tomorrow morning, he sees Carlos's box and he figures out who broke in.

Cotil. Are you sure it'll work?

Elias. Aren't I Elias Macias? Hey, babe, by tomorrow Carlos will be fired. We'll have put him in his place. It's taken time to settle accounts with that goody-goody. Say, babe, can't you stay awhile?

Cotil. I have to get home. I just wanted to make sure everything is going okay.

Elias. Will you think of me?

Cotil. I do every night, Elias, just before I go to sleep.

Elias. Really?

Cotil. Yeah, now go on . . . listen to the radio . . . for a sign from me . . .

Elias. Cotil, the guys don't believe I have a girlfriend. How come you don't want to go out with me in public? (Cotil *looks away from him with an annoyed expression.*) Well, okay . . . until tomorrow. We'll celebrate the downfall of that plaster saint. There's no one worse than someone who smiles a lot with phony goodness . . . Goodnight, Cotil.

Cotil. Goodbye. Make sure that all goes well. (*She exits.*)

Elias. My Cotil . . . will you dedicate a song for me tonight? Ay! (*He sighs and exits with* Carlos's *box.*)

[It is now about eight P.M. Everyone starts to arrive. By the side of the road stand four old women in black, who later become The Birds, Tin, Tan, Ton, *and* Mabel.]

Woman One (*referring to the boys coming in for work at the tortilla factory*). Those boys, it's disgraceful . . .

Woman Two. Where is he?

Woman Three. Who?

Woman Four. The boy.

Woman Two. I don't see him.

Woman One. The rascally thin one, over there, over there.

Woman Four. His parents were killed when he was nothing . . .

Woman One. He was very small, wrinkled from his mother . . .

Woman Three. Full of his father's sweat . . .

Woman Two. They were killed?

Woman Four. He's always been alone, like the sore on the side of the mouth, turned inside with a life of its own . . .

Woman One. There he goes . . .

Woman Two. Who?

Woman Four. He's all alone . . .

Woman Three. The boy . . .

[The boys come up. Tudi *is the first to arrive. He opens up the tortilla factory, turns on the lights and the machines.* Bennie *and* Oscar *are behind him, followed by* Carlos *and* Elias. Nora *wanders in last.* Elias *is carrying a paper bag with the cigar box inside. He and* Oscar *wink to each other.]*

Tudi. Hello, boys!

All. Hello, Tudi!

Carlos. How are you, Tudi?

Tudi. I just said hello.

Nora. Hello, hello. I'm fine.

Tudi. I'm ready for work. How about everyone else?

[Various grumbles, moans, sighs, and a belch can be heard.]

Oscar. I'm ready to go out on the town, to do anything but slave in this furnace.

Elias *(looking at* Oscar*).* We'll have to set off some fireworks later on, eh, Oscar? Won't we?

Tudi. What's this? All of a sudden two fighting dogs become friends. It must be the end of the world.

Elias. We've come to an understanding.

Oscar. Some common ground.

Tudi. Probably some common hate. Don't forget about rule number three: socializing too much.

Oscar. Oh, yes, sir, Mr. Tudi.

Nora. Hello, hello, hello. I'm fine.

Tudi. Okay, okay, let's get to work. *(Talking to* Oscar*)* Are you setting up, Oscar?

Elias. Yes, we've got it all worked out . . . right, Oscar?

Tudi. Ready, Carlos . . . Nora?

Nora. Ready, Tudi, ready.

Carlos. I'm glad to see you and Oscar have become friends, Elias.

Tudi. Something must be wrong.

Elias. Finally something is right. We discovered a way to settle old debts.

Tudi. Get to work, you bums. We've been here ten minutes and you haven't done a bit of work. Hurry up there, Nora!

Nora. Okay, Tudi, I hurry.

Oscar. Here it comes, folks . . . THE TORTILLA EXPRESS!!

[The action is speeded up. The machines roar, night goes by. Suddenly, it is early morning and the work is done. Tudi *is beginning to turn off the lights and lock up.]*

Elias. Hey, Oscar, did you hear about Neno?

Oscar. What happened, man?

Elias. You were right.

Tudi. You guys must really be sick. Are you actually agreeing with him, Elias?

Elias. Neno's got the corn rot.

Oscar. He does?

Carlos. What's this, Elias? What's wrong?

Elias. Neno's got the rot. He's in bed. He's really sick. They don't know if he's going to make it.

Tudi. He was always sickly. The first time I saw him he looked like a stale sausage, very dark with bloody eyes. He was never healthy.

Oscar. I've said it again and again . . . it'll get you sooner or later. It gets into your blood after awhile and then there's no going back. You're lost.

Carlos. Neno is really sick? We should go see him.

Elias. Not me! I might get the rot from being near him.

Oscar. He was never a friend of mine. Too puny and dark.

Elias. I never knew him that well.

Nora. Nora all finished with work. She go home.

Carlos. I'll walk you, Nora.

Oscar. Uuucheee, it's too funny!

Elias. They're sweethearts, Oscar!

Tudi. Get out of here, you worms! I haven't got all day to put up with a bunch of lazy, rascally caterpillars. I have to lock up.

Carlos (*speaking gently to* Nora). Neno's sick.

Nora. Where's Nenito?

Oscar. Why do you bother with her? She can't understand you. One . . . two . . . three . . . four . . . five . . . six . . . seven . . . eight . . . nine . . . ten . . . eleven . . . twelve — that's all she understands. The two of you keep trying to make sense, and no one can understand.

Carlos. Let's go, Nora.

Nora. Goodbye, my friends.

Tudi. Go on, I have my work to do.

Carlos. Have a nice day, Tudi!

Tudi. Haven't you left yet?

Elias. I'm going.

Tudi. Well, hurry up!

Elias. Bye, you guys.

Carlos. Bye, Elias.

Elias (*to* Oscar). Hey, man, I'll walk with you.

Tudi. So goodbye already . . . this must be the end of the world.

Oscar. Let's go.

✳
Things to Know

T.V.I. Technical and Vocational Institute, p. 450

Juan de Oñate Trail route of the Spanish explorer who led an expedition north in 1598 and took possession of New Mexico for the Spanish king, p. 454.

[*They exit and disappear around the building. They wait until* Tudi *has locked up and has gone.* Carlos *and* Nora *have left.*]

Oscar *and* Elias *emerge from the shadows and furtively slip into the doorway.* Oscar *begins fiddling with the door lock.]*

Elias. Where'd you learn that?

Oscar. You think I've been making tortillas all my life? I'm a T.V.I. graduate.

Elias. I never knew you were so smart, Oscar.

Oscar. Haven't I told you all this time?

Elias. But who listens?

Oscar. Did Cotil come?

Elias. She gave me something that will put our Carlos in real trouble. See, it's a box with his name on it. When we get inside the office, we'll drop it on the floor for Tudi to find. It's all settled. We'll get him yet!

[They go inside quietly. Once they open the office door, they rummage around the room, dropping the box, and then leave as quietly and as quickly as possible. While they have been doing this, Nora *has returned, looking for* Neno. *She sees what is going on but does not fully comprehend its significance. She slips away. Meanwhile,* Carlos *has returned to wait for* The Tortilla Man *under the same stoop. He is tired and sleepy. He sits back, leaning up against the door, and falls into a heavy sleep. He hears the sounds of voices, then a solitary voice—first far away, then near. It is a soothing, melodious voice, the type one hears in dreams. It has a sweet clarity and richness that comes from a height and flows past the dreamer until it is there beside him.* Carlos *feels a coolness and a movement but is unsure of where he is. Suddenly he feels a warm tingling sensation on his face.* Carlos *is startled and jumps up. This sudden movement jars him out of the dream. He is now awake.]*

Carlos. Where am I? *(Although he finds himself in mid-air, on a smooth disc, he is reassured to see* The Tortilla Man.*)*

Tortilla Man. Don't be impudent, boy. Where do you think you are?

Carlos. Where am I?

Tortilla Man. Why do you ask so many questions? Just look around. Open your eyes and really see. We're flying over the Rio Grande now.

Carlos. We are??? *(He jumps around and makes the Flying Tortilla take a nose dive).*

Tortilla Man. I wouldn't do that if I were you, Carlossssss . . .

(The Tortilla Man *looks nervous, but quickly regains control of the ship.* Carlos *holds on for dear life. He is glued to the firm spongy mass under him and stares, wide-eyed. The Flying Tortilla is a flat spongy disc about six feet across and four feet wide. It is a blue color, with multicolored spots. Tough and durable, it has been made by a Master Tortilla Maker,* Mr. Juan *himself. It has no seats to speak of, just two slightly raised air pockets that serve as seats.* The Tortilla Man *is wearing a historical costume of the fifteenth century, complete with armor. He looks proud and distinguished and a bit older than before. On the side of the Flying Tortilla is a flag of an unknown country with a feather on top. At the sides are rudders of dough. In the middle are several large sacks of baking powder, used to raise and lower the ship, much like the sand bags used in balloons. Once airborne, the Magic Blue Corn Tortilla floats on air currents and the occasional boost from various birds who happen to be flying by.)* You should never do that, Carlos!

Carlos. Are we on an airplane or a ship?

Tortilla Man. I must have asked questions, too, when I was a boy, so I'll have to be patient. Yes, we are on a ship. The Magic Flying Blue Corn Tortilla. There seems to be no satisfying you with answers . . . that's good. Yes, Carlos, right now we are . . . let me see . . . *(The Tortilla Man looks at a compass, checks the feather, and moistens his finger with saliva, then holds it up a foot or so from his face.)* We are about two miles due west of Cuchillo as the birds fly.

Carlos *(embracing* The Tortilla Man *with a mixture of fear and glee).* We are?

Tortilla Man. Boy, once you get over your wonder, you can start dealing with life. Sit up there . . . you're slouched over like you're afraid.

Carlos *(peering over the edge of the Flying Tortilla).* I am!

Tortilla Man. You, my young explorer, afraid of this . . . (The Tortilla Man *begins to jump up and down on the tortilla.*)

Carlos *(begging* The Tortilla Man *to stop).* Oh please, Mr. Juan, won't you stop doing that? I think I'll just sit here, if you don't mind.

Tortilla Man. This isn't like you, Carlos. We're on an adventure. You just can't sit there and watch the birds fly by. You have to jump in or, in this case, fly on . . .

Carlos. How far up are we?

Tortilla Man. About three cloud lengths and a half . . . I can check . . . (*He makes a motion to go to the back of the ship.*)

Carlos. No, that isn't necessary. Is this . . . a . . . tortilla?

Tortilla Man. Nothing but the best for me . . . blue corn.

Carlos. How does it fly?

Tortilla Man. Up, Carlos, up! Now then, here we have the front and lateral rudders. I had a lot of trouble perfecting them. It seems the birds would fly by and nibble on them between meals. Lost a lot of rudders that way. I used to carry a parachute for safety. But since I've put those letters on the side, it's been better.

Carlos. M.F.T.V.F. What does it mean, Mr. Juan?

Tortilla Man. Glad to see you relaxing, Carlos. I hate to see tense young people. Why, those letters mean MAGIC FLYING TORTILLA VERY FATTENING. Birds are very conscious of their figures. To an extreme you might say. They never stop talking about it, but oh, how they love to eat! You don't do that, do you, Carlos?

Carlos. Do you really talk to the birds?

Tortilla Man. Yes, and usually in a loud voice. They're hard of hearing. I talk to them when I have time. We're always so busy. Now for the rest of the tour. How you do ask questions! The best thing is not to ask but to listen. You'll find out things much faster that way. Not enough listening these days. Here is my flag, Carlos. My compass and baking powder bags. (*He pauses and looks at* Carlos.) I'm waiting for questions.

Carlos. What flag is that?

Tortilla Man. Why it's my own, of course. It's the flag of growth. *(The flag is in burnt desert colors. It shows the mountains, the rivers, and the plants of the desert. In the fore-front is a plant with its root system exposed.)* This is the land, dry and burnt. To someone who doesn't know its ways, it is like thirst — there is no in-between. Our land is a land of mountains and rivers, dry things and grow-ing things. Our roots are in the earth and we feel the nourishment of the sky. This is *my* flag . . . what's yours?

Carlos. I don't have a flag of my own.

Tortilla Man. You don't? Well, then you shall have to make one.

Carlos *(discovering his box on the Flying Tortilla).* My cigar box! What is it doing here?

Tortilla Man. You were thinking about it, perhaps?

Carlos. Why, that's my feather up there with your flag!

Tortilla Man. I needed a compass. You see, birds tell the direction by the way their feathers blow, and besides, it's a nice feather.

Carlos. My father calls it an old ugly chicken feather.

Tortilla Man. Has he ever had his own feather? (Carlos *shakes his head no.)* Well, then, how would he know?

Carlos. It *is* an old feather!

Tortilla Man. Don't let the birds hear you say that. They may never forgive us! They don't exactly hold grudges, but it'll go better for us if we keep on their good side; the other side can be most uncomfortable. They give us a push now and then when the air current is low, so we can really use their help. You see, we fly by current. I ignite special minerals and then sprinkle that mixture over baking power and whoosh! We are off! The staying up part is the only thing I've never really quite figured out yet.

Carlos. Ohhhh! *(He looks down fearfully.)* How do you land?

Tortilla Man. By dropping bags of powder much the way a balloon drops sand.

Carlos. But, Mr. Juan, that's not the way it works!

Tortilla Man. It isn't? Oh, what does it matter? Why must everything work the same way for everybody?

Carlos. All of this is hard to believe.

Tortilla Man. Just look down there . . . isn't it breath-taking? That's my trail down there. The Juan de Oñate Trail. That's the way I came up through Mexico and all the way north to Santa Fe. When I came through here, there was nothing . . . Imagine that!

Carlos. Oñate, the explorer? We learned about him in school. He was from Spain, but he came up from Mexico to explore. He was a conquistador. I did a report on him.

Tortilla Man. Him? You mean me!

Carlos. You? But you're The Tortilla Man, Mr. Juan.

Tortilla Man. So I am.

Carlos. How can you be two people at once? Mexican and Spanish? Modern and old?

Tortilla Man. Carlos, my boy, when are you going to stop asking questions? Too many questions! *(He pushes out two bags of baking powder.)* We're going to land and walk around. *(He adjusts the compass.)* Now then, take a seat, Carlos. The landing may be a bit rough. I think a bird heard you earlier.

Carlos. You mean about the feather?

Tortilla Man. Ssshhh! Birds are terrible spellers, so kindly spell out that word henceforth. Very good diction but lousy spellers. *(The Magic Tortilla floats down and lands on a rocky hill.)* I thought you'd like this place. I understand you collect fossils.

Carlos. Yes, I do!

Tortilla Man. Well, look around you, Carlos. We have some good ones here. This used to be under water many, many years ago. All of this was once part of a great vast ocean.

Carlos. Where are we now?

Tortilla Man. It's hard to believe, I know, but we are at the bottom of the sea! Find your fossil. We have all the time in the world. Find your fossil!

[*They stand together a moment.* Carlos *picks up a fossil and puts it in his cigar box. They wander about collecting fossils for a while and then reboard the ship and head due north to an area of white sand.* The Tortilla Man *has brought a lunch, and they take a break. They collect some sand, which* Carlos *puts in his box, then head back to Cuchillo.]*

Tortilla Man. It's getting late, Carlos. Are you tired? We must go on . . .
Carlos. I could never be tired with you, Mr. Juan. I'm too happy.
Tortilla Man. You're a good boy, Carlos.
Carlos. That's the problem! I don't want to be a good boy! I want to be a person. Nobody really likes good boys.
Tortilla Man. That *is* a problem. I see what you mean. It seems you can't be too good or too bad. It's hard. The solution is just to be yourself. Be truthful, and you won't have to worry about being at any far end. You'll be in the middle with yourself.
Carlos. But it's so hard!
Tortilla Man. When will you learn not to be impudent, boy! Trust me, and trust yourself above all. Here we are!

[They drag the Flying Tortilla with a rope that is attached. They then sit by the side of the river, happy but exhausted.]

Carlos. I want this time to last forever!
Tortilla Man. It will, my friend, but shhh! Let's listen to the birds. They're talking . . . see, there they are on the Magic Flying Tortilla . . .

[The Four Old Women, *now* Birds, *peck at the Flying Tortilla.]*

Ton. I'm hungry, Tin . . .
Tin. Me too, Ton.
Tan. I haven't eaten in days.
Mabel. Weeks . . .
Ton. Months . . .
Tin. Years . . .
Tan. When was it, anyway?
Mabel. When The Flying Tortilla Man was on his way South . . .

Ton. I don't know if I would have lasted if he hadn't come
by . . .

Tin. I was dying for even a moldy, dried-out crust, a few
crumbs . . . anything!

Tan. How about a nice big juicy earthworm?

Mabel. I am a vegetarian.

Ton. Against your religion, eh?

Mabel. No, against my waistline.

Tin. Always prancing about with her airs she is!

Ton. Look who's talking!

Tin. What about you, Ton-Tona?

Ton. Don't call me that, please.

Tin. Against your religion?

Tan. Oh, yes, a nice big juicy baked earthworm would
be nice, with lots of gravy and a bird's nest salad . . .
(She cries out.) Bird does not live by bread alone!

Mabel. Stop it! I feel faint!

Tan. Can it be? Can it be? Oh, dear, The Tortilla Man is
coming back this way. He's spotted us. See him, Mabel?
Girls, take courage. Here he comes. *(They all bow.)* Oh,
great Tortilla Man!

Ton. Image of hope, blessed Tortilla!

Tin. Blessed be the Holy Name of Tortilla.

Mabel. Thank you, Mr. Juan. *(She stuffs her face with some
tortilla.)* Food!

Tin. Now who's watching her figure?

Tan. Not me, I don't have problems!

Ton. Nor me!

Mabel. You're all as crazy as magpies!

Tin. That's a terrible insult, Mabel!

Tan. Will you be quiet! They're just about ready to take
off, and I'm still hungry! I'm still so hungry I can't think
or move!

Ton *(speaking to the others).* She never could!

Mabel. Girls, please, we have to be off. Mr. Juan is nearly
ready to leave. Settle down and get in formation. That's
right!

[They dress right and do a drill. Then, they fly off.]

Birds. Thank you, Mr. Juan!

Tortilla Man *(as he inspects the ship).* Rudders don't look too damaged. Really, those birds are all right, Carlos. They do give me a push now and then. Now hop aboard . . . we have to go home.

Carlos. Do we have to, Mr. Juan?

Tortilla Man. We have things to do. We have our work, our families. And there's the fiesta coming up. I have to get ready for that.

Carlos. I don't have a real family, and I'm so tired of making tortillas!

Tortilla Man. There you go again. It's not what you do but how you do it. And as for having a family, you have people who love you . . . and you have yourself. So many people don't have themselves, Carlos. So what does it matter how many brothers and sisters you have? Why all of us are brothers and sisters!

Carlos. I've heard all those things before!

Tortilla Man. Yes, but did you listen to them? Or ask yourself *why* people were saying such things? Now be still with yourself and don't talk about you know what—because our friends might be listening. They might think we're saying one thing when we really mean another. Carlos, are you tired? Rest there on the Magic Tortilla. Before you know it, we'll be in Cuchillo. Close your eyes, sleep, sleep!

[Carlos *is getting sleepy, almost against his will.*]

Carlos. I'm not really sleepy. It's been the happiest day of my life!

Tortilla Man. Stretch out there and rest!

Carlos. Just for a moment, Mr. Juan. A little nap, that's all I need. You won't leave me, will you?

Tortilla Man. No, I won't leave you, ever . . . remember these things, Carlitos, and sleep, sleep . . .

Carlos *(in a far away voice).* Mr. Juan, where's my box? I had it right here . . .

Tortilla Man. Sleep . . . you need it, boy, to be strong . . .

SCENE 4

Outside the factory the next morning. Carlos *wakes to find himself in the same position he was in on the Flying Tortilla. His body is cold and cramped. He is surprised to find himself on the steps of the tortilla factory.* Tudi *shakes him as* Oscar *and* Elias *stand nearby.*

Tudi. Wake up! Wake up, you rascal!

Carlos. Mr. Juan, where is my box? I had it right here.

Elias. There you are, Tudi. He admits his guilt.

Oscar. It was Carlos who broke into your office, Tudi, and tried to get in the safe.

Elias. Oscar and I were walking by and noticed the lights were still on. Then we saw Carlos sleeping here. That's when we called you, Tudi.

Tudi. Thank you, boys! I'll make it up to you. Fortunately, the snake wasn't able to get into the safe, but he sure made a mess of things. How did you get in Carlos? Oh, you're going to be sorry that you ever saw this place. You'll never forget this day!

Carlos. I don't understand. I was with Mr. Juan!

Elias. Don't lie to us, you thief!

Oscar. He's a sneaky one. Don't believe him, Tudi.

Elias. I'm very surprised, Tudi. He always seemed so good.

Carlos. I don't understand all this . . . what's happening?

Tudi. Don't lie to me, Carlos. And here I was thinking of promoting you. Vandal, you broke into my office and tried to rob my safe; and when you couldn't break in, you made a mess of things!

Elias. And you dropped this . . . (*He shows off* Carlos's *cigar box.*)

Carlos. My box, where did you find it?

Oscar. He admits it! Remember this, Elias. We're witnesses!

Elias. We'll sue! Won't we, Tudi?

Tudi. We'll sue! You'll be sorry you were ever born. They'll probably send you to the boys' home in Springer.

Oscar. Not that!

Elias. That's where all the hardened criminals go. A cousin of mine is there, so I know.

Carlos. You're all wrong! I wasn't here at all. I was flying with Mr. Juan.

Elias. Who is this Mr. Juan, anyway?

Carlos. He's a friend of mine.

Oscar. Listen to that story, would you, Tudi!

Tudi. Stop lying to us, Carlos. You're making up these crazy stories to lead us off the track.

Carlos. You've got it all wrong. I can show you. Give me the box, please.

Elias. Oh no, that's important evidence.

Oscar. If you were flying around, show us your wings. Show us your wings! That's a funny one!

Tudi. Let's go!

Carlos. Where? I'm not guilty. I tell you, I'm not guilty!

Tudi. This is a matter for the Sheriff's Office.

Oscar (*he turns to* Carlos, *almost impressed*). You little thief, you've hit the big time!

Elias. Is Fatty in today? I thought he went fishing on Wednesdays.

Tudi. The law is always at hand.

Oscar. What does that mean?

Tudi. Sounds good, doesn't it?

Carlos. But you have it all wrong!

Oscar. Man, if I were you, I'd start praying. No one can face Fatty Campbell and not feel helpless fear.

Tudi. Go on, march. March, there. Go on, march! Oscar, you run ahead and tell Bertina and Hermano Gil. They'll want to hear about this. Tell them to meet us at the Sheriff's Office. Forward now, to justice!

SCENE 5

The Sheriff's Office. It is near the Plaza on Calle del Sol street. It consists of several rooms. The lobby has a desk and chairs and a long, orange plastic couch for visitors. A magazine rack is near the couch and has old copies of Ford Times, The Ranch News, *and last Thursday's paper. On the wall is a calendar from*

Corney Hawkins Olds. Next to that is a Navy picture of
Company 1435, U.S. Naval Training Center, Great Lakes,
Illinois, and beside that is a horseshoe and a picture of President
John F. Kennedy.

Fatty. Where were you the night of the 10th?

Carlos. With Mr. Juan.

Elias. There he goes again with that fabulous story.

Fatty *(He admonishes* Elias*).* Whoa there, boy. Order in the
court. What do you mean speaking out of turn!

Elias. Tell us the truth now, Carlos!

Carlos. I *have* been telling the truth.

Bertina. No child of mine was ever a disgrace to our
home, son.

Hermano Gil. Please, Carlos, tell Mr. Fatty the truth.

Fatty. Order, order in the court! (Elias, Bertina, Hermano
Gil *and the others settle down and look at* Fatty.) Ahem. It's
about time. *(To* Carlos) Were you not found near the
scene of the crime by these two young fellows? *(He peers
at* Elias *and* Oscar *very closely.)* I think I know you two
from somewhere.

Carlos. Yes, I was, Mr. Fatty. I fell asleep with Mr. Juan,
and he must have carried me back to the factory.

Fatty. *Who* is this mysterious Mr. Juan?

Hermano Gil. Pay no attention to him, Sheriff.

Elias. He keeps talking about a Mr. Juan who flies.

Tudi. He's unstable. That's all there is to it. He needs help.

Bertina. Oh, shut your mouth, Tudi.

Hermano Gil. Bertina, my love . . . Bert, settle down.

Carlos. Mr. Juan is a friend of mine.

Tudi. It's all your fault, Bertina, I shouldn't have listened
to you and given the boy a chance at the factory. Now
look what he's done! He's ruined my business.

Bertina. It's not *your* business, you little toad. Nothing
was stolen, your honor.

Hermano Gil. My love, please.

Fatty. Settle down, folks. I know emotions run high, but
this is a court of law . . . and I am the law. Settle down
there, folks!

Hermano Gil. Can we settle this out of court, Mr. Fatty?

Cotil. Of course not, Papa! This is a matter of public concern.

Hermano Gil. Nothing was stolen except a bag of frozen tamales . . . that's all . . .

[Elias *looks at* Oscar, *who shrugs his shoulders as if to say, "I was hungry."*]

Tudi. That's all! I'll sue, Gil. My reputation is ruined. Have you seen that mess in the office? I'll sue! I'll sue!

Fatty. Whoa there. As judge and jury, I take the reins of the law in my hands. Having viewed the evidence and spoken to the accused and the witnesses, I now proclaim the verdict of this court, Filmore P. Campbell presiding, this eleventh day of June, in the year of, etcetera. Isn't it about time for lunch, Gil? What time do you have?

Bertina. He's just a boy! He never meant to hurt anyone. He's a good boy, your honor.

Elias. So what's the verdict?

Fatty. Don't I know you from somewhere, sonny?

Cotil. Mama, we have to abide by the verdict.

Hermano Gil. I can't believe a boy of mine could do this. How could you, son?

Carlos. Papa . . . you must believe me . . . I'm innocent!

Elias. As innocent as a snake!

Cotil. He's a liar, Papa. Don't you know that already?

Elias. Sentence him!

Oscar. Show no mercy!

Fatty. I hereby sentence you, Carlos Campo, to a week's labor on the Plaza, early curfew, and a fine of twenty dollars for court costs. Case closed. We have the fiesta coming up, and we'll need all the help we can get. Report at five A.M. to Fernando at the water tower. Court dismissed. (*He speaks to* Elias.) I know you from somewhere. Don't you have a cousin . . . ?

Elias. You must be thinking of someone else, Mr. Fatty.

Tudi. I demand a retrial! Who's going to clean up my office? What about the tamales? My mother made them for me, and I was taking them home. I demand a retrial!

Fatty. Go back and sell a few tortillas!

Tudi. I'll sue!

Bertina. He's just a child! Can't you understand that?

Fatty. Clear the court . . . clear the court. It's my lunchtime. Someone mention tamales?

Tudi. *This* is justice?

Fatty. Insulting the court — five dollars!

Tudi. I'll write my congressman.

Fatty. Threatening the law — ten dollars.

Tudi. Now wait a minute!

Fatty. Harassing the court — fifteen dollars.

Elias. Man, Tudi, you better leave while you can. It doesn't look good for you.

Hermano Gil. After all these years, son, how could you break your father's heart? You were my only hope, Carlos. I felt as if you were my true son, my flesh and blood. Now you're a stranger!

[He walks away with Bertina *and* Cotil, *who is gloating.]*

Cotil. Papa, I told you he was a sneak!

Carlos. Papa! I'm innocent!

Hermano Gil. Don't talk to me. Let's go, Bert.

Bertina. That's all right, son. Dinner's at six. We're having papitas con chorizo.

Hermano Gil. How can anyone eat with a mouthful of sand?

Cotil. Hey, Carlos, bad luck!

Elias. Where are you going now, Cotil?

Cotil. I'm busy. I'm going home with Mama. So don't you bother me.

Elias. How can you say that to me after all I've done for you?

Cotil. You were always too young for me.

Oscar. Hey, Elias, I know something we can do.

Elias. Leave me alone, man.

Oscar. So what happened to our friendship?

Elias. I have better things to do. Out of my way.

[*They all exit.* Carlos *and* Fatty *are left in the courtroom.*]

Fatty. Come on, sonny, cheer up. It's not the end of the world. When I was a kid, I got into a few scrapes. What's it matter, huh? You want part of a tuna fish sandwich? Some chips? Now, cheer up. Here's the evidence. Don't tell anyone I gave it back to you. Run along now. I haven't got all day. I haven't eaten my lunch yet. Now, sonny, you watch those stories . . . they'll get you in a mess of trouble.

Carlos. They aren't stories . . . it's the truth! It's really the truth!

✳
Spanish Words

papitas con chorizo potatoes with sausage, p. 462

Loca en la cabeza crazy, p. 465

Jusephe an Indian scout who was a guide on one of Juan de Oñate's expeditions, p. 467

SCENE 6

Carlos's *room late that night. He is sitting on the bed, when he decides to get up and get his box from the chest of drawers.*

Carlos (*looking up at the ceiling*). Where were you, Mr. Juan, when I needed you? Where are you now? Why do you always leave me? (*Dejectedly*) I am as lonely and sad as the day the men from the church carry the body of God around the Plaza in that wooden box on Good Friday. The people are all in black, singing with dried voices and moaning to themselves. They stop in front of doors that are closed. He said many things but not where he was from or where he went. He comes and goes, and I want to be angry with him, but I can't. I can feel him close sometimes, when it matters. He knows, he really knows me . . . and he cares. Mr. Tortilla Man, come back. Stay awhile with your Carlos. He needs friends. Because people hate him when he is good and love him when he is bad. (*He looks down at the cigar box.*) Should I open it? What of our fossils and sand? Will they be there? (*He opens the box.*) Where are they? What's this? It's a little note. "Remember, Carlos. Your friend,

Mr. Juan, The Flying Tortilla Man." That's all, just a note and this—a small hard edge of tortilla. Of what use is it? *(He throws the tortilla away and then retrieves it.)* Oh, well. It's something! He said many things, but not where he came from and where he went. He said many things . . . "Remember," he said, "remember." But what? What?

[*Carlos goes to sleep and has fitful dreams. The* Old Women/ Birds *call out his name in a dream sequence. "There he is . . . who . . . ," and he sees all the people from the court scene. He wakes up in a sweat, clutching the cigar box; then he drifts off to sleep again.*]

SCENE 7

The next morning in the Plaza. Carlos *is sweeping the band-stand. He looks forlorn and miserable.* Nora *comes up to him.*

Nora. What's wrong with boy?
Carlos. Hello, Nora.
Nora. What's wrong with Carlitos?
Carlos. I lost my job.
Nora. So sad. I miss Carlos at job. Oscar and Elias no like Nora—make fun all time. Neno? Neno?
Carlos. He's still very sick.
Nora. Neno! I look for him last night. Saw Oscar and Elias at the job.
Carlos. What was that, Nora?
Nora. Neno good boy—lose job? I look for him last night after Carlos walk Nora home. See Oscar and Elias make mess.
Carlos. They said I tried to break into Tudi's office last night.
Nora. Oh no, no. Oh no, that Elias and Oscar do.
Carlos. No, Nora. They said that about *me*.
Nora. Oscar and Elias go in and throw things around.
Carlos. What are you saying?
Nora. Nora see them.
Carlos. Have you told anyone?
Nora. I tell you. Nora see Elias and Oscar make mess.

Carlos (*grabbing her hand*). Let's go, Nora. Let's go see Fatty!

Nora. I don't know Fatty.

SCENE 8

The Sheriff's Office.

Fatty. This is a highly unusual case. I've taken the liberty to call in two witnesses.

Carlos. Nora told us how she saw Elias and Oscar break into Tudi's office and throw things around.

Fatty. That's fine, son; but what proof do we have?

Carlos. Nora told us! She's a witness!

Fatty (*taking* Carlos *aside*). Son, she's not well. Loca en la cabeza. You know what I mean? I think she made it up to help you. (*He speaks to* Oscar *and* Elias.) What do you boys say?

Elias. Carlos is trying to defend himself. It was a good try, but it won't work.

Nora. Oscar with Elias.

Oscar. Go away, Nora.

Nora. She see. She see. Elias call Oscar stupid fat boy behind his back.

Elias. Don't listen to her, Oscar. She's not all there.

Nora. Elias hate Oscar. He told me. (*She looks at* Oscar.) Say that night that you a stupid boy and he smart one.

Elias. Don't believe her, Oscar!

Oscar. Well, how do you like that! After all we've been through! You never did like me, man. He was there, Fatty. He made me do it!

Elias. You stupid fool! Why'd you take those tamales? I told you not to!

Oscar. I was hungry! Fatty, it was Elias's idea. He told me about it and asked me to help. We were trying to get back at Carlos for being such a baby. I thought Elias was my friend, but he's the type that talks about you behind your back. He's just a lousy tortilla bum with the rot!

Elias. Will you shut up!! He's the sick one, Sheriff. He's got the rot. He's making things up!

Oscar. I'm smarter than you, Elias, you little punk. I can pick any lock I want to. What can you do besides give directions and tell people what to do? What do you know, anyway?

Nora. Carlos come back to work now?

Carlos. I was innocent all the time, Mr. Fatty.

Fatty. So it seems. The law is never tricked. Justice rules. Call Bertina, Gil, and Tudi. Court's in session. The retrial is about to begin.

Carlos. Why did you do this, Elias?

Elias. It was Cotil's idea. She made me do it. She wanted to get back at you for everything.

Oscar (*looking at* Carlos). You were always a better friend to me than Elias, Carlos.

Carlos. It's all right, Oscar. I forgive you.

Oscar. It was Elias's fault. He's full of poison blood.

Elias. It's the rot, man. I got the rot! It was Cotil made me do it . . .

Carlos. I forgive you too, Elias.

Elias. You always talked too much, Nora.

Nora. Thank you, all my friends! Go to work now?

SCENE 9

The Fossil beds. Carlos *and* The Tortilla Man *are sitting on a rock shelf reviewing the past few days' events. It is a peaceful twilight in New Mexico.*

Carlos. And so, Mr. Juan, everything finally worked out. Where were you all that time? You could have told the Sheriff that I wasn't guilty.

Tortilla Man. When will you learn not to be impudent, boy? The truth of the matter is that I was getting ready for the fiesta, and anyway, you handled things pretty nicely.

Carlos. I don't know what I would have done without Nora.

Tortilla Man. I told her to take care of you.

Carlos. Do you know her?

Tortilla Man. Oh, blessed tortillas, yes! We're dear old friends. And besides, I was with you all the time.

Remember that night you looked inside your cigar box? You were thinking of me, and I heard you. I said hello. I'm sorry I had to take the sand and the fossil. You see, I thought it was the best way. Things can't be too easy for us, or we don't appreciate them. We don't grow that way! Here's your fossil and the sand. (*The Tortilla Man hands them to* Carlos.) Remember me when you see them.

Carlos. Will you go away before the fiesta, Mr. Juan? Neno was to play the part of the Indian scout, Jusephe, but he's still a little weak, so they asked me to take the role. This is my first time in the fiesta play. When I grow up, I want to play the part of Oñate. But how can anyone play that part, if you're the real Oñate? Why don't *you* play the part?

Tortilla Man. We'll have to work out something by that time, Carlos.

Carlos. Elias and Oscar have to work in the Plaza now, in my place, but the Sheriff is letting them take part in the parade. All of us have roles in the pageant play! Will you be in the parade? You said something about getting ready for the fiesta.

Tortilla Man. Oh, I have a very small part. Nothing that anyone couldn't play if they really wanted to.

Carlos. Will I see you?

Tortilla Man. If you don't, I shall be very sorry. Now, remember to see, not to look. I might seem a bit different from myself, but it's me. You can never really change a person inside, no matter what you do.

Carlos. Mama is making the costumes. Cotil is playing the part of a Señorita, but she still won't talk to me.

Tortilla Man. She'll get over it.

Carlos. Even if you're not good, some people still don't like you.

Tortilla Man. Remember what I said, we're all from the same country. We have the sky which covers our heads and the earth which warms our feet. We don't have time to be anywhere in between where we can't feel that power. Some people call it love. I call it I.W.A.

Carlos. I.W.A.? What does that mean?

Tortilla Man. Inside We're Alike. Now I must leave you.

Carlos. Can we go for a ride on the Flying Tortilla some time?

Tortilla Man. Anytime you like, Carlos.

[*The Magic Tortilla takes off with a huge blast, and soon* Carlos *and* The Tortilla Man *are floating in space. Flash to the Plaza, the town fiesta, in honor of the founding of Cuchillo by Don Juan de Oñate. The Plaza is decorated with bright streamers and flowers, and booths completely circle it. There are food booths as well as game booths. The parade begins at North Cotton Street. First come the Spanish soldiers in costume, with* Tudi *leading.* Elias *and* Oscar *wear a cow costume and are led by a radiantly beautiful* Nora. Hermano Gil *plays the part of one of Oñate's generals, and* Bertina *is a noblewoman. She is followed by* Cotil, *and behind* Cotil *is* Fatty, *in a tight-fitting suit of armor and a helmet with the insignia of the Spanish army. He is the Master of Ceremonies. The parade marches forward.* Jusephe, *played by* Carlos, *leads the Royal Entourage.* Carlos *is followed by Don Juan de Oñate* (The Flying Tortilla Man), *a small old man with twinkling eyes.*]

Elias. Hey, Oscar, who's that old man next to Carlos?

Oscar. Let me see. (Oscar *sticks his head out of the cow's rear end.*) That's El Boss, Señor López—he owns the factory. He lives at one of those rest homes, but every year he comes out and plays Oñate. He's been doing it as long as I can remember.

Elias. So that's the original Tortilla Man, eh? He looks as old as the hills and as dusty.

Oscar. I can't go on much longer . . . it's hot!

Elias. So go work in an ice plant. Get it? Man, you have no sense of humor.

Oscar. You wouldn't have a sense of humor if you were back here!

[*They march forward, and when* Fatty *gets to the bandstand, he makes an announcement.* Carlos *sees* Neno *and yells to him.*

Neno *is sitting on the side, resting in the sun, and looks much better.]*

Carlos. Hey, Neno! Neno, how are you?
Neno. I'm getting better, Carlos . . . I'm going to make it!
Elias. Move over, Oscar. There's Neno. I don't want germs to float over this way.
Nora. Come on, little cow; go see Neno.
Oscar. Can't you do anything, Elias? She's going near you-know-who-with-you-know-what. The Rot!
Nora. Neno, Neno!
Fatty. As Master of Ceremonies and Sheriff of the Cuchillo Municipality, I, Filmore P. Campbell, welcome you inhabitants to our annual fiesta in honor of the founding of Cuchillo by Don Juan de Oñate.

[The crowd cheers, and there is a great noise of firecrackers and shouts. The Birds are seen from a distance, viewing all the festivities.]

Mabel. There he is . . .
Tin. Who?
Tan. The boy.
Ton. Are you going to start that again?
Mabel. I don't know what you're talking about.
Tan. What are they doing down there?
Tin. Who?
Mabel. The people in the Plaza.
Tan. They're laughing and having a good time.
Tin. You mean the ones out there? *(She peers into the audience.)*
Mabel *(looking out as well).* Oh, yes, they've been here awhile, haven't they?
Tan. I think they've had a good time, too. Don't you, Ton?
Ton. They look a little happier than when they came in.
Tin. Do you think so?
Tan. But what about the people in the Plaza? What's all that about down there? That parade and all the noise?
Mabel. Horses make me nervous.

Ton. Everything makes you nervous or unhappy or fat.

Mabel. I like a good story now and then, something to pass the time.

Ton. Oh, you and your time!

Tan. It's so nice to just sit here and smell the sky and the sunshine, and feel the sounds of life . . .

Mabel. How can you smell the sky, you crazy bird? You have it all mixed up!

Ton. Leave Tan alone, Mabel. She's all right. She's just being Tan.

Mabel. I guess you're right. She just can't help being Tan. Poor dear!

Tin. Are they getting nervous out there? *(Referring to the audience)*

Ton. No, but I think it's time to go home now.

Tin. Why? I was having so much fun!

Ton. It's just time.

Tan. Will we come back here again?

Tin. We'd better. I'm getting hungry just thinking about it.

Mabel. What are you silly birds talking about?

Tan. What's all the noise about anyway?

[They fly off.]

Ton. When will you listen, silly bird?

Tan. What was that? I couldn't hear you! "Listen." Did you say, "listen"? *(In a faraway voice)* Can't you just smell the sky?

RESPONDING

1. **Personal Response** The Tortilla Man says, "Things can't be too easy for us, or we don't appreciate them. We don't grow that way." Explain what he means and tell whether or not you agree, based on your experience.

2. **Literary Analysis** *Magical realism* refers to a type of literature that introduces fantastic (bizarre and unbelievable) elements within a real world. Find elements of magical realism in this play.

3. Multicultural Connection Explain why the fiesta and parade are important to the community. If your community or another one you know about has similar celebrations, describe them to the class.

LANGUAGE WORKSHOP

Stage Directions The opening *stage directions* in *The Flying Tortilla Man,* indicated in italics, help describe the setting and the characters. Where does this story take place? What do you learn about Carlos? Bennie? Neno? Oscar? Elias? Tudi? Nora?

WRITER'S PORTFOLIO

The dreamers of the world need to have jobs just like everyone else. Think about a job for which Carlos is well suited, given his kindness, sensitive character, and imagination. Then write a job description customized for him.

DREAMS AND REALITIES

Projects

SURVEY

As a class project, brainstorm a list of ten "dreams" that you think are important to Americans today. Then make a list of ten "nightmares" that pose a threat to the future of the American dream, such as crime, pollution, and depletion of natural resources. Using these lists, construct a survey that asks respondents to rank items from most to least important. Allow room for an "Other" category so respondents can indicate their own dreams and nightmares. In teams, administer the survey to students in your school. Compile the results in graph form and post on a bulletin board. Discuss the results in class.

DREAM T-SHIRT

Design your own dream T-shirt illustrating your dreams, hopes, and goals. You might use permanent-ink markers to draw or write, as well as iron-on art. You can also sew on small objects that express your dreams. Wear the finished product and give a T-Talk for the class, explaining items on your shirt.

DREAMS AND REALITIES

How do your dreams and the realities you encounter while pursuing them compare with those of characters in this unit? Are your dreams easier or harder to attain? more or less realistic? Do you have a dream-maker of your own that is comparable to Carlos's flying tortilla? Which of your dreams do you think you will achieve in twenty years? Organize your thoughts and write an essay.

Further Reading

The following titles focus on the dreams of people and the realities they encounter in pursuing these dreams.

Brown, Wesley, and Ling, Amy, eds. *Visions of America: Personal Narratives from the Promised Land.* Persea Books, 1993. This is an excellent multicultural anthology of personal essays and autobiographical accounts written from 1900 to the present.

Gonzalez, Ray, ed. *Mirrors Beneath the Earth: Short Fiction by Chicano Writers.* Curbstone Press, 1992. These are exciting tales of discovery and the supernatural from established writers and new voices.

King, Laurie, ed. *Hear My Voice.* Addison-Wesley, 1994. Thematically arranged units include fiction, nonfiction, and poetry, providing a glimpse into the hopes and frustrations that are part of life.

Lesley, Craig, ed. *Talking Leaves: Contemporary Native American Short Stories.* Dell, 1991. Stories written by thirty-five Native Americans focus on the dreams and realities of contemporary life.

Rico, Barbara, and Mano, Sandra, eds. *American Mosaic: Multicultural Readings in Context.* Houghton Mifflin, 1991. Voices, old and new, of diverse cultural backgrounds, speak within important historical and literary contexts in this collection.

Twain, Mark. *Huckleberry Finn.* Random, 1985. In this novel, first published over a century ago. Huck pursues his dreams and freedom as he travels on the Mississippi.

GLOSSARY

aberration (ab ́ə rā ́shən), *n.* a deviating from the right path or usual course of action

absolute (ab ́sə lüt), *n.* fundamental

acacia (ə kā ́shə), *n.* a locust tree of North America

accede (ak sēd ́), *v.* give in; agree

accomplice (ə kom ́plis), *n.* person who aids another in committing a crime or wrong act

ad hoc (ad hok ́), Latin word meaning "for a specific purpose"

adobe (ə dō ́bē), *n.* brick made of sun dried clay

affluent (af ́lü ənt), *adj.* wealthy; rich

aggressor (ə gres ́ər), *n.* one that begins an attack or pursuit

agility (ə jil ́ə tē), *n.* liveliness; nimbleness

alma mater (al ́mə mä ́tər), *n.* school, college, or university at which one is or has been a student

amnesia (am nē ́zhə), *n.* partial or entire loss of memory

amoral (ā môr ́əl), *adj.* unable to distinguish between right and wrong

anemia (ə nē ́mē ə), *n.* lack of vigor or strength; weakness

anguish (ang ́gwish), *n.* great suffering

apartheid (ə pärt ́hāt), *n.* racial segregation, especially as practiced in the Republic of South Africa

apprehensive (ap ́ri hen ́siv), *n.* fearful about the future

arbiter (är ́bə tər), *n.* judge

arpeggio (är pej ́ē ō), *n.* the sounding of the notes of a chord in rapid succession instead of simultaneously

arroyo (ə roi ́ō), *n.* a dry gulch

articulate (är tik ́yə lit), *adj.* able to put one's thoughts into words easily and clearly

assail (ə sāl ́), *v.* come over

assemblage (ə sem ́blij). *n,* group of persons gathered together

atrocity (ə tros ́ə tē), *n.* monstrous wickedness or cruelty

audacity (ô das ́ə tē), *n.* reckless daring

avail (ə vāl ́), *n.* use; help

bandolier (ban ́dl ir ́), *n.* a broad belt worn over the shoulder and across the breast

barrio (bär ́ē ō), *n.* section of a city inhabited chiefly by Spanish-speaking people

bastion (bas ́chən), *n.* any strongly fortified or defended place

befit (bi fit ́), *v.* suit

bemuse (bi myüz ́), *v.* confuse

bereaved (bi rēvd ́), *adj.* mourning the death of a loved one

berth, give a wide berth to, keep well away from

blasphemy (blas ́fə mē), *n.* abuse or contempt for God or sacred things

boardwalk (bôrd ́wôk), *n.* a wide sidewalk or promenade, usually made of boards

bop (bop), *n.* bebop — a form of jazz

bravado (brə vä ́dō), *n.* a show of courage or boldness

bray (brā), *v.* make a loud, harsh sound

briny (brīn ́ē), *adj.* salty

broach (brōch), *v.* begin conversation about

brocade (brō kād ́), *n.* an expensive cloth woven with raised designs on it, used for clothing or upholstery

brogue (brōg), *n.* a strongly marked accent or pronunciation peculiar to any dialect

brutal (brü ́tl), *adj.* savagely cruel, inhuman

bulbous (bul ́bəs), *adj.* rounded and swelling

buoyancy (boi ́ən sē), *n.* power to float

bureau (byúr ́ō), *n.* office for transacting business

burl (bėrl), *n.* a large knot in some kinds of wood

Cajun (kā ́jən), *n.* a descendant of the French who came to Louisiana from Acadia; something related to these people, such as their cooking

Cantonese (kan ́tə nēz ́), *n.* a Chinese dialect

carnivore (kär ́nə vôr), *n.* mammal that feeds chiefly on flesh

cassock (kas ́ək), *n.* a long outer garment worn by clergy

castanets (kas′tə netz′), *n.* a pair of instruments clicked together to beat time for dancing or music

Caucasian (kô kā′zhən), *adj.* of or having to do with the so-called white race

cavernous (kav′ər nəs), *adj.* large and hollow, like a cavern

cessation (se sā′shən), *n.* a stopping

chafe (chāf), *n.* irritation

checkerberry snuff (chek′ər ber′ē snuf′), *n.* a powdered tobacco made from the red berries of the wintergreen plant

Chicano (chi kä′nō), *n.* an American of Mexican descent

chisel (chiz′əl), *v.* cut with a sharp edged blade making clear and sharp outlines

clabber (klab′ər), *n.* thick, sour milk

cliché (klē shā′), *n.* a timeworn expression or idea

cloister (kloi′stər), *n.* a building in which nuns live

collards (kol′ərdz), *n. pl.* the fleshy leaves of this plant, cooked as greens

composure (kəm pō′zhər), *n.* self-control

concoct (kon kokt′), *v.* make up; devise

condolence (kən dō′ləns), *n.* expression of sympathy

congenial (kən jē′nyəl), *adj.* getting on well together

conniving (kə nīv′ing), *adj.* giving aid to wrongdoing by not telling of it or by helping it secretly

conquistador (kon kwis′tə dôr′), *n.* a Spanish conqueror in North or South America during the 1500s

consciousness (kon′shəs nis), *n.* all the thoughts and feelings of a person or group of people

console (kon′sōl), *n.* a radio, television, or phonograph cabinet, made to stand on the floor

constitutional (kon′stə tü′shə nəl), *n.* a walk taken for one's health

context (kon′tekst), *n.* circumstances in which something takes place

continuum (kən tin′yü əm), *n.* a continuous quantity, series, etc.

corral (kə ral′), *v.* surround; capture

covey (kuv′ē), *n.* a small group; brood

cow (kou), *v.* frighten

cower (kou′ər), *v.* crouch in fear or shame

coy (koi), *adj.* acting more shy than one really is

coyote (kī ō′tē), *n.* a small wolflike mammal of the dog family; **coyote-smooth** refers to the coyote's slyness

CPR cardiopulmonary resuscitation

credential (kri den′shəl), *n.* a letter of introduction

crony (krō′nē), *n.* a very close friend

croup (krüp), *n.* inflammation of the throat and windpipe, especially in children

crystalline (kris′tl ən), *adj.* clear like a crystal

curlicue (kėr′lə kyü), *n.* a fancy twist, curl, or flourish

cursive (kėr′siv), *adj.* written with the letters joined together

cursory (kėr′sər ē), *adj.* hasty and superficial

curtailment (kėr′tāl′mənt), *n.* the act of cutting off some of

dasher (dash′ər), *n.* a device for stirring the cream in a churn

decadent (dek′ə dənt), *adj.* declining; decaying

deceased, the (di sēst′), *n.* a dead person

decry (di krī′), *v.* express strong disapproval

delude (di lüd′), *v.* trick or deceive

delve (delv), *v.* search carefully for information

demitasse (dem′i tas′), *n.* a very small cup

demographic (dē′mə graf′ik), *adj.* having to do with the science of human populations — distribution, etc.

deprivation (dep′rə vā′shən), *n.* condition of being kept from having or doing

derail (dē rāl′), *v.* cause to run off the tracks

derange (di rānj′), *v.* make insane

deride (di rīd′) *v.* make fun of

desecrate (des′ə krāt), *v.* disregard the sacredness of; profane

diabetes (dī′ə bē′tis), *n.* disease characterized by excessive sugar in the blood and urine

dicey (dī′sə), *adj.* risky

diction (dik′shən), *n.* manner of pronouncing words

diffidence (dif′ə dəns), *n.* lack of self-confidence; shyness

diffuse (di fyüz′), *v.* spread out so as to cover a large space

dignitary (dig′nə ter′ē), *n.* a person who has high rank or a position of honor

dilapidated (də lap′ə dā′tid), *adj.* fallen into ruin or disrepair

dimensional (də men′shə nəl), *adj.* having to do with length, breadth, or thickness

dire (dīr), *adj.* desperately urgent

disassociate (dis′ə sō′shē āt), *v.* separate

disclaimer (dis klā′mər), *n.* denial

discordant (dis kôrd′nt), *adj.* not in harmony

discreet (dis krēt′), *adj.* having or showing good judgment; wisely cautious

disdain (dis dān′), *n.* feeling of scorn

disembodied (dis′em bod′ēd), *adj.* separated from the body

dispensation (dis′pən sā′shən), *n.* official permission to disregard a rule

dissect (di sekt′), *v.* cut apart

dissension (di sen′shən), *n.* disagreement in opinion that produces strife; discord

dissipate (dis′ə pāt), *v.* disappear

dissolution (dis′ə lü′shən), *n.* a breaking up

dissuade (di swād′), *v.* persuade not to do something

distraught (dis trôt), *adj.* in a state of mental conflict and confusion

dock (dok), *v.* cut short

documented (dok′yə mən təd), *v.* proved or supported by the means of documents

doily (doi′lē), *n.* a small piece of lace or other material put on furniture

drove (drōv), *n.* many people moving along together

eccentric (ek sen′trik), *adj.* peculiar

ecstasy (ek′stə sē), *n.* condition of great joy

elaborate (i lab′ər it), *adj.* worked out with care

elicit (i lis′it), *v.* draw forth

encase (en kās′), *v.* cover completely

enthrall (en thrôl′), *v.* fascinate; charm

entity (en′tə tē), *n.* being

enunciate (i nun′sē āt), *v.* pronounce

epiphany (i pif′ə nē), *n.* manifestation; perception

epithet (ep′ə thet), *n.* an insulting or contemptuous word or phrase

eradicate (i rad′ə kāt), *v.* get rid of entirely

errant (er′ənt), *adj.* wrong

espresso (e spres′ō), *n.* a very strong black coffee brewed in a special machine

essence (es′ns), *n.* that which makes a thing what it is

eulogy (yü′lə jē), *n.* speech in praise of a person

expansionist (ek span′shə nist), *n.* a person who believes in spreading out

explicit (ek splis′it), *adj.* definite

expound (ek spound′), *v.* make clear; explain

expurgated (ek′spər gāt əd), *adj.* free of objectionable passages or words

extemporize (ek stem′pə rīz), *v.* speak or sing, composing as one goes along

falsetto (fôl set′ō), *n.* an artificially high-pitched voice

familial (fə mil′yəl), *adj.* having to do with family

fanatical (fə nat′ə kəl), *adj.* unreasonably enthusiastic or zealous

fastidious (fa stid′ē əs), *adj.* dainty in taste

feign (fān), *v.* make believe; pretend; **feigned** *adj.* pretended

feint (fānt), *v.* pretend

fester (fes′tər) *v.* form pus

fiasco (fē as′kō), *n.* ridiculous failure

flintrock (flint′rok), *n.* anything very hard or unyielding

florid (flôr′id), *adj.* showy; highly colored with red; ruddy

foppish (fop′ish), *adj.* vain

furrow (fėr′ō), *n.* a long, narrow groove cut in the earth by a plow

furtive (fėr′tiv), *adj.* sly, stealthy; **furtively,** *adv.* in a sly manner

gangly (gang′glē), *adj.* awkwardly tall and slender

gangrene (gang′grēn′), *n.* decay of human tissue when the blood supply is cut off

gape (gāp), *v.* stare with the mouth open

geisha-girl (gā′shə), *n.* a young woman trained to be a professional entertainer and companion for men (in Japan)

gelid (jel′id), *adj.* cold as ice; frozen

generic (jə ner′ik), *adj.* general; not special

genuflect (jen′yə flekt), *v.* bend the knee as an act of reverence or worship

ghetto (get′ō), *n.* section of a city where any racial or other minority group lives

goatee (gō tē′), *n.* a pointed, trimmed beard on a man's chin

gourd (gôrd), *n.* any of various squash-like fruits that grow on vines

hacienda (hä′sē en′də), *n.* a large ranch or landed estate

hallucination (hə lü′sn ā′shən), *n.* an imaginary thing heard or seen

haughtiness (hô′tē nəs), *n.* pride; arrogance

heresy (her′ə sē), *n.* opinion opposed to what is generally accepted

hierarchy (hī′ə rär′kē), *n.* organization of persons or things arranged one above the other according to rank or importance

horde (hôrd), *n.* a great number

hostilities (ho stil′ə tēz), *n. pl.* fighting

huffily (huf′ ə lē), *adv.* angrily

ideograph (id′ē ə graf), *n.* a graphic symbol that represents a thing or an idea directly

idiom (id′ē əm), *n.* phrase or expression whose meaning cannot be understood from the ordinary meanings of the words

immobile (i mō′bəl), *adj.* motionless

immovable (i mü′və bəl), *adj.* that cannot be moved

impertinent (im pèrt′n ənt), *adj.* rudely bold

impoverished (im pov′ər isht), *adj.* very poor

impudence (im′pyə dəns), *n.* great rudeness; shameless boldness

inanimate (in an′ə mit), *adj.* lifeless

incoherence (in′kō hir′əns), *n.* disconnected thought or speech

incompatible (in′kəm pat′ə bəl), *adj.* inconsistent; opposed in character

indignant (in dig′nənt), *adj.* angry at something unworthy or unjust

indignity (in dig′nə tē), *n.* lack of respect of proper treatment

indisputably (in′dis pyüt′ə blē), *adv.* undoubtedly

ineducable (in ej′ə kə bəl), *adj.* incapable of being educated

infatuated (in fach′ü ā′tid), *adj.* foolishly in love

infringe (in frinj′), *v.* act contrary to or violate

ingenuity (in′jə nü′ə tē), *n.* cleverness

ingrain (in grān′), *v.* fix deeply and firmly

initiate (i nish′ē āt), *v.* induct

inlay (in′lā′), *n.* decoration set in the surface

innumerable (i nü′mər ə bəl), *adj.* too many to count

insouciant (in sü′sē ənt), *adj.* free from care or anxiety

installment (in stôl′mənt), *n.* part of a debt to be paid at certain times

insularity (in′sə lar′ə tē), *n.* narrow-mindedness

integration (in′tə grā′shən), *n.* inclusion of people of all races on an equal basis in schools, parks, neighborhoods, etc.

interim (in′tər im), *n.* temporary

interscholastic (in′tər skə las′tik), *adj.* between schools

intimate (in′tə mit), *adj.* very familiar

intimidation (in tim′ə dā′shən), *n.* the act of frightening

introverted (in′trə vèr′tid), *adj.* more interested in one's own thoughts than in what is going on around one

intuition (in′tü ish′ən), *n.* immediate understanding; without reasoning

jauntily (jôn′tə lē), *adv.* in a carefree manner; sprightly

jovially (jō′vē əl lē), *adv.* good-humoredly

kowtow (kou′tou′), *v.* kneel and touch the ground with the forehead in respect

laboriously (lə bôr′ē əs lē), *adv.* with much effort

labyrinth (lab′ə rinth′), *n.* a confusing, complicated state of affairs

labyrinthine (lab′rin′thən), *n.* confusing and complicated; mazelike

lacerate (las′ə rāt), *v.* deeply indenting

lacquer (lak′ər), *n.* wooden articles coated with a special varnish

laggard (lag′ərd), *n.* a backward person

languid (lang′gwid), *adj.* drooping; weak

latitude (lat′ə tüd), *n.* freedom from narrow rules

latrine (lə trēn′), *n.* toilet or privy

lethality (li thal′ə tē), *n.* deadliness

lexicon (lek′sə kən), *n.* vocabulary

lilt (lilt), *v.* sing or play a tune in a light, tripping manner

litany (lit′n ē), *n.* a repeated series

lithe (liᴛ͟H), *adj.* supple

llano (lä′nō), *n.* a broad, grassy, treeless plain

loathsome (lōᴛ͟H′səm), *adj.* disgusting

luminous (lü′mə nəs), *adj.* full of light

lunar zodiac (lü′nər zō′dē ak), *n.* an imaginary belt of the heavens around the apparent path of the moon

lurk (lèrk), *v.* move about in a sly manner

macabre (mə kä′brə), *adj.* horrible; ghastly

malice (mal′is), *n.* active ill will; wish to hurt or make suffer

maniacal (mə nī′ə kəl), *adj.* violently insane

mannequin (man′ə kən), *n.* figure of a person used by stores

martyr (mär′tər), *n.* a person who chooses to die or suffer rather than renounce a religious belief

maze (māz), *n.* network of paths through which it is hard to find one's way

meager (mē′gər), *adj.* poor or scanty

mediocrity (mē′dē ok′rə tē), *n.* average or lower than average quality

medley (med′lē), *n.* mixture of things that ordinarily do not belong together

melee (mā′lā), *n.* a confused struggle

memoir (mem′wär), *n.* biography

menacingly (men′is əng lē), *adv.* threateningly

mentor (men′tər), *n.* a wise and trusted advisor

meretricious (mer′ə trish′əs), *adj.* attractive in a showy way

mesa (mā′sə), *n.* a small, high plateau with a flat top and steep sides

mesmerize (mez′mə rīz′), *v.* hypnotize

mestizo (me stē′zō), *n.* person of mixed descent

midden (mid′n), *n.* dunghill or garbage heap

minstrel show (min′strəl), *n.* show in which the performers blackened their faces and played music, sang songs, and told jokes

minutely (mī nüt′lē), *adv.* very slightly

miscalculate (mis kal′kyə lāt), *v.* estimate incorrectly

misnomer (mis nō′mər), *n.* error in naming

mission (mish′ən), *n.* a group of people sent by a religious organization to spread its beliefs; group of people sent on some special business by their government

mole (mōl), *n.* a large piece

momentum (mō men′təm), *n.* impetus resulting from movement

monumental (mon′yə men′tl), *adj.* important; lasting

morose (mə rōs′), *adj.* gloomy; sullen

mortified (môr′tə fīd), *adj.* ashamed

mosaic (mō zā′ik), *n.* decoration made of small pieces of stone, glass, wood, etc., inlaid to form a picture

moult (mōlt), *v.* shed skin, feathers, etc.

musk (musk), *n.* substance with a strong odor, found in the glands of some animals

natatorium (nā′tə tôr′ē əm), *n.* a swimming pool

nave (nāv), *n.* the main part of a church

noncommittal (non′kə mit′l), *adj.* not revealing one's opinion

nuclear family (nü′klē ər), *n.* a family consisting of father, mother, and children

ogle (ō′gəl), *v.* make eyes at

ominously (om′ə nəs lē), *adv.* threateningly

outré (ü trā′), *adj.* bizarre

overlay (ō′vər lā′), *n.* covering; decoration

pampers (pam′pərz), *n.* disposable diapers

pantomime (pan′tə mim), *n.* a play without words

Papago (pap′ə gō′), *n.* a member of a North American Indian people closely related to the Pima

paradox (par′ə doks), *n.* statement that may be true but seems to say two opposite things

paragon (par′ə gon), *n.* model of excellence or perfection

parishioner (pə rish′ə nər), *n.* a member of a particular church

parlance (pär′ləns), *n.* talk

partitioned (pär tish′ənd), *adj.* divided into parts

passionate (pash′ə nit), *adj.* having or showing strong feelings

patent (pat′nt), *v.* get a government grant that gives a person sole rights to make or sell a new invention

pedestrian (pə des′trē ən), *n.* dull; commonplace

perception (pər sep′shən), *n.* understanding that is the result of observing

perilous (per′ə ləls), *adj.* dangerous

permeate (pėr′mē āt), *v.* spread through the whole of

perpetrator (pėr′pə trā′tər), *n.* one who commits a crime or anything bad

perpetuity (pėr′pə tü′ə tē) *n.* existence forever

perplexity (pər plek′sə tē), *n.* bewilderment

pert (pėrt), *adj.* bold

perverse (pər vėrs′), *adj.* contrary and willful

pharmaceutical (fär′mə sü′tə kəl), *adj.* a medicinal drug

philosophical (fil′ə sof′ə kəl), *adj.* wise; reasonable

phonetic (fə net′ik), *adj.* having to do with speech sounds

pidgin (pij′ən), *n.* one of several forms of English, with simplified grammatical structure and often a mixed vocabulary

pigment (pig′mənt), *n.* coloring matter

pilaf (pi läf´), *n*. a Middle Eastern dish consisting of rice or cracked wheat boiled often with mutton, fowl, or fish, and flavored with spices, raisins, etc.

placid (plas´id), *adj*. peaceful; **placidly** *adv*. quietly

plagiarist (plā´jər ist), *n*. a person who takes the work of another person and uses as one's own

plowshare (plou´sher´), *n*. blade of a plow

poignantly (poi´nyənt lē), *adv*. intensely

pollinated (pol´ə nāt əd), *adj*. containing pollen

pomade (pə mād´), *n*. a perfumed ointment for the scalp and hair

pompadour(pom´pə dôr), *n*. arrangement of a woman's hair in which it is puffed high over the forehead

porcelain (pôr´sə lin), *n*. a very fine earthenware; china

precarious (pri ker´ē əs), *adj*. not safe

precedent (pres´ə dənt), *n*. action that may serve as an example or reason for a later action

precocious (pri kō´shəs), *adj*. occurring before the natural time

preconception (prē´kən sep´shən), *n*. idea formed beforehand

preempt (prē empt´), *v*. secure before someone else can

prelude (prel´yüd), *n*. an introduction

proclamation (prok´lə mā´shən), *n*. a public declaration

prodigious (prə dij´əs), *adj*. very great

prodigy (prod´ə jē), *n*. a remarkably talented child

project (proj´ekt), *n*. group of apartment houses built and run as a unit, especially as part of public housing

pronouncement (prə nouns´mənt), *n*. formal statement

proprietor (prə pri´ə tər), *n*. owner

protestation (prot´ə stā´shən), *n*. a solemn declaration

psychic (sī´kik), *adj*. especially susceptible to mental influences

pudgy (puj´ē), *adj*. short and fat or thick

pumice (pum´is), *n*. a porous, glassy lava

purveyor (pər vā´ər), *n*. person who supplies anything

quarry (kwôr´ē), *n*. prey

quarters (kwôr´tər), *n. pl*. place to live

quest (kwest), *v*. search

quirk (kwėrk), *n*. a peculiar way of acting

raconteur (rak´on tėr´), *n*. person clever in telling stories

randomly (ran´dəm lē), *adv*. without a definite plan

raunchy (rôn´chē), *adj*. shabby; vulgar

realm (relm), *n*. kingdom

ream (rēm), *v*. stretch

rebuke (ri byük´), *n*. expression of disapproval; scolding

recoil (ri koil´), *n*. draw back; shrink back

reconcile (rek´ən sīl), *v*. make friends again

regalia (ri gā´lē ə), *n. pl*. clothes, especially fine clothes

reincarnated (rē´in kär nā´tid), *v*. reborn

replica (rep´lə kə), *n*. a copy

reproach (ri prōch´), *n*. blame or censure

reproof (ri prüf´), *n*. blame or disapproval

resemblance (re zem´blens), n. similar appearance

residency (rez´ə dən sē), *n*. position of a doctor who continues practicing in a hospital after completing an internship

resonant (rez´n ənt), *adj*. resounding

retch (rech), *v*. make efforts to vomit

retrospect (ret´rə spekt), *n*. thinking about the past

reverie (rev´ər ē), *n*. dreamy thoughts

rivulet (riv´yə lit), *n*. a very small stream

roan (rōn), *adj*. yellowish- or reddish-brown sprinkled with gray or white

roil (roil), *v*. stir up sediment

R S V P, abbreviation for the French *répondez s'il vous plaît* meaning "reply, if you please"

rudder (rud´ər) *n*. a flat piece of wood or metal hinged vertically to the rear end of an aircraft and used to steer it

russet (rus´it), *adj*. yellowish-brown or reddish-brown

sacrilege (sak´rə lij), *n*. an intentional injury to anything sacred

salt lick block of salt set out for animals

samurai (sam´u ri´), *n*. the military in feudal Japan, consisting of the retainers of the great nobles

sandhog (sand´hog´), *n*. a person who works either underground or underwater

scrutinize (skrüt´n īz), *v*. examine closely

searing (sir´ing), *adj*. burning; withering

serial (sir´ē əl), *n*. story broadcast one part at a time on a radio or television

sestina (se´stē nə), *n*. a lyrical fixed form of six six-line, usually unrhymed, stanzas

six six-line, usually unrhymed, stanzas

shaman (shä′mən), *n.* a man in American Indian tribes who is believed to have close contact with the spirit world

Shangri-La (shang′gri lä′), *n.* an idyllic earthly paradise

shiner (shī′nər), *n.* a small American freshwater fish with glistening scales

shoyu (shō′yü′) *n.* Japanese word meaning "soy sauce"

sibling (sib′ling), *n.* a brother or sister

sibyl (sib′əl), *n.* prophetess; fortuneteller

simian (sim′ē ən), *adj.* apelike

sloe (slō), *adj.* shortened form of sloe-eyed — having very dark eyes

smugness (smug′nəs), *n.* condition of being too pleased with one's own goodness

snide (snīd), *adj.* spiteful in a sly way

sniveler (sniv′əl ər), *n.* one who sniffles or whimpers

solace (sol′is), *n.* comfort or relief

sonata (sə nä′tə) *n.* piece of music, for one or two instruments, having three or four movements in contrasted rhythms

staccato (stə kä′tō), *adj.* disconnected

stanchion (stan′shən), *n.* an upright support for a roof

stoically (stō′ə kəl lï), *adv.* with self-control

stricture (strik′chər), *n.* a binding restriction

stucco (stuk′ō), *n.* plaster which sets with a hard, stonelike coat

study (stud′ē), *n.* thing to be investigated

subterfuge (sub′tər fyüj), *n.* trick; excuse

succor (suk′ər), *n.* help; aid

tabloid (tab′loid), *n.* a newspaper of small size, having many pictures, short articles, and large, often sensational headlines

Tarahumara (tär′ə hü mär′ə), *n.* a member of an American Indian people of the Sierra Madre region of the state of Chihuahua

tarp (tärp), *n.* a sheet of canvas or other heavy waterproof material

taunt (tânt), *v.* jeer at; mock

tenement (ten′ə mənt), *n.* apartment building in a poor section of a city

testify (tes′tə fī), *v.* give evidence

titter (tit′ər), *v.* laugh nervously; giggle

trachoma (trə kō′mə), *n.* a contagious eye disease caused by a virus

tranquil (trang′kwəl), *adj.* peaceful

transmittal (tran smit′l), *n.* passing along

trek (trek), *v.* travel

truculent (truk′yə lənt), *adj.* eager to fight

tsking, *v.* making a clicking sound by sucking in while the tongue is on the teeth, used to express impatience

turmoil (tėr′moil), *n.* disturbance

tyranny (tir′ə nē), *n.* cruel or unjust use of power

unassailable (un′ə sāl′ə bəl), *adj.* not able to be attacked

undertow (un′dər tō′), *n.* strong current below the surface, moving in a direction different from the surface current

uninflammatory (un in flam′ə tôr′ē), *adj.* not tending to excite or arouse

unnerving (un nėrv′əng), *adj.* cause to become nervous

utilitarian (yü til′ə ter′ē ən), *adj.* designed for usefulness

vagrant (vā′grənt), *adj.* wandering

vaguely (vāg′lē), *adv.* indefinitely; indistinctly

vanquish (vang′kwish), *v.* to overcome

vaudeville (vôd′vil), *n.* theatrical entertainment featuring a variety of acts

vendor (ven′dər), *n.* seller; peddler

venerable (ven′ər ə bəl), *adj.* worthy of reverence

vengeance (ven′jəns), *n.* revenge; with great force

venom (ven′əm), *n.* spite; malice

virago (və rā′gō), *n.* a violent, bad-tempered woman

vulnerable (vul′nər ə bəl), *adj.* sensitive to criticism; open to attack

wall (wôl), *v.* cause one's eyes to become wide open and staring

wan (won), *adj.* pale

warbling (wôr′bləng), *v.* singing with trills

wariness (wer′ē nis), *n.* caution

warrenlike (wôr′ən lik′), *adj.* having a maze of passageways; like a rabbit's warren

wary (wer′ē), *adj.* cautious or careful; **warily**, *adv.* cautiously

weathervane (weᴛʜ′ər vān′), *n.* a device that moves with the wind and indicates its direction; **weathervaned** *v.* initiated; expressed

whence (hwens), *adv.* from where

wile (wil), *n.* a trick to deceive

wry (ri), *adj.* turned to one side; twisted

INDEX OF AUTHORS AND TITLES

ACKNOWLEDGMENTS

vii Foreword by Rita Dove © 1994 by ScottForesman, Glenview, Illinois.
3 "American History" from *The Latin Deli: Prose & Poetry* by Judith Ortiz Cofer. Copyright © 1993 by Judith Ortiz Cofer. Published by The University of Georgia Press.
15 From *Donald Duk* by Frank Chin, Coffee House Press, 1991. Copyright © 1991 by Frank Chin. Reprinted by permission of the publisher.
25 "Black Men and Public Space" from *Just Walk on By* by Brent Staples, 1986. Reprinted by permission of the author.
31 From "Chicago: Southside Summers" from *To Be Young, Gifted and Black* by Lorraine Hansberry In Her Own Words. Adapted by Robert Nemiroff. Copyright © 1969 by Robert Nemiroff. Reprinted by permission of the publisher, Prentice Hall/A Division of Simon & Schuster, Englewood Cliffs, N.J.
37 "West Side" from *Hugging the Jukebox* by Naomi Shihab Nye. Copyright © 1982 by Naomi Shihab Nye. Reprinted by permission of the author.
38 "The Real Thing" from *Selu: Seeking the Corn-Mother's Wisdom* by Marilou Awiakta. Copyright © 1993 by Marilou Awiakta. Reprinted by permission of Fulcrum Publishing.
40 "Merritt Parkway" from *Collected Earlier Poems 1940-1960* by Denise Levertov. Copyright © 1960 by Denise Levertov. Reprinted by permission of New Directions Publishing Corp.
43 "Stoplight" by Steve Chan-No Yoon. Copyright © 1992 by Steve Chan-No Yoon. Reprinted by permission of the author.
59 From *Through the Ivory Gate* by Rita Dove. Copyright © 1992 by Rita Dove. Reprinted by permission of Pantheon Books, a division of Random House, Inc.
68 "Dear John Wayne" from *Jacklight* by Louise Erdrich. Copyright © 1984 by Louise Erdrich. Reprinted by permission of Henry Holt and Company, Inc.
70 "Picture Bride" from *Picture Bride* by Cathy Song. Copyright © 1983 by Cathy Song. Reprinted by permission of Yale University Press.
73 "The Day the Cisco Kid Shot John Wayne" from *The Day the Cisco Kid Shot John Wayne* by Nash Candelaria. Copyright © 1988 by Bilingual Press/Editorial Bilingue. Reprinted by permission of Bilingual Press/Editorial Bilingue, Arizona State University, Tempe, Arizona.
93 "Getups" from *Wouldn't Take Nothing for My Journey Now* by Maya Angelou. Copyright © 1993 by Maya Angelou. Reprinted by permission of Random House, Inc.
97 "Appearances Are Destructive" by Mark Mathabane. Copyright © 1993 by Mark Mathabane. Reprinted by permission of FiFi Oscard Agency.
101 "Rain Music" by Longhang Nguyen. Copyright © 1992 by Longhang Nguyen. Reprinted by permission.
107 "Only Approved Indians Can Play: Made in USA" by Jack Forbes. Copyright © 1983 by Jack Forbes. Reprinted by permission of the author.
111 "Who Said We All Have to Talk Alike" by Wilma Elizabeth McDaniel. Reprinted by permission of The Seal Press.
123 From *Bless Me, Ultima* by Rudolfo A. Anaya. Copyright © 1972 by Rudolfo A. Anaya. Reprinted by permission of the author.
134 "For Misty Starting School" by Lucy Tapahonso from *A Breeze Swept Through*. Copyright © 1987 by Lucy Tapahonso. Reprinted by permission of West End Press.
136 "We Real Cool" from *Blacks* by Gwendolyn Brooks. Copyright © 1991 by Gwendolyn Brooks. *Blacks* is published by Third World Press, Chicago. Reprinted by permission of the author.
139 "Getting the Facts of Life" by Paulette Childress White. Reprinted by permission of the author.
153 "Not Knowing and Not Wanting to Know" from *Black Men: Obsolete, Single, Dangerous?* by Haki R. Madhubuti. Copyright © 1990 by Haki R. Madhubuti. Reprinted by permission of Third World Press.
157 "Puzzle Solving" from *The Lost Garden* by Laurence Yep. Copyright © 1991 by Laurence Yep. Reprinted by permission of the publisher, Julian Messner, a division of Silver Burdett Press, Inc., Simon & Schuster, Englewood Cliffs, N.J.
171 "The Man to Send Rain Clouds" from *Storyteller* by Leslie Marmon Silko. Copyright © 1981 by Leslie Marmon Silko. Reprinted by permission of Wylie, Aitken & Stone.
179 "Everyday Use" from *In Love & Trouble: Stories of Black Women* by Alice Walker. Copyright © 1973 by Alice Walker. Reprinted by permission of Harcourt Brace & Company.
191 "The Chandelier" by Gregory Orfalea. Copyright ©1984, 1990 by Gregory Orfalea. Reprinted by permission of the author.
207 Excerpt from *Rain of Gold* by Victor Villaseñor is reprinted with permission from the publisher of *Rain of Gold*. Arte Público Press-University of Houston, 1991.
215 "The Struggle to Be an All-American Girl" by Elizabeth Wong. Reprinted by permission of Writers & Artists Agency.
220 "Becoming American" by Vern Rutsala. Copyright © 1992 by Vern Rutsala. Reprinted by permission of the author.
222 "Without Title" from *Iron Woman* by Diane Glancy. Copyright © 1990 by Diane Glancy. Reprinted by permission of the author.